D0484772

THE CRAFT OF
INTERNATIONAL HISTORY

THE CRAFT OF INTERNATIONAL HISTORY

A GUIDE TO METHOD

MARC TRACHTENBERG

PRINCETON UNIVERSITY PRESS

PRINCETON AND OXFORD

Library of Congress Cataloging-in-Publication Data

Trachtenberg, Marc. 1946–
    The craft of international history: a guide to method / Marc Trachtenberg.
        p.   cm.
    Includes bibliographical references and index.
    ISBN-13: 978-0-691-12501-5 (cl : alk. paper)
    ISBN-10: 0-691-12501-5 (cl : alk. paper)
    ISBN-13: 978-0-691-12569-5 (pb : alk. paper)
    ISBN-10: 0-691-12569-4 (pb : alk. paper)
1. International relations—History.   I. Title.
    JZ1329.5.T73 2005
    327′ 072′ 2—dc22   2005051469

British Library Cataloging-in-Publication Data is available

This book has been composed in Goudy
Printed on acid-free paper. ∞
pup.princeton.edu

Printed in the United States of America

10   9   8   7   6   5   4   3   2   1

CONTENTS

PREFACE

My goal in this book is to provide a practical guide to the historical study of international politics—a guide to how historical work in this area can actually be done, a guide which people working in this field might actually find useful.

Is there any real need for a book of this sort? Historians have gotten by quite well over the years, or so it would seem, without paying much attention to issues of method. Charles Gillispie, the distinguished historian of science, remembered how he was trained in graduate school: "All that we students of history were taught to do, was to go look at the sources, all of them."[1] That was my experience too. What we historians got in terms of formal methodological training was fairly minimal. And yet isn't there more that can be given by way of guidance than just the simple piece of advice: "go look at the sources"? The sources, after all, cannot be approached in a totally mindless way. So isn't there something useful that can be said about how they *should* be approached?

I think there are things worth saying. One key point, for example, is that the evidence needs to be approached with specific questions in mind. To draw meaning from the sources you examine, you need to pose questions. But questions arise in your mind because you come to the subject at hand armed with a kind of theory, that is, with a general sense for how things are supposed to work. And to present conclusions—to make sense of the sources, to bring out the meaning of what was going on—you also have to draw on a certain sense for how things work.

It is for that reason that historical work, if it is to be of real value, has to have a strong conceptual core. That basic claim is scarcely original. I remember Sheldon Wolin arguing, when I was an undergraduate at Berkeley in the 1960s, that at the heart of every great work of history lies a certain political theory, a certain conception of how politics works. (He was referring specifically to Thucydides.) I remember Edward Segel, in another class I took at about that time, pointing out that at the core of some major works of history lay a certain conception of "what makes history run." (He was referring to Churchill's *The Gathering Storm*.) A good deal of what I am going to say in this book is nothing but a long footnote to points of that sort—to insights I absorbed as an undergraduate forty years ago.

Those insights are a point of departure for thinking seriously about issues of method. They imply in particular—and this is a major theme that will run

---

[1] Charles C. Gillispie, "A Professional Life in the History of Science," *Historically Speaking* 5, no. 3 (January 2004): 3.

through these pages—that the art of doing historical work, and maybe even the art of studying international politics in general, consists in large measure of finding some way of getting the conceptual and the empirical sides of the scholarly effort to connect with each other.

But general points of that sort, as important as they are, can only take you so far. To understand how historical work is done, you need to have the doors of the workshop thrown open. You need to be exposed not just to nice, neat, finished products. You need instead to see for yourself the sort of thought process the historian goes through before he or she puts anything down on paper.

It is for that reason that I've included the chapter on America's road to war in 1941 in the book. That chapter is not a finished product at all. It is about twice as long as it would be if it were a finished piece of work. But for my purposes here I wanted to leave a lot of the scaffolding up. I wanted to show what goes into an historical interpretation. I wanted to give some sense for the process by which an interpretation takes shape.

The focus of the book, in other words, is on the nuts and bolts of what the famous historian Marc Bloch called the "historian's craft." Many of the things I am going to talk about here I learned the hard way. Many of them are purely practical in nature. My hope is that by reading a book of this sort, a young scholar will not have to go through everything that I went through and will instead be able to work efficiently right from the start—more efficiently, at any rate, than I was able to when I was starting out.

This book is in fact intended mainly for younger scholars, especially for graduate students and advanced undergraduates in both history and political science. I am particularly interested in speaking to people in that latter field. I think political scientists, or at least those studying international relations, need to know how to do historical work. They may need to know other things as well, but it is hard to see how they can hope to understand international politics if they do not know how to do historical analysis in a fairly serious way.

Is that point contentious? Most political scientists, I think, would agree in principle that a certain level of historical understanding is important for their purposes. But at the same time they take it for granted that in practice there is a limit to what they can realistically hope to achieve. Given the nature of their field, they have to concern themselves primarily with relatively broad issues and that means that it is hard for them to study specific questions in depth. They have so much ground to cover that it is almost impossible for them to study particular historical episodes the way historians would. They also tend to assume that they just do not have the training needed to do serious historical work. They seem to think there is a set of relatively arcane skills historians learn in graduate school and that historical work produced by scholars who have never been taught those skills is bound to be hopelessly amateurish.

I don't think either assumption is valid. I think there is a method for reaching relatively solid conclusions about major historical issues in a reasonable amount of time—say, in about three or four months of uninterrupted work. This, in fact, is the basic point of chapters 3 and 4. And I don't think there is any great mystery to doing historical work. There *are* skills involved, but most are quite prosaic, and there is nothing really arcane about any of them. In any event, one of my main goals here is to demystify historical work so that political scientists can feel less inhibited about doing it.

This book took shape gradually over a fifteen-year period. When I first started to write about these issues of method, I had no idea that I would end up producing a book of this sort. I was teaching a course at Yale for first-year graduate students in history, and my goal was to show the students in that class how historical work on international politics during the period covered in the course (the Cold War period) could in practice be done. I didn't want to spend a lot of time in class talking about purely practical matters—about what sources were available or about how to do bibliographical work—and it seemed to me that the easiest way to deal with those matters was just to write up what I had to say and have it photocopied and distributed as a coursepack. And since I was having the students buy that coursepack anyway, I thought it would make sense to have it include a number of other things I had accumulated over the years—information, for example, about various microfilm publications, about how to use the Freedom of Information Act, and about how to apply for a research grant from one of the presidential libraries. The response was positive, and I ended up using a version of that coursepack in a number of undergraduate seminars I taught at the University of Pennsylvania in the 1990s. Toward the end of that decade, when people began using the internet and a number of sources and finding aids started to become available online, I developed an online version of that guide. At that time, as it happened, I was also writing a book on the Cold War, and I included that guide—it was, after all, a guide to doing Cold War history—in the "internet supplement" I set up for that book, updating it from time to time and adding new sources as I found them.[2]

By that point, I had also begun to spend a lot of time with political scientists. The ones I got to know were very interested in history, and were actually quite interested in learning about how historical work is done—and indeed in learning a bit more about history as a discipline with an intellectual personality of its own. I would occasionally talk with them about those issues, and I even wrote a paper in 1985 that dealt with questions of this sort.[3] So some of the issues this book is concerned with were in the back of my mind for some time. But it was not until 1999 or so that I decided to write a book

---

[2] That guide is still available online: http://www.polisci.ucla.edu/faculty/trachtenberg/guide/guidehome.html.

of this sort. I did not make that decision entirely on my own. Alexander George of Stanford University urged me to write this kind of book—political scientists, he thought, really needed some guidance in this area—and if it hadn't been for him, this book probably would never have been written. But when I agreed to write a methods book, I didn't quite realize how much of a commitment I was taking on. I didn't think at that time that writing a book on historical method would be a particularly difficult thing to do. After all, my old Cold War guide had already been written, and having worked in this field ever since I was an undergraduate, I thought I knew the ropes well enough to write a book of this kind fairly quickly. To be sure, there were certain things I felt I needed to do. In particular, I wanted to provide a sort of "philosophical" basis for what I had to say, and that obviously would call for a certain amount of work. Still, I thought I should be able to have a finished manuscript ready in about a year.

As it turned out, the book took me about five years to complete. I spent a lot of time working on the text—rethinking key arguments and rewriting key chapters as I saw how people reacted to what I had to say. I was writing this book for other people, and other people played a major role in making it what it is. I got feedback at various points as it was being written—from Alex George and Bob Jervis, from Bruce Kuklick and Steve Van Evera, from Andy Moravcsik and Mark Sheetz and Fred Logevall—and for all that help, some of which was quite extraordinary, I am of course very grateful. I also tried out some of the ideas here with graduate and undergraduate students, at Yale, at Penn, at Columbia, and especially over the last few years at UCLA. And after a draft of the book had been written, I gave a number of talks laying out some of the arguments here before groups of students (and faculty) at Chicago, MIT, and SAIS. Those experiences were extremely valuable, at least for me. It was the only way I could actually see what resonated with people or what struck them as problematic. So I want to thank all those students just for reacting to what I had to say—for taking the arguments seriously and for giving me some sense for what they actually found useful.

[3] "Making Sense of the Nuclear Age," written for a conference held at Columbia University's Institute of War and Peace Studies in 1985 and published in Marc Trachtenberg, *History and Strategy* (Princeton: Princeton University Press, 1991).

THE CRAFT OF
INTERNATIONAL HISTORY

Chapter One

THE THEORY OF
HISTORICAL INQUIRY

THIS IS A BOOK about method. It's about the techniques historians use to understand international politics. But issues of method cannot be dealt with in a vacuum. To see *how* historical work needs to be done, you first have to have some sense for *what* it is exactly that historians should be trying to do. What's the aim of historical analysis? What's the point of this whole branch of intellectual activity? These questions are of fundamental importance, even in practical terms. To understand the goal of historical work—to know what historical understanding is and what historical explanation is—can be of great value to the working historian. That knowledge can serve as a kind of beacon. It can help the historian see how to proceed.

Does the philosophy of history literature provide historians with the guidance they need? This question is the focus of the first two sections in this chapter, but in a word the answer is no. Does that mean that the philosophers have nothing much to offer the historians? Again, the answer is no. There are important insights available, but they are to be found in the philosophy of *science* literature. That these writings are of real value to the practicing historian is the point of the argument in the final section of this chapter. In that section I want to draw out some of the insights to be found in that literature and show how they apply to historical work.

The Classic Tradition: Hempel versus Collingwood

In 1942 the philosopher Carl Hempel published a paper called "The Function of General Laws in History" in which he laid out a theory of historical explanation.[1] In history as in science, Hempel said, explanation meant deduction. An explanation would show that certain initial conditions existed and would lay out general laws that governed what would happen if those conditions were met; the occurrence of the event in question would follow as

---

[1] Carl Hempel, "The Function of General Laws in History," *Journal of Philosophy* 39 (1942): 35–48; reprinted in Patrick Gardiner, ed., *Theories of History* (New York: Free Press, 1959), pp. 344–56. Further references are to the text as it appeared in the Gardiner book.

a matter of course from those laws and those initial conditions. Unless a historical account had that form, Hempel wrote, that account could not be considered a real explanation. It would at best be a mere "explanation sketch." This theory of explanation, the "covering law" theory as it is often called, was a focus of philosophical discussion until about 1970.[2] Indeed, as one leading scholar noted, the Hempel paper was so fundamental that most participants in the debate on historical explanation "quickly found themselves classified as either pro-Hempelian or anti-Hempelian."[3]

This theory was attractive because it appealed to people's sense for what an explanation should be. If an account does not explain why an event *had* to happen, if it simply explains why it *might* have happened, then, in a certain sense, it is not a real explanation at all. As one leading philosopher of history put it: "If what we give in explanation of an event does not rule out the possibility of that event's failing to occur, then we can scarcely claim that we know why in that particular case it *did* occur: why in that case, in other words, the possibility of its not occurring was not realized instead. The only way we can rule out such a possibility is by arguing that the event *had* to occur: that it *necessarily* occurred. And that is what the deductive requirement of scientific explanation insures."[4]

This point, however, carried little weight with most historians. Their feeling was that the Hempel approach was abstract and formalistic and did not take actual historical practice as its point of departure. It did not look at what explanation meant to the historian and then try to build out from there. Hempel, with his emphasis on social scientific "laws," would force interpretation into much too rigid a mold. He did not seem to have any real feel for

[2] See William Dray, *Laws and Explanation in History* (Oxford: Oxford University Press, 1957). Alan Donagan characterized this view as the "Popper-Hempel" theory. Alan Donagan, "The Popper-Hempel Theory Reconsidered," *History and Theory* 1 (1964): 3–26, reprinted with minor changes in *Philosophical Analysis and History*, ed. William Dray (New York: Harper and Row, 1966), pp. 127–59; further references are to this latter version of the article. It should be noted, however, that by the time this article came out, Popper was very critical of what he called "historicism," which he defined as "an approach to the social sciences which," among other things, was concerned with discovering the laws "that underlie the evolution of history." Karl Popper, *The Poverty of Historicism* (London: Routledge, 1961), p. 3. He later went out of his way to praise Donagan "for fighting this danger [of historicism] so forcefully." Paul A. Schilpp, ed., *The Philosophy of Karl Popper*, 2 vols. (La Salle, Ill.: Open Court, 1974), 2:1174. The term "historicism," of course, has been used in many different ways. See Georg Iggers, *The German Conception of History* (Middletown, Conn.: Wesleyan University Press, 1968), pp. 287–90 (or pp. 295–98 in the revised edition published in 1983), and the references cited there.

[3] William Dray, *On History and Philosophers of History* (Leiden: Brill, 1989), p. 13. See also Donagan, "Popper-Hempel Theory," p. 127.

[4] William Dray, *Philosophy of History* (Englewood Cliffs, N.J.: Prentice-Hall, 1964), pp. 6–7 (emphasis in original). Dray was here paraphrasing another philosopher's argument.

history as a discipline with an intellectual personality of its own.[5] And a number of philosophers sympathized with the view that standards were not to be arbitrarily imposed on the discipline from the outside.[6] They rejected the idea that what could not be "cut down to analytic size" in terms of those standards was to be "stripped of the epaulets of cognitive honor" and agreed that a field like history was to be taken essentially on its own terms.[7] Their feeling was, as one of them put it, that the social sciences in general and history in particular were not to be remodeled into "deformed likenesses of physics."[8] And they sympathized with the historians' view that the covering-law approach was unacceptable because it failed to allow for human agency—for the role that individual human beings play in shaping the course of events.[9]

Those philosophers, moreover, were able to show that the Hempel theory was not particularly impressive, even on its own terms. Alan Donagan, for example, in one section of his well-known article on the "Popper-Hempel theory," effectively demolished Hempel's assumption that covering laws were readily available. Among other things, he showed that one example Hempel had given in his original article—an explanation drawing on three explicit covering laws—did not hold up because "all three were obviously false"![10] A more basic problem was that Hempel, by his own admission, did not even purport to show what an explanation *was*. All he did was to point to one of the things that an explanation of an event in his view had to be. It needed, he said, to provide a *sufficient* basis for expecting that that event had occurred. The problem here, as he himself pointed out, was that "certain kinds of information"—the "results of a scientific test," for example—might provide a sufficient basis for believing that some event had occurred "without in the least explaining why."[11] A certain barometric reading might predict a worsening of the weather, but it could scarcely be said to cause the change in atmospheric conditions. Predictive power was just not enough for something to qualify as a real explanation. Something more was needed, but what? This was a fundamental problem, but Hempel essentially walked away from it.

---

[5] See especially J. H. Hexter, "The One That Got Away," *New York Review of Books*, February 9, 1967.

[6] See, for example, Dray, *Laws and Explanation in History*, p. 12, and Alan Donagan, "Can Philosophers Learn from Historians?" in *Mind, Science, and History*, ed. Howard Kiefer and Milton Munitz (Albany: State University of New York Press, 1970), p. 244.

[7] Marvin Levich, "Interpretation in History," *History and Theory* 24 (1985): 61.

[8] Donagan, "Popper-Hempel Theory," p. 157.

[9] William Dray, "The Historical Explanation of Actions Reconsidered," in *Philosophy and History: A Symposium*, ed. Sidney Hook (New York: New York University Press, 1963), p. 133.

[10] Donagan, "Popper-Hempel Theory," p. 142.

[11] Carl Hempel, "Reasons and Covering Laws in Historical Explanation," in Hook, *Philosophy and History*, p. 146. See also N. R. Hanson, *Observation and Explanation: A Guide to Philosophy of Science* (New York: Harper, 1971), pp. 39–49, esp. pp. 42, 48–49.

This does not mean that the sort of thinking represented by the Hempel article is devoid of practical value. The Hempel approach might have been overly rigid in the reliance it placed on social scientific laws, but (as will be seen) the argument that causal explanation is closely related to logical deduction is in fact quite important. And the Hempel approach does shed some light on some second-order issues. Hempel's point, for example, that explanation and prediction are cognate concepts—that to explain an event is to be able to predict, given some general principles and certain particular conditions, that that event would occur—translates into an important point of method.[12] At any given point in a historical argument, the historian can ask, given what was said up to that point, whether it would be possible to predict how things would develop. This provides a useful test of the *power* of the argument: a strong interpretation should have a certain predictive force. An interpretation, moreover, generates expectations: if it is valid, then what else would one expect to find? Consciously or unconsciously, the historian will be making predictions about what as yet unexamined sources would reveal, and those predictions can provide a useful yardstick for judging the *validity* of the argument.

So the Hempel tradition is not to be dismissed out of hand. The fact remains, however, that on the central issues the practicing historian will not find much of value here. But this was not the only approach the philosophers of history were able to come up with. There was, in fact, one basic alternative to the Hempel doctrine, the approach associated with the British philosopher R. G. Collingwood. Indeed, in the philosophy of history literature in the 1950s and 1960s, Collingwood's ideas were often treated as the only real alternative to Hempel's. But did this alternative approach give the historians what they needed?

The Collingwood theory was quite extraordinary. According to Collingwood, the historian was concerned not with events as such but with actions—that is, with "events brought about by the will and expressing the thought of a free and intelligent agent." The historian, he said, "discovers this thought by rethinking it in his own mind." The "reliving of past experiences" through the "rethinking" of past thought: this for Collingwood was what history was about, and this was what historical explanation amounted to. "An historical fact once genuinely ascertained," he argued, "grasped by the historian's reenactment of the agent's thought in his own mind, is already explained. For the historian there is no difference between discovering what happened and

---

[12] Hempel, "Function of General Laws," pp. 347–48. Popper argued along similar lines. See Karl Popper, *The Open Society and Its Enemies*, 4th ed. (London: Routledge, 1962), 2:262. The relationship between the two concepts, however, is not as simple as Hempel thought. See the chapter on "Explaining and Predicting" in N. R. Hanson, *The Concept of the Positron: A Philosophical Analysis* (Cambridge: Cambridge University Press, 1963), pp. 25–41.

discovering why it happened." When a historian asks, for example, "'Why did Brutus stab Caesar?' he means 'What did Brutus think, which made him decide to stab Caesar?' The cause of the event, for him, means the thought in the mind of the person by whose agency the event came about: and this is not something other than the event, it is the inside of the event itself."[13]

This, according to Collingwood, was one of the things that distinguished history from science. "The processes of nature," he wrote, could be "properly described as sequences of mere events, but those of history cannot. They are not processes of mere events but processes of actions, which have an inner side, consisting of processes of thought; and what the historian is looking for is these processes of thought." The historian discovered them by rethinking those thoughts "in his own mind." To understand why Julius Caesar, for example, did certain things, the historian tries "to discover what thoughts in Caesar's mind determined him to do them. This implies envisaging for himself the situation in which Caesar stood, and thinking for himself what Caesar thought about the situation and the possible ways of dealing with it." "The history of thought," he concluded, "and therefore all history, is the re-enactment of past thought in the historian's own mind."[14]

The historian's goal was thus to bring the past back to life by rethinking past thoughts in the present. Indeed, according to Collingwood, that was the historian's *only* goal. History, he insisted, was "*nothing but* the re-enactment of past thought in the historian's own mind." The thoughts that a historian "can re-think for himself" are "*all* he can know historically." "Of everything other than thought," he said, "there can be no history." Human reason was the only factor of interest to the historian. Montesquieu, he said, had "misunderstood the essential character" of the differences between various nations and cultures: "instead of explaining their history by reference to human reason, he thought of it as due to differences in climate and geography." "History so conceived," he argued, "would become a kind of natural history of man, or anthropology, where institutions appear not as *free inventions of human reason* in the course of its development, but as the necessary effects of natural causes." To be sure, he admitted, there was "an intimate relation between any culture and its natural environment; but what determines its character is not the facts of that environment, in themselves, but what man is able to get out of them; and that depends on what kind of man he is."[15]

This whole approach would today, I think, strike even the most conservative historians as narrow and dogmatic and in fact as a bit bizarre. Philosophers

---

[13] R. G. Collingwood, *The Idea of History* (New York: Oxford University Press, 1956), pp. 175–78, 214–15.

[14] Ibid., p. 215.

[15] Ibid., pp. 78–79, 218, 228, 304 (emphasis added).

have traditionally tended to view the Collingwood approach more sympathetically, but even some philosophers have found that approach a little hard to take.[16] How could Collingwood simply assume, for example, that social institutions were "free inventions of human reason"? How could he be so dismissive of factors having little to do with "action" and "rational thought" in his sense? Collingwood would simply lay it down as a basic principle that "so far as man's conduct is determined by what may be called his animal nature, his impulses and appetites, it is non-historical."[17] But this view was obviously rather arbitrary. To be sure, conscious thought plays a role, sometimes a very important role, in shaping the course of events, and one of the historian's basic techniques is to try to look at things through the eyes of the people he or she is studying. But the historian's goal is to make sense of the past—to see how things fit together, to understand the logic underlying the course of events—and often that logic has a great deal to do with nonintellective factors. Demographic change, economic growth, shifts in the distribution of power among states: developments of that sort are obviously of fundamental historical importance. To explain why Brutus stabbed Caesar (to take Collingwood's own example), the historian would want to see what was going on in Rome at the time socially, economically, culturally and above all politically: the goal would be to see not just what was in Brutus's mind at a particular moment, but to understand the whole process that had led up to the assassination of Caesar. Or to put the point in more general terms: historical evolution, like evolution as a whole, is not always driven by intent; the "structure selects," the environment, both human and natural, plays a key role, and the "why" questions are thus not always answered by looking essentially to conscious thought.[18]

So for most historians the Collingwood theory was not taken too seriously. And what this meant was that neither the Collingwood school nor the Hempel school gave the historians much that they found useful in the way of philosophical guidance. The two schools represented opposite ends of a spectrum: one emphasized structure and law-like regularity, and the other free will and human agency. But every practicing historian knows that both sorts of factors come into play. Part of the art of doing history is being able to figure

[16] See especially R. F. Atkinson, *Knowledge and Explanation in History* (Ithaca: Cornell University Press, 1978), pp. 26–27.

[17] Collingwood, *Idea of History*, p. 216.

[18] This simple point lies at the heart of evolutionary theory. For the application of this type of thinking to political life, see Kenneth Waltz, *Theory of International Politics* (New York: McGraw-Hill, 1979), esp. pp. 76–77, 82–88, 118; the phrase quoted is on p. 92. Note also the general approach taken in Robert Axelrod's *The Evolution of Cooperation* (New York: Basic Books, 1984). Axelrod approached his problem in evolutionary terms and thus did not assume intelligence shaped action. An organism, as he put it, "does not need a brain to play a game," and his theory of "cooperation" applied to bacteria as well as to human beings. Ibid., p. 18; note also chapter 5.

out how exactly in any particular case the balance between them is to be struck, and this of course is an empirical and not a philosophical problem. The two schools together had dominated Anglo-American philosophy of history in the 1950s and 1960s, but from the point of view of the practitioners, neither tradition had generated much in the way of insight into what history should be.

THE CONSTRUCTIVIST CHALLENGE

Practicing historians by the late 1960s had thus come to have a fairly low opinion of the philosophy of history literature. J. H. Hexter, for example, referred in 1967 to the "long-standing failure of a considerable number of talented philosophers writing about history to say anything of much interest to historians."[19] Many other historians felt much the same way. But the tradition Hexter was criticizing was already petering out, and within the space of a few years a very different body of theory had emerged. This time the theorists *were* saying things of considerable interest to historians. But did this new body of theory actually meet their needs any better than the body of theory it had replaced?

The new movement was based on the idea, not particularly new in itself, that history is not so much discovered as invented.[20] The argument was that the past itself no longer exists; what happened in the past cannot be perceived and is not directly knowable; it therefore takes an act of the imagination to create a picture of the past. That picture could take many different forms, all equally legitimate. As Hayden White, the leading figure in the movement, put it: "any historical object can sustain a number of equally plausible descriptions or narratives of its processes."[21]

Indeed, White contended, one could never take it for granted that there is any coherent story that captures the historical reality of the subject being

[19] Reply to Morton White, *New York Review of Books*, March 23, 1967, p. 29.

[20] The British philosopher Michael Oakeshott, for example, argued in 1933 that "the historian's business is not to discover, to recapture, or even to interpret: it is to create and construct." Michael Oakeshott, *Experience and Its Modes* (Cambridge: Cambridge University Press, 1933), p. 93. Collingwood, incidentally, considered the chapter in which Oakeshott had made this argument to be "the most penetrating analysis of historical thought that has ever been written." Quoted in David Boucher, "The Creation of the Past: British Idealism and Michael Oakeshott's Philosophy of History," *History and Theory* 23 (1984): 193.

[21] Hayden White, *The Content of the Form: Narrative Discourse and Historical Representation* (Baltimore: Johns Hopkins University Press, 1987), p. 76. For a discussion of the surprisingly common argument about the "non-existence" of the past, see Atkinson, *Knowledge and Explanation in History*, pp. 51–53.

studied: "the conviction that we can make sense of history stands on the same level of epistemic plausibility as the conviction that it makes no sense whatsoever."[22] Because the material the historian has to work with grossly underdetermines the sort of interpretation that is produced, historical writing was much more inventive than the historical profession had traditionally been willing to admit. It followed, he argued, that "if one treated the historian's text as what it manifestly was, namely a rhetorical composition, one would be able to see not only that historians effectively *constructed* the subject of their discourse in and by writing, but that, ultimately, what they actually wrote was less a report of what they had found in their research than of what they had *imagined* the object of their original interest to consist of."[23]

Old-fashioned historians were thus wrong, in White's view, to think that narrative discourse was "a neutral medium for the representation of historical events." It was instead "the very stuff of a mythical view of reality"; in fact, the literary structure of the historical text carried the meaning.[24] The "factual" content, such as it was, was not to be taken too seriously; "every historical narrative" was to be regarded as "allegorical"—that is, "as saying one thing and meaning another."[25] The historian, according to White, in adopting a rhetorical strategy, performs "an essentially *poetic* act, in which he *pre*figures the historical field and constitutes it as a domain upon which to bring to bear the specific theories he will use to explain 'what was *really* happening' in it."[26] In White's view, as one commentator put it, the heart of the interpretation was "packed into the historian's original creative act."[27] Since "the possible modes of historiography," White argued, were "in reality *formalizations* of poetic insights that analytically precede them," and since none of these poetic insights had a more legitimate claim to being "realistic" than any of the others, the historian's choice of an interpretative strategy did not depend on what best captured "reality": the choice was "ultimately aesthetic or moral rather than epistemological."[28] The conclusion, shocking to old-fashioned historians, was that "we are free to conceive 'history' as we please, just as we are free to make of it what we will."[29]

[22] White, *Content of the Form*, p. 73.

[23] Hayden White, response to Arthur Marwick, *Journal of Contemporary History* 30 (April 1995): 240 (emphasis in original).

[24] White, *Content of the Form*, pp. ix, 43–44.

[25] Ibid., p. 45.

[26] Hayden White, *Metahistory: The Historical Imagination in Nineteenth-Century Europe* (Baltimore: Johns Hopkins University Press, 1973), p. x (emphasis in original).

[27] Maurice Mandelbaum, "The Presuppositions of *Metahistory*," *History and Theory* 19, Beiheft (1980): 46.

[28] White, *Metahistory*, p. xii (emphasis in original).

[29] Ibid., p. 433.

Historical narratives were thus to be treated as "verbal fictions"; there was no fundamental difference between history and myth.[30] The basic concepts people normally used to distinguish between the two, concepts like "truth" and "reality," were themselves problematic. Here people like White drew freely on the writings of literary theorists like Roland Barthes, who had challenged the idea that one could meaningfully distinguish between historical and fictional discourses and who had insisted that thought was a captive of language.[31]

People who argued along these lines, as White himself pointed out, were often charged with promoting "a debilitating relativism that permits any manipulation of the evidence as long as the account produced is structurally coherent." Such an approach, the critics alleged, would for example permit a Nazi version of history, a version that would even deny the reality of the Holocaust, "to claim a certain minimal credibility." Wasn't it the case, those critics asked, that according to his theory whether or not the Holocaust had actually occurred was "only a matter of opinion," and that one could "write its history in whatever way one pleases"?[32]

White did not quite say no. Indeed, he admitted that "the kind of perspective on history" he favored was "conventionally associated" with "the ideologies of fascist regimes." But this, he said, was no reason for shying away from it: it was important, in his view, to "guard against a sentimentalism that would lead us to write off such a conception of history simply because it has been associated with fascist ideologies." He still insisted "that when it comes to apprehending the historical record, there are no grounds to be found in the historical record itself for preferring one way of construing its meaning over another."[33] But once again this raised the issue of whether a Nazi interpretation of history was as legitimate as any other.

White dealt with that issue not directly but rather by considering the question of whether the Nazis' victims, the Jews, could legitimately concoct a historical interpretation for their own political purposes. His answer was that they could. Israeli ideologists, he said, had adopted the theory that the Holocaust was the inevitable outcome of life in the Diaspora. "The totalitarian, not to say fascist, aspects" of Israeli policy on the West Bank, according to White, might be rooted in that theory, but it should nonetheless be considered as a "morally responsible response to the meaninglessness" of Jewish history in the Diaspora. It was not to be dismissed as an "untruth." Indeed,

---

[30] Hayden White, *Tropics of Discourse: Essays in Cultural Criticism* (Baltimore: Johns Hopkins University Press, 1978), p. 82.

[31] White, *Metahistory*, p. xi; White, *Content of the Form*, pp. 35, 37. A quotation from Barthes ("le fait n'a jamais qu'une existence linguistique") was used as the motto for that latter book.

[32] White, *Content of the Form*, p. 76; White, *Metahistory*, p. 433.

[33] White, *Content of the Form*, pp. 74–75.

"its truth, as a historical interpretation, consists precisely of its effectiveness in justifying a wide range of current Israeli political policies that, from the standpoint of those who articulate them, are crucial to the security and indeed the very existence of the Jewish people." And how, in White's view, did that sort of history compare with history that purports to be objective—with history that claims "to have forgone service to any specific political cause and simply purports to tell the truth about the past as an end in itself," and that claims to provide a relatively impartial view that might lead to "tolerance and forbearance rather than reverence or a spirit of vengefulness"? The more politicized approach was actually to be preferred. The balanced view, the view that suggests that the "desire for revenge" be put aside, is the sort of view, he says, that "always emanates from centers of established political power," but the kind of tolerance it recommends "is a luxury only devotees of dominant groups can afford." The attempt to write history objectively is thus ruled out on *political* grounds—ruled out precisely because it would lead to mutual tolerance. The truth was not to be sought "as an end in itself"; the test of validity was political effectiveness.[34]

White was not the only scholar to argue along these lines, and some writers were even more extreme. Hans Kellner, for example, argued that the belief in "historical objectivity" was not just a form of self-deception. The set of norms associated with that concept was actually an instrument of repression. "'Truth' and 'reality,'" according to Kellner, "are, of course, the primary authoritarian weapons of our time."[35]

The effect of this type of thinking was to sanction a highly politicized form of historiography. For if it were true, as Michel Foucault argued, that "we cannot exercise power except through the production of truth," then one could try to gain power by creating one's own "truth"—that is, by shaping a text so as to serve one's own political purposes.[36] And this had to be the goal of writing history, because the competing conception of what the goal of history was—the old-fashioned idea that the aim was to "tell the truth about the past as an end in itself"—had been so thoroughly discredited. From this point of view, the historian did not even have to try to be honest. "White's view of history" was thus praised by one of his supporters for allowing "for those 'creative, interpretive distortions' which, optimistically, go beyond orthodox ways of reading the past the present and the future in *utopian* ways."[37] The point

---

[34] Ibid., pp. 80–81; see also p. 73.

[35] Hans Kellner, "Narrativity in History: Post-Structuralism and Since," *History and Theory* 26, Beiheft 26 (December 1987): 6.

[36] Michel Foucault, *Power/Knowledge* (New York: Pantheon, 1980), p. 93.

[37] Keith Jenkins, On *"What Is History?"*: *From Carr and Elton to Rorty and White* (London: Routledge, 1995), p. 42 (emphasis in original).

of doing history, the argument ran, was therefore not "to get the story straight" but rather to "get the story *crooked*."[38]

Given how sharply these views diverged from traditional notions of what historical scholarship was supposed to be, it was scarcely to be expected that they would be accepted uncritically. As it turned out, in their pure form they had only a negligible impact on what historians actually did. White's writings, for example, as his own supporters note with chagrin, have had "virtually no discernible influence" on historical work. "Inadequately read, rarely reviewed in journals read by historians, infrequently cited, little discussed, and then routinely and grossly misunderstood"—that was the upshot of one such study of White's impact.[39] Those writers had their own ideas about why this was so, but perhaps the basic reason was that White's theory, and especially the idea of the historian performing an "an essentially *poetic* act," did not ring true in terms of the historians' understanding of their own work. An interpretation can take years, and sometimes decades, of intense study to work out. The whole intellectual process of making sense of the evidence seemed to the people engaged in it to play a fundamental role in shaping the final product. Practicing historians could scarcely admit that interpretation ultimately boiled down to a simple "poetic act."

So most historians found these arguments hard to accept, and yet the movement was not without consequence. Many of the notions with which it was associated were broadly accepted, albeit in watered-down form. The view that it was legitimate for historical work to be shaped, at least to some degree, by a political agenda became quite respectable.[40] The old ideal of historical objectivity, on the other hand, fell into disrepute. It was often taken for granted that the belief that historical work could be objective was a delusion; the inference was sometimes drawn that there was little point to even trying for objectivity and that the important thing was to make one's own biases explicit.

---

[38] Stephen Bann, quoted in Hans Kellner, *Language and Historical Representation: Getting the Story Crooked* (Madison: University of Wisconsin Press, 1989), p. 3, and also quoted in J. L. Gorman's review of the Kellner book in *History and Theory* 30 (1991): 359 (emphasis in original).

[39] Nancy Partner, "Hayden White (and the Content and the Form and Everyone Else) at the AHA," *History and Theory* 36 (1997): 104, and Richard Vann, "The Reception of Hayden White," *History and Theory* 37 (1998).

[40] See, for example, Joyce Appleby, Lynn Hunt, and Margaret Jacob, *Telling the Truth about History* (New York: Norton, 1994), p. 4: "We seek a vision of the past and an intellectual stance for the present that will promote an ever more democratic society." See also Thomas L. Haskell, *Objectivity Is Not Neutrality: Explanatory Schemes in History* (Baltimore: Johns Hopkins University Press, 1998), p. 150, and the cases cited in Peter Novick, *That Noble Dream: The "Objectivity Question" and the American Historical Profession* (Cambridge: Cambridge University Press, 1988), p. 598.

Why were ideas of this sort taking hold even among mainstream historians? For one thing, the general intellectual climate was changing rapidly in
the late twentieth century. There was a growing tendency throughout the humanities in the 1970s and 1980s especially to challenge the very idea of
truth, and to mount that challenge in a rather radical way. "The secret of theory," according to one leading theorist (Baudrillard), is "that truth does not
exist."[41] According to another even more famous theorist (Foucault), "reality
does not exist," "only language exists."[42] And this kind of thinking was by no
means limited to a number of well-known French writers.

In America as well, there was a certain tendency, as represented, for example, in the work of the philosopher Richard Rorty, to downgrade notions like
"rationality" and "objectivity," to blur the distinction between knowledge
and opinion, and to insist that "there is no way to get outside our beliefs and
our language." For Rorty, terms like "truth" and "knowledge" were simply
"matters of social practice"—mere "compliments" paid to "beliefs we think so
well justified that, for the moment, further justification is not needed."[43] Insofar as there was a difference between knowledge and opinion, for Rorty it
was simply the difference between ideas that are generally shared and ideas
"on which agreement is relatively hard to get."[44] From his point of view, "the
desire for objectivity" was thus simply "the desire for as much intersubjective
agreement as possible."[45] To reach for something more—"to explicate 'rationality' and 'objectivity' in terms of conditions of accurate representation"—is
just a "self-deceptive effort to eternalize the normal discourse of the day."[46]
Indeed, according to Rorty, the archaic vocabulary of Enlightenment ratio-
nalism had become an "impediment to the progress of democratic societies":
it was "obsolete" and should be replaced by a new way of speaking more in
line with our current political values.[47] These views were quite influential.
They served in particular to give a veneer of philosophical respectability to
the new antiobjectivist view of history.[48]

[41] Jean Baudrillard, interview with Sylvere Lotringer, "Forgetting Baudrillard," *Social Text*,
no. 15 (Fall 1986): 142.

[42] This widely quoted remark originally appeared in the "Débat sur le roman," published in *Tel
Quel* 117 (Spring 1964): 45, and reprinted in Michel Foucault, *Dits et Ecrits, 1954–1988*, vol. 1
(Paris: Gallimard, 1994), p. 380.

[43] Richard Rorty, *Philosophy and the Mirror of Nature* (Princeton: Princeton University Press,
1979), pp. 10, 11, 178, 385; Richard Rorty, *Objectivism, Relativism, and Truth* (Cambridge:
Cambridge University Press, 1991), p. 24.

[44] Rorty, *Objectivism, Relativism, and Truth*, p. 23.

[45] Ibid.

[46] Rorty, *Philosophy and the Mirror of Nature*, p. 11.

[47] Richard Rorty, "The Contingency of Community," *London Review of Books*, July 24, 1986, p. 10.

[48] See especially Jenkins, *On "What Is History?": From Carr and Elton to Rorty and White*. Note
also John Searle's discussion of Rorty's influence on the humanities in general in his "The Storm
over the University," *New York Review of Books*, December 6, 1990, p. 40.

But there was something quite odd about Rorty's whole line of argument. Who, for example, really thinks that the belief that the earth was flat was no less "true" in its day than the opposite belief is today? But people tended to be somewhat bowled over by Rorty's prestige and by the claim that his views had come to represent something of a consensus. Who, it was asked, still actually believed in such notions as "reality" and "truth"? "Metaphysical prigs" of that sort, according to people like Rorty, had become increasingly hard to find.[49]

The Rorty view, however, did not represent anything like a consensus. There were many philosophers, including some quite well-known ones, who took a position on these issues much more in line with common sense.[50] John Searle, for example, one of America's most distinguished contemporary philosophers, even had the temerity to declare that the "idea that there is a real world independent of our thought and talk" and "the idea that our true statements are typically made true by how things are in the real world" were "essential presuppositions of any sane philosophy."[51]

These were not, of course, new issues for the philosophers. The problem of the nature of knowledge had been at the top of their agenda since ancient times. And during those centuries of philosophical debate, certain key points had become clear. One such point was that there was no way to disprove the claims of the skeptic. There was no way, for example, to rule out the possibility "that the world sprang into being five minutes ago, exactly as it then was, with a population that 'remembered' a wholly unreal past."[52] Knowledge was therefore never absolute. There was no way to prove that the external world even exists. But the point was trivial. It simply meant that everything we do of an intellectual nature is premised on the assumption that we are not being systematically misled: we take as our point of departure the assumption that

[49] Richard Rorty, "Deconstruction and Circumvention," in his *Philosophical Papers*, vol. 2, *Essays on Heidegger and Others* (New York: Cambridge University Press, 1991), p. 86. This paper was originally published in *Critical Inquiry* (September 1984).

[50] W. V. Quine, for example, explicitly repudiates the view Rorty attributes to him (the "claim that there is no 'matter of fact' involved in attributions of meaning to utterances"); he says that the meaning of sentences is "very much a matter of fact." Donald Davidson says: "We can accept objective truth conditions as the key to meaning, a realist view of truth, and we can insist that knowledge is of an objective world independent of our thought or language." W. V. Quine, "Let Me Accentuate the Positive," and Donald Davidson, "A Coherence Theory of Truth and Knowledge," in *Reading Rorty: Critical Response to Philosophy and the Mirror of Nature (and Beyond)*, ed. Alan Malachowski (Oxford: Blackwell, 1990), pp. 117, 120–21.

[51] John Searle, *The Construction of Social Reality* (New York: Free Press, 1995), p. xiii. An argument supporting these propositions is laid out in chapters 7–9 of that book.

[52] Bertrand Russell, *The Analysis of Mind* (London: George Allen and Unwin, 1921), p. 160. Arguments of this sort are common in epistemology. Descartes, for example, raised the specter of "a deceiver of supreme power and cunning who is deliberately and constantly deceiving me." René Descartes, *The Philosophical Writings of Descartes*, trans. John Cottingham, Robert Stoothoff, and Dugald Murdoch (Cambridge: Cambridge University Press, 1984), p. 17.

our basic beliefs about reality—about the existence of an external world knowable through the mind and through the senses, acting in tandem—are in fact correct. As Hume put it: "'tis in vain to ask, *Whether there be body or not?* That is a point, which we must take for granted in all our reasonings."[53] The skeptic is not refuted; the basic epistemological problem is recognized, but the normal assumptions—about the existence of reality and the possibility of knowledge—are made, and we just move on from there.

Because these basic conclusions apply to knowledge in general, they apply to historical knowledge in particular. But does the problem end there, or is there a distinct problem of *historical* knowledge that needs to be considered—distinct because historical knowledge is essentially different from other forms of knowledge? In particular, is historical knowledge fundamentally different from scientific knowledge? If not, then perhaps the philosophy of science can give us the guidance we are looking for.

PHILOSOPHY OF SCIENCE AS PHILOSOPHY OF HISTORY

How does historical analysis differ from scientific analysis? Is science different because it deals with the natural world, whereas history deals with the human world?[54] This is obviously not the case: many sciences—experimental psychology, for example—take human beings as objects of study. Is science different because in science truths are discovered "through observation and experiment exemplified in what we actually perceive, whereas the past has vanished and our ideas about it can never be verified as we verify our scientific hypotheses"?[55] Again the answer is no. Science often deals with the vestiges of past phenomena. This is as true of astrophysics as it is of evolutionary biology, geology, and many other fields. The biologist has a fossil record to work with, and the historian has a documentary record. From an epistemological point of view, how is the one body of evidence essentially different from the other?

It is often argued that the real difference has to do with the level of generality at which a subject is studied. The historian, it is often said, is concerned with the particular, and the scientist's concern is with general phenomena—that the scientist's aim is to "formulate a system of general laws," whereas the historian's "central preoccupation" is with "the precise course of individual

[53] David Hume, *A Treatise of Human Nature*, ed. L. A. Selby-Bigge, 2d ed. (Oxford: Clarendon, 1978), p. 187.

[54] As claimed, for example, by Anthony O'Hear in his *Introduction to the Philosophy of Science* (Oxford: Clarendon, 1989), p. 6.

[55] Collingwood, *Idea of History*, p. 5.

events."[56] But most scientists, to judge from the sorts of articles published in their journals, are concerned with very specific matters—to be sure, in the context of a more far-reaching set of interests. The same point, however, applies to the historians: the topic may be relatively narrow, but fundamental conceptual issues are rarely entirely absent.

Sometimes the argument is that historical analysis is necessarily selective and is therefore subjective and unscientific.[57] But as one philosopher points out, it is "wholly mistaken to hold that history is selective and science not. In truth the sciences are much more rigorous and explicit in selecting the facts or aspects of fact which concern them than history ever is."[58]

Sometimes professional consensus is taken as the key indicator. Scientists, it is said, have "evolved a standard way of thinking" about their subject matter; as a result, scientific thinking is "impartial and impersonal"; assumptions and principles are shared, and the conclusions reached are accepted by all competent scientists. This, it is argued, is one of the main things that makes a field like physics "scientific" and why it is that natural science can be said to provide "objective knowledge."[59] Historians, on the other hand, commonly disagree sharply among themselves on many important issues; history, the argument runs, therefore cannot be considered a science.

But consensus is not a measure of quality in the natural sciences: the most impressive advances in physics, for example, took place during times when no consensus existed and when fundamental claims were vigorously disputed, and the same kind of point can be made about evolutionary biology in our own day. Nor would it necessarily be a sign of scientific status and a higher level of objectivity if historians, for their part, did accept standard interpretations on a whole range of issues. Degree of consensus is very much a surface indicator. Scientific status really depends on the nature and the quality of argumentation: on whether insights can be developed in a logically compelling way and on whether those insights are rooted in the empirical evidence at hand.

The scientific status of a discipline turns therefore on the nature of the method used. In that regard history and science have more in common than one might think. Collingwood developed the point quite effectively:

Francis Bacon, lawyer and philosopher, laid it down in one of his memorable phrases that the natural scientist must "put Nature to the question." What he was denying,

[56] W. H. Walsh, *An Introduction to the Philosophy of History* (London: Hutchinson's, 1951), pp. 24, 38. See also Maurice Mandelbaum, *The Problem of Historical Knowledge: An Answer to Relativism* (New York: Liveright, 1938), p. 3.

[57] This familiar point goes back at least to Descartes; see the passage quoted in Collingwood, *Idea of History*, p. 59.

[58] Atkinson, *Knowledge and Explanation in History*, p. 79.

[59] Walsh, *Introduction to the Philosophy of History*, pp. 96–97, 114.

when he wrote this, was that the scientist's attitude towards nature should be one of respectful attentiveness, waiting upon her utterances and building his theories on the basis of what she chose to vouchsafe him. What he was asserting was two things at once: first, that the scientist must take the initiative, deciding for himself what he wants to know and formulating this in his own mind in the shape of a question; and secondly, that he must find means of compelling nature to answer, devising tortures under which she can no longer hold her tongue. Here, in a single brief epigram, Bacon laid down for all the true theory of experimental science.[60]

Collingwood's real insight here was that the point did not just apply to science. Bacon, he said, had also hit upon the "true theory of historical method." And Collingwood stressed the point, both in *The Idea of History* and in his earlier work, that historical analysis should, like science, be question-driven. "You can't collect your evidence before you begin thinking," he noted, and because thinking meant "asking questions," nothing was evidence "except in relation to some definite question."[61]

This point is of absolutely fundamental importance. In doing historical work, if you are doing it the right way, you are not just studying a topic. You are trying to answer a question, or perhaps a set of questions. And it really matters how those questions are framed. Questions need to be set up in such a way that the answers turn on what the evidence shows. There is little point in setting out to answer essentially trivial questions—that is, in doing what historians contemptuously refer to as "antiquarian" work. If the goal is to get some insight into the really big issues (such as what makes for war, or for a stable international system), then the particular questions the historian sets out to answer should have some larger importance, in the sense that the way they are answered should shed some light on one of those basic issues. This does not mean, of course, that the historian should try to tackle some very broad issue in a very direct way. To do that is like grabbing at a cloud. To get at such an issue, the scholar has to try to bring it down to earth and give it some concrete content: not just "what makes for war?" but "what caused the First World War?" or even "why did events take the course they did during the July crisis in 1914?" The narrower the question, the more studiable it is. But in defining the question more narrowly, it is important not to lose sight of the more basic conceptual issue. The historian's findings need to have some broader importance. But this point applies not just to historical work but to science as a whole.

So there is less to the distinction between science and history than meets the eye, and indeed the sense that the two fields are radically different is rooted in a rather old-fashioned and idealized sense for what science is. Science, according to that traditional view, was based on observed fact. Facts had a kind

---

[60] Collingwood, *Idea of History*, p. 269.
[61] Ibid., p. 281.

of elemental quality: once discovered, they could not be disputed, and they were the basic building blocks used to construct theories. Scientists might disagree about theoretical matters, but fact, discovered through experiment, was a "court of final appeal": observation would decide the issue and would decide it in a way that was intellectually compelling. There was, in other words, a method, practically an algorithm, linking empirical observations to theoretical conclusions. That meant that the theory produced by that method was in no sense arbitrary: the natural world was being revealed for what it really was.[62]

That whole view was basically abandoned in the 1960s. The logic of scientific development, the argument ran, was much looser than people had thought, and the whole notion of an algorithm did not come close to capturing the way science actually worked. For one thing, the basic idea that facts were what they were, independent of theory, came to be seen as somewhat problematic: an observation was meaningful only in the context of a set of theoretical assumptions, so the line between fact and theory was not nearly as sharp as the old positivist tradition had assumed.[63] And theory itself never took shape in a kind of mechanical way from facts gathered up "like pebbles on the beach." The facts never just "speak for themselves."[64] That certainly was Einstein's view. There was, he said, "no inductive method which could lead to the fundamental concepts of physics"; "in error are those theorists who believe that theory comes inductively from experience."[65]

But if theory is not a simple product of observation, what, if anything, makes a particular theory intellectually compelling? The test of evidence is not quite as decisive as it might seem. Since observations do not just "speak for themselves" and have to be interpreted, theoretical assumptions inevitably come into play. So there is a certain problem of circularity here. And theories,

---

[62] Thomas Kuhn, *The Trouble with the Historical Philosophy of Science* (Cambridge, Mass.: Harvard History of Science Department, 1991), pp. 4–5; Stephen Toulmin, "From Form to Function: Philosophy and History of Science in the 1950s and Now," *Daedalus* 106, no. 3 (Summer 1977): esp. 147, 150–51.

[63] This is one of the basic themes of N. R. Hanson's work. See Hanson, *Observation and Explanation*, pp. 1–15, esp. 4–5; N. R. Hanson, *Patterns of Discovery: An Inquiry into the Conceptual Foundations of Science* (Cambridge: Cambridge University Press, 1958), chaps. 1 and 2; and N. R. Hanson, *Perception and Discovery: An Introduction to Scientific Inquiry* (San Francisco: Freeman, Cooper, 1969), parts 2 and 3. This way of looking at things was by no means entirely new; the key ideas had, in fact, been laid out a half century earlier by Pierre Duhem. See especially Pierre Duhem, *La Théorie physique, son objet, sa structure* (Paris: Chevalier et Rivière, 1906), and published in English as *The Aim and Structure of Physical Theory* (Princeton: Princeton University Press, 1954); note especially part II, chaps. 4 and 6.

[64] Hanson, *Perception and Discovery*, pp. 220, 237. See also the quotations in Hanson, *Patterns of Discovery*, pp. 183–84.

[65] Albert Einstein, "Physics and Reality," in Albert Einstein, *Ideas and Opinions* (New York: Crown, 1954), pp. 301, 307. This article was first published in 1936.

it turns out, are not abandoned simply because evidence turns up that seems to contradict them. Evidence of that sort can often be written off with ad hoc arguments, and, even when it cannot be dealt with in that way, a theory can be adjusted to accommodate observations which, in its original form, it had been unable to account for.[66] So the method of justification—the method for treating the "facts" as a kind of final arbiter—is much weaker than one might think. But if all this is true, what then *does* determine theory choice? Does all this mean that theory choice is an essentially arbitrary process?

For the philosophers concerned with these issues in the 1950s and early 1960s, people like N. R. Hanson, Stephen Toulmin, and Thomas Kuhn, it seemed that the history of science might point the way to some answers. The older formalist tradition had been largely ahistorical. That tradition had emphasized the "context of justification." The assumption had been that methodology had to do with the rational justification for theories in their final form; it was concerned with the formal methods for establishing the validity of such theories. Questions about discovery—about the actual historical process through which theory took shape—were dismissed as matters of "mere psychology."[67] Karl Popper, for example, although he wrote a book called *The Logic of Scientific Discovery*, was not really interested in the historical process that led to the emergence of new theories.[68] Hanson made fun of that kind of approach. What Popper and other scholars in that school were interested in, he said, was not so much the "*logic of discovery*" as the "*logic of the Finished Research Report*."[69] But one of the assumptions of the new, more historicist approach was that such distinctions were much too sharp and that the "logic of discovery" was of a piece with the "logic of justification."

If theories, however, were the product of a historical process, a process that could have developed in more than one way, what did this imply about their epistemic status? It seemed that to admit that the issue of theory choice is not decided in a purely rational and objective way—to admit that theory choice "depends on a mixture of objective and subjective factors"[70]—was to open the floodgates. How could the truth claims of science survive the admission

[66] See especially Imre Lakatos, "Falsification and the Methodology of Scientific Research Programmes," in *Criticism and the Growth of Knowledge*, ed. Imre Lakatos and Alan Musgrave (Cambridge: Cambridge University Press, 1970), pp. 100–101.

[67] Imre Lakatos, quoted in Stephen Toulmin, *Human Understanding*, vol. 1 (Princeton: Princeton University Press, 1972), p. 482n.

[68] Karl Popper, "Normal Science and Its Dangers," in Lakatos and Musgrave, *Criticism and the Growth of Knowledge*, pp. 57–58. Kuhn quotes (and criticizes) this passage in one of his own contributions to that volume, ibid., p. 235.

[69] N. R. Hanson, *What I Do Not Believe, and Other Essays* (Dordrecht: Reidel, 1972), pp. 288–89.

[70] Thomas Kuhn, *The Essential Tension: Selected Studies in Scientific Tradition and Change* (Chicago: University of Chicago Press, 1977), p. 325. One scholar quotes this passage as

that theory had no purely rational basis, compelling in itself? Wouldn't the "door to subjectivism" be "wide open"?[71]

Thomas Kuhn was the best-known champion of the new approach, and in his amazingly successful book *The Structure of Scientific Revolutions* he presented the new thinking in a particularly sharp form. Kuhn's analysis focused on what he called "paradigms"—that is, basic frameworks for scientific thinking during a particular stage in the history of science.[72] Science, in his view, developed in two distinct ways. There was "normal science," the work that took place in the context of a particular paradigm, and "revolutionary science," the process leading to the replacement of old paradigms by newer ones. His fundamental claim was that new paradigms did not emerge, and older ones were not overthrown, for purely rational reasons; the "issue of paradigm choice," he wrote, "can never be unequivocally settled by logic and experiment alone."[73] Instead, he saw a process of anomalies piling up as "normal science" ran its course; normal science was unable to deal with these anomalies, precisely because it took the existing paradigm as given and could therefore not question it. The resulting crisis could therefore only be resolved through a kind of revolution: the emergence of a new paradigm and the "conversion" of large numbers of scientists to it.

That whole process, Kuhn argued, was not to be understood in entirely rational terms. Crises are terminated, he says, not by a lengthy process of "deliberation and interpretation" but "by a relatively sudden and unstructured event"—by a kind of "gestalt switch," by means of which everything is suddenly seen in an entirely new light. "Scientists then often speak," he says, "of the 'scales falling from the eyes' or of the 'lightning flash' that 'inundates' a previously obscure puzzle, enabling its components to be seen in a new way that for the first time permits its solution. On other occasions the relevant illumination comes in sleep. No ordinary sense of the term 'interpretation' fits these flashes of intuition through which a new paradigm is born."[74] The new view, he wrote, is essentially accepted "on faith";[75] the old view is not exactly shown to be false, and its adherents are not convinced to abandon their view

---

evidence for his point that, for Kuhn, "all theory choices in science are subjective"! Larry Laudan, *Beyond Positivism and Relativism: Theory, Method, and Evidence* (Boulder, Colo.: Westview, 1996), p. 249.

[71] R. W. Newell, *Objectivity, Empiricism and Truth* (London: Routledge, 1986), pp. 2–3, 115 n. 1. See also Toulmin, *Human Understanding*, 1:19.

[72] Kuhn was not the first scholar to use the term in this sense. See, for example, Stephen Toulmin, *Foresight and Understanding: An Enquiry into the Aims of Science* (New York: Harper, 1961), p. 16.

[73] Thomas Kuhn, *The Structure of Scientific Revolutions*, 2d ed. (Chicago: University of Chicago Press, 1970), p. 94. The first edition was published in 1962.

[74] Ibid., pp. 122–23.

[75] Ibid., p. 158.

through an essentially rational process of argument. Indeed, in such discussions the two parties generally talk past each other; the scientists involved find it hard to "make complete contact with each other's viewpoints."[76] (This Kuhn called the problem of "incommensurability.") The new view gradually wins out, in large part (although not exclusively) for "subjective and aesthetic" reasons.[77] Resistance is intellectually legitimate; there is no point at which it becomes "illogical or unscientific."[78] It dies out because the supporters of the older paradigm die out; the assumption is that the older paradigm is never really vanquished intellectually.

Kuhn's argument was certainly overstated. Consider, for example, his argument about how in science new insight emerges in a "relatively sudden" way through a kind of "gestalt switch."[79] It was Hanson who had introduced the basic concepts of Gestalt psychology to the philosophy of science in his *Patterns of Discovery*, and Kuhn in his discussion of the issue took Hanson's work as his point of departure. But Hanson had taken great pains to demonstrate that important new theories did *not* emerge in a "relatively sudden" way.[80] In his more sober view, the rational element was fundamental: the whole point of his close analysis of the long and intellectually strenuous process that led to the formulation of Kepler's laws was that the emergence of a major new way of looking at things was a lengthy and difficult process, with a distinct logic of its own.[81]

But Kuhn's argument was framed in more extreme language and thus provoked rather unrestrained counterarguments. Imre Lakatos, for example, charged that "*in Kuhn's view scientific revolution is irrational, a matter for mob psychology.*"[82] Such accusations Kuhn categorically rejected and, in his later work especially, he took pains to distance himself from the idea that the development of science was not at all to be understood in rational terms. That point of view he considered "absurd," an "example of deconstruction gone

---

[76] Ibid., p. 148.

[77] Ibid., p. 156.

[78] Ibid., pp. 152, 159.

[79] Ibid., p. 122.

[80] Hanson, *Patterns of Discovery*, pp. 8–19, 90; note also the references to the psychology of perception literature on pp. 180–81. Kuhn, *Structure of Scientific Revolutions*, p. 113, for the reference to Hanson.

[81] Hanson, *Patterns of Discovery*, pp. 72–85, for the discussion of Kepler. Note also his comment that "Galileo struggled for thirty-four years before he was able to advance his constant acceleration hypothesis with confidence" (p. 72) and his remark that the "initial suggestion of an hypothesis" is "not so often affected by intuition, insight, hunches, or other imponderables as biographers or scientists suggest" (p. 71).

[82] Lakatos, "Falsification and the Methodology of Scientific Research Programmes," p. 178 (emphasis in original).

mad," and he was disturbed by the fact that it was "developed by people who often called themselves Kuhnians."[83]

Kuhn was not an irrationalist. In his view of scientific development, rational factors loomed large. But in themselves they were not decisive. Indeed, they could not be decisive. That point seemed to put him on the relativist side of the fence. But this was a fence that he was in reality trying to straddle, and that was the heart of the problem. On the one hand, the process of scientific development was what it was: somewhat loose and not wholly determined by purely rational factors. On the other hand, there was clearly something quite extraordinary about science, something that gave it (to use Toulmin's phrase) a "genuine intellectual authority over us."[84] How could this sort of process lead to such results? Given the way science actually worked, how could it produce the conclusions it did, "true or probable conclusions about the nature of reality"? This Kuhn took to be a "serious question," and he admitted that our "inability to answer it is a grave loss in our understanding of the nature of scientific knowledge."[85]

That problem was fundamental, not just for Kuhn but for other pioneers of the new approach, like Toulmin and Hanson. They too were looking for a "via media," a "middle way," between relativism and absolutism.[86] They too viewed the development of science in historicist terms. Like Kuhn, they were not comfortable with the notion of scientific "truth" and preferred to talk instead about the rationality of the process. Theory choice was a social phenomenon; individual scientists made up their minds on the basis of a whole series of criteria, which they were free to weigh differently.[87] Those criteria—"accuracy,

---

[83] Thomas Kuhn, "Reflections on My Critics," in Lakatos and Musgrave, *Criticism and the Growth of Knowledge*, pp. 259–64; Kuhn, *Essential Tension*, pp. 320–21; and Kuhn, *Trouble with the Historical Philosophy of Science*, pp. 3, 8–9. The constructivist view is indeed sometimes pushed to extremes. Note for example Bruno Latour's denial of the existence of the tuberculosis bacillus prior to its discovery by Robert Koch in 1882, discussed in Alan Sokal and Jean Bricmont, *Fashionable Nonsense: Postmodern Intellectuals' Abuse of Science* (New York: St. Martin's, 1998), pp. 96–97. For another example, see Richard Dawkins, "The Moon Is not a Calabash," *Times Higher Education Supplement*, September 30, 1994, p. 17. Dawkins had once asked a social scientist about a hypothetical tribe that believed that the "moon is an old calabash tossed just above the treetops." Did he really believe that that tribe's view would be "just as true as our scientific belief that the moon is a large Earth satellite about a quarter of a million miles away?" The social scientist replied, according to Dawkins, that "the tribe's view of the moon is just as true as ours."

[84] Toulmin, *Human Understanding*, 1:50.

[85] Kuhn, *Trouble with the Historical Philosophy of Science*, p. 8.

[86] Toulmin, *Human Understanding*, 1:88; Hanson, *Observation and Explanation*, pp. 1, 13.

[87] See, for example, Toulmin, *Human Understanding*, 1:135 and 139 (for his evolutionary perspective), 168–70 and 225–26 (for his attitude toward "truth"), and 229 (for the standard criteria). For Kuhn's attitude toward "truth," see his *Structure of Scientific Revolutions*, pp. 170–71 and 206, and his "Reflections on My Critics," pp. 264–65.

simplicity, fruitfulness and the like"[88]—might be, as Kuhn put it, "subjective and aesthetic" in character.[89] But that did not in itself mean that the decision was irrational. Quite the contrary: the fact that choice is made by a scientific community—the fact that the decision is rooted in the mature judgment exercised by the members of that community—is the closest we can come to guaranteeing the rationality of the process.[90] Even Lakatos, as Kuhn pointed out, stressed the importance of "decisions governed not by logical rules but by the mature sensibility of the trained scientist."[91]

What does all this mean to the historian? First of all, it gives us a reasonable standard by which to assess the rationality and scientific status of historical work: science as it actually is, not science as it was supposed to be. And there is no reason to assume that historical work can never measure up to that more modest standard. Historians exercise judgment, but so do scientists, and if the process is rational in science, it can be just as rational in history.[92] The demoralizing assumption that objectivity is impossible, that the mere fact that interpretation is unavoidable means that historical work can never be free from the "taint of subjectivity," and that there is perhaps therefore little point in even trying to be objective—all this is no more warranted in history than it is in science.

But beyond that, the basic point that science and history are not all that different in epistemic terms means that the insights developed by philosophers of science—about truth and knowledge and understanding and explanation—carry over directly into corresponding notions about history. This act of translation yields, if not quite a ready-made philosophy of history, then at least a very useful framework for thinking about the sorts of problems we are concerned with here.

[88] Kuhn, *Structure of Scientific Revolutions*, p. 199.

[89] Ibid., pp. 155–56, 158. The emphasis scientists place on aesthetic considerations is in fact quite striking. One Nobel Prize–winning scientist told a story about a 1957 meeting at which the physicist Murray Gell-Mann was describing a new theory of the weak interactions that he had just worked out with Richard Feynman. There were three recorded experiments that contradicted that theory, but "Gell-Mann boldly asserted that these three experiments must be faulty, *because his new theory was too beautiful to be wrong.* And future experiments decisively proved that Gell-Mann was right." That scientist then went on to quote another famous physicist (Dirac), who said that it was "more important to have beauty in one's equations than to have them fit experiments." Jerome Friedman, "Creativity in Science," in Jerome Friedman et al., *The Humanities and the Sciences*, ACLS Occasional Paper No. 47 (New York: American Council of Learned Societies, 1999), pp. 12–13 (emphasis added). See also Toulmin, *Foresight and Understanding*, p. 81.

[90] Kuhn, "Reflections on My Critics," pp. 237–38, 262–64, and Toulmin, *Human Understanding*, 1:227, 229, 242–43, and esp. 482.

[91] Kuhn, "Reflections on My Critics," p. 233. Note also Toulmin's discussion of Lakatos in *Human Understanding*, 1:482, and Toulmin's own reference to the "judgement of authoritative and experienced individuals," ibid., p. 243.

[92] See Toulmin, *Human Understanding*, 1:371.

Above all, there is the question of the historian's fundamental goal. Is the aim to get at the truth? It is (or at least used to be) commonly assumed that this was the goal, but it was also taken for granted that this goal was essentially unreachable. The well-known Dutch historian Pieter Geyl made this common point in a lecture he gave at Yale in 1954. The goddess History, Geyl said, "may be in possession of the truth, the whole truth and nothing but the truth," but to the historian she will at best "vouchsafe a glimpse. Never will she surrender the whole of her treasure. The most that we can hope for is a partial rendering, an approximation, of the real truth about the past." The reason was, according to Geyl, that to make the past intelligible, to *understand* the bare facts, the historian had to "use his material by choosing from it, ordering it, and interpreting it. In doing so he is bound to introduce an element of subjectivity; that is, he will tamper with or detract from the absolute, unchanging truth."[93]

"The absolute, unchanging truth": philosophers like Kuhn and Toulmin were uncomfortable with such notions, and justifiably so.[94] The very concept of "the truth" is both highly problematic and unnecessary in practical terms. What does it mean to talk about the "truth" about some aspect of nature or some period in history? The term seems to imply that the object of study has a kind of well-defined essence, wrapped up in a neat package somewhere, but never quite discoverable in its entirety—a treasure, as Geyl put it, that can be glimpsed but never actually acquired. But the vision conjured up by such metaphors scarcely makes sense, and the concept is certainly not needed for any practical purpose. Reality is what it is; the past was what it was; and what is being studied can be studied on its own terms. The coming of the First World War, for example, can be studied as a problem in its own right; there is no need to say that the goal is learn the truth about the origins of the First World War.

So the idea that the aim is to learn the truth about the object of study can safely be abandoned. But if the concept drops away, then the whole notion that the effort to understand is tainted because it does violence to the "absolute, underlying truth" also has to be abandoned. Understanding then emerges as the central goal in its own right—as the end in itself, not as the means for getting at the mysterious and ultimately unreachable goal of the "truth." Making the past intelligible is, in that case, not to be viewed à la Geyl as a source of distortion. Instead it should be seen as the heart of the historical enterprise. This, and not the uncovering of the "truth," is what the historian should be striving to achieve.

---

[93] Pieter Geyl, *Use and Abuse of History* (New Haven: Yale University Press, 1955; reprint, Archon Books, 1970), pp. 62–64 (emphasis in original).

[94] See the references cited in note 87 above.

But what exactly does "understanding" mean? Hanson's work is a major source of insight here, and for him understanding essentially meant seeing how things fit together. The scientist, as Hanson lays out the argument, begins with observations, and "they set the problem."[95] The aim is to explain the data: the physicist's "goal is a conceptual pattern in terms of which his data will fit intelligibly alongside better-known data."[96] And that is how theories are generated:

> Physical theories provide patterns within which data appear intelligible. . . . A theory is not pieced together from observed phenomena; it is rather what makes it possible to observe phenomena as being of a certain sort, and as related to other phenomena. Theories put phenomena into systems. They are built up "in reverse"— retroductively. A theory is a cluster of conclusions in search of a premiss. From the observed properties of phenomena the physicist reasons his way towards a keystone idea from which the properties are explicable as a matter of course.[97]

A theory was thus a deductive system, one that "guarantees inferences from cause to effect."[98] Indeed, one needed this sort of guarantee to claim that a causal relationship existed: it was "this logical guarantee that theories place upon causal inferences that explains the difference between truly causal sequences and mere coincidences."[99] For two phenomena to be related to each other as cause and effect, there had to be a *necessary* connection between the two, and that element of necessity could only be supplied by a theory. Only a theory—precisely because it was a deductive system—could show you why cause and effect *had to be* related to each other: "the necessity sometimes associated with event-pairs construed as cause and effect is really that obtaining between premisses and conclusions in theories which guarantee inferences from the one event to the other."[100]

How does this differ from what Hempel said? For Hempel, explanation also meant deduction, but he essentially just left it at that. For Hanson, the Hempel approach was just too mechanical, too formalistic, and he insisted that theories that were mere "predicting devices"—and those theories met Hempel's basic criterion for what theories should be—would not provide genuine explanations. A theory had to do something more. People also had to have the sense that something was really being explained—that thanks to

[95] Hanson, *Patterns of Discovery*, p. 72.

[96] Ibid.

[97] Ibid., p. 90. "Retroduction" (or "abduction" as the concept is also called) means "studying facts and devising a theory to explain them." The term is defined in a passage from the philosopher Charles Sanders Peirce, quoted ibid., p. 85.

[98] Hanson, *Perception and Discovery*, p. 309.

[99] Ibid., pp. 292, 309 (for the quotation).

[100] Hanson, *Patterns of Discovery*, p. 90.

the theory, they understood something they had not understood before.[101] Suppose, for example, that your goal is to understand why for a particular right triangle the sum of the squares of the two short sides is equal to the square of the long side. It would not do simply to measure the sides of a large number of right triangles, note that for all those cases the square of the hypotenuse was equal to the sum of the squares of the two remaining sides, proclaim that as an empirical "law," and then "explain" the case you are interested in by citing that "law." But if you studied the Pythagorean theorem—if you followed the proof, if you saw how the conclusion followed from relatively plausible assumptions—you would understand why things had to be as they were. The observed phenomenon would be explained: you would have a certain "sentiment of comprehension" that would otherwise be missing.[102]

There are other important points to be taken away from Hanson's analysis—points about the importance of theory in causal explanation, about the nature of understanding, and about whether understanding can ever be "objective." Hanson was trying to get at what such concepts as understanding, explanation, and causation actually meant, and in his analysis he wanted to get away from an overly mechanistic approach to these issues.

In particular, he wanted to get away from mechanistic (or "causal-chain") models of causation. He was trying to view causation not as a phenomenon that could be observed directly in the real world but rather as something that had meaning only in the context of a theory. "Causes certainly are connected with effects," he wrote, "but this is because our theories connect them, not because the world is held together by cosmic glue."[103] Even billiard-ball interactions are not self-explanatory. As Maupertuis argued in 1732: "people are not astonished when they see a body in motion communicate this motion to others; the habit that they have of seeing this phenomenon prevents them from seeing how marvellous it is."[104] One needed to have some theory of nature ("however primitive," as Hanson says) to interpret such phenomena in causal terms.[105]

Theory thus existed in people's heads. The "locus of causal-talk," Hanson wrote, was "not in the physical world." "There is nothing we can see, touch, or kick in nature that will answer to the name 'causal connection.'" But one

---

[101] Hanson, *Observation and Explanation*, pp. 41–49, esp. pp. 42–44 and 48–49.

[102] Ibid., p. 44. Note also Hanson's comment in *Patterns of Discovery*, p. 71: "The reason for a bevelled mirror's showing a spectrum in the sunlight is not explained by saying that all bevelled mirrors do this." The Pythagorean theorem example, however, is mine.

[103] Hanson, *Patterns of Discovery*, chap. 3 (p. 64 for the quotation); N. R. Hanson, "Causal Chains," *Mind* 64 (1955): 289–311; and Hanson, *Perception and Discovery*, pp. 312–13.

[104] Maupertuis (1732), quoted in Alexandre Koyré, *Newtonian Studies* (Cambridge, Mass.: Harvard University Press, 1965), p. 162.

[105] Hanson, *Perception and Discovery*, p. 292.

could not kick a fact or a true statement either. That did not mean, however, that there was anything "grossly subjective" or "chimerical" about such notions: "facts, true statements, and causal connections are all what they are because the world is what it is" and there was "nothing subjective about arguing validly to true conclusions."[106]

But this was not quite an objectivist view. And indeed, for Hanson the goal of theory was not to provide an exact mirror of reality. The accumulation of factual material, he argued, was not an end in itself. The aim was to understand. One therefore had to prevent the picture from being cluttered by extraneous detail. "The more like a reflection a map becomes," he pointed out, "the less useful it is as a map."[107] A theory was like a model. The main purpose of a model was to provide a kind of "awareness of structure." A theory also had to try to bring out what was of fundamental importance in the object of study. A degree of stylization was thus needed not just for a model to be a model, but also for "theories to *be* theories" and even for "sciences to *be* sciences."[108]

A premium thus had to be placed on simplicity. The aim was to develop an explanatory system based on a handful of relatively simple assumptions: "The great unifications of Galileo, Kepler, Newton, Maxwell, Einstein, Bohr, Schrödinger and Heisenberg were pre-eminently discoveries of terse formulae from which explanations of diverse phenomena could be generated as a matter of course."[109] The reaching for simplicity was reflected in a reaching for mathematical form, an attitude captured by Kant's famous dictum that "in every specific natural science there can be found only so much science proper as there is mathematics present in it."[110]

If the goal was understanding, the criteria for theory selection therefore *had* to what they were. Those fundamental criteria—analytical elegance, explanatory fertility, and the like—were not just arbitrary guidelines, reflecting the subjective and aesthetic preferences of the scientific community. They performed a *rational* function.[111] A simple, elegant structure, where a handful of core assumptions had broad and far-reaching implications, allowed hypotheses to be developed deductively; those hypotheses could be tested experimentally, even when the core assumptions could not be tested directly.[112] If a particular hypothesis turned out to be valid, this tended to strengthen the theory; but even if it failed, that finding could be of considerable value.

---

[106] Ibid., pp. 312–13.

[107] Hanson, *Patterns of Discovery*, p. 28.

[108] Hanson, *Observation and Explanation*, pp. 81–82 (emphasis in original).

[109] Hanson, *Patterns of Discovery*, p. 109.

[110] Ibid., p. 193.

[111] Hanson, *What I Do Not Believe*, p. 300.

[112] Hanson, *Perception and Discovery*, pp. 230–36.

Because the hypothesis had been inferred from general assumptions, its failure would have general implications. It is structure that generates insight: a random observation is of little importance, but the failure of a hypothesis drawn from a larger body of theory could force people to deal with basic issues. "Truth," as Bacon said, "emerges more readily from error than from confusion."[113]

Analytical elegance and explanatory fertility are thus not arbitrary, subjective criteria at all. To develop a powerful deductive system is not just something that people do for essentially aesthetic reasons. The goal of such a system is to provide a certain "awareness of structure": the aim is to see how things fit together. And all this is important because this is *what understanding is*: this is *what it means* to understand a phenomenon.

How much of this applies to historical work? A historian also begins with observations, and those observations "set the problem." A war breaks out: how is it to be explained? The physicist's goal "is a conceptual pattern in terms of which his data will fit intelligibly alongside better-known data."[114] The historian also tries to develop such a pattern—to understand the logic underlying the course of events. In science, "an event is explained when it is traced to other events which require less explanation" and "when it is shown to be part of an intelligible pattern of events."[115] In history, too, the goal is to show how particular events are part of an "intelligible pattern of events." When dealing with events that are at first glance hard to explain (the Pearl Harbor attack, for example), a successful explanation will make those events intelligible by tracing them to causes that are not quite so hard to understand—that is, by constructing a story.

A historical interpretation is the analogue of a physical theory. The aim of an interpretation is also to provide a framework "within which data appear intelligible." A historical interpretation, like a physical theory, "is not pieced together from observed phenomena; it is rather what makes it possible to observe phenomena as being of a certain sort, and as related to other phenomena." The facts in history as in science never just "speak for themselves." And historical interpretations are built up the same way Hanson says physical

---

[113] Cited in Kuhn, *Structure of Scientific Revolutions*, p. 18. Kuhn does not give the reference, but for the original quotation see Francis Bacon, *The New Organon*, ed. Lisa Jardine and Michael Silverthorne (Cambridge: Cambridge University Press, 2000), p. 173 (book II: XX). The British logician Augustus De Morgan made a similar point: "Wrong hypotheses rightly worked from, have produced more useful results than unguided observation." Quoted in Hanson, *Perception and Discovery*, p. 236. Note also what Karl Popper says in the very first sentence of his *Conjectures and Refutations*, 2d ed. (New York: Basic Books, 1965): "The essays and lectures of which this book is composed are variations upon one very simple theme: the thesis that *we can learn from our mistakes*" (p. vii; emphasis in original).

[114] Hanson, *Patterns of Discovery*, p. 72.

[115] Ibid., p. 94.

theories are. The physicist, he says, "rarely searches for a deductive system *per se*, one in which his data would appear as consequences if only interpreted physically. He is in search, rather, of an explanation of these data; his goal is a conceptual pattern in terms of which his data will fit intelligibly alongside better-known data." Similarly, the historian rarely sets out to develop a particular interpretation; the interpretation emerges naturally as the historian tries to understand what was going on and to make sense of what the data show.[116]

For Hanson, theories were deductive systems; phenomena were explained by deducing their occurrence from a handful of relatively simple axioms. Such systems placed a heavy premium on simplicity: the "elegance" of a theory was a key measure of its value. In history too, there is a certain premium placed on simplicity and analytical elegance—that is, in giving a picture of the past that does not try to be a photographic reproduction but rather seeks to bring out what was really important. If an interpretation can account for a good deal of what was going on in terms of a few relatively simple and plausible premises, that is very much to its credit; if those premises explain much that is otherwise puzzling or unexpected, then that is even stronger evidence of its power.

So to a certain degree an attempt to understand some historical phenomenon may lead to the construction of a deductive system. And historical explanation—a formalization of the sort of understanding that is reached in the course of doing historical work—should to the extent possible have a kind of deductive structure. To explain the Eisenhower administration's basic policy toward Europe, for example, the historian could begin by showing that President Eisenhower wanted to pull out of Europe in the not-too-distant future. He or she could then go on to show how this implied that western Europe should constitute a "third great power bloc" in world affairs, able to stand up to Soviet power without direct American support. The different aspects of America's European policy in that period—the support for European integration, the interest in reducing American troop levels in Europe, the nuclear sharing policy, and so on—could then be shown to follow logically from that basic policy choice. This counts as explanation, even though no social scientific law à la Hempel comes into play. What makes it an explanation is the logic that links the general with the specific—that given Eisenhower's basic thinking, the specific policies he pursued followed "as a matter of course."

The historian, however, in reaching for such a structure, has to take care not to push the effort too far. In historical processes, contingent factors loom large; the logic of historical change is never as tight as the logic of a mathe-

---

[116] Ibid., pp. 72, 90. For the facts not "speaking for themselves": Hanson, *Perception and Discovery*, p. 200, and also Hanson, *Observation and Explanation*, p. 25.

matical theorem. The goal might be to see the degree to which a wide variety of observed phenomena can be accounted for by a handful of relatively simple factors. But at the same time the historian needs to be careful not to read more structure into historical reality than is actually there.

The reality test is thus fundamental. Historical interpretations are constructs. They exist in people's minds. But, as Hanson said about causal statements in general, this does not in itself mean that there is anything "grossly subjective" and therefore arbitrary or chimerical about such notions: "they are what they are because the world is what it is."[117] It is not as though observations are like dots on a piece of paper that can be connected to each other however one pleases. Only certain connections can legitimately be drawn: the sort of picture that can legitimately be painted on the basis of those data is limited by the fact that "the world is what it is"—or, in the case of history, by the fact that the past was what it was.

How far can a scholar go in constructing an interpretation that is both powerful and intellectually compelling? The answer turns on a whole series of factors. It depends on the nature of the particular subject being studied and on the sort of evidence that is available. But it also depends on the skill and the training of the scholar doing the work. And those skills can be developed. There is a method for dealing with historical problems, a method people can actually learn how to use.

[117] Hanson, *Perception and Discovery*, pp. 312–13.

Chapter Two

DIPLOMATIC HISTORY AND INTERNATIONAL RELATIONS THEORY

A HISTORICAL INTERPRETATION has to have a conceptual core. The facts never really just "speak for themselves." The historian thus has to make them "speak" by drawing on a kind of theory—by drawing, that is, on a certain sense for how things work. But what does this mean in practice? What role does theory in that broad sense play in actual historical work? And how does a particular conceptual framework take shape in the mind of the historian in the first place? How *should* historians go about developing the sort of theoretical framework they need to make the past intelligible? Should they try to grapple with basic conceptual issues in a relatively direct way, by studying international relations theory and coming to terms with the arguments they find in that literature? Or are less direct, less formal, methods good enough for their purposes?

As for the theorists, what, if anything, can they hope to get by studying history? How can historical analysis be brought to bear on the study of theoretical issues? What in general can the theorists get from the historical literature? If historical interpretation has a conceptual core, doesn't that imply that that literature should not be viewed just as a great storehouse of factual material that can be drawn on for the purposes of theory testing? Doesn't that imply that the theorists might be able to get a lot more from it if they approach it the right way?

THE HISTORIAN AND INTERNATIONAL RELATIONS THEORY

This chapter will be concerned with questions of this sort—questions about the relationship between history and theory—and I want to begin by looking at this set of issues from the historian's point of view. How, first of all, does the historian actually use theory? In very broad terms, the answer is simple: theory is above all an instrument of analysis and, depending on what that analysis reveals, can also serve as the basis for interpretation. But that point is very general, so let me explain what I mean by giving a specific example. It relates to a passage in an article written more than seventy-five years ago by the French historian Elie Halévy, perhaps the finest historian of his generation.

Halévy in that article—it was actually one of the Rhodes lectures he gave at Oxford in 1929—summed up the origins of the First World War in a single but quite remarkable paragraph. By 1914, he wrote, Austria's leaders had come to believe that the problem of Slav nationalism could be dealt with only if Serbia was crushed militarily. "But everyone knew, who chose to know, that, whenever Austria declared war upon Serbia, Pan-Slavist sentiment would become too strong for any Russian government to resist its pressure," and "everyone knew, who chose to know, that whenever Russia gave so much as a sign of declaring war upon Austria, Pan-German feelings would compel the German government to enter the lists in its turn." "It was likewise common knowledge," he went on to point out, "that Germany, whenever she declared war upon Russia, was resolved not to tolerate the existence in the west of an army that was after all the second best army in Europe; that she would first march upon Paris and annihilate France as a military power, before rushing back to the east, and settling matters with Russia." It was also clear that, in order to implement that plan, the German army felt it would have to march through Belgium. But "everybody understood that if ever the Belgian coast and the northern coast of France were to fall under the domination of Germany, Great Britain, feeling her prestige and her security in danger, would enter the war on the side of Belgium and France." What all this meant was that by 1914 war had become virtually inevitable: "everyone knew, who wished to know, not only that a European war was imminent, but what the general shape of the war would be."[1]

Halévy was a truly great historian, and it is amazing how much he was able to pack into that one paragraph. A mere decade after the fighting had ended, he was able to analyze the coming of the war with Olympian detachment. He had a sense of tragedy. Events unfolded in accordance with a certain inexorable logic, and it was the historian's job not to blame one side or the other for the war but simply to show what that logic was. But as impressive as this was, you still have to wonder about some of the points he made. Russia was bound to come to the aid of Serbia *no matter what*, even if such a policy meant war with both Germany and Austria? Wouldn't Russia's decision depend on whether it had a good chance of winning such a war, and wouldn't that depend in large measure on whether it could count on the active military support of Britain and France? And wouldn't the western powers, for their part, have a certain interest in holding Russia back? Wouldn't they want to avoid a war if they could, because of the risks they would run and the price they might have to pay? And part of that price might be political: even total victory in such a war might not be an unalloyed blessing. Would it

[1] Elie Halévy, "The World Crisis of 1914–1918: An Interpretation," first published in 1930, and reprinted in Elie Halévy, *The Era of Tyrannies: Essays on Socialism and War* (London: Allen Lane, 1967), pp. 161–90. The paragraph in question is on p. 179.

really be to their interest to destroy the German counterweight to Russian power in Europe? Wouldn't some kind of balance of power in Europe be much better than war? Perhaps those sorts of considerations came into play, and if so, maybe things might have developed in all kinds of different ways. And that point makes you wonder. Wasn't there much more of a story here than Halévy had made out?

For me, having worked in this field for more than forty years now, such questions come to mind quickly. Implicit in those questions is a certain view of international politics. I read the Halévy passage and think to myself: *this just can't be*. I find it hard to believe that the Russians would have gone to war for the sake of Serbia no matter what. My strong suspicion, without looking at a single document, is that their policy on this issue *had to* depend very much on their sense for what France and Britain would do. My assumption, in other words, is that power factors of that sort were *bound* to be of fundamental political importance—that European leaders *could not* simply ignore such considerations and allow their policies to be shaped essentially by Pan-Slav or Pan-German sentiment.

Those italicized terms are a tip-off. They show that an element of *necessity* has been brought into play, and thus (as we saw in the previous chapter) that a causal theory has been brought to bear on the problem. Of course, I am using my terms rather loosely. There is no physical or logical impossibility here. It is not absolutely out of the question that Halévy was essentially right. So when I say to myself that power factors *had to be* more important than Halévy thought, all I really mean is that I find it very hard to believe that they did not come into play in a major way. But even bearing these caveats in mind, it is clear that, in reacting to Halévy that way, I am drawing on a kind of theory—on a rough sense for "what had to be," rooted in a general sense for how international politics works.

But note the role that that theory, if you can call it that, actually plays. It does not provide any ready-made answers. Instead, it serves to generate a series of specific questions you can only answer by doing empirical research. What, for example, did the Russians actually think France and Britain would do if they went to war over Serbia, and were those calculations in their minds when they decided on a course of action in July 1914? The theory, in other words (if it is used correctly), is not a substitute for empirical analysis. It is an *engine* of analysis. It helps you see which specific questions to focus on. It helps you see how big issues (like the origins of the First World War) turn on relatively narrow problems (like what Russia calculated about Britain and France, and how that affected its behavior in the crisis). It thus helps you develop a sense for the "architecture" of the historical problem you are concerned with and helps you see how you can go about dealing with it. It thus plays a crucial role in the development of an effective research strategy.

To see the point, just compare this approach with its alternative—an approach to research that is not rooted in any particular conceptual framework. If you adopt that sort of method, how do you go about doing your work? Do you just plunge into the sources and begin looking around in a totally mindless way, not having the slightest idea of what you are looking for, hoping that some interpretation will more or less automatically take shape when you have absorbed enough information? After all, in history as in science, it does not make sense to simply gather up a mass of facts "like pebbles on the beach." In history as in science, a conceptual framework does not emerge in a purely mechanical way from a simple piecing together of empirical observations. But what that means is that a lot of thought has to go into the research effort— that it has to be question-driven. You therefore need to develop some sense for what the questions are—that is, you need something that can help generate those questions. And it is in this area that some theory—some sense, that is, for how international politics works—is really indispensable.

But there are dangers here. Theory can be misused. If you rely on a certain theory, you run the risk of seeing only what that theory says is important or of trying to force the evidence into some preconceived theoretical structure. You might fall in love with a certain way of looking at things and interpret the past accordingly. But problems of this sort are not unmanageable. The important thing here is to realize that theory, in itself, does not provide answers and that its main function is to bring questions into focus.

How does this process work in practice? As you deal with a particular historical problem, you are constantly trying to see how things fit together. You never want to interpret history as just a bunch of events strung together over time. Your goal instead is to understand the *logic* that underlies the course of events. And it's in that context that theoretical notions come into play.

Suppose, for example, you want to understand the origins of the First World War. You know that Russian policy in the Balkans is an important part of the story. Russia, of course, went to war in 1914 to protect Serbia. But what exactly *was* Russian policy in that area? How did it take shape, and why? It turns out, when you study the issue, that Russia did not pursue a purely defensive, status quo–oriented policy in that area in the years before World War I. The Russians, for example, helped set up the Balkan League in 1912. But as French prime minister Poincaré pointed out at the time, the treaty establishing the Balkan League "contained the seeds not only of a war against Turkey, but of a war against Austria as well."[2] Given that Germany

[2] Poincaré, notes of meeting with Russian foreign minister Sazonov, August 1912, *Documents diplomatiques français (1871–1914)*, 3d ser., vol. 3(Paris: Imprimerie nationale, 1931), p. 34. For the key evidence on Russia's Balkan policy at the time, see Barbara Jelavich, *Russia's Balkan Entanglements, 1806–1914* (Cambridge: Cambridge University Press, 1991), pp. 246–47; Bernadotte Schmitt, *The Coming of the War, 1914*, 2 vols. (New York: Scribner's, 1930), 1:135; and Luigi Albertini, *The Origins of the War of 1914*, 3 vols. (London: Oxford University Press, 1952–57), 1:375, 486.

was Austria's ally, the Russians were obviously playing with fire. How then is that Russian policy to be understood?

In dealing with that question, you need to draw on certain assumptions of a theoretical nature. Russia was too weak to take on Germany by itself. Such a course of action would have been suicidal, and you assume that power realities *had to* be taken into account. But Russia was not alone: it could count on the support of France, and perhaps of Britain as well. The attitude of the western powers was crucial, but why would they be willing to go to war for the sake of Russia's Balkan policy? The French, it turns out, had been far more cautious in that area during the early days of the Franco-Russian alliance in the 1890s. Why the shift? Didn't the answer have to do with Germany or, more precisely, with the deterioration of Franco-German (and Anglo-German) relations in the decade before World War I? It stands to reason—and this is another essentially theoretical assumption—that as relations between Germany and the western powers deteriorated, Britain and France would become more dependent on Russia. They would have to worry about what Russia would do if war broke out in the west, and even in peacetime they would have to worry about the possibility of Russia mending fences with Germany if they did not give it more or less unconditional support. For similar reasons, Germany also had a certain interest in trying to wean Russia away from the western powers. And all this, the theory would suggest, would tend to put Russia in the driver's seat. It would tend to increase its freedom of action—the freedom, that is, to pursue a forward policy in the Balkans.

So using your theory, you generate a series of hypotheses—about French policy, German policy, Russian policy, and British policy. Those hypotheses tell you what to look for when you start studying the sources. Did the French really feel that they had to support Russia no matter what? If so, was this a result of the way their relations with Germany had developed? Did the Russians feel that both sides were courting them, and did this have any effect on what they thought they could get away with in the Balkans? The theory, once again, does not provide you with the answers, but it does give you some sense for what the questions are—that is, for which questions should lie at the heart of the analysis.

But suppose you are able to answer those questions. Suppose, in fact, that the hypotheses that you had started out with ring true in terms of the evidence. You would then have an interpretation of what was going on. You would have been able to pull together a whole series of different things—the events leading to the deterioration of relations between Germany and the western powers, and increased Russian assertiveness in the Balkans. And that interpretation would draw on a theory—in fact, on the very theory that was used to generate those hypotheses in the first place.

In other words, in developing that interpretation—in explaining why things took the course they did before 1914—you would be drawing on certain principles of a theoretical nature. The basic principle in this case is this: when relations between powers, or blocs of powers, deteriorate, the position of third powers necessarily improves, and in each case those shifting power relations have an important effect on policy. This principle is not just an empirical regularity à la Hempel which you just happen to observe. With a little reflection, you can see why things more or less *have* to work that way.

You can use this basic theoretical principle in historical work in all kinds of different contexts. Suppose, for example, you were interested in great power politics in the late 1960s and early 1970s. You know, of course, that Sino-Soviet relations deteriorated dramatically just prior to that period. And using that theory, you can hypothesize that the course of Sino-Soviet relations had a good deal to do with the coming of détente in Europe and with the improvement in America's relations with both Russia and China by around 1970. Without looking at a single document but just by drawing on very general knowledge and on assumptions of a theoretical nature, you can generate a hypothesis which, depending on what the sources show, you might be able to develop into a historical interpretation.

But your basic understanding of how things work is by no means set in concrete. It is not just "there," fixed for all time, just waiting for you to draw on it. It takes shape—it evolves—as you grapple with fundamental conceptual issues in specific historical contexts. It develops, in particular, as you react to what other people have to say, and especially as you react to historical arguments with a certain theoretical resonance.

How, for example, is the war of 1939 to be understood? For many years it was taken for granted that this question had a very simple answer: Hitler was to blame for that conflict, and not much more needed to be said on the subject. But in 1961 A.J.P. Taylor mounted an attack on that piece of conventional wisdom in his famous book *The Origins of the Second World War*. According to Taylor, the problem after 1919 "was not German aggressiveness or militarism, or the wickedness of her rulers."[3] The real problem in his view was that Germany was basically so much stronger than any other power in continental Europe. Fascist war lust was not a crucial factor; indeed, it *could not be* the crucial factor: "Even the Fascist dictators would not have gone to war unless they had seen a chance of winning."[4] Power realities therefore *had to be* of fundamental importance: "the essential problem" in interwar Europe, Taylor wrote (in what was probably the most important sentence in the book), "was political, not moral"—that is, it had to do with power realities and not with aggressive intent.[5]

[3] A.J.P. Taylor, *The Origins of the Second World War* (New York: Atheneum, 1961), p. 24.
[4] Ibid., p. 103.
[5] Ibid., p. 24.

Taylor obviously took the argument too far (and I show why in some detail in the next chapter), but as you grapple with that argument, it becomes clear that his basic claim that it did not make sense to think of Hitler as pushing ahead without regard to the political and military conjuncture *had to* be correct. The structure of power as a whole, both what it was at any particular point and the way it was changing over time, *was bound* to come into play. To understand the origins of the war, the story of international politics in the 1930s therefore had to be reconstructed, and this was a story whose logic had a good deal to do with power realities. What gives this point a certain bite is the fact that it is at odds with what was at least at one time the conventional wisdom—at odds with a view of the origins of the war that indeed focused heavily on moral considerations and did not adequately take power factors into account.

That last point is very important for our purposes. You develop your understanding of how things work by seeing things that you had not seen before. You are convinced by certain *ideas*—by certain lines of argument—about the way things work. But you also develop your thinking by reaching certain conclusions of a purely factual nature. Thomas Kuhn at one point talked about why philosophers of science of his generation had become interested in the history of science: "we were already dissatisfied with the prevailing tradition and were seeking behavioral *clues* with which to reform it." The history could serve as a kind of springboard for grappling with the philosophical issues. Indeed, it eventually became clear to Kuhn that "many of the most central conclusions we drew from the historical record [could] be derived instead from first principles."[6] Historical conclusions are often "clues" in that sense. They are the clues you use to work your way back to a more basic understanding of international politics. They force you, as Hanson would put it, to reach for the fundamental principles from which those findings would follow "as a matter of course."

And those findings can have a quite extraordinary impact on your thinking when they are dramatic and unexpected, and especially when they differ sharply from what you yourself had believed. When this happens—when you reach the conclusion that you were wrong on some important issue—it's like finding gold in your hands. It forces you to think about the source of the error and to rethink your basic assumptions; it thus enables you to deepen your understanding of how international politics works.

So your basic thinking evolves as you do historical work. You react to the arguments historians make. What is to be made of the fundamental assumptions that lie at the heart of particular interpretations? You try to think the issues through for yourself. And as you do your own empirical work, you are

---

[6] Thomas Kuhn, *The Trouble with the Historical Philosophy of Science*, (Cambridge, Mass.: Harvard History of Science Department, 1991), pp. 6, 10 (emphasis added).

in effect testing out various general ideas. What rings true in terms of the evidence? Which ideas do not seem to count for much, in terms of their ability to explain what was going on in the real world? Sometimes your assumptions turn out to be wrong. Why exactly were you mistaken? Was there something important you had missed? As you go through this process, you automatically develop a certain sense for how things work.

So in that way a conceptual framework takes shape in your mind. But should the historian also try to approach the issue in a more direct way? Political scientists and other theorists have had a lot to say about the big issues historians need to be concerned with. Does it make sense for historians to study what they have written and to try to come to terms with their arguments, or is the homegrown theory of the sort I have been alluding to so far all the historian really needs?

Many historians have a low regard for the sort of work the theorists do, just as many theorists tend to look down on historians as mere fact-mongers.[7] I don't think that those attitudes are warranted in either case, but for now let me just say that taking international relations theory seriously can benefit diplomatic historians in a number of ways. First, and most obviously, there are certain basic issues that the historian needs to be able to sort out, and theoretical writings can provide important guidance. Suppose, for example, that you are studying international politics in the nuclear age. You realize you need to learn something about nuclear weapons and about the impact they have on international political life. Do they simply "cancel each other out"? Are they a force for peace or a source of instability? In coming to terms with such problems, the works of theorists like Thomas Schelling and Bernard Brodie are of absolutely fundamental importance.

So certain theoretical works can help the historian deal with particular issues. But that's not the only reason the historian should study the international relations literature. I talked a few paragraphs back about "dramatic" findings, and in fact philosophers of science often emphasize the importance of findings of this sort.[8] But what makes a finding "dramatic" is not just that it

---

[7] For the view of some historians, see, for example, Paul Schroeder's letter to the editor, *International Security* 20, no. 1 (Summer 1995): 195. The attitude of some theorists comes out in some remarks made in passing. Thus Martin Wight says: "Guicciardini was a historian; he described but did not analyse." Martin Wight, "The Balance of Power and International Order," in *The Bases of International Order*, ed. Alan James (London: Oxford University Press, 1973), pp. 88–89. Hans Morgenthau makes the same kind of very sharp distinction. "But where is the line to be drawn," he asks, "between the similar, which is susceptible to theoretical understanding, and the unique, which is the proper province of history?" Hans Morgenthau, "The Purpose of Political Science," in *A Design for Political Science: Scope, Objectives, and Methods*, ed. James Charlesworth (Philadelphia: American Academy of Political and Social Science, 1966), p. 64.

[8] The point played a particularly important role in the writings of Imre Lakatos. See, for example, Lakatos, "Falsification and the Methodology of Scientific Research Programmes," p. 116; Imre Lakatos, "History of Science and Its Rational Reconstructions," in *Method and*

differs, even radically, from what people had previously believed. If the issue were trivial, findings of that sort wouldn't count for much. The finding has to be *important*, and what makes a finding important is the way it bears on fundamental beliefs—in this case, beliefs about how international politics works.

The importance of a particular finding will therefore register in your mind with particular force when you've grappled directly with the fundamental conceptual issues that lie at the heart of this area of inquiry. Only then will you really see why a certain finding is surprising and therefore important. Only then will you be able to hear the alarm bells sound and understand why certain findings matter. If surprise is important, then theory has to be important. The two go hand in hand. As Robert Jervis says: "Without a theory, you can't be surprised by anything—i.e., events are surprising because they do not fit our expectations, and these can only come from implicit or explicit theories. People sometimes think that not being surprised is evidence for a great deal of knowledge; in fact, it is the reverse. People who know nothing cannot be surprised by anything."[9]

Let me be clear about what I'm arguing here. When I say that historians should grapple with basic theoretical issues, I'm not implying that they should simply buy into the worldview of the theorists. Most of them would not be able to do that in any case, for the simple reason that the theorists just do not look at the world the same way the historians do.[10] But for that very reason you can profit enormously, if you're a historian, by going into the intellectual world of the theorist and trying to come to terms with the ideas found there. Even if you ultimately reach the conclusion that the political scientists are basically wrong on some issue, the process that led to that conclusion can be quite rewarding. And when it turns out that you yourself had been wrong, as it sometimes does, the payoff can be quite extraordinary.

Appraisal in the Physical Sciences: The Critical Background to Modern Science, 1800–1905, ed. Colin Howson (Cambridge: Cambridge University Press, 1976), pp. 7, 11; Imre Lakatos, "Lectures on Scientific Method," in Imre Lakatos and Paul Feyerabend, *For and Against Method: Including Lakatos's Lectures on Scientific Method and the Lakatos-Feyerabend Correspondence*, ed. Matteo Motterlini (Chicago: University of Chicago Press, 1999), p. 99, 100; and Lakatos quoted in Brendan Larvor, *Lakatos: An Introduction* (New York: Routledge, 1998), p. 55. But Lakatos was not the only philosopher of science to stress the importance of results of this sort. See, for example, Karl Popper, *Conjectures and Refutations* (New York: Basic Books, 1962), p. 36, and Thomas Kuhn, *The Structure of Scientific Revolutions*, 2d ed. (Chicago: University of Chicago Press, 1970), p. 155.

[9] Jervis, email to the author, February 1, 2005.

[10] On this issue, see the very interesting exchange between Robert Jervis and Paul Schroeder in Colin Elman and Miriam Fendius Elman, eds., *Bridges and Boundaries: Historians, Political Scientists, and the Study of International Relations* (Cambridge, Mass.: MIT Press, 2001), pp. 385–416.

HISTORY AND THE THEORIST

Now let's look at the issue from the other side. Why exactly should the theorist study history? It's not hard to come up with some fairly obvious answers. History can provide the theorist with examples that can serve to illustrate particular theoretical points. Those examples can clarify the theorist's meaning and also provide a degree of empirical support for the particular point the theorist is making. Empirical examples, whether cited by the theorist or not, can also help someone who is grappling with important conceptual issues to see the power of a theoretical argument. Thus Kenneth Waltz in his *Theory of International Politics* made an important argument, very much in the spirit of his basic structural approach to international politics, about the role of competitive pressure in shaping political behavior.[11] Suppose you are familiar with this argument and then come across the case of a top Prussian official (Prince Hardenberg) arguing in 1807 that his country had been unable to stand up militarily to France because the Revolution had "brought the French people a wholly new vigor" and that Prussia, if it hoped to survive, could not simply cling to the old order. The force of the new revolutionary principles was such, according to Hardenberg, "that the state which refuses to acknowledge them will be condemned to submit or to perish."[12] That way of thinking, it turns out, had a lot to do with the very important reforms Prussia adopted at that time. You note these things, and you're struck by the way they relate to Waltz's argument. His theoretical point takes on a certain reality quality. The historical example suggests that Waltz had not just come up with an interesting intellectual construct but rather that the argument he develops can actually help you understand how things work in the real world.

And studying history can help theorists see things they might not otherwise see. In international relations theory, an important body of thought "emphasizes the dangers that arise when the offense is strong relative to the defense."[13] You might find that basic idea quite plausible. But if you study the Anglo-Russian relationship in the nineteenth century, a defense-dominant

[11] Kenneth Waltz, *Theory of International Politics* (New York: McGraw-Hill, 1979), esp. pp. 76–77, 127–28.

[12] Hardenberg Riga Memorandum, quoted in Mack Walker, ed., *Metternich's Europe* (New York: Walker, 1968), p. 8. See also Thomas Nipperdey, *Germany from Napoleon to Bismarck, 1800–1866* (Princeton: Princeton University Press, 1996), p. 20.

[13] Stephen Van Evera, "The Cult of the Offensive and the Origins of the First World War," *International Security* 9, no. 1 (Summer 1984): 63, and the sources cited there in Van Evera's n. 25. See also James Morrow's review article, "International Conflict: Assessing the Democratic Peace and Offense-Defense Theory," in *Political Science: The State of the Discipline*, ed. Ira Katznelson and Helen Milner (New York: Norton, for the American Political Science Association, 2002), esp. pp. 183–91.

relationship if there ever was one, you might be struck by how bellicose key British leaders were at various points—for example, during the Near Eastern crisis in 1877.[14] In that case, a rather different idea might take shape in your mind. Could it be that the danger in this case had to do with the fact that this was a *defense*-dominant relationship—that it was precisely *because* the risks for both sides were limited that statesmen could approach war in a relatively cavalier, and indeed frivolous, way? Of course, even if that were true in this case, that in itself would not mean that the general argument about offense-dominance being destabilizing was necessarily wrong. But the example could nonetheless provide some food for thought. It might suggest that the theoretical issue was more complex (and perhaps even more interesting) than you had originally thought.

Of course, theorists can use history in such ways: historical examples can illustrate theoretical points, and the study of historical cases can serve as a spur to theoretical analysis. But if, from the theorists' point of view, that was essentially all that history was good for, it would scarcely make sense for them to go into historical issues in any great depth. Historical analysis, if that were the case, could scarcely play a fundamental role in theoretical work. So if historical work *is* important, it has to be because it gives the theorists something more than what I have been talking about so far. It has to give them something fundamental, something that relates to their core intellectual aspirations.

What then do the political scientists who study international relations really want to do? They would like, by and large, to do more than just say intelligent things about how international politics works. Their goal, by and large, is to move beyond the "essay tradition." They would like their field to be a kind of science. Their aim is to develop not just an intellectually respectable body of thought but a body of *theory*.[15] And their approach to history is often rooted in such aspirations. On the whole, they tend to be positivists at heart. They generally take it for granted that theories are tested by looking at the facts, and they often approach historical work from that point of view. Their assumption is that history can serve up the facts that are needed to test theories.

But one of the key insights to be drawn from the philosophy of science literature is that the very notion of "theory testing" is far more problematic than you might think. The problem derives from the fact that theories are not *supposed* to give as accurate a picture of reality as possible. The goal

[14] See especially R. W. Seton-Watson, *Disraeli, Gladstone, and the Eastern Question* (London: Macmillan, 1935), pp. 217–18.

[15] See, for example, Kenneth Waltz, "Realist Thought and Neorealist Theory," *Journal of International Affairs* 44, no. 1 (Summer 1990).

instead is to cut to the core—to simplify, to focus on what is driving things, to bring out what was really important in what is being studied. Theories therefore have to provide a kind of model, a somewhat stylized view of reality. And that model has to differ from the chunk of reality it is supposed to help you understand. "Completely eliminating *all* differences between the model and the original state of affairs," as Hanson says, would destroy "the very thing the model was meant to achieve—namely, the provision of an 'awareness of structure' absent from the original confrontation with a complex of phenomena."[16]

This is as true in the study of international politics as it is in science as a whole. Explanatory power, as Waltz points out—and part of his eminence has to do with the fact that his approach to theory is rooted in an exceptionally sophisticated understanding of these philosophy of science issues—"is gained by moving away from 'reality,' not by staying close to it," so it is a mistake to think that the best model "is the one that reflects reality most accurately."[17] Is the theory of gravitation defective because it fails to explain "the wayward path of a falling leaf"? Is classical economic theory to be faulted because it is based on a theoretic construct, "the famous 'economic man,'" which, as every sensible economist knows, "does not exist"?[18] To say that theory should try to replicate reality, "to say that a 'theory should be just as complicated as all our evidence suggests,'" Waltz notes, "amounts to a renunciation of science from Galileo onward."[19]

What then are we to make of the simple idea that theories should be tested by looking at the empirical evidence? A test consists of a comparison between what the theory implies and what observations show. If a theory is supposed to offer only a stylized picture of reality, a gap between the two is to be expected. How then can a discrepancy, even in principle, be said to falsify the theory? Such gaps, moreover, are generally not hard to deal with. As philosophers of science have noted for more than a hundred years, ad hoc explanations can easily be developed to save theories from falsification.[20] The

[16] Hanson, *Observation and Explanation*, p. 81, and more generally, pp. 79–83 (emphasis in original).

[17] Waltz, *Theory of International Politics*, p. 7.

[18] Ibid., pp. 89, 121.

[19] Kenneth Waltz, "Evaluating Theories," *American Political Science Review* 91, no. 4 (December 1997): 914; the internal quotation is from a well-known book on method, Gary King, Robert Keohane, and Sidney Verba, *Designing Social Inquiry: Scientific Inference in Qualitative Research* (Princeton: Princeton University Press, 1994), p. 20. Waltz, of course, is not the only political scientist who makes this point. Note, for example, the line of criticism developed in Jonathan Bendor and Thomas H. Hammond, "Rethinking Allison's Models," *American Political Science Review* 86, no. 2 (June 1992): esp. 318.

[20] The argument, worked out originally at the end of the nineteenth century, that any theory "can be permanently saved from 'refutation' by some suitable adjustment in the background

well-known philosopher of science Imre Lakatos tells a story (imaginary, but based on a number of real historical episodes) to illustrate the point. The path of a newly discovered planet is calculated using Newton's laws, but the actual path of the planet is different. The Newtonian astronomer conjectures that the deviation is due to the existence nearby of another hitherto unknown planet, but new and more powerful telescopes fail to disclose its existence. The astronomer then "suggests that a cloud of cosmic dust" accounts for the fact that the telescopes were unable to detect it. A satellite is sent up to look for this "conjectural cloud," but the result is another failure leading to another ad hoc conjecture. The process, he says, can go on indefinitely. Success at any point would be treated as a great victory for the Newtonian theory, but failure can always be explained away. At no point does failure mean that the basic theory has been refuted.[21]

Lakatos's point is that testing in science is not nearly as straightforward a concept as one might suppose. People think that a sharp distinction can be drawn between the theoretician and the experimenter, that "the theoretician proposes" and that "the experimenter—in the name of nature—disposes." "Man proposes a system of hypotheses," as one writer put it. "Nature disposes of its truth or falsity. Man invents a scientific system, and then discovers whether or not it accords with observed fact."[22] But, as Lakatos argues, things are just not that simple. Ad hoc explanations can always be put forward: "the prime target remains hopelessly elusive."[23] "Nature may shout no," but human ingenuity "may always be able to shout louder."[24] And it is for that reason, he says, that in science "falsifications are somehow irrelevant."[25] What really matters, according to Lakatos, are "dramatic" results, predicted by the theory, otherwise unexpected, and confirmed by observation. And he gives the example here of the 1919 experiment that showed that light rays from distant stars were deflected by the gravitational force of the sun, just as Einstein's theory of relativity had predicted—a stunning result that played a key role, he says, in winning scientists over to the Einstein theory.[26]

---

knowledge in which it is embedded," came to be called the "Duhem-Quine thesis." The thesis has, as Lakatos pointed out, both a strong and a weak form. But even the weak version "asserts the impossibility of a direct experimental hit on a narrowly specified theoretical target and the logical possibility of shaping science in indefinitely many ways." See Lakatos, "Falsification and the Methodology of Scientific Research Programmes," pp. 184–85.

[21] Ibid., pp. 100–101; Lakatos, "Lectures on Scientific Method," pp. 69–70.

[22] Lakatos, "Falsification and the Methodology of Scientific Research Programmes," pp. 96–97. Lakatos is quoting here from a book by Braithwaite.

[23] Ibid., p. 102.

[24] Lakatos, "History of Science and Its Rational Reconstructions," p. 10.

[25] Lakatos, "Lectures on Scientific Method," p. 95.

[26] Ibid., pp. 99–100. On p. 99, Lakatos gave another example, having to do with the astonishingly accurate prediction of the reappearance of Halley's comet after a seventy-two-year lapse.

This general argument is certainly too extreme, and testing plays a greater role in natural science than Lakatos was prepared to admit. The 1919 experiment, for example, though very important, was not taken as absolutely conclusive. The relativity theory had also predicted the displacement of certain spectral lines, and Einstein himself recognized that the experimental test of that prediction was of crucial importance. "If it were proved that this effect does not exist in nature," he wrote, "then the whole theory would have to be abandoned."[27] Similarly, the Darwin theory of the "survival of the fittest" is often said to be tautological (because fitness is defined in terms of survivability) and therefore untestable. Darwin himself, however, took pains to point out ways in which his theory could be tested empirically—ways in which the empirical evidence would cause the theory to "break down."[28]

But even though Lakatos took the argument too far, there certainly was something to what he was saying, and in fact his basic point applies with greater force to a field like international relations theory than it does to fields like physics or even biology. In international relations theory, hard-and-fast predictions are rarely made; such theories thus cannot be confirmed or falsified in a relatively simple, straightforward way, as the term "testing" implies. Even in natural science, theories are normally not defeated instantly in a "simple battle" with the facts.[29] In the international politics literature, where general claims are much less precise, the assessment process is even less cut-and-dry. It is really the spirit of a theory that is being assessed—whether it gives you some real insight into how the world works, whether it helps you see things you otherwise would have been unable to see, whether it can explain things that you otherwise might find hard to understand. And the key point here is that such judgments simply cannot be made in a mechanical

---

Newton's theory had served as the basis for that calculation, so the amazing accuracy of the prediction provided powerful support for the theory. Kuhn gives a number of similar examples, one of which was particularly striking. In France, he says, resistance to the wave theory of light "collapsed suddenly and relatively completely when Fresnel was able to demonstrate the existence of a white spot at the center of the shadow of a circular disk. That was an effect that not even he had anticipated but which Poisson, initially one of his opponents, had shown to be a necessary if absurd consequence of Fresnel's theory." Kuhn, *Structure of Scientific Revolutions*, p. 155.

[27] Einstein to Eddington, December 15, 1919, quoted in A. Vibert Douglas, *The Life of Arthur Stanley Eddington* (London: Thomas Nelson, 1956), p. 41.

[28] See Richard Alexander, *Darwinism and Human Affairs* (Seattle: University of Washington Press, 1979), pp. 7–8.

[29] Lakatos, "History of Science and Its Rational Reconstructions," p. 31. For a good example of current thinking on the subject, see the section on "Problems of Falsifiability," in Alex Rosenberg, "Biology and Its Philosophy," in *Philosophy of Science: Contemporary Readings*, ed. Yuri Balashov and Alex Rosenberg (London: Routledge, 2002), pp. 28–31; originally published in Alexander Rosenberg, *The Structure of Biological Science* (Cambridge: Cambridge University Press, 1985), pp. 6–8.

way. Even in a field like physics, such judgments are governed "not by logical rules but by the mature sensibility of the trained scientist."[30] So in a field like international relations, where there is even less reason to assume that such decisions can be made in an essentially mechanical way, serious judgments have to draw on the "mature sensibility" of the trained scholar.

This is the real reason why history is important for the theorist. History is not to be thought of as a great reservoir of facts that can be gathered up like "pebbles on the beach" and drawn on for the purpose of theory testing. It is important because by studying history the scholar can develop the kind of sensibility that makes intelligent judgment possible. Indeed, it is hard to see how a scholar *can* develop that kind of sensibility without studying history in a more or less serious way. Purely abstract analysis can only take you so far. It can sometimes take you quite far.[31] But at some point theory has to connect up with reality. At some point, it has to help you understand something important about the real world. So the key thing is to do the sort of work that can draw theory and history together.

Doing that kind of work allows you to take your measure of particular theoretical approaches and thus to develop your own sense for the sort of general theoretical framework appropriate for the analysis of the questions you are concerned with. You might in some cases be surprised by the degree to which a particular theory helps you understand a particular historical episode. You might be struck by how well the history and the theory resonate with each other. You might, in those cases, say to yourself: "I wouldn't have expected to find something like this, but lo and behold, there it is, a finding very much in line with the way that theoretical argument says the world works." When this happens, you sense that the theorist might be on to something important, something you previously had not seen. On the other hand, when the theory

---

[30] See chapter 1, p. 22 above.

[31] In science itself, it is amazing how far the greatest thinkers were able to go on sheer brainpower. Galileo's disproof of the Aristotelian theory that heavier bodies fell more quickly than lighter ones is one extraordinary case in point. See James Robert Brown, *The Laboratory of the Mind: Thought Experiments in the Natural Sciences* (London: Routledge, 1991), pp. 1–3. The origin of the relativity theory provides another important example. The famous Michelson-Morley experiment of 1887, often cited in this context as a "crucial experiment," in fact played a minor role in shaping Einstein's thinking. The real source of the theory was Einstein's intuitive sense, a sense he had even as a teenager, for the way things had to be. Leo Sartori, *Understanding Relativity: A Simplified Approach to Einstein's Theories* (Berkeley: University of California Press, 1996), pp. 51–54, and esp. p. 53; Gerald Holton, "Einstein, Michelson, and the Crucial Experiment," in his *Thematic Origins of Scientific Thought: Kepler to Einstein* (Cambridge, Mass.: Harvard University Press, 1973). In international relations theory, the work of Thomas Schelling is probably the best example of a penetrating body of thought that was generated essentially by pure brainpower. See especially Thomas Schelling, *The Strategy of Conflict* (Cambridge, Mass.: Harvard University Press, 1960), and Thomas Schelling, *Arms and Influence* (New Haven: Yale University Press, 1966).

does not help you understand much of anything, that also has to be taken into account when you are making up your mind about these issues—that is, when you are developing your own understanding of how international politics works. Both positive and negative results feed into the assessment, and in both cases the real world connection is crucial.

Or to put the point another way: theorists often come up with interesting ideas about how international politics works—indeed, with ideas that are at times at odds with each other. But the fact that an idea is interesting or clever does not mean that it necessarily tells you much about how things work in the real world. You thus have to develop some sense for how important these various dynamics are. You need to develop some sense for how they stack up against each other, and thus for what dominates the international political process. Only by studying history in some depth can you make those kinds of judgments. This is particularly important because a major body of theory commonly makes a kind of meta-claim: the theorists who hold those ideas are in effect asserting that what they are emphasizing counts for more than many people think. Indeed, a body of theory needs to make that sort of meta-claim if it is to be of real value: theories that simply sum up what everyone already knows are not worth much. So one of the things that normally characterizes a theory in this field is that it is not universally accepted. Realists, for example, in effect claim that power political factors are a good deal more important than many people are prepared to admit. But judgments about the relative importance of various sets of factors can only be made when you get a real sense for how things actually work, and you can develop that sense only by studying the historical record.

But how exactly do you go about doing this? The basic technique is to take some major theoretical claim, bring it down to earth by thinking about what it would mean in specific historical contexts, and then study those historical episodes with those basic conceptual issues in mind. Exercises of this sort—exercises that bring the conceptual and empirical sides of the broader intellectual effort together—are a way of getting a handle on a problem. Abstract argument, as I said before, has a certain cloudlike quality. Theoretical claims are hard to deal with on a very general level. But those general claims translate, or should translate, into expectations about what you are likely to find if you study a particular historical episode. You can then look at that episode with those expectations in mind. The problems are now more concrete. The questions, being narrower and more specific, are more answerable. And given the way you have set up the question, the answers you reach are bound to give you a certain insight into the more general issues to which those questions are connected.

This is a very standard way of approaching major theoretical problems. In chapter 6, I'll talk more about how in practice this sort of work can actually be done, but for now let me just say that in principle it is generally not that hard to see what theoretical claims "translate into," in terms of specific historical interpretations. Indeed, theorists themselves often give historical examples as a way of backing up their arguments. If your goal is to assess those arguments, the historical cases they themselves cite are the first ones you would want to study. Waltz, for instance, says that one of the reasons why bipolar international systems are more stable than multipolar ones is that, under multipolarity, the "weaker or the more adventurous party" to an alliance can drag its partner into a war. He then cites Austro-German relations in the "prelude to World War I" as a case in point.[32] If your goal is to assess Waltz's argument about multipolarity, one of the first things you would want to do is to see what relations between Austria and Germany during the July crisis were actually like. You would like to see whether Austria was able to drag a reluctant Germany into the war. Did the Austrians, for example, feel that they could do whatever they wanted, knowing that the Germans would not be able to abandon them no matter what happened, or did they feel that they had to clear things with the Germans before they did something that might get them into real trouble with Russia? Did the Germans feel that they would have to support Austria no matter what, or did they feel that Austria could not move ahead unless Germany first gave the green light? These are all studiable issues, and answering them will throw some light not just on Waltz's historical claim about the July crisis but also on the general argument that that claim was meant to support.

The basic point here is that if you want to get a real handle on a major theoretical issue, you often need to go into key historical questions in some depth. You've been exposed to all sorts of historical arguments in the course of your education, but many of them have to be taken with a grain of salt. Waltz might have been taught that Austria dragged Germany into war in 1914; I also remember hearing something like that when I was in college. But historical arguments you pick up in that way are often very much open to question. For serious academic purposes, it scarcely makes sense to take them at face value. If you accept them uncritically, you'd be building on an unnecessarily weak base.

Let me give what to my mind is a particularly striking example of a failure on the part of theorists to do the sort of historical work I am talking about. For me this case is of particular interest because it involves two of the theorists I most admire. In 1965 Thomas Schelling was writing his book *Arms and Influence*, and one of his key arguments in that book had to do with the role the military system could play in bringing on a war. Both sides in a conflict, in Schelling's view, could be trapped by the sort of military system in place

---

[32] Waltz, *Theory of International Politics*, p. 167. See also Waltz's "The Origins of War in Neorealist Theory," *Journal of Interdisciplinary History* 18, no. 4 (Spring 1988): 621.

during a crisis. That system, he thought, could bring on a war that no one really wanted. This was a very important argument, with all kinds of major implications, and the coming of war in 1914 was the one great historical example Schelling gave to support it. The first seven pages of the chapter in which he made that argument were in fact devoted to a discussion of that case.[33]

Schelling sent a draft of that chapter to his friend Bernard Brodie, another giant in the strategic studies field, and Brodie wrote back with detailed comments. He suggested that Schelling, in that section, use the famous story about how, on the eve of the First World War, the Kaiser, thinking that it might be possible to fight the war only in the east, tried to get General von Moltke, the chief of the general staff, to change the plan calling for an initial attack in the west, but was told that this was impossible. (Brodie himself had used that story to make a point about how a rigid military mind-set could bring on a war that "no one wanted" in an article he had published a decade earlier.) Barbara Tuchman, Brodie told Schelling, had described the incident her recent best seller, *The Guns of August*. Schelling replied that he had "thought of using that business about the Kaiser's being told the trains couldn't be turned around," but he "had a nagging impression that Barbara Tuchman or somebody thought the story was possibly undocumented, and maybe a little too good to be true," so he "let it go." If, however, Brodie or some "other genuine scholar" could assure him "that the story was correct" or tell him "where to find a reference," he said he would like to use it. But he was too busy to try to "trace down any documented version" himself.[34]

This exchange I found quite revealing. I was struck, first of all, by what it showed about Brodie. The evidence (including the evidence that Tuchman had presented in her discussion of this particular episode, if you read it with any care) shows very clearly that it was Moltke and not the Kaiser who was overruled on the key issue of whether the attack on France had to proceed as planned without regard to changed political conditions. The Kaiser, having been led to believe that Britain might stay out of the war if it were fought only in the east, decided to call off the attack in the west. Moltke pleaded with him to change his mind, but as Tuchman herself points out, "despite all his pleading, the Kaiser refused to budge." "'Crushed,' Moltke says of himself," Tuchman writes (quoting from Moltke's own memoir), "he returned to the General Staff and 'burst into bitter tears of abject despair.'" The orders calling for an attack in the west were canceled, and it was only after new

[33] Schelling, *Arms and Influence*, pp. 221–27.

[34] Brodie to Schelling, February 8, 1965, and Schelling to Brodie, February 19, 1965, Bernard Brodie Papers, box 2, UCLA Research Library, Los Angeles; and Bernard Brodie, "Unlimited Weapons and Limited War," *Reporter*, November 18, 1954, p. 21.

information came in from Britain showing that an east-only war would not be possible that the attack in the west was allowed to proceed as planned.[35]

So Brodie had missed the real point of the story, but why? The problem might have had something to do with the way the Tuchman book was written. Tuchman had framed the issue in a way that probably led Brodie to think that her analysis supported his view of the incident. Here, for example, is the concluding paragraph from her short but very dramatic introduction to the part of the book dealing with the outbreak of war:

> War pressed against every frontier. Suddenly dismayed, governments struggled and twisted to fend it off. It was no use. Agents at frontiers were reporting every cavalry patrol as a deployment to beat the mobilization gun. General staffs, goaded by their relentless timetables, were pounding the table for the signal to move lest their opponents gain an hour's head start. Appalled upon the brink, the chiefs of state who would be ultimately responsible for their country's fate attempted to back away but the pull of military schedules dragged them forward.[36]

This is the kind of passage that makes an impression on people. Tuchman's account of the confrontation between the Kaiser and Moltke might have been factually accurate, but, in terms of what people took away from the book, what mattered was not the detailed account but the way it was packaged. *"The pull of military schedules dragged them forward"*—this, according to Tuchman, was the point of the story, and unless you are in the habit of reading historical texts critically, you tend to assume that this was what her detailed account actually showed. And that, of course, is a major reason for getting into the habit of reading such texts critically. But let's not focus too narrowly on the reference to the Tuchman book. The more serious point is that Brodie had never really studied the July crisis the way it should have been studied, above all by an expert of his stature, and was content to repeat the standard clichés.

What makes this case particularly striking is that Brodie was unusual among strategic theorists of his generation in that he *did* pay a lot of attention to history, believed deeply in the importance of historical study, and criticized many of his fellow strategists for not knowing much about diplomatic or military history.[37] And yet here was Brodie himself, perhaps the most historically minded of the leading American strategic theorists, making a historical argument that he would never have made if he had studied this very

---

[35] Barbara Tuchman, *The Guns of August* (New York: Macmillan, 1962), p. 81. A detailed discussion of this episode could also be found in what was then by far the most thorough account of the immediate origins of the war available in English, Albertini's *The Origins of the War of 1914*, 3:171–81 and 3:380–86.

[36] Tuchman, *Guns of August*, p. 72.

[37] Bernard Brodie, *War and Politics* (New York: Macmillan, 1973), p. 475.

specific but fundamental issue—the role of the military system in bringing on the war in 1914—the way it ought to have been studied.

The case of Schelling was perhaps even more striking. Here he was, producing a book that was destined to be the single most important work in the field, but he could not be bothered to do the work needed to get to the bottom of the issue that Brodie had raised. He could not even go to the library or to a bookstore and look up the story in the Tuchman book. It was as though the historical evidence had purely ornamental value. If this story did not work, then there was no need to use it. Although he talked a lot about the July crisis in that key chapter in *Arms and Influence*, an accurate understanding of what happened in July 1914 was not seen as crucial in its own right.

But Schelling was writing a work of theory, so why, you might ask, was it important for him to get to the bottom of these historical issues? After all, one *could* imagine the Kaiser giving way to Moltke. The standard account of this episode has a certain plausibility, and for the purposes of theory building, isn't that all that really matters? But there is obviously something wrong with the notion that from the point of view of the theorist, fiction, as long as it is plausible, is as good as history.[38] To take one of the key issues people like Brodie and Schelling were concerned with: doesn't it matter, from the standpoint of the theorist, whether war was in reality often brought on by the workings of the military system in place at the time, or whether war is virtually never to be interpreted in such terms? Given the role the story about the confrontation between Moltke and the Kaiser plays in supporting the view that military factors could play a key role in bringing on a war that nobody wanted, doesn't it matter whether that story is correct or not? Suppose you couldn't find any historical evidence at all to support that view, and all you had to go on were purely fictional accounts of how a war could begin virtually by accident. Wouldn't the absence of powerful historical evidence be an important "clue" in Kuhn's sense? Shouldn't the absence of evidence, in that case, play a certain role in shaping your thinking about what makes for war?

So doesn't all this mean that people like Brodie and Schelling could have done better, as theorists even, if they had gone into what for them were important historical questions in greater depth? I think not only that they could have done better but also that it would not have been all that hard for them to have done so. And this, in fact, is one of the main points I want to make in this book. You might think that I am asking too much. You might think

[38] Note what Schelling says in the preface to *Arms and Influence* (p. vii): "I have used some historical examples, but usually as illustration, not evidence. For browsing in search of ideas, Caesar's *Conquest of Gaul* is rich reading and Thucydides' *Peloponnesian War* the best there is, whatever their historical merits—even if read as pure fiction."

that I am in effect saying that theorists need to become historians. And you might feel that that expectation is not just unrealistic but that it ignores the fact that international relations theory is a field with an intellectual personality of its own—that no one can do everything and that those who choose to do theory simply cannot be expected to become historians and do professional-quality historical work.

But to do the kind of work I am talking about, a theorist does not have to become a historian. A theorist can reach relatively solid conclusions on key historical issues in a reasonable amount of time, provided he or she uses the right method—and in the next two chapters, I want to show you what that method is.

Chapter Three

THE CRITICAL ANALYSIS OF
HISTORICAL TEXTS

There's a method for tackling historical problems, a method for reaching relatively solid conclusions more quickly and more efficiently than you might have thought possible. That method is based on the analysis of what historians call secondary sources—not documents and other "primary" or "original" sources produced at the time, but books and articles written mainly by the historians themselves.

My main goal in this part of the book is to show what that method is and how it can be used to reach conclusions on major historical issues. I want to show in this chapter how historical texts can be analyzed and in the next, how that method of textual analysis can be used to arrive at an interpretation of an important historical episode. The basic point of these two chapters, taken as a whole, is that that method can take you much further than you might imagine, given the limited amount of time you can reasonably devote to the study of a particular issue. For many purposes it's the only method you'll need to use. At times you may want to study a particular problem in greater depth, and in such cases you'd obviously want to work extensively with original sources. But even then it would probably still make sense to begin your project by examining the historical literature using the method I'm going to outline here.

To use that method, though, you first have to figure out which works to read. But how exactly do you do that? How do you develop a sense for what the important texts are in a given area of scholarship? How, in other words, do you get your bearings in what may for you be an entirely new field? The section that follows is concerned with these relatively prosaic, nuts-and-bolts questions.

THE LAY OF THE LAND

No one does scholarly work in a vacuum. If you're interested in a particular problem, you naturally want to see what scholars have had to say on that subject. Indeed, one of the first things you want to do when you begin work in a particular field of scholarship is to get a sense for the lay of the land—a sense for what the most important works are, for who says what, and for how scholarly debate in that field is structured. You need to do this because you form views of your own by *reacting* to what other people say: *their* arguments provide the framework within which you can at least begin to work out your own answers to basic historical problems.

But how do you identify the main works dealing with the particular subject you're interested in? Your goal is to come up with a relatively short list of key works and perhaps also to get some sense for the basic arguments with which those works are associated. There are two main techniques you can use to generate such a list, one based on articles and the other on books. Let me talk about the article-based method first.

When you begin a new project, it's a good idea to start with the periodical literature. There are a number of journals which deal with international politics and military affairs, and I list some of the most important ones in appendix I.[1] Take a look at that list when you start a project. Which journals are most likely to publish articles related to your topic? Then go through those journals, looking for three main things: review articles, especially those that survey a whole subfield of scholarly work; articles related to the subject you are interested in; and reviews of books that deal with that general topic. The review articles are particularly important for obvious reasons. A good survey article can save you an enormous amount of time. A lot of your bibliographical work will have been done for you. Some collections of survey articles dealing with American foreign policy have been published as books: Gerald Haines and J. Samuel Walker, eds., *American Foreign Relations: A Historiographical Review* (1981); Robert Schulzinger, ed., *A Companion to American Foreign Relations* (2003); and two books edited by Michael Hogan: *America in the World: The Historiography of American Foreign Relations since 1941* (1995), and *Paths to Power: The Historiography of American Foreign Relations to 1941* (2000). There are, incidentally, similar volumes covering the political science literature.[2]

The importance of such articles is obvious. But even ordinary scholarly articles are an important source because it is standard practice for an author to explain at the outset how the work presented in that article relates to prevailing ideas in the field as a whole. Major works—works that are well regarded, works that have had a certain impact on the field, works by well-known scholars—are often cited in that context. Note that to get what you need for this phase of the project, you do not need to read such articles in their entirety. For your present purposes, you just zero in on what an author says in the first few pages of the article.

You can often find articles of interest just by looking through the relevant journals for the past five or ten years. You can also identify them by using a

---

[1] See pp. 207–208 below.
[2] See pp. 205–206 below.

number of computerized search engines: JSTOR, Project MUSE (both of which have full texts available online), the Social Science Citation Index, and the Expanded Academic ASAP (Infotrac). These are available through most American research libraries, and I'll explain how they work in appendix I.[3]

You might also want to spend a little time looking at the book review sections in the main journals covering the subject you are interested in. Not every book published in the field is worth reviewing, so the book review section in recent issues of the journal can give you a sense for what are considered the most significant books that have appeared in the past few years. If a particular book looks interesting, you can check it out. Recent books will obviously provide a lot of information about recent work in the field. After you have identified a number of important books in a given field, no matter how you have come up with that list, you might want to see quickly what their arguments are and how they are regarded by other scholars. In that case, you can look up the reviews of those books; a number of computerized search engines now make this a relatively easy thing to do. I'll show you how this is done in appendix I.[4]

The second basic avenue of attack also has to do with books, but relies on standard computerized library catalogues. You need not limit yourself to your own home library's search engine, since practically all of them are available online. My basic advice here is that you should become familiar not just with your home university catalogue but also with some other catalogue with very extensive listings. Your best bet here, I think, is to familiarize yourself with Eureka (sometimes called RLIN), the union catalogue for the Research Libraries Group, which lists the combined holdings of the major American research libraries. Eureka is not publicly available and to use it you generally have to go through your home library website. If for some reason your library is not a subscriber, you could instead use the catalogue of some library that does have massive holdings, like the Library of Congress or the Harvard University Library. Both of those search engines (and others as well, such as MELVYL, the union catalogue for the University of California system) are accessible through the internet.[5]

---

[3] See pp. 208–211 below.

[4] See pp. 214–215 below.

[5] The Harvard Library URL is http://lib.harvard.edu/; click into the link for the HOLLIS catalogue on the bottom left. The URL for the Library of Congress catalogue is http://catalog.loc.gov/. In these search engines, and in most others as well, you can opt to do a simple search or a more complex search—that is, you can search in more than one field at the same time. In different catalogues, this is referred to in various ways. The Library of Congress catalogue calls it a "guided search"; HOLLIS refers to it as an "expanded search"; MELVYL, the union catalogue for the University of California system (http://melvyl.cdlib.org), calls it an "advanced search." But whatever your university catalogue calls it, I recommend that you get to know how it works and use it for all your searches. You can do everything you can do with a simple search, and a lot more besides.

Your goal with all of these catalogues is to do a subject search, but it's often hard to know which subject terms to search for, or even which subject words to search for, since the subject headings a book is listed under are often assigned in a fairly arbitrary way. So it makes sense to start with a book that you know is related to your topic. If you don't know of a single book on the subject, you can do a search for a key individual associated with the topic. If your topic, for example, is American intervention in the First World War, then you can do a subject search, or even a title search, for "Woodrow Wilson." You can then see which books relate most directly to whatever you are interested in. It scarcely matters what those books are, because once you get your foot in the door, you can spread out very quickly. Let me explain how.

When you call up a particular listing, you go into what computerized catalogues call the "long display," the "full view," or something of that sort. The more complete listing that comes up shows you the subject headings that book is listed under. You then click into the links for those subject headings and see which books turn up. You then repeat the process for those books in that new list which are of particular interest. When you do this work, be sure to use the catalogue's "save" command. You mark and save the most interesting titles. At the end of the session, you print out or save the list you've generated, making sure that that list includes the books' call numbers.

By examining those call numbers, you'll notice that the books you're interested in are concentrated in certain parts of the stacks, and you then go to where they cluster. As you get used to the cataloguing system, you might even be able to go to certain areas of the stacks directly, without even looking anything up. In the Library of Congress cataloguing system, used by many university libraries, the E183.8 x call number is given to books dealing with U.S. relations with a country whose names begin with x: the E183.8 G3 section will have books on U.S.-German relations, the E183.8 G7 section will have books on U.S. relations with Great Britain, and so on. When you get to the areas in the stacks where books relating to your topic are concentrated, pick out those that seem to be most useful for your present purposes. You should pay particular attention to books that look relatively new and have been published by university presses.

Now go through those books and see which ones have annotated bibliographies or bibliographical essays. By reading those bibliographies, you will probably be able to get a certain sense for the structure of the field—for what the main works are, and maybe also for how they differ from each other in terms of the arguments they make. Authors, moreover, have a certain interest in explaining why their books are important, and thus in explaining how their conclusions differ from, or otherwise relate to, those of major works in the field; they therefore often talk about the field as a whole, commonly toward the beginning of the book. One trick here is to pay special attention during this phase of the project to the footnotes for the preface or introduction.

Are you interested, for example, in the Vietnam War? You can get a certain sense for the literature on that subject just by reading the six pages of notes appended to the preface of Fredrik Logevall's *Choosing War: The Lost Chance for Peace and the Escalation of the War in Vietnam.*[6]

Even relatively narrow studies somewhat outside your area of interest can help you get a sense for the scholarly lay of the land in a particular field. Here's another trick you can use: get a book dealing with the subject you want to study, but one that begins its detailed coverage at a slightly later point in time. A book of this sort might well have an introductory chapter or section dealing with the immediately preceding period. The discussion there will be highly selective, which for these purposes is a good thing, and the references cited there will probably be of interest.

The more narrowly focused monographic studies are not, of course, the only sorts of books you'll want to look at. Major works of synthesis, or at least books with a fairly broad scope, might also be worth checking out, especially if they are written by well-known scholars. Using the index or table of contents, you can go directly to the part of the text dealing with the issue of interest to you. The broader the scope of the book as a whole, the shorter the passage dealing with your specific subject is likely to be. The author's interpretation of the subject should be fairly succinct, and you can generally tell from the way that interpretation is framed whether the account simply reflects the conventional wisdom, or whether the author is taking issue with standard views. General surveys, moreover, are particularly useful for their bibliographies, especially if the author does more than simply give you a long list of books and articles relating to the subject matter covered in that work. Bibliographical essays and annotated bibliographies found at the end of such books, as well as bibliographical footnotes, are also generally quite valuable—and again, for these purposes the more opinionated they are, the better. I remember at one point being particularly struck by Maurice Baumont's reference in a book of this sort to William Langer's important work on international politics in the late Bismarckian period, *European Alliances and Alignments* (1931). This, Baumont noted in a bibliographical footnote, was a major work to be sure but was marred by "too systematic an admiration for Bismarck"—a very pithy remark, and one that was absolutely on target.

General surveys are often written as parts of a series—the old "Rise of Modern Europe" series, for example, the French "Peuples et Civilisations" series (in which the Baumont book appeared), the various Oxford and Cambridge history series, and so on. The authors, in such cases, are generally senior scholars who were asked to take on the job because they have devoted a good chunk of their lives to the study of that field. You can thus be fairly confident

---

[6] Fredrik Logevall, *Choosing War: The Lost Chance for Peace and the Escalation of War in Vietnam* (Berkeley: University of California Press, 1999), pp. 417–22.

that they are quite familiar with the relevant scholarly literature. Warren Cohen's *America in the Age of Soviet Power, 1945–1991* (1993), volume 4 in *The Cambridge History of American Foreign Relations*, is a good case in point. Even if you did not know that the author was a major figure in the field, you could tell right away this was a highly respectable work. Anyone asked to write a volume in something called the "Cambridge History of American Foreign Relations" would have to be an important person in the field, someone whose judgments about work produced in the field would carry particular weight.

Those are the two basic avenues of attack, but when you are doing bibliographical work, there are various other techniques you can use. Let me talk briefly about two of them: dissertations and syllabi. Dissertations as a rule have excellent bibliographies, and they frequently have sections (often the first chapter, or a long introduction, or an annotated bibliography) discussing the scholarly literature in the field. So getting a good dissertation, especially a recent one, may save you a lot of time because the author may have done a good deal of your bibliographical work for you. And finding a good dissertation might also enable you to do a bit of quality control on yourself: in your literature search, have you missed any important sources that another scholar had been able to turn up? Dissertations are easy to identify and easy to get hold of. They are published in various formats by University Microfilms Incorporated (or UMI), now part of ProQuest, and you can use the UMI website to identify dissertations you might want to see. The procedure for using the search engine there will be discussed in appendix I.[7]

You can also look at syllabi developed for courses that relate to the subject you are interested in, especially courses taught by well-known figures in the field. If you do not know who they are, you might want to check out syllabi for courses offered at prestigious universities, and there are also some "syllabus archives" you might want to check out.[8] Syllabi are very useful because they give you some sense for what the instructor thinks are the most important works in the field, or at least those most worth reading.

Using these techniques, you quickly (in a day or two) get a feel for what a particular area of historical scholarship is like—for who the key people are, for which books and articles are of fundamental importance, and often for what the major issues are and for who says what. You don't need to use every one of these techniques whenever you begin a new project. You use whatever combination works for you—that is, whichever methods take you to where you want to go easily and quickly.

These techniques are pretty basic. They can be used in a variety of fields. They can be used, for example, by political scientists, both to get some feel

[7] See pp. 212–213 below.
[8] See pp. 213–214 below and the sources cited there.

for the lay of the land in a certain corner of their own discipline and also at the start of a project that will draw on both theory and history. But no matter which field you are in, the key thing to bear in mind is that your goal at this point in the research process is strictly limited. Your goal is just to develop a rough sense for what a particular area of scholarship is like. When you see what it is like—when you see what the important works are—you can put the bibliographical effort aside and move into phase two of the project. You can begin to read the texts you consider fundamental. But you will need to read them *critically*.

You may, of course, need to do additional bibliographical work later on. Generally, as you read books and articles, one work leads to another. You can go into a particular issue more deeply by looking at the works cited in foot-notes appended to the passages dealing with that issue. But you might also want to do a more exhaustive search for what has been published on a partic-ular question. One way you can do that is by using published book-length bibliographies. You can often find bibliographies dealing with a particular subject by doing a search for that subject in a computerized library catalogue, but with the word "bibliography" added as a search term, or perhaps even simply tacked on to the subject heading. You might, for example, want to see if there is any published bibliography that covers Japan's decision to go to war against America in 1941. You can look up one of the standard books dealing with that subject—say, Robert Butow's *Tojo and the Coming of the War*. In the "long display" or "full view," you see the subjects this book is listed under. One of them is "World War, 1939–1945—Japan." So you then do a subject search for "World War, 1939–1945—Japan—Bibliography." A number of titles come up, one of which is John Sbrega's *The War against Japan, 1941–1945: An Annotated Bibliography* (1989). Going into the "long display" for that listing, a number of additional subject links turn up, listing additional bibliographical works in related areas.

As you become familiar with your library's cataloguing system, you can do this kind of search just by adding the term "bibliography" to a standard subject. For example, if you do a subject search for "United States—Foreign relations—bibliography," a whole series of listings turns up, and some—for example, Richard Dean Burns's *Guide to American Foreign Relations since 1700* and its successor volume, Robert Beisner's *American Foreign Relations since 1600: A Guide to the Literature*—are clearly of particular importance.[9] For "United States," you can of course substitute the name of some other country you are interested in, and sometimes useful listings turn up.[10]

[9] Richard Dean Burns, *Guide to American Foreign Relations since 1700* (Santa Barbara, Calif.: ABC-CLIO, 1983); Robert Beisner, *American Foreign Relations since 1600: A Guide to the Litera-ture* (Santa Barbara, Calif.: ABC-CLIO, 2003).
[10] For further discussion, see pp. 201–203 below.

Another way to generate references of this sort is to do a title search—that is, a search for books whose titles contain phrases like "Arab-Israeli" or "Sino-Soviet" and words like "bibliography," "guide," or "handbook." Or you can go to the part of the stacks in the reference section of the library containing books with call numbers corresponding to your area of interest—that is, the call numbers where works dealing with your subject tend to cluster—and you will often find bibliographies there. Let me also mention here the single most important published bibliography for people working on twentieth-century international politics: the *Bibliographie zur Zeitgeschichte*, which is published as a kind of supplement to the main German journal for scholarly research in this area, the *Vierteljahrshefte für Zeitgeschichte*. This is a very well-organized list, put out now on an annual basis, with works basically in English, German, and French. It is easy to use even for people who do not know much German.

You may at some point in a research project want to find out as much as you can about what's been written on a particular subject. In appendix I, I'll talk about how detailed bibliographical work can be done and I'll also tell you about some specific bibliographies you might want to use when the time comes. But as a general rule exhaustive bibliographical work should *not* be done at the beginning of a project. When you're starting out, all you want to do is develop a certain sense for what a particular area of scholarship is like—for what the important works are and, if possible, for what arguments they make.

Textual Analysis: The Method Explained

After identifying the major works in a given area of scholarship, what do you do next? Should you just read those works cover to cover, trying to absorb as much factual information as you can? If your goal is to develop your own understanding of a particular subject, it's important to approach those texts in a very different way. You need a more active method, a method that allows you to react to arguments and weigh them against each other. That method will not only help you make up your own mind up about these historical issues but also enables you to absorb the evidence presented in those texts more effectively. A piece of evidence will register in your mind when you understand what it means. And you're better able to understand what it means when you see it in the context of an argument.

The first thing you want to do, therefore, is to develop some sense for the overall argument of a particular historical text. "What's the point here?" you ask. "What's the author driving at?" If the work in question is any good at all, the core argument should not be hard to find. An author, after all, has an interest in displaying it prominently. If the reader is to be convinced, he or she has to see what the author is driving at. So the heart of the argument is summed up in those places in the text which the reader is most likely to read attentively: the title or subtitle of the work, the titles of particular chapters or sections, the introduction, the conclusion, the first and last paragraphs in the book or article, and the first and last paragraphs (or even sentences) in each chapter or section. So these are the first things you should read when you pick up a particular work. Your first goal is simply to find an answer to the question: what is the basic argument—the central thesis—of this particular book or article? What is the author trying to get me to believe?

The next step is to get some sense for the structure or "architecture" of the argument. The core argument rests on a number of key specific claims. Those claims in turn rest on empirical evidence—on documents and other historical sources, generally cited in footnotes. Your goal now is to understand something about how these different elements in the text relate to each other—about what those specific claims are and about the sort of evidence that supports them. You begin by looking at the table of contents or by skimming through the work to see how it is broken down into sections. Do the various parts of the work fit into some overarching structure? Is there a logic that pulls the different elements in the text together? Many works have a "road map" passage, often located toward the end of the introduction, that can be quite useful in this context.

Once you have some sense for the structure of an argument, you can begin to read the text in a relatively active way—that is, with specific questions in mind. As you go through it, you ask yourself how the various passages you read and the main claims made in those passages relate to the larger argument. Is a specific passage really crucial for the purposes of that argument? Or are you wading through a lot of extraneous material, of no particular importance from the point of view of the argument as a whole? It is generally not hard to see what the point of a passage is, although sometimes you have to think a bit before you understand how it relates (or fails to relate) to the overarching argument of the work as a whole.

Because your main goal at this point is to assess the central argument of the book or article in question, passages of marginal relevance can be read quite quickly. But passages that are of fundamental importance in that context need to be read with great care and again with a view toward answering certain very specific questions.

Those questions fall into two categories. The first has to do with the *logic* of the argument. Even if the specific claim made in a particular passage is valid, does it really support the general argument made in that book or article, even if the author suggests it does? Do the various claims the author is making all fit neatly into one broader argument, or do they seem to pull in different directions? Is the argument internally consistent, or does the author say different things—things at odds with each other—in different places?

The second set of questions has to do with the nature and adequacy of the *evidence* supporting the various specific claims that are made. Does the evidence, assuming the author is reading it properly, really prove what the author wants you to think it proves? Is enough evidence given to support the point being made? Is that point perhaps contradicted by other evidence you have seen elsewhere, including evidence presented in other sections of the same book or article? To answer some of these questions, you naturally want to pay special attention to the footnotes. Weak documentation is always a bad sign. When points are supported by a good deal of direct evidence, especially archival evidence and other documentary evidence, your opinion of a work generally goes up.

When a particular claim plays a key role in the general argument, it might make sense to check the references given to back up that point. You normally do this only rarely, when you have some doubt about a particular claim. But checking sources nowadays is generally not hard to do. Even many archival sources are readily available on microfilm or in some electronic format. But checking references can be very eye-opening. It not only helps you form an opinion on the substantive issue at hand but also gives you some sense for the quality of the work as a whole.

The method is thus fairly straightforward. You identify the heart of the argument, you try to understand its structure, and you then try to see what is to be made of the argument in terms both of its internal logic and of the adequacy of the evidence supporting key specific claims. But getting a general sense for how the method works is just a beginning. To understand how to use it, you need to see how in practice specific historical arguments can be analyzed.

A.J.P. TAYLOR AND THE ORIGINS OF THE SECOND WORLD WAR

A.J.P. Taylor's *The Origins of the Second World War* is one of the most famous works of history ever written. Even today, more than forty years after it was originally published, it still looms large in the scholarly literature on the origins of the war of 1939. If you are interested in understanding what led to that conflict, this book is certainly one you would want to analyze.

Taylor's goal is implicit in the book's title—to explain the origins of the Second World War or, more precisely, as he himself points out, the origins of the war that broke out in September 1939. So what, according to Taylor, caused that war? You find the answer (or at least something that points to the answer) at the very end of the book. Summing up his argument, Taylor says in that concluding passage: "Such were the origins of the second World war, or rather of the war between the three Western Powers over the settlement of

Versailles; a war which had been implicit since the moment when the first war ended."[11]

What does he mean, you wonder, when he says that the war was over Versailles? Is he implying that it came about as the result of an attempt by Germany to throw off the constraints on German power contained in the Treaty of Versailles, the peace treaty imposed on Germany following its defeat in World War I? You look at the table of contents. You note that chapter 4, dealing with the 1933–35 period, is called "The End of Versailles." You also note, using the technique of paying special attention to first and last sentences, that the very next chapter, the one that deals with 1935–36, begins with the sentence: "Versailles was dead." How then can the war be said to have broken out "over . . . Versailles" when the Versailles system, by Taylor's own account, had been dead for four years?

You might be puzzled, but to try to understand what he had in mind, it occurs to you that it would probably make sense to see what he meant by the final phrase in that passage at the end of the book, a phrase that might help shed some light on the part of the sentence that preceded it. What does Taylor mean there about a new war being "implicit since the moment when the first war ended"? To get the answer, you naturally turn to the first chapter in the book, the chapter called "The Legacy of the First World War." What Taylor says in that chapter allows you to answer that question. "The decision which ultimately led to the second World war was taken," he writes, "a few days before the first war ended" in 1918.[12] This was the decision to leave Germany intact. "The armistice settled the question of German unity," he says, "so far as the first World war is concerned."[13] It was not the (alleged) harshness of the Versailles peace treaty of 1919 that was important. "The most important thing" about that treaty was that "it was concluded with a united Germany."[14] This, he says, "was the decisive, fateful, outcome of the armistice and the peace treaty"—hence the reference to the war being over Versailles. It was important because it made the German problem "more acute":

This problem was not German aggressiveness or militarism, or the wickedness of her rulers. These, even if they existed, merely aggravated the problem; or perhaps actually made it less menacing by provoking moral resistance in other countries. The essential problem was political, not moral. However democratic and pacific Germany might become, she remained by far the greatest Power on the continent of Europe; with the disappearance of Russia, more so than before. She was greatest

[11] A.J.P. Taylor, *The Origins of the Second World War* (New York: Atheneum, 1962), p. 278.
[12] Ibid., p. 21.
[13] Ibid., p. 23.
[14] Ibid., p. 24.

in population—65 million against 40 million in France, the only other substantial
Power. Her preponderance was greater still in the economic resources of coal and
steel which in modern times together made up power.[15]

So there it is, the core argument of the book. "The essential problem was political, not moral": political realities, *power* realities, played the key role in
shaping the course of events. Taylor's basic idea here was that Germany was
basically such a strong country that, if things developed in the normal way,
"nothing could prevent the Germans from overshadowing Europe, *even if they
did not plan to do so.*"[16]

If you've been exposed to any international relations theory at all, that
argument might have a familiar ring. The type of regime Germany had,
according to Taylor, was not particularly important. Nor did German political
culture count for much. The structure of power was by far the most important
factor at work in international politics. You've probably heard these kinds of
arguments before. If so, you would probably have little trouble picking up the
fact that Taylor's interpretation is rooted in a certain theory of international
politics. And that implies that an analysis of his argument is bound to have
certain theoretical implications. Taylor's interpretation, it seems, with its emphasis on power and its minimizing of everything else, is rooted in a realist
understanding of international politics. An analysis of his argument might
therefore shed some light on the sorts of issues associated with that general
approach to international politics.

One of Taylor's basic assumptions is that regime type was not of fundamental importance. Indeed, as you read the book, you are struck by the fact that
Taylor argues explicitly that it did not matter, in terms of foreign policy, that
Germany was being run by the Nazis. You're struck by this argument because
you had earlier absorbed the conventional view that the fact that Hitler
was in control of German policy from 1933 on mattered a great deal. But in
Taylor's view foreign policy was the one sphere in which Hitler "changed
nothing." Hitler's foreign policy, Taylor writes, "was that of his predecessors,
of the professional diplomats at the foreign ministry, and indeed of virtually
all Germans. Hitler, too, wanted to free Germany from the restrictions of the
peace treaty; to restore a great German army; and then to make Germany the
greatest power in Europe from her natural weight."[17] And as you think about
it—as you think about how these claims relate to his overall argument—you
quickly come to see how that specific view about Hitler is linked to a certain
theory of how international politics works, a theory that takes the structure
of power as fundamental. When Germany was weak, German policy was

---

[15] Ibid.
[16] Ibid. (emphasis added).
[17] Ibid., p. 68.

restrained. Even Fascist dictators, Taylor points out, would not go to war unless they saw "a chance of winning."[18] But as Germany recovered its strength, opportunities were bound to appear. There was no need for Hitler to make plans, and he did not "make plans—for world conquest or for anything else."[19] As the fruit ripened on the tree, it would basically just fall into his lap, with only the most minimal effort on his part. Hitler himself, in Taylor's view, was simply a medium through which basic structural changes—fundamental shifts in the structure of power—produced their effects. Hitler did not even have to be aware of what was going on. "The greatest masters of statecraft," he writes, "are those who do not know what they are doing."[20] And Taylor repeatedly insists that Hitler was not actually driving the course of events. "Despite his bluster and violent talk," Hitler was "a master in the game of waiting." He did not "make precise demands," he simply "announced that he was dissatisfied; and then waited for the concessions to pour into his lap, merely holding out his hand for more."[21] "It was never Hitler's method," he says, "to take the initiative. He liked others to do his work for him; and he waited for the inner weakening of the European system, just as he had waited for the peace settlement to crumble of itself."[22]

You thus come to see how the different levels of Taylor's argument hang together—that is, how his interpretation has a certain "architecture." Not only is there a direct connection between his view of Hitler's role and his general theory of how international politics works, but that view is in turn linked to his interpretation of a series of specific episodes in the run-up to the war: the Austrian and Czech crises in 1938, and the German seizure of Prague and the Polish crisis in 1939. In the chapter on the Austrian crisis, Taylor says that Hitler was not forcing the pace, that the Austrian Nazis were acting on their own, and that "even Hitler's orders could not stop" Nazi agitation in Austria.[23] In the chapter on the Czech crisis, Taylor says that the ethnic Germans in Czechoslovakia, the Sudeten Nazis, generated the problem on their own. "Even more than in the case of Austria," he says, "Hitler did not need to act. Others would do his work for him. The crisis over Czechoslovakia was provided for Hitler. He merely took advantage of it."[24] And he reiterated the point, in perhaps even more extreme form, at the very start of the final chapter: "The Sudeten Nazis, like the Austrians before them, built up the tension gradually without guidance from Hitler."[25]

[18] Ibid., p. 103.
[19] Ibid., p. 134.
[20] Ibid., p. 72.
[21] Ibid., p. 71.
[22] Ibid., p. 108.
[23] Ibid., p. 139.
[24] Ibid., p. 152.
[25] Ibid., p. 248.

So you see the architecture of the argument. Taylor's basic interpretation of the origins of the war is supported by a particular view of Hitler's policy. That view rests in turn on a series of specific claims about German policy in the crises of the late 1930s. But those specific arguments need to be backed up by empirical evidence. By examining how well the evidence Taylor gives supports his specific claims, you're thus not just assessing the validity of those claims. Because you understand the structure of the argument, you're also assessing the validity of the general interpretation they support—and, indeed, you're also, to a certain extent, taking your measure of the general theory of international politics with which that general interpretation of the origins of the war is associated.

How then can key specific claims be examined? Taylor's claim about how even "Hitler's orders" could not stop the Austrian Nazis is not supported by any reference, and the absence of a footnote raises doubts in your mind. You realize you could check this by doing some very targeted work using scholarly studies of the Austrian crisis and maybe also by doing some highly targeted research in the published documents. But with regard to the Czech crisis, you can draw conclusions without having to look at outside sources. Taylor, for example, as I just noted, says explicitly that the Sudeten Nazis "built up the tension gradually *without guidance from Hitler*." And yet Taylor himself shows—to be sure, in another part of the book—that Hitler played a very active role. On March 28, Taylor writes, Hitler "received the Sudeten representatives and appointed Henlein, their leader, his 'viceroy.' They were to negotiate with the Czechoslovak government; and, in Henlein's words, 'we must always demand so much that we can never be satisfied.'" So by Taylor's own account, Hitler was giving the Sudeten Nazis very clear guidance. Indeed, Taylor himself notes at this point that Hitler "screwed up the tension in the hope that something would give somewhere."[26]

When you notice contradictions of this sort, alarm bells go off. There's a basic problem with the argument. It seems that the author is trying to square a circle. The argument and the evidence pull in opposite directions. And because of the way the analysis has developed, to point out such a contradiction is not just to take a potshot at the book. Taylor's claim about Hitler's relative passivity, a fundamental element in his interpretation of the origins of the war, turns on his account of just a few historical episodes. His claims about those episodes are the pillars on which his larger argument rests. If those pillars collapse—if those claims are discredited by evidence Taylor himself presents in the book—the core argument of the book as a whole also collapses.

And you can hardly help noticing how Taylor contradicts himself on some very fundamental issues. What, for example, does Taylor have to say about

[26] Ibid., p. 153.

Hitler's basic goals? This is obviously an important issue and bears directly on the central question the book is concerned with. Did the Nazi leader, according to Taylor, seriously intend to carve out a great empire in the east and thus to conduct a great war of conquest against Russia? The main thrust of Taylor's argument is to play down the idea that such goals really mattered in terms of effective policy. Goals of that sort are dismissed as "day-dreams."[27] Policy, in Taylor's view, is shaped by the immediate problems of the present, not by grandiose ambitions of that sort. Hitler, he says flatly, "did not plan" a war against the USSR, and he talks as though the Germans were caught by surprise when a war with that country actually broke out: "the Germans had to improvise furiously when they went to war against Soviet Russia in June 1941."[28] To be sure, there was violent talk, but it was all bluster, not to be taken at face value.[29] Evidence of Hitler's warlike goals is generally written off with one argument or another.[30] In every crisis Hitler was simply aiming at victory in a war of nerves.[31] His ultimate goal was merely to "make Germany the greatest power in Europe from her natural weight."[32]

On the other hand, Taylor often does seem to admit that there was more to German policy than that—that Hitler *was* pursuing a warlike policy and that he *did* take the goal of creating a great empire in the east quite seriously. Hitler, Taylor says, "probably intended a great war of conquest against Soviet Russia so far as he had any conscious design."[33] "Eastern expansion," he writes, "was the primary purpose of his policy, if not the only one."[34] Sometimes Taylor seems to think that the German demand for *Lebensraum*, for "living space," needs to be taken seriously. He says that the argument about *Lebensraum* was "plausible enough to convince Hitler himself."[35] But he then goes on to dismiss the idea that the demand for *Lebensraum* helped bring on the war by arguing that it made little economic sense. *Lebensraum*, he concludes, "did not drive Germany to war. Rather war, or a warlike policy, produced the demand for *Lebensraum*."[36] So now he's admitting that Germany was pursuing a "warlike policy"?

As you try to get a handle on this issue, you read particular passages with special care, passages that relate directly to the question of how warlike Germany's policy actually was. At one point, for example, Taylor is trying to refute a particular argument that purported to explain why Germany

---

[27] Ibid., pp. 69, 132.
[28] Ibid., p. 219.
[29] Ibid., pp. 71, 131–32.
[30] Ibid., pp. 166, 170–71, 192–93.
[31] Ibid., pp. 153, 216.
[32] Ibid., p. 68.
[33] Ibid., p. 103.
[34] Ibid., p. 70.
[35] Ibid., p. 105.
[36] Ibid., p. 106.

supposedly pursued a warlike policy in 1939. The argument is that the Germans pursued an aggressive policy in 1939 because they knew that for them it was a question of now or never. The Germans knew, the argument runs, that as the western powers rearmed, Germany's lead in armaments would waste away. Hitler, Taylor notes, "himself used this argument, but only in the summer of 1939 *when already committed to war*," but this he says is not to be taken seriously. Hitler, in fact, Taylor goes on to say, did not care about the military balance, because "he was intending to succeed without war, *or at any rate only with a war so nominal as hardly to be distinguished from diplomacy*." The claim made in passing at the beginning of the paragraph, about Hitler being "committed to war" in 1939, has thus begun to evolve. By the end of the paragraph the evolution is complete. "The state of German armament in 1939," Taylor writes, "gives the decisive proof that *Hitler was not contemplating general war, and probably not intending war at all*."[37] What is important here is not this particular argument, but rather the series of claims Taylor makes in passing, the claims I just italicized. In the course of a single paragraph, he goes from saying that Hitler was "committed to war" to saying that he was probably "not intending war at all."

Does all this mean that the book is so deeply flawed that it is a waste of time even reading it? By no means: even with all its problems, you can still learn a lot by analyzing it in this way. The fundamental idea that in the interwar period the basic problem was "political, not moral" is worth taking quite seriously, especially since it runs counter to what was for many years the conventional wisdom in this area. Taylor obviously took it too far. He got himself into trouble because he was trying too hard to be clever. The structural theory in that extreme form was simply incapable of carrying the load.

And indeed when you think about it, you realize that a structural argument of the sort Taylor made could not possibly explain the origins of the Second World War. For Taylor, the war of 1939 was implicit in the fact that Germany had been left intact after World War I. The idea that Germany was bound to become "the greatest power in Europe from her natural weight" implied that the western countries had no choice ultimately but to acquiesce in a resurgence of German power. It implied, that is, that they would *not* use the military strength they had at the time to keep German power limited. But if their acquiescence could be taken as given, why then was there a problem? The theory that fundamental power realities shape the course of international politics might account for the collapse of the Versailles system. It might account in large measure for the resurgence of Germany as the strongest country in Europe. But if the western countries were bound to accept those basic power realities, how could that theory possibly explain the coming of the Second World War?

[37] Ibid., pp. 217–18 (emphasis added).

What this means, however, is just that the theory has its limits. It does not mean that it is devoid of value. The basic idea that international life is to be understood in political and not moral terms is in fact a powerful source of insight. As the analysis of the Taylor book shows, it's obviously important to avoid pushing that idea too far, but that of course does not mean that it is to be ignored entirely. The main lesson to draw from the exercise is that in doing historical work in this area, you always need to strike a balance. Power realities are of fundamental importance, but statecraft also has a major impact on the course of events, and in doing history both invariably have to be taken into account.

Fritz Fischer and the Origins of the First World War

In the study of international politics, one of the most basic problems has to do with the relationship between war and aggression. People often talk about wars as being "started" by one side or the other. But do you really need an aggressor to have a war, or can a war break out even if no major power wants one? Can war, that is, result from the clash of essentially defensive, status quo–oriented policies? Those who think that war is not necessarily the product of aggression point above all to the coming of war in 1914, but not everyone agrees that the First World War broke out even though no one really wanted it to. Many scholars, in fact, believe that the war of 1914 was a war of aggression and, in particular, that it was a war of *German* aggression. To support that view, the scholars who argue along those lines generally cite the work of the German historian Fritz Fischer. Fischer is said to have shown that Germany engineered the war.

To get at this very important issue, it thus makes sense to examine Fischer's work closely. Fischer, it turns out, published two long books dealing with the subject, first *Germany's Aims in the First World War* (1961) and then *War of Illusions* (1969). Each of those books had a single chapter that dealt directly with the July crisis of 1914—that is, with the question of the immediate origins of the war. If your goal is to assess the Fischer thesis, those are the key chapters to focus on, because if Germany actually engineered the war, you'd expect that point to be borne out by a close study of German policy in that crisis.

Your first goal then is to see what exactly Fischer was arguing in those chapters. Did he actually claim that the German government deliberately engineered a major European war? If so, how did he support that conclusion? What were the specific claims on which that general conclusion rested? Are those claims adequately supported by the evidence he presents? With those questions in mind, you turn to the texts and begin by focusing on those places in the text where you'd expect the author to lay out his basic argument.

By looking in those key places, you can see right away what his thesis is. At the very end of the first part of the chapter on the July crisis in the *War of Illusions* book, Fischer, for example, refers to the "war which the German politicians started in July 1914," and says there that that war "was an attempt to defeat the enemy powers before they became too strong, and to realise Germany's political ambitions which may be summed up as German hegemony over Europe."[38] In the first sentence in another section in that chapter, he talks about how "the German government was determined from early July 1914 onwards to use this favourable opportunity"—that is, the opportunity created by the assassination at Sarajevo of Archduke Franz Ferdinand, heir to the Austrian throne—"for a war against France and Russia."[39] And in the concluding paragraph of the chapter, talking about the period in early August 1914 when the war had just begin, he refers to "the plan decided on a month previously to use the favourable opportunity of the murder at Sarajevo for the start of the continental war which Germany regarded as necessary," a plan which he says had been "carried out successfully."[40] In an earlier passage, he had also alluded to the "decision taken in early July to start the war at this moment in time."[41]

Fischer's argument here is thus fairly precise. It is therefore testable. He had fleshed out his thesis by making a specific claim: that the German government had actually decided *in early July*—that is, very soon after the archduke's assassination—to start a continental war. To examine the argument supporting that claim, you therefore want to focus on the part of the chapter dealing with that early period when the decision was supposedly made. You thus turn to the section called "The Occasion Is Propitious—The First Week in July." That seven-page section can be examined quite closely. As you read it, you want to approach it with a particular question in mind: does Fischer really show there that the Germans had decided at that point on a plan to start a war?

So what exactly do you find when you examine that passage with some care? Fischer begins by paraphrasing the report of a conversation between a high Austrian Foreign Ministry official and the well-connected German publicist Viktor Naumann. The document is presumably important for Fischer's purposes, since it is the first piece of evidence presented in this key section, is discussed at length, and contains the phrase about the occasion being "propitious," which Fischer had used as the title of the section and which related to a key element of his argument. Naumann happened to be in Vienna when the

[38] Fritz Fischer, *War of Illusions: German Policies from 1911 to 1914* (New York: Norton, 1975), p. 470.
[39] Ibid., p. 480.
[40] Ibid., p. 515.
[41] Ibid., p. 494.

archduke was assassinated on June 28, and he met with the Austrian official a couple of days later. Fischer has Naumann picturing the German government as ready, even eager, for war. Naumann was sure, Fischer writes, "that unlike the year before not only the military but also the Foreign Ministry and the Emperor no longer objected to a preventive war against Russia and that public opinion would moreover force the government into a war." "In the Foreign Ministry," his paraphrase continues, "'the moment [was considered] propitious for the great decision.' Naumann warned that if Austria-Hungary failed to use this opportunity Germany would drop Austria as an ally."[42]

Given the role it plays in Fischer's argument, this document might be worth checking out. You can see from a footnote Fischer appends to this passage that the Naumann document was published in a volume of documents on the crisis edited by Imanuel Geiss. When you look up the reference, you quickly discover that a version of the Geiss collection was also published in English translation, and it turns out that the document is included in that collection as well. And when you read it, you are struck by the fact that there is quite a gap between Fischer's paraphrase and the text of the document itself. Fischer, for example, has Naumann saying that the "Foreign Ministry and the Emperor no longer objected to a preventive war against Russia," but all Naumann had actually said was that "not only in army and navy circles but also in the Foreign Ministry the idea of a preventive war against Russia was regarded with less disfavour than a year ago," which is considerably weaker than Fischer's paraphrase. And Naumann had not said anything at all about the *emperor's* feelings about preventive war.

What about Naumann's supposed comment that public opinion would "force the government into a war" against *Russia?* All Naumann had said was that public opinion would force the Foreign Ministry to support Austria in a showdown with *Serbia*, which again was rather different from Fischer's paraphrase. The phrase about this being a propitious time for the "great decision" referred in context to the Serbian issue, and not, as Fischer had implied, to a decision to engineer a great European war. Finally, there is Fischer's claim that Naumann had warned that if Austria did not act, Germany would drop it as an ally. Again, the corresponding passage was much weaker. No threat of that sort was actually made. Naumann had simply remarked that Austria would be "finished as a Monarchy and as a Great Power if she does not take advantage of the moment"—a point his Austrian interlocutor basically agreed with.[43]

That particular document thus scarcely proves that the German leadership had decided in early July to "use the favourable opportunity of the murder at

[42] Ibid., p. 473.

[43] Imanuel Geiss, ed., *July 1914: The First World War, Selected Documents* (New York: Scribner's, 1967), pp. 65–66.

Sarajevo" to start a European war. The German government, it was clear, was being made to appear more bellicose than that first piece of evidence really warranted. Did Fischer then give any other evidence in that section to show that the Germans had decided at that specific time to provoke a European war? The general staff, according to one report he cites, thought "it would not be too bad if there was a war now"; according to another report, the military authorities were pressing for "a war now while Russia is not yet ready."[44] But the political leadership, according to one of those reports, did not agree: the emperor was said to be "in favour of preserving the peace," meaning, in Fischer's context, peace with France and Russia. But Fischer says that that account of the emperor's views was incorrect, and the proof, he says, was the emperor's handwritten comment on a report from the German ambassador in Vienna: "now or never . . . we must make a clean sweep of the Serbs and soon." The emperor's comment, however, scarcely proves (as Fischer had implied both here and in his use of the phrase in the subtitle of the chapter) that the emperor wanted a *European* war. The "now or never" referred simply to a showdown between Austria and Serbia, which was not the same thing at all. And there is in fact very little evidence in this section to support the view that the German government, and especially the German political leadership, had consciously decided at this point to provoke a European war.

Does Fischer, you then wonder, present compelling evidence to the effect that Germany wanted to engineer a general war anywhere in either of his two chapters on the July crisis? You read those chapters with that question in mind. In *Germany's Aims*, he does cite one document which makes the German leadership appear quite bellicose—a letter of July 18 from the German foreign secretary, Jagow, to the German ambassador in London, Lichnowsky. That letter, Fischer says, sums up the German attitude in the crisis "in a nutshell."[45] According to Jagow (as Fischer paraphrases the document):

> The struggle between Teuton and Slav was bound to come (a thought which often reappeared in Jagow's utterances at critical junctures during the war); which being so, the present was the best moment for Germany, for "in a few years Russia . . . will be ready. Then she will crush us on land by weight of numbers, and she will have her Baltic fleet and strategic railways ready. Our group meanwhile is getting steadily weaker."[46]

This is a key piece of evidence. The letter, as Fischer paraphrases it, clearly suggests that the German political leadership wanted to engineer a war with Russia. It's thus important enough to make you want to read the text of the

---

[44] Fischer, *War of Illusions*, p. 475. For the emperor's comment, see his note on the margin of Tschirschky to Bethmann Hollweg, June 30, 1914, in Geiss, *July 1914*, pp. 64–65.

[45] Fritz Fischer, *Germany's Aims in the First World War* (New York: Norton, 1967), p. 60.

[46] Ibid., p. 59.

letter itself. But when you read it in the Geiss collection, what you find is a little shocking. It turns out that Jagow had said nothing here about a war between "Teuton and Slav" being unavoidable. He had merely noted that "the feeling of the Slavic element [in Russia] is becoming more and more hostile to Germany," which again was a much weaker point.[47] Indeed, Jagow's point in talking about how the military balance was shifting was not that this would be the "best moment" to provoke a general war. He was making exactly the opposite point that because Germany was still relatively strong, Russia and its allies would probably back off and thus that the Serbian problem could be brought to a head without provoking a general war. Fischer's paraphrase had thus turned the Jagow argument upside-down.

As you do this kind of analysis, you reach the conclusion that there is very little direct evidence to support the view that the German government had consciously decided to provoke a European war. The fact that Fischer had to twist the evidence the way he did is in itself a strong indicator of the weakness of that argument. But you don't want to just leave it at that, because you sense that something else is going on here. Fischer repeatedly interpreted the strong evidence that Germany wanted Austria to move militarily against Serbia as evidence that what Germany really wanted was a European war, a war with France and Russia. The "now or never" about a showdown with Serbia became a "now or never" about a European war, but why, you wonder, did he conflate these two very different things? What assumption would allow him to go from what the evidence showed—namely, that the Germans wanted Austria to bring matters to a head in the Balkans—to the much less well-established point that Germany was really trying to engineer a general European war?

As you think about what it takes to bridge that gap between evidence and conclusion, you realize that there is only one answer. The implicit assumption had to be that the Germans realized that there was no way Austria could crush Serbia without Russian intervening. All you have to do is make that assumption for evidence that the Germans wanted a showdown in the Balkans to become evidence that what they really wanted was a European war. So you ask yourself whether Fischer ever explicitly makes this assumption. If you can find that claim expressed directly, you would expect the evidence and argument supporting it to be in that same passage. You would then be able to examine it closely to see whether you find it convincing.

So you search these two chapters for a passage where that argument is laid out, and sure enough you find Fischer saying at one point that "as innumerable documents show, Germany knew that Russia would never allow Austria-Hungary to act in the Balkans unopposed."[48] A claim of that sort, asserted at

---

[47] Jagow to Lichnowsky, July 18, 1914, in Geiss, *July 1914*, p. 123.

[48] Fischer, *Germany's Aims*, p. 63.

the beginning of a paragraph, is in effect a promise to the reader that at least one or two of these "innumerable documents" will be summarized in the passage that follows. So you look to see what does follow. What the evidence there shows, however, was that the Germans realized European complications were possible, not that they thought escalation would be inevitable. Indeed, the main document cited in this passage—a document Fischer presumably considers important, since he gives an extract from it as a block quotation—begins with Jagow saying that "we want to localise the conflict between Austria and Serbia," which scarcely supports the view that the German government understood that "localization" was a political impossibility. And, indeed, Jagow (you might remember) had made the argument that localization was possible in his July 18 letter to Lichnowsky, the letter that Fischer a few pages earlier had said summed up Germany's attitude "in a nutshell."

But are those remarks about the desirability of localization to be taken at face value? You might wonder about that, and you might therefore want to dig more deeply into this particular issue. The Germans might have pretended, even among themselves, to believe that localization was possible while at the same time realizing that it was not. The pretense might have served a certain political or psychological purpose. It therefore makes sense to consider whether it was a simple political reality that Russia was bound to intervene. If that was the case, and if the situation was obvious to anyone with any political sense, then, regardless of what the Germans were saying even among themselves at the time, one might reasonably conclude that a bellicose policy vis-à-vis Serbia could therefore be taken as proof of Germany's desire to provoke a general war.

Your focus thus shifts to the question of whether Fischer gives any evidence bearing on the issue of Russian intervention. With that question in mind, you pay special attention to what Fischer has to say about Russian policy, and you note that he has a section in the *War of Illusions* chapter dealing with Russia. It turns out that Fischer in that section says in passing that as late as July 24, the Russians thought that Serbia should be advised that "if Austrian troops entered Serb territory it should to begin with offer no resistance but withdraw its troops."[49] The Russians were thus not absolutely determined to go to war as soon as Serbia was invaded. You might want to explore this subject further by consulting other accounts of the crisis. But, for your present purposes, what it means is that there was still a bit of softness in the Russian position even late in the crisis, and that it consequently might have made sense for the Germans to think that a localized war was not out of the question. Evidence that the Germans were pressing for a war in the Balkans thus cannot be taken as evidence that the Germans were really trying to engineer a European war.

[49] Fischer, *War of Illusions*, p. 489.

So that's how the method of critical analysis works. You first identify the author's general thesis. You then try to understand the structure of the argument that supports that thesis. In particular, you try to see how general conclusions rest on more specific claims. You then evaluate those specific claims in terms of the evidence that the author gives to support them. It is all very straightforward. Along the way, you are taking your measure of the intellectual quality of the work as a whole, and when you find someone twisting the evidence, your opinion of the work plummets.

But note that you're not just evaluating a particular historical work. You're also learning something about the subject itself. In this case, you've assessed a particular interpretation of the coming of the First World War. A conclusion that that interpretation is quite weak is bound to have a certain bearing on your understanding of the origins of the war. If even the most famous exponent of a particular interpretation is not able to make an effective case, then you have to wonder whether a compelling case is to be made at all. Beyond that, you have begun to reach certain substantive conclusions in specific areas. You might conclude, for example, that the Germans probably did take "localization" seriously, and that there was some basis for the hope that Austria could crush Serbia without Russia and France intervening. But you also note that the Germans were willing to run the risk of a European war—an attitude that was rooted in their understanding of the military balance, both what it was and the way it was changing over time. Conclusions of that sort affect your understanding of the war-origins question as a whole. Because of the way you've framed the analysis—because you understand how the big questions turn on relatively narrow issues—the conclusions you reach on those specific issues are bound to have a certain broader significance. They may even shed some light on the most basic problem in the study of international politics, the problem of what makes for war or for a stable international order.

RICHARD NEUSTADT AND THE SKYBOLT AFFAIR

As you do historical work, you have to deal with a whole series of relatively minor problems. You might, for example, be interested in the post–Cuban missile crisis period. You read various historical accounts and you get a sense for what the major events of that period were. The missile crisis was settled in late October 1962. It was followed by the Skybolt-Nassau affair of December 1962, and then by de Gaulle's veto of British admission to the European Common Market the following month and by an important Franco-German treaty signed a week after that. President Kennedy's famous trip to Germany followed in June 1963, and the nuclear test ban treaty was signed in July. When you do history, you try to figure out how things fit together. So if you are studying this period, you have to wonder how all these events related to each other. How do they fit into the larger story of what was going on at that time?

To answer those questions, you have to study those specific episodes one by one. In particular, you have to learn what you can about the Skybolt affair. If you proceed in the usual way, you will come across a number of references to a long report on the Skybolt affair that the distinguished political scientist Richard Neustadt wrote for President Kennedy in 1963. That, it rapidly becomes clear, is the most important work ever written on the subject. So one of the first things you want to do is to analyze Neustadt's argument with some care.

Or you might come to the Neustadt report in a very different way. Perhaps you're a political scientist and you're interested in the bureaucratic politics theory of policy making—that is, in the idea that the state is a congeries of semiautonomous bureaucratic fiefdoms, each pursuing its own parochial interests, and that what passes for policy is simply the outcome of an intragovernmental process in which interagency conflicts are worked out. Policy, from that point of view, has a certain mindless quality. According to that general line of argument, rational thought—the sort of thinking that takes places at the center, as the political leadership tries to chart a course in line with what it views as the country's most basic interests—does not play a really fundamental role in shaping policy, because the political leadership does not really dominate the policy-making process.

If valid, the bureaucratic politics theory would have all kinds of important implications, not just for political scientists but for historians as well, so you might be interested in seeing how valid that theory is. One basic way to do that is to assess interpretations of specific historical episodes that reflect the bureaucratic politics point of view. In general, in assessing a given theory, you want to do what you can to bring it down to earth—to give it some concrete content, to "translate" it into specific interpretations of particular historical episodes—because that's the only way to get a real handle on it. But defenders of a given theory also have a certain interest in showing how it applies to the real world and often develop historical interpretations that seem to support that theory. It makes sense, therefore, to focus on those interpretations and especially on the best of them. If an argument is to be made at all, the champions of a theory are the ones who should presumably be able to make it. In their work, the strongest arguments are presumably to be found.

As you learn about this area of scholarship—that is, the body of work rooted in the bureaucratic politics paradigm—you see references to Neustadt's writings and in particular to his study of the Skybolt affair. And that study, you quickly discover when you get your hands on it, is an exceptionally interesting piece of work. There are many books and articles that interpret specific episodes in bureaucratic politics terms, but the Neustadt report really stands out, because of the intelligence of the author, the sharpness of the argument, and the quality of the empirical evidence that supports it. Clearly, if you are interested in reaching an opinion of your own about the bureaucratic politics theory of policy making, this work is worth focusing on.

But no matter how you come to the topic, you have to begin with the basics. What is the standard account of the Skybolt affair? Skybolt was an air-to-surface nuclear-tipped missile which the Americans were developing in the late 1950s and early 1960s. The British had been told they could buy the missile if production turned out to be technically feasible. They wanted to buy it because having Skybolt would give their bomber-based deterrent force, threatened with obsolescence because of improving Soviet air defenses, a new lease on life. The weapon thus played a central role in British defense planning. The Americans, however, decided in 1962 to cancel the Skybolt program. The question then was what if anything Britain would be offered as a substitute. The U.S. government, according to the standard interpretation, was not very forthcoming, and British prime minister Harold Macmillan decided to bring the matter to a head when he met with President Kennedy at Nassau in December 1962. At Nassau, the British were angry and defiant. Macmillan demanded that America provide Britain with the sea-based Polaris missile, one of America's most advanced weapons, as a substitute for Skybolt. If America refused, Britain would be forced to go ahead on its own, but that course, Macmillan said, "would lead to a deep rift with the United States."[50] Faced with that threat, the Americans gave way and the British were essentially offered Polaris as a substitute for Skybolt.

The basic problem here is to explain why events had taken this course. Neustadt's answer was laid out in the introduction to his report. "'Skybolt' as an issue between Washington and London," he says, was caused by "successive failures on the part of busy persons to perceive and make allowance for the needs and wants of others: failures among 'Chiefs' to share their reasoning with 'Indians'; failures among Indians to sense—or heed—the reservations of their Chiefs; failures among Americans to comprehend restraints upon contingency-planning in London; failures among Englishmen to comprehend imperatives of budgeting in Washington; failures on all sides to consider how A's conduct might tie B's tongue."[51] From this point of view, the showdown at Nassau was not rooted in a genuine political conflict—that is, in a clash between what the American government wanted and what the British were prepared to accept. It came about instead because of the way governments work—that is, because of the way large bureaucracies function. Policy is not really controlled from the center. In Neustadt's account, you note, the president plays only a minor role. Midlevel officials, on the other hand, receive a

---

[50] Quoted in Richard Neustadt, *Report to JFK: The Skybolt Crisis in Perspective* (Ithaca: Cornell University Press, 1999), p. 91.

[51] Ibid., pp. 26–27.

good deal of attention. They make sure key policy documents contain sentences in line with their thinking. They then use these documents as "hunting licenses" to pursue their own policy objectives. They even issue "instructions" to top government officials (like Secretary of Defense Robert McNamara) by drafting documents reflecting their own views and then getting the secretary of state to sign off on them, instructions you can tell Neustadt thinks were important simply because he spends so much time talking about them.[52]

This basic interpretation is developed in the body of the report. Why, Neustadt wonders, were the two sides unable to reach a mutually acceptable arrangement well before the issue came to a head at the Nassau conference? The British had been warned that Skybolt might well be canceled on November 8. The recriminations did not begin until just after McNamara met with his British counterpart, Defence Minister Peter Thorneycroft, in London on December 11. The two sides thus had plenty of time to agree on a substitute for Skybolt, and there was no fundamental political obstacle to an agreement. President Kennedy was by no means dead set against giving the British an adequate substitute for Skybolt. "He himself," as Neustadt notes, "had never been disposed to withhold an agreement on POLARIS if there were no other way to meet the British problem."[53] If that was Kennedy's attitude, the two sides should have been able to work out some kind of deal before the matter got out of hand. The British could have gone to the Americans, made their concerns clear, and tried to work out a deal. Or the Americans could have taken the initiative and approached the British. But neither side took that kind of action. Why not?

Neustadt's answer is that both sides were "immobilized" by internal bureaucratic pressures.[54] Thorneycroft could not "step out" onto Polaris until the Americans offered it. If he had done so, he would have come across internally as favoring Polaris in principle. He would be viewed by various elements within his own government, and especially by his own air force, as "selling SKYBOLT down the river." That course of action would be viewed as "tantamount to treason" by those elements in the bureaucracy. He therefore "calculated that POLARIS must be brought to him; he could not go for it."[55] McNamara, Neustadt says, "had precisely the same notion in reverse." In McNamara's view, the British needed to take the initiative. "Rather than precipitate a row with his associates," Neustadt writes, "he meant to let the British press POLARIS on him."[56] So nothing was done, and when the two men met on December 11 and Polaris was not offered, the British exploded.

[52] Ibid., pp. 41–44, 47–48, 115–16.
[53] Ibid., p. 93.
[54] Ibid., p. 55
[55] Ibid., pp. 49, 70.
[56] Ibid., p. 69.

How is this general interpretation to be assessed? Was McNamara really "immobilized" because midlevel officials opposed the policy of offering Polaris to the British? The answer is no, and the point emerges quite clearly from Neustadt's own evidence. When McNamara met Thorneycroft on December 11, he had no real problem broaching the issue. "Would you buy POLARIS systems," he asked the British defence minister, "if we could make them available?" And as for the British, it is also quite clear, even from the evidence Neustadt himself presents, that Thorneycroft also had no trouble bringing up the possibility of a Polaris solution. The British minister, according to his own account, in fact "used the *word* 'POLARIS'" in a November 9 telephone conversation with McNamara.[57]

So neither side was held back in any really fundamental way by bureaucratic factors. McNamara, to be sure, was not as direct as he might have been, and his decision not to deal with the issue in a straightforward way might have led to certain problems in that meeting with his British counterpart. But it was clear enough how he wanted things to end up: the British would get Polaris, and although the force would be under their own control, it would be assigned to NATO. By the end of the meeting with Thorneycroft, the Americans had in effect suggested an arrangement of this sort, an arrangement that Thorneycroft in principle found acceptable.[58]

But if what was going on is not to be understood à la Neustadt in bureaucratic politics terms, then that suggests that the real explanation lies elsewhere. You might not know what that explanation is, but the very fact that you are puzzled helps drive the research process. You now know more precisely what needs to be explained. You have thus gotten something of value from the exercise.

The point is worth stressing because it might seem at first glance that the method of critical analysis is purely destructive. It certainly does give you a way to dissect other people's arguments, but it's important to realize that doing so is not an end in itself. The method has to be viewed in more positive terms, and there are, in fact, a number of ways in which it can play a very positive role. For one thing, it helps you see how to separate the wheat from the chaff. You come to see what makes for a good argument and thus get a sense for the sort of approach you might want to emulate. You also see what makes an argument fail—in other words, you see the sort of thing you might want to avoid. Without any conscious effort on your part, certain standards

---

[57] Ibid., pp. 39, 73.

[58] Ibid., pp. 70–74. The document Neustadt quotes from here, the Rubel notes of the December 11, 1962, McNamara-Thorneycroft meeting, is now available in its entirety online (through subscribing libraries) on the Declassified Documents Reference System website. The DDRS is discussed in detail in appendix II on pp. 228–229 below. The DDRS record number for this document is CK3100078274.

take shape in your mind, standards you automatically internalize and apply to your own work.

When you do this kind of analysis, moreover, you pay special attention to the big issues. You focus on the basic argument and try to understand why it's important—that is, how it relates to the fundamental question of how international politics works. You come to see how a particular historical argument can have a certain conceptual dimension, and your analysis of that argument will thus often give you some insight into an important conceptual issue. If you're a political scientist, this point is of obvious importance. But historians also need to develop a certain conceptual framework in order to do their work, and that framework more or less automatically takes shape when they do this kind of analysis. And beyond that, reading texts critically, as I said before, turns out to be an efficient way to absorb important factual information. Things stick in your mind when you see the role they play in the elaboration and analysis of arguments. Those same things often do not register when you are just gliding along the surface of a text in the usual passive way.

All these things are important, but the real reason this method is worth mastering is that it enables you to develop your own understanding of what was going on in a particular historical period and to do so in a very efficient way. By grappling with other people's arguments, you can penetrate to the heart of a historical problem. You're then in a position to tackle it head on and possibly even answer it. The method is thus a source of empowerment. It puts you in the driver's seat. You no longer have to accept what other people say on faith. In principle, and perhaps even in practice, you can decide these historical issues for yourself.

Chapter Four

DEVELOPING AN INTERPRETATION
THROUGH TEXTUAL ANALYSIS:
THE 1941 CASE

Is REAL INSIGHT into basic historical questions beyond the reach of those who are not prepared to spend many years studying them? I don't think so. I think that scholars who are not prepared to make that kind of investment can still develop a certain level of historical understanding—a level no one would call superficial—provided they approach historical problems the right way.

How then are such problems to be approached? Not passively: you can't just read a lot of books and articles and documents, absorbing what you can and throwing everything into the hopper, and expect that something called "historical understanding" will almost automatically come out the other end. Historical problems instead need to be approached *actively*. That means that you have to put *questions* to the material you are working with. And to come up with the right questions, you are going to have to do a lot of *thinking*. This is not a particularly easy thing to do, but if you work that way, you might be surprised by how effective this method is—by how far it will take you and by how quickly it will get you where you need to go.

How in practice should you proceed? In principle, the answer is simple. You tackle an issue by identifying the most important historical works that deal with it. You then analyze that body of work using the method outlined in the previous chapter: seeing what the core arguments are, seeing how basic theses are supported by key claims, and then examining those claims, paying special attention to the evidence given to back them up. The questions thus emerge in a very natural way: are a particular author's claims correct? What's to be made of the argument that supports them? Does the evidence really prove what it's supposed to prove? And when authors disagree, as they usually do on important issues, you ask: who's right? Who makes the stronger case? Above all, you'll want to think about how different claims relate to each other, and in particular about how major arguments are related to relatively narrow claims. The more concrete the question, the more studiable it is. Your goal, therefore, is to see how broad issues of interpretation turn on relatively narrow claims. The conclusions you reach when you examine those claims in

the light of the evidence will then automatically have relatively broad implications. The big questions will gradually get answered, and an interpretation
will gradually take shape in your mind.

All this is very general, and if you're to understand how this method
works, you're going to have to see it in operation. So in this chapter, I want
to show how it can be used to develop an interpretation of an important
episode in the history of international politics, America's road to war in
1941.

AMERICA AND GERMANY IN 1941

Let's say that your goal is to explain how America ended up at war with
both Germany and Japan in December 1941. Where do you start? You can
begin by reacting to certain notions you've absorbed from the general culture.
You might have been led to believe, for example, that the United States
was a peace-loving country that sought to avoid foreign entanglements,
that Germany and Japan were aggressor states, and that America's entry
into the war was a product of Axis aggression pure and simple. You look at
what scholars have had to say on the subject. A.J.P. Taylor, for example, in
the very last paragraph of *The Origins of the Second World War*, says that
Hitler's decision to go to war with America was "gratuitous," and that the
United States was a country that "asked only to be left alone."[1] You perhaps
note that this type of interpretation is still widely accepted and that even
scholars from time to time still argue along those lines.[2]

Claims of that sort are a kind of springboard. You react to that sort of argument, drawing on your general sense for how international politics works.
Why on earth, you wonder, would Hitler have declared war on America,
involved as he was in his war with the Soviet Union, if the United States
had really "asked only to be left alone"? Why on earth would he have "gratu-
itously" embarked on an armed conflict with a power as strong as the United
States? Your whole understanding of international politics leads you to
think that things just could not have been so simple, that the German
decision to go to war with America almost certainly had something to do
with American policy, and that America was in all probability more deeply
involved in European affairs by that point than Taylor, for example, was
suggesting.

[1] A.J.P. Taylor, *The Origins of the Second World War* (New York: Atheneum, 1962), p. 278.
[2] Note, for example, Randall Schweller's use of that passage from the Taylor book in his article
"Bandwagoning for Profit: Bringing the Revisionist State Back In," *International Security* 19,
no. 1 (Summer 1994): 94–95.

This sort of thinking, however, simply defines the questions. Only the evidence can provide answers. So to find out what was going on, you begin by turning to what you identify (using the method outlined in the previous chapter and elaborated on in appendix I) as the most important accounts of U.S. policy in this period. It soon becomes clear that the American government, especially in late 1941, was anything but passive. The United States, it turns out, was fighting an undeclared war in the Atlantic against Germany at that time. One of the most important works dealing with the subject is in fact called *The Undeclared War*.[3] But how, you wonder, is that behavior to be understood? What was the American political leadership trying to do? Did President Roosevelt and his top advisers simply want to defend the sea lanes in order to keep Britain from falling? Perhaps they did not want to go any further if they could help it? Or maybe Roosevelt's goal actually was to bring the United States into the war on Britain's side, and maybe the naval operations are to be understood in terms of that objective?

Scholars, you note, are divided on the issue. The majority view is that Roosevelt, certainly from mid-1941 on, "steadily maneuvered the country in the direction of war."[4] It is commonly assumed that public opinion was a key factor here. Most Americans, it seems, wanted to keep out of the war but also supported strong action even if it meant risking war, and Roosevelt's policy was framed with an eye on that situation. The argument is that rather than present the issue of intervention to the country directly, he preferred to maneuver in a way that would allow people to believe (or at least half believe) that the country was being pushed into the conflict.[5]

What sort of evidence, you wonder, supports that view? Well, for one thing, Roosevelt actually *said* he wanted to go to war with Germany. Robert Dallek, author of the most important book on Roosevelt's foreign policy, supports his claim that the president by late 1941 "now wished to take the United States into the war" by citing the record of Roosevelt's meeting with the British prime minister, Winston Churchill, at the Atlantic Conference in

[3] William Langer and S. Everett Gleason, *The Undeclared War, 1940–1941* (New York: Harper, 1953), esp. chap. 14, 18, 23.

[4] Patrick Hearden, *Roosevelt Confronts Hitler: America's Entry into World War II* (DeKalb: Northern Illinois University Press, 1987), p. 201.

[5] Robert Dallek, *Franklin D. Roosevelt and American Foreign Policy, 1932–1945* (Oxford: Oxford University Press, 1979; paperback edition, 1981), pp. 265, 267, 285–89. On the idea that the American people, while themselves unwilling to make the tough decisions, basically understood (and approved of) what Roosevelt was doing, see Warren Kimball's September 22, 1999, post on H-Diplo (http://www2.h-net.msu.edu/~diplo/). For a detailed study of the role of public opinion during this period, see Steven Casey, *Cautious Crusade: Franklin D. Roosevelt, American Public Opinion, and the War against Nazi Germany* (Oxford: Oxford University Press, 2001).

August 1941. Roosevelt had explained to Churchill that he was "skating on pretty thin ice" with Congress, and that if he asked for a declaration of war Congress would spend three months debating the issue. He therefore would not go that route. He would instead "wage war, but not declare it." "He would become more and more provocative." His goal, he said, was to "force an 'incident.'" He "made it clear that he would look for an 'incident' which would justify him in opening hostilities."[6] And this, you notice, was not just an isolated remark. Roosevelt, in fact, often spoke in such terms at the time.[7]

But perhaps Roosevelt's comment to Churchill is not to be taken at face value? Waldo Heinrichs, the author of another important book on the subject, says that Roosevelt at that point was not "seeking war" and that when the president had earlier talked about how American patrolling of the North Atlantic would lead to an "incident, which would not be unwelcome," he was probably just trying "to be encouraging."[8] And David Reynolds, author of an important study of Anglo-American relations in this period, quotes Roosevelt's remarks to Churchill at length but argues that, even as late as November and early December 1941, the president did not want "to provoke hostilities" with Germany.[9]

Faced with these differences of opinion, how do you get to the bottom of the issue? The answer is simple. You look for evidence, when reading these historical accounts, that bears both directly and indirectly on the question. You try to understand Roosevelt's basic thinking about what a German victory in Europe would mean, both for America and for the world as a whole, and you think about what that implied about the sort of policy America should adopt. You look at the tenor of what he and his closest advisers were saying, both in public and in private—his statement, for example, on September 1, 1941, that "we shall do everything in our power to crush Hitler and his Nazi forces,"[10] or the remark by his close adviser Harry Hopkins in November 1941 that it was going to take much more than a lend-lease program to defeat Hitler.[11] You pay special attention to what the U.S.

[6] Dallek, *Roosevelt*, p. 285.

[7] See David Reynolds, *The Creation of the Anglo-American Alliance, 1937–41: A Study in Competitive Co-operation* (Chapel Hill: University of North Carolina Press, 1982), pp. 202, 208, and esp. 347 n. 38. See also Hearden, *Roosevelt Confronts Hitler*, pp. 196, 200–202; and Dallek, *Roosevelt*, p. 286.

[8] See Waldo Heinrichs, *Threshold of War: Franklin D. Roosevelt and American Entry into World War II* (New York: Oxford University Press, 1988), pp. 78, 151.

[9] Reynolds, *Anglo-American Alliance*, pp. 214, 219.

[10] Quoted in Langer and Gleason, *Undeclared War*, p. 743.

[11] Robert E. Sherwood, *Roosevelt and Hopkins: An Intimate History* (New York: Harper, 1948), p. 410. Note also Hopkins's criticism in a note to Roosevelt of a public statement by an army general about U.S. military unpreparedness. This sort of thing, he said, was doing "a good deal of harm" because it made people reluctant "to go all the way"—a comment that reflects the implicit assumption that both men wanted the country to "go all the way." Ibid., p. 377.

government was actually doing: what sorts of military forces were being built, what kind of planning was going on, what sort of diplomacy was being practiced, what kinds of military operations, if any, were being conducted. Above all, you want to see whether all these things fall into a *pattern*—that is, whether you can make sense of what was going on by seeing how all these things fit in with each other.

What emerges when you do this exercise? First, how did Roosevelt approach these basic issues of foreign policy? You look at the key sources cited by writers who deal with these issues, and when you read that material, you see certain themes sounded over and over again. The United States, Roosevelt felt, could not afford to think in strictly defensive terms. America, that is, could not just sit on its hands until it was attacked. America's security was deeply affected by what was going on elsewhere in the world. If Britain went down, the Axis powers would control the resources of the entire Old World. The New World would then "be living at the point of a gun—a gun loaded with explosive bullets, economic as well as military."[12]

The threat was particularly acute—and this was a theme that came up repeatedly in his remarks in the 1939–1941 period—because of the nature of modern warfare. The oceans might have been "reasonably adequate defensive barriers" in the past. But given the range of modern bombers and the speed with which attacks could be mounted, this was no longer the case. The United States had in effect been brought much closer to Europe, and its interests were thus more deeply bound up with what went on there. The country had to face up to the problem this posed before it was too late. One could not allow things to deteriorate to the point where the nation would be forced to fight "a last-ditch war for the preservation of American independence" sometime in the future. It would be "suicide" to wait until the enemy was "in our front yard." His basic premise was that it made sense to deal with the problem before it became unmanageable. America had to defend itself in a more "dynamic" way and not just at the borders. Implicit in this whole line of argument was the idea that Nazi power had to be broken: the Nazis could not be allowed to build up their power by consolidating their position and drawing on the resources of all of Europe; a policy of simply preventing the defeat of Britain—even assuming that Britain would fight on forever once it became clear that America would never enter the war—would not be good enough. By late 1941 what was implicit before had become explicit. Hitler had to be

[12] Frank Freidel, *Franklin D. Roosevelt: A Rendezvous with Destiny* (Boston: Little, Brown, 1990), p. 311; *The Public Papers and Addresses of Franklin D. Roosevelt*, comp. Samuel Rosenman, vol. 9 (for 1940) (New York: Macmillan, 1941), pp. 2–4, 231, 324, 635–36 (for the quotation), 665–66, and vol. 10 (for 1941) (New York: Harper, 1942), pp. 183–84, 188; Roosevelt to Cudahy, March 4, 1939, *The Roosevelt Letters*, ed. Elliott Roosevelt with Joseph Lash, vol. 3 (London: Harrap, 1952), pp. 256–57.

defeated; there could be no thought of "any peace founded on a compromise with evil itself"; the Nazi threat had to be "struck down."[13]

It turns out, moreover, that that was not just Roosevelt's view. His top military advisers were thinking along similar lines. They were if anything more willing than the president to dot the i's and explicitly accept the implications of this line of argument. Admiral Stark, the chief of naval operations, argued strongly, beginning in late 1940, for a policy of bringing the United States into the war with Germany, an approach that General Marshall, the army chief of staff, basically accepted. And the evidence strongly suggests that Roosevelt himself, very secretly, made it clear to Stark that he shared his point of view. Seeing what the thinking was in such circles helps you interpret what was actually done, especially in the area of naval operations in the North Atlantic. And as you try to make sense of that story, you pay special attention to certain key pieces of evidence. You note, for example, Admiral Stark's comment, as early as February 1941, that "the question as to our entry into the war now seems to be when and not whether"[14]—a remark that is of particular importance in this context, given that Stark, as CNO, was in a good position to know what the president's thinking on naval operations in the Atlantic actually was. As the different elements in the story gradually fall into place, a general picture takes shape.[15]

But before you commit yourself to a particular interpretation, you want to examine the arguments on the other side. Not everyone believes that Roosevelt, in 1941, wanted to take the country into the war, and some first-rate scholars take the opposite view. Gerhard Weinberg, for example, in his important book *A World at Arms* gives a picture of "Roosevelt trying and hoping to avoid war." While "some of Roosevelt's advisors did think the

---

[13] Wesley Craven and James Cate, *The Army Air Forces in World War II*, vol. 1 (Chicago: University of Chicago Press, 1948), p. 118; Roosevelt, *Public Papers*, 9:198–99, 633, 636, 665, and 10:183, 185, 189, 367–435. Roosevelt to White, December 14, 1939, *Roosevelt Letters*, 3:293.

[14] Quoted in Jonathan Utley, *Going to War with Japan, 1937–1941* (Knoxville: University of Tennessee Press, 1985), p. 138, and also in Mark Stoler, *Allies and Adversaries: The Joint Chiefs of Staff, the Grand Alliance, and U.S. Strategy in World War II* (Chapel Hill: University of North Carolina Press, 2000), p. 41.

[15] There are a number of excellent historical works dealing with U.S. strategic thinking in this period. See especially Stoler, *Allies and Adversaries*, and James Leutze, *Bargaining for Supremacy: Anglo-American Naval Collaboration, 1937–1941* (Chapel Hill: University of North Carolina Press, 1977). For Roosevelt's endorsement of Stark's thinking, see esp. Leutze, *Bargaining for Supremacy*, pp. 202–5, 219, 296 n. 12; note also B. Mitchell Simpson, *Admiral Harold R. Stark: Architect of Victory, 1939–1945* (Columbia: University of South Carolina Press, 1989), p. 75, and Maurice Matloff and Edwin Snell, *Strategic Planning for Coalition Warfare, 1941–1942* (Washington, D.C.: Center of Military History, 1999; originally published 1953), p. 28 n. 43. Note also Roosevelt's positive reaction to an October 8, 1941, memorandum by Admiral Stark calling for the United States "to enter the war against Germany as soon as possible"; see Sherwood, *Roosevelt and Hopkins*, pp. 379–80.

United States should or would have to enter the war to assure the defeat of Hitler," Weinberg says, there is "no evidence that the President himself abandoned his hope that the United States could stay out."[16] The key argument he makes to support that conclusion has to do with American naval policy in 1941. Thanks to British intelligence cooperation, as Weinberg points out, from April 1941 on the Americans were able to read intercepted German naval messages. The knowledge the U.S. government acquired in this way, he writes, "was regularly and carefully utilized to *avoid* incidents, when it could very easily have been used to *provoke* them." Roosevelt's famous order "to shoot at German submarines on sight," he says, "was more to frighten them off than to provoke them." "Aware of German orders to submarines to avoid incidents," he argues, Roosevelt "could push forward with his program of aid to Britain knowing that at worst there might be isolated incidents in the Atlantic."[17] This is a point, he believes, that nearly everyone has overlooked, in spite of the fact that the "relevant records have been available for decades" and had been analyzed in an account the German scholar Jürgen Rohwer published "many years ago."[18]

These specific claims about naval operations thus play a key role in supporting Weinberg's general argument about Roosevelt's policy and are thus worth examining closely. So to pursue the issue, you look up the footnotes for the passages in which those claims are made. You immediately notice something odd. In the key footnote Weinberg admits that his interpretation "differs somewhat" from Rohwer's own interpretation. What then, you wonder, does Rohwer actually claim, and what exactly does he show, especially in the particular passages Weinberg cites in his footnotes?

So you look up those passages, and it turns out that Rohwer, like most historians who have studied the question, sees a gradual movement toward belligerency. He divides American policy on the European war into three periods. During the first period, which ended with the fall of France in the spring of 1940, Roosevelt wanted to keep out of the war. He was not a pure

---

[16] Gerhard Weinberg, A *World at Arms: A Global History of World War II* (Cambridge: Cambridge University Press, 1994), pp. 240–41.

[17] Ibid. (emphasis in original).

[18] Gerhard Weinberg, H-Diplo post, October 5, 1999. Note also his comment about how Rohwer's findings about how the German intercepts were used "to avoid incidents as much as possible . . . invalidates many standard readings of FDR's policy." Gerhard Weinberg, "World War II: Comments on the Roundtable," *Diplomatic History* 25, no. 3 (Summer 2001): 492. The H-Diplo post turned up in an H-Diplo search for "Pearl Harbor," a keyword useful in searching for writings related to the origins of the Pacific War; the *Diplomatic History* article turned up in a Social Science Citation Index search for articles that cited the Rohwer article. That latter search, incidentally, also turned up a reference to a review article, which would be valuable if you wanted to pursue the issue further: J. Rohwer, "Signal Intelligence and World War II: The Unfolding Story," *Journal of Military History* 63, no. 4 (October 1999): 939–51.

isolationist even then, but in Roosevelt's view at that time Britain and France would be able to keep Hitler from winning with only limited American support. After the fall of France in 1940, according to Rohwer, American policy entered a second phase. The Americans began to build up a strong military force, and support for Britain was greatly intensified. A third phase began in the early spring of 1941: Roosevelt was moving toward a policy of undeclared war against Germany.[19]

But putting all this aside, it's still fair to ask what Rohwer's evidence actually showed. To get at that issue, you need to focus on the specifics, so you read Rohwer's account closely. What emerges is a picture of a very active American policy in late 1941. In July, for example, it was decided that German warships that threatened U.S.-protected convoys were to be attacked, and according to Rohwer depth charges were dropped on real or suspected German submarines on at least eighty separate occasions.[20] That policy and those tactics were apparently adopted before anyone knew how Hitler would react. To be sure, the number of incidents was limited by the fact that the main task of the naval authorities, both British and American, was to get the convoys through safely, and that meant that they took full advantage of the information they acquired through their intelligence operations to steer the convoys away from German U-boats.[21] The Americans, however, had clearly not opted for a policy of avoiding confrontations with German warships. As Rohwer shows, it was through pure chance—in one important case, through simple mechanical problems on the German side—that attacks on major German vessels did not take place in the immediate pre–Pearl Harbor period.[22] It was not as though the Americans had learned from intercepted German naval communications exactly how far they could go without provoking Hitler to declare war and went that far but no further.

---

[19] Jürgen Rohwer, "Die USA und die Schlacht im Atlantik 1941," in *Kriegswende Dezember 1941*, ed. Jürgen Rohwer and Eberhard Jäckel (Koblenz: Bernard and Graefe, 1984), pp. 81–89.

[20] Ibid., pp. 94, 97. Other accounts support Rohwer's basic point that the Americans, from mid-1941 on, were pursuing a very active policy in the Atlantic. See, for example, Douglas Norton, "The Open Secret: The U.S. Navy in the Battle of the Atlantic, April–December 1941," *Naval War College Review* 26 (January–February 1974): esp. pp. 71–73, reprinted in Walter Hixson, ed., *The United States and the Road to War in Europe* (New York: Routledge, 2002). On the eve of Pearl Harbor, the German navy had in fact noted "that the Battle of the Atlantic had become so intensive that a declaration of war between Germany and the United States remained only a formality." Holger Herwig, *Politics of Frustration: The United States in German Naval Planning, 1889–1941* (Boston: Little, Brown, 1976), p. 234. Admiral Stark, looking back a few years later, characterized the situation in much the same way. U.S. Congress, Joint Committee on the Investigation of the Pearl Harbor Attack, *Hearings*, 79th Cong., 1st sess. 1945–46, pt. 5, p. 2292.

[21] Rohwer, "Die USA," pp. 97, 99, 101–2.

[22] Ibid., pp. 99–101. See also Leutze, *Bargaining for Supremacy*, p. 258.

It seems quite clear, in fact, that the policy of using the intelligence to get the convoys through by routing them around German submarine concentrations cannot be taken as proof of a desire on Roosevelt's part to avoid war with Germany. It was the British (as Rohwer notes) who played the key role in deciding how the convoys would be routed.[23] If the British government, which certainly wanted America to come into the war, opted for such a policy, why should the fact that the Americans pursued that same policy be taken as proof that they wished to avoid war with Germany? So the evidence in the Rohwer article does not prove that Roosevelt was trying to keep America out of the war. If anything, it suggests exactly the opposite. Doing that exercise—seeing what Weinberg's interpretation is based on and analyzing a key text *he* cites to support that view—thus helps you develop your own understanding of the substantive issue at hand.

Let me step back a minute and make two comments about what has been going on here. Weinberg tends to interpret the story in terms of aggressors and victims, pure and simple. But you might think not just that U.S. policy was far more assertive than he makes out but also that it *had* to be more assertive, because that is the way international politics works. The Americans, you might assume, could not just remain passive in the face of what the Nazis were doing in Europe, because of its long-term effect on their own security position. The different historical interpretations might thus reflect different assumptions of a theoretical nature. But that does not mean that the theory is logically prior to the history—that one opts for a particular theoretical approach, that the history is interpreted accordingly, and that it could just as easily be interpreted the other way. You decide the historical issue by analyzing key bodies of evidence, and the way it's decided then helps you make up your mind about the theoretical assumptions you use to interpret these historical issues.

The second comment relates to the way an issue of this sort is analyzed. You look at a key claim—a claim that plays a major role in supporting one of the book's basic arguments—and you then focus on the evidence the author gives to back it up. You thus turn to the footnotes appended to the passages in which that claim is made, look up the sources cited there, and read them with some care, perhaps even examining the sources *they* cite. In unraveling the Watergate scandal, Bob Woodward and Carl Bernstein were given a famous piece of advice: "follow the money." But if you want to get to the bottom of a historical issue, it's not the money that you should follow. It's the footnotes.

But to return now to the historical analysis: suppose you reach the conclusion, using these techniques, that Roosevelt's policy in 1941 was to take the country into the war with Germany. This conclusion is important, but in the final analysis it's just one element in the story. You're still a long way from

[23] Rohwer, "Die USA," pp. 97, 102.

understanding how America became involved in the Second World War. The naval operations in the Atlantic, after all, did not lead directly to war with Germany. For Hitler in late 1941, the war with Russia was the top priority and that meant that for the time being war with America was to be avoided if at all possible. The German navy (as Weinberg notes) was thus kept on a short leash. "Under no circumstances," the German naval commander noted, did the Führer "wish to cause incidents which would result in U.S. entry into the war."[24] And it was of course only after the Japanese attack on Pearl Harbor that Hitler declared war on the United States.

ROOSEVELT AND JAPAN

So you obviously have to pay attention to U.S.-Japanese relations in 1941. How does that story fit in to the larger story of global politics in this period? To get at that question, the first step is to try to learn what you can about what was going on between American and Japan in this period—to try to understand at a very rudimentary level how one thing led to another, until finally the Japanese attacked the American fleet at Pearl Harbor on December 7, 1941. Using the techniques outlined in the previous chapter, a number of books can be identified as academically respectable accounts. You read those books, and perhaps some key collections of documents as well, and you quickly get a sense for what the basic story was.

What, in brief, was the story here? In late July 1941 the Japanese moved into southern Indochina. The Americans responded by freezing Japan's assets in the United States. The freezing of assets quickly turned into a full economic embargo. In particular, deliveries of petroleum and petroleum products were suspended, and those shipments were embargoed not just by the United States but by America's friends Britain and Holland as well. But Japan was dependent on oil imports from sources controlled by those countries. Those oil imports were particularly important for military (including naval) purposes. Japan had been engaged in an undeclared war in China since 1937. Without liquid fuels, its military effort there would grind to a halt. If the effort in China was not to be abandoned, the Japanese would need to find some way to get the oil they needed. That they could do either by reaching an agreement with the United States that would allow oil shipments to resume or by seizing the oil fields in the Dutch East Indies. But it was clear enough in late 1941 that an attack on the Indies would in all probability mean war with the United States.[25]

---

[24] Quoted in Hearden, *Roosevelt Confronts Hitler*, p. 203.

[25] Certain explicit warnings about further Japanese expansion, and in particular a move into the Indies, were in fact issued. The most important ones were given by Roosevelt in a meeting with the Japanese ambassador on July 24, 1941, and by Under Secretary of State Sumner Welles

The Japanese-American talks in late 1941 were thus of fundamental importance. To avoid both war with America and a collapse of its position in China, Japan needed a negotiated settlement with the United States. Indeed, it needed the issue to be resolved relatively quickly. As its oil reserves dwindled, Japan felt "like a fish in a pond from which the water was gradually being drained away."[26] But the Americans were unwilling to give the Japanese what they wanted. The China question turned out to be the nub of the problem. The Americans insisted on a complete Japanese withdrawal from China proper, but as the U.S. government itself realized, this was something

---

in a meeting with another Japanese diplomat on August 4. These widely cited documents were published in U.S. Department of State, *Foreign Relations of the United States* (FRUS), *Japan: 1931–1941*, 2 vols. (Washington, D.C.: GPO, 1943), 2: 527, 543. Note also the final paragraph in the Oral Statement Roosevelt handed to the Japanese ambassador on August 17, 1941, in ibid., p. 556. Secretary of War Henry Stimson viewed this as a "virtual ultimatum." Henry Stimson Diaries, microfilm edition, handwritten annotation at top of entry for August 19, 1941. But even if those warnings had not been issued, the basic situation would still have been fairly clear. Given the general picture as everyone understood it, it was reasonable to assume that a Japanese attack on the Indies would probably lead to war with America. What is the thinking that that conclusion is based on? The U.S. government, first of all, was obviously calling the shots on the western side. Britain and Holland, in imposing embargoes of their own, were simply following the American lead. How then could America leave them in the lurch if they were attacked by Japan for doing precisely that—that is, for cooperating with the U.S. policy and thus for provoking Japan to attack? This, you might assume, was the sort of calculation people would have made at the time. The Japanese, you might further assume, could reasonably calculate that the Dutch and the British could pursue a tough policy on the oil issue only if they were backed by America; given the European situation, they would have had to take a much softer line if they had had to stand entirely on their own. The fact that they took a tough line could thus be taken as confirming that general point about an attack on the Indies being casus belli for the United States. And military arguments about the Philippines—about the importance for the Japanese of neutralizing American bases in the area if they were to attack the Indies, given the fact that there was a certain risk of war with America if they did so—would also have to be taken into account in this context, both in Tokyo and in Washington. All these things, you might calculate, would have a certain bearing on people's estimates of the risk that a Japanese seizure of the Indies would lead to a U.S.-Japanese war. By considering these sorts of issues, you can thus begin to reach certain judgments about how people "must have" analyzed the situation at the time, even in the absence of hard empirical evidence. But this kind of analysis also helps you get a handle on the evidence. It serves as a kind of "searchlight." It directs your attention to certain specific questions—for example, to the question of what inferences the Japanese in fact drew from what they observed about British and Dutch policy, or to questions about the role the Philippine issue played in their calculations. And that in turn helps you see things you might not otherwise have seen—and indeed helps you understand how what you see bears on the basic issues at hand. On these matters, note the evidence presented in Scott Sagan, "From Deterrence to Coercion to War: The Road to Pearl Harbor," in *The Limits of Coercive Diplomacy*, ed. Alexander George and William Simons (Boulder, Colo.: Westview, 1994), pp. 77–78.

[26] Quoted in Heinrichs, *Threshold of War*, p. 182, and Robert Butow, *Tojo and the Coming of the War* (Stanford: Stanford University Press, 1961), p. 245. The source of the metaphor is an article written after the war by Sato Kenryo, in 1941 chief of the Military Affairs Section of the War Ministry.

the Japanese found hard to accept. As U.S. under secretary of state Sumner Welles put it in November 1941, the Japanese leaders had to provide "some justification to their own people after four years of national effort and sacrifice" in China. Welles therefore "could not believe" that the Japanese would "agree to evacuate China completely." But "nothing less," he said, would "satisfy [the] United States."[27] The Japanese had thus been backed into a corner. They were in effect forced to choose between war with the United States and capitulation on the China issue.

American policy was thus an important element in the story of the coming of the Pacific war. The U.S. oil embargo, most scholars seem to agree, had the effect of putting the United States on a collision course with Japan. Yet the scholars who have studied the subject most closely all seem to think that the last thing U.S. leaders wanted at the time was an armed conflict with that country. "No one during the fall of 1941," Jonathan Utley says, "wanted war with Japan."[28] Even those writers who believe that Roosevelt was trying to take the country into the European war think that war with Japan was not on his agenda. Indeed, in their view, the fact that Roosevelt was moving toward war with Germany made it more important than ever to avoid a second war with Japan. "From the fall of 1940 to the summer of 1941," Dallek writes (in the first paragraph of his chapter on the subject), Roosevelt wanted to "keep things as quiet as possible in the Pacific"; in June and July 1941, the president's "desire to avoid greater involvement in the Pacific" was "undiminished."[29] But Roosevelt was pushed "toward a confrontation with Japan" by "pressures beyond his control."[30] Even after the embargo was imposed, the president still sought to avoid, or at least to postpone, a conflict in the Pacific. "Scarce resources," Roosevelt felt, needed to "be marshaled to fight Hitler."[31] Waldo Heinrichs makes the same general point about American policy toward Japan at the time the embargo was imposed. The Americans, he says, "were on the point of intervening in the Battle of the Atlantic, but could not fight two wars

---

[27] Australian Minister to the United States R. G. Casey to Australian Department of External Affairs, November 14, 1941, Australian Department of Foreign Affairs, *Documents on Australian Foreign Policy, 1937–49* (Canberra: Australian Government Publishing Service, 1982), 5:197. See also British Ambassador Halifax to the British Foreign Office, November 12 and 15, 1941, FO 371/27911, available in the Scholarly Resources microfilm publication (Wilmington, Del., 1978), *British Foreign Office: Japan Correspondence, 1941–1945*, series for 1941, reel 7. The crucial importance of the China issue was commonly recognized very early on. As Paul Schroeder wrote in an important 1958 book: "There is no longer any real doubt that the war came about over China. Even an administration stalwart like Henry L. Stimson and a sympathetic critic like Herbert Feis concur in this." Paul Schroeder, *The Axis Alliance and Japanese-American Relations, 1941* (Ithaca: Cornell University Press, 1958), p. 200.

[28] Utley, *Going to War*, p. 157.

[29] Dallek, *Roosevelt*, pp. 269, 273.

[30] Ibid., p. 273.

[31] Ibid., pp. 275–76.

at once. Somehow Japan must be boxed in and neutralized; East Asia must be disconnected from the central problems of war and defense."[32]

American policy toward Japan is thus interpreted essentially as one of containment. The goal, it is argued, was to deter Japan from making further advances, both toward the south and toward Russia.[33] But knowing what the basic story was, you wonder whether it really makes sense to interpret American policy in those terms. The Americans, after all, were insisting that Japan withdraw from China, which, to use the idiom of a later period, looks more like rollback than containment. If the policy had been simply to deter the Japanese from pursuing a policy of expansion, the U.S. government would have had to make it clear to them that a continuation of their expansionist policy would lead to war with America. But if that had been American policy, U.S. officials would have also had to make it clear that if the Japanese agreed to refrain from further expansion, the two countries could live with each other as they had in the period before the embargo was imposed. The deterrent threat, after all, could carry weight only if the Japanese understood that they could avoid war if they bowed to the threat. If war would result even if they agreed to forgo further advances, what incentive would they have to pursue a moderate policy?

Your goal at this point, in other words, is simply to try to figure out what a policy of containment and deterrence would have been in this context. If the United States had threatened to impose sanctions *if* the Japanese continued their advance, then the American would have been pursuing a strategy of deterrence. If the Americans had embargoed oil shipments temporarily and then soon replaced the embargo with a licensing arrangement, then that too could be thought of as a policy of deterrence: those measures would have suggested to Japan that a full embargo could be reimposed *if* it proceeded with its expansionist policy. Even a strategy of maintaining the sanctions in full force, pending an agreement with Japan in which that country agreed to forgo *further* aggressive action, if not a deterrent strategy in the normal sense of the term, could certainly be used to support a policy of containment.

Thus *thinking* plays a fundamental role in the analysis of the issue. When you think through the issue in this way, key historical points are more likely to register in your mind. You are more likely to see the importance of some of the "dogs that didn't bark"—of the fact, for example, that Japan was not threatened with sanctions if (but only if) it *continued* its advance; of the fact that the Americans decided explicitly *not* to warn the Japanese that sanctions would be imposed if they moved into southern Indochina; and of the

[32] Heinrichs, *Threshold of War*, p. 126.

[33] See, for example, Dallek, *Roosevelt*, p. 299; Weinberg, *World at Arms*, p. 245; Butow, *Tojo*, p. 223; Akira Iriye, *The Origins of the Second World War in Asia and the Pacific* (London: Longman, 1987), p. 147; and especially Heinrichs, *Threshold of War*, p. 145 and title of chap. 5.

fact that the sanctions were not lifted when the Japanese government made it clear that it was willing to halt its advance (including a possible advance north against the USSR) rather than face war with the United States.[34] The significance of a couple of other key facts—the fact that the oil embargo came as a surprise to most Japanese leaders and the fact that the Japanese were told that they might not be able to avoid war simply by refraining from further acts of expansion, because actions "already undertaken" might well be the problem—also becomes clearer when you see them in this context.[35] In that way, the story gets fleshed out in your mind and your understanding of what was going on gradually deepens.

But the main thing to note here is the way thinking drives the research process. Just by thinking through the problem, you come to see why conventional interpretations of U.S. policy cannot be accepted uncritically. The thinking doesn't give you the answers, but it does help bring the real historical problem into focus. The basic conclusion you reach here—that the U.S. government had *not* opted for a simple strategy of containment and deterrence—helps define the question and thus sets the stage for yet further work: if the goal was not containment, if the aim was not to prevent *further* Japanese advances, then what was it?

But what leads you to try to consider this problem in this way in the first place? This kind of thinking could be triggered in various ways. You might, for example, have noticed that some major writers seemed to be a little uncomfortable with the conventional characterization of American policy as a policy of containment and deterrence. Heinrichs, for example, seemed to think

---

[34] Two weeks before the Japanese move, Welles told the British ambassador that he had advised the president to place a "complete economic embargo on Japan as soon as the Japanese committed any overt act." Welles, however, "was not in favour of telling the Japanese in advance that this would be the United States attitude." Halifax to Eden, July 9, 1941, *British Documents on Foreign Affairs: Reports and Papers from the Foreign Office Confidential Print* [BDFA], Part III (1940–45), Series E (Asia), vol. 4 (Bethesda, Md.: University Publications of America, 1997), p. 330. See also Tsunoda Jun, *The Final Confrontation: Japan's Negotiations with the United States, 1941*, the fifth and final volume in *Japan's Road to the Pacific War*, ed. James Morley (New York: Columbia University Press, 1994), p. 162. (Tsunoda's name, however, is not given on the title page.) On Japan's willingness to forgo further expansion, note especially the Japanese Government Statement handed to the president on August 28, 1941, FRUS Japan 2: 575.

[35] For the point that key Japanese leaders did not expect the move into southern Indochina to lead to a full embargo, see Butow, *Tojo*, p. 210; Tsunoda, *Final Confrontation*, pp. 162–63; Nobutaka Ike, ed., *Japan's Decision for War: Records of the 1941 Policy Conferences* (Stanford: Stanford University Press, 1967), pp. 48, 50, 107; and Takushiro Hattori, *The Complete History of the Greater East Asia War* (translated by the U.S. Army, 500th Military Intelligence Service Group, 1953), pp. 123, 130–31, 166. Hattori was chief of the Operations Sections at Japanese Army headquarters during the war, and then worked as an official historian during the postwar period; his account is based on both documentary sources and on conversations with former Japanese officers. For the point about measures "already undertaken," see Welles memorandum of meeting with Wakasugi, August 4, 1941, FRUS Japan 2:545.

that the Americans had not just opted for a simple strategy of deterrence. The embargo, he says, "was a deterrent, or, if stringently applied, powerfully coercive," and he makes it clear that it was applied very stringently indeed.[36] Or perhaps you were trying to figure out what to make of one of the key arguments found in the Heinrichs book, the claim that in opting for a "hard policy" toward Japan, Roosevelt was trying to head off a Japanese attack on the Soviet Union.[37] If Roosevelt's primary goal was to "keep Japan off Russia's back," couldn't he, you wonder, have just threatened to take measures that would lead to war if Japan moved north? Couldn't he have tried to reach a deal with Japan that included a Japanese promise not to attack the USSR— a deal secured by the threat that an embargo would be imposed if Japan reneged on that promise, a promise, in fact, which Japan seemed ready to make to avoid war with America?[38] Wouldn't the Japanese be more likely to do what America (supposedly) wanted—that is, remain at peace with Russia, while also avoiding war with the United States—if the price of compliance were relatively low than if Japan were being pushed to the wall on the China issue? The Americans might have wanted to contain Japan in the north as well as in the south. But if that was basically all that Roosevelt wanted in this area, did he really need to run a serious risk of a Pacific war?

Or you might have been sensitized to these basic questions about U.S. policy in 1941 by some exposure to deterrence theory, especially to the works of Bernard Brodie and Thomas Schelling. You might have absorbed from that literature the idea that in policies that depend on threat making, the fears and expectations that are generated are far more important than the actions actually taken—that the actions, no matter how harsh, have no coercive or deterrent value, except insofar as they shape expectations about what might happen in the future. The two atomic bombs that were dropped on Japan, for example, did not in themselves, Brodie pointed out, have a coercive effect. What led the Japanese to surrender, in his view, was the "threat of more to come"—the threat posed by the "nonexistent additional bombs which the Japanese didn't know we didn't have."[39] Brodie's basic insight here was of

---

[36] Heinrichs, *Threshold of War*, p. 145.

[37] Ibid., pp. 142, 159–60, 179, 189, 199.

[38] See Japanese Government Statement handed to Roosevelt on August 28, 1941, FRUS Japan 2:575. For the Japanese decision in August not to go to war with the USSR, see Tsunoda, *Final Confrontation*, pp. 152–57. Concerns about how America would react if Japan did attack Russia—indeed, the U.S. reaction to preparations for war in the north—were evidently factored into that decision. Note especially the emperor's comments on July 31 about the "bad impression" certain military measures of that sort were making in "other countries"—meaning, of course, the United States—quoted ibid., p. 156.

[39] Bernard Brodie, "Changing Capabilities and War Objectives," lecture given to Air War College, April 17, 1952, pp. 28–29, Bernard Brodie Papers, box 12, UCLA Research Library, Los Angeles.

fundamental importance, and it bears directly on the question of what a policy of deterrence would have been in 1941. In principle, of course, you can try to think the issue through on your own, simply by asking yourself what terms like "containment" and "deterrence" actually mean. But it really helps to have a prepared mind, a mind attuned to this sort of problem by exposure to the relevant body of theory.

Suppose then that in thinking through the problem of how American policy toward Japan in 1941 is to be interpreted you come to the conclusion that whatever it was, it was not a policy of containment and deterrence. You have cleared away a bit of the underbrush, and the central issue has been brought into focus: if the aim was not just containment, what then was the U.S. government trying to do? You note again that the effect of American policy was to put the United States on a collision course with Japan, but you also note that practically every serious scholar who has studied the subject thinks President Roosevelt and his top advisers wanted to avoid war with that country. That simple juxtaposition brings the problem into even sharper focus: how are these two points to be reconciled? How could such a policy have been pursued if the goal was to avoid war in the Pacific?

That question serves as a kind of searchlight. It points you in a certain direction. It tells you what to look for when you go back and read the main historical texts on the subject. How exactly do their authors deal with the problem? With that question in mind, you notice that the answers fall into two categories. Some scholars argue that Roosevelt did not understand the implications of the embargo. The claim is that he did not think the embargo would lead to war, because no matter how severe the economic sanctions were, the Japanese would not dare to attack the western powers. Other scholars, however, make a very different sort of argument. In their view, the political leadership had lost control of policy. The embargo, they say, was imposed without Roosevelt's knowledge or consent, and that by the time he found out what was going on, it was too late to do anything about it.

Both of these arguments purport to explain how the U.S. government could have adopted a policy that led directly to a war Roosevelt very much wanted to avoid. But when you think about how these arguments relate to each other, it gradually dawns on you that those are the only two possible explanations. For suppose Roosevelt *had* in fact been calling the shots from July 1941 on. Given that the embargo had in effect put the United States on a collision course with Japan, how then could you defend the idea that the president wanted to avoid war with Japan? In one and only one way: you'd have to argue that Roosevelt had miscalculated. You'd have to make the case that the president just did not understand what effect the embargo would have. For if Roosevelt *had* understood that the embargo would put the United States on a collision course with Japan, and if he *had* been in effective control of policy, then U.S. policy toward Japan in late 1941 would have to be seen as deliberate. You'd have to conclude, in that case, that the American political leadership had opted for a policy that led directly to war with Japan knowing full well what it was doing. So to deny that U.S. policy is to be understood in such terms, you therefore have to argue *either* that the president did not understand the implications of his actions *or* that he was not in effective control of his own government. Both of these claims could then be examined in the light of the evidence. If both were rejected, the implications would be far-reaching. What that would mean is that the American government had deliberately adopted a policy which its leaders knew might well lead to a U.S.-Japanese war.[40]

You thus come to have a sense for the architecture of this particular historical problem. You come to see how you can reach conclusions on important historical issues by breaking them down into problems that are more concrete and thus more studiable. But you develop that sense not by trying to work out the structure of the problem entirely on your own. Instead, you try to understand how specific claims that you see historians making relate both to each other and to the larger historical issue at hand. Getting a sense for the architecture of a problem is of fundamental importance, but in practice developing that sense is generally more a "bottom-up" than a "top-down" process.

When you have broken a major historical problem down into its component parts, you are in a position to study those specific issues one by one. In this case, you can begin with the claim that the U.S. political leadership did not understand the implications of the embargo and, in particular, that it did not believe it would lead to a U.S.-Japanese war. The president, one scholar writes, "was convinced that Japan would not fight the United States and the British empire simultaneously. This judgment was fundamental to his decisions after July 1941."[41] "The United States government," another scholar says, "did not believe that the Japanese reaction to the freezing order against their trade would go as far as an attack on British or Dutch possessions."[42] You understand the importance of those claims—that is, how they relate to a more general historical problem—but you now have to zero in on the question of whether they are in fact correct.

What, you thus wonder, did the U.S. political leadership think the effect of the embargo would actually be? That question again tells you what to

---

[40] For another example of how a major issue can be analyzed in this way, see my "The Coming of the First World War: A Reassessment," in my book *History and Strategy* (Princeton: Princeton University Press, 1991), pp. 72–95.

[41] Norman Graebner, "Hoover, Roosevelt, and the Japanese," in *Pearl Harbor as History: Japanese-American Relations, 1931–1941*, ed. Dorothy Borg and Shumpei Okamoto (New York: Columbia University Press, 1973), p. 49. See also Christopher Thorne, *Allies of a Kind: The United States, Britain and the War against Japan, 1941–1945* (New York: Oxford University Press, 1978), p. 83.

[42] Llewellyn Woodward, *British Foreign Policy in the Second World War*, 5 vols. (London: HMSO, 1970–), 2:140.

search for and which passages to focus on. And it turns out, perhaps to
your surprise, that Roosevelt and his closest advisers understood that an oil
embargo would in all probability lead to a Japanese attack on the Indies and
thus to war. As the president himself said, an embargo "would simply drive
the Japanese down to the Dutch East Indies, and it would mean war in
the Pacific."[43] In 1940 and 1941, he repeatedly made the point that an embargo would lead to a Japanese attack on the Indies, both in public and in
private.[44] And by late 1941 it had become increasingly clear that an attack
on the Indies would mean war with the United States. By that point, top
U.S. officials had come to the conclusion that tough economic sanctions
would, as Welles put it on July 9, "provoke Japan to war" with America "before long."[45]

Roosevelt thus knew that an oil embargo would probably lead to war with
Japan. If, as is generally assumed, his goal was to avoid war with that country,
why then did the United States pursue the embargo policy? Given the way
your thinking has developed so far, you understand that there can now be
only one answer to that question. The argument has to be that Roosevelt had
lost control of policy, and in fact a number of scholars argue that this was in
fact the case. Jonathan Utley's *Going to War with Japan*, for example, develops
this sort of argument, and you note that various other scholars either explicitly endorse Utley's argument or themselves argue along similar lines.[46] The
Utley argument is thus worth analyzing closely.

[43] Quoted in Hearden, *Roosevelt Confronts Hitler*, p. 211. See also Dallek, *Roosevelt*, p. 274, and
John Morton Blum, *From the Morgenthau Diaries: Years of Urgency, 1938–1941* (Boston:
Houghton Mifflin, 1965), p. 377.

[44] See, for example, Dallek, *Roosevelt*, pp. 271, 273. Note also Roosevelt's well-known confrontation with Secretary of the Interior Harold Ickes on the issue in June 1941. The documents
were published in *The Secret Diary of Harold L. Ickes*, 3 vols. (New York: Simon and Schuster,
1954–55), 3:553–60. On that episode, see Utley, *Going to War*, p. 131; Hearden, *Roosevelt Confronts Hitler*, p. 210; and Dallek, *Roosevelt*, p. 273. The president made the point in public on July
25, 1941; see FRUS Japan 2:265.

[45] Casey to Menzies and Stewart, July 9, 1941, *Documents on Australian Foreign Policy,
1937–49*, 5:6.

[46] The argument was laid out independently by Utley and Irvine Anderson. See Utley, *Going
to War*, pp. 153–56, 180; Jonathan Utley, "Upstairs, Downstairs at Foggy Bottom: Oil Exports
and Japan, 1940–41," *Prologue* 8 (Spring 1976): 17–28; Irvine Anderson, "The 1941 De Facto
Embargo on Oil to Japan: A Bureaucratic Reflex," *Pacific Historical Review* 44 (1975): 201–31;
and Irvine Anderson, *The Standard Vacuum Oil Company and United States East Asian Policy,
1933–1941* (Princeton: Princeton University Press, 1975). The Utley-Anderson argument has
been accepted by a number of major scholars. See, for example, Reynolds, *Anglo-American
Alliance*, pp. 235–36; Iriye, *Origins of the Second World War in Asia and the Pacific*, p. 150; and
Dallek, *Roosevelt*, p. 275. The bureaucratic politics theorists naturally also accept this general
interpretation. See, for example, Graham Allison and Morton Halperin, "Bureaucratic Politics:
A Paradigm and Some Policy Implications," in "Theory and Policy in International Relations,
ed. Raymond Tanter and Richard Ullman," *World Politics* 24, Supplement (Spring 1972): 67.

Utley's goal is to "explain why a nation that never wanted to fight Japan ended up doing so."[47] Even during the fall of 1941, he says, no one "wanted war with Japan," but war broke out because the bureaucracy could not be kept in line.[48] Neither Secretary of State Cordell Hull nor President Roosevelt, he writes, "managed to maintain control over the constantly growing and increasingly complex foreign policy bureaucracy. By losing control over the execution of policy, they lost control over the direction the nation moved."[49] The actions actually taken did not necessarily reflect "high-level policy decision"; effective policy was the result of what the bureaucrats did. "Rather than a smoothly functioning, harmonious machine, the foreign policy establishment in the Roosevelt administration" was, in Utley's view, "a snake pit of influential leaders and faceless bureaucrats working at cross-purposes, striking deals, and not infrequently employing sleight of hand in order to move the nation in the direction each thought most appropriate."[50]

The oil embargo is by far the most important case in point. Roosevelt and Hull, according to Utley, did not want a total halt to oil deliveries, but an embargo was nonetheless engineered by midlevel officials—above all, by Assistant Secretary of State Dean Acheson—who had their own ideas "about what should be done with Japan."[51] When Japan's assets were frozen in late July, the president's idea was that the freeze would simply lay the basis for a licensing arrangement. The deliveries were to resume as licenses were issued. But without anyone quite realizing what was going on, Acheson saw to it that the funds the Japanese needed to pay for the oil were not released. In that way, Utley writes, "the policy that was supposed to avoid provoking Japan was transformed into full-scale economic warfare that led to the attack four months later on Pearl Harbor."[52] It was only on September 4, he says, that Hull discovered how complete the embargo was, "but by then it was too late" to do anything about it: "To have reopened the flow of oil after a month's cut-off would have sent the wrong message to Tokyo and reinforced the position of the Japanese hard-liners, who claimed that the United States would give in."[53] Acheson had arrogantly "alter[ed] presidential orders" on his own and had "got away with it."[54] The results were disastrous. America went to war with Japan, not because of policy choices made by the nation's political leadership, but because irresponsible officials like Acheson had been able to hijack the policy process and, in effect, to make policy on their own.

[47] Utley, *Going to War*, p. xiii.
[48] Ibid., p. 157.
[49] Ibid., pp. 179–80.
[50] Ibid., pp. xii–xiii.
[51] Ibid., p. 153.
[52] Ibid., p. 154.
[53] Ibid., p. 156.
[54] Ibid.

If valid, these conclusions would be extraordinarily important for all kinds of reasons. But can it really be, you wonder, that American policy in late 1941 was shaped in such a haphazard way? Could Roosevelt really have been so out of touch with what was going on, given his understanding of what was at stake? The president, after all, had earlier made it quite clear that he considered this a very delicate area of policy, an area in which he intended to exercise control.[55] Why would he change his mind and suddenly become *less* involved, now that the situation had become even *more* serious? And could he possibly *not* have known until September that the Japanese were getting no oil? Even if Acheson was not reporting what he was doing, given the seriousness of this business, wouldn't Roosevelt have found out in some other way—for example, through the Japanese diplomatic correspondence, which the Americans had been able to intercept and decipher?

But even if he did not find out until September that his policy had been subverted from within his own government, was it really too late at that point to loosen the embargo and allow some oil shipments to resume? His attitude at the time Japanese assets had been frozen in late July was that licenses would be granted and the flow of oil would continue, but that policy, he said, "might change any day and from there on we would refuse any and all licenses."[56] His feeling at that point was that, rather than drawing "the noose tight," it was better "to slip the noose around Japan's neck and give it a jerk now and then."[57] To relax the embargo after six weeks would have been in line with that policy: a temporary cutoff would have given the Japanese a very strong "jerk" without actually driving them to war. And if for some reason Roosevelt in September felt unable to relax the sanctions—if he felt trapped by the actions that officials like Acheson had taken, ignoring the policy guidelines he had laid down—you would expect some evidence of that. If Acheson had behaved that way, you would expect Roosevelt and Hull to have been furious when they found out what he had done. These expectations are again a kind of searchlight. They help you focus in on evidence that might help resolve the issue. But when you find nothing, that makes you wonder about whether Roosevelt and Hull had really lost control of policy and about whether the embargo had been imposed contrary to their wishes.

The absence of evidence to that effect might make you wonder, but it is in no sense conclusive. Indeed, all these musings are in no sense conclusive. But they are important because they help you assess the inherent plausibility of the Utley argument and thus give you a sense for how high the evidentiary bar has to be. And this sort of thinking also gives you a sense for the specific questions you would like the evidence to answer. It thus helps you figure out

[55] See especially the June 1941 Roosevelt-Ickes correspondence, in Ickes, *Secret Diary*, 3:553–60.

[56] In cabinet meeting, July 24, 1941, quoted in Langer and Gleason, *Undeclared War*, p. 649.

[57] Ickes, *Secret Diary*, 3:588, a passage quoted in many accounts.

which issues, which passages, and even which bodies of source materials you need to focus in on.

What in particular, you might wonder, does the evidence show about how the political leadership really felt about a full embargo at that point? The freezing of assets was originally supposed to lay the basis for a licensing system that would allow the flow of oil to continue. That was the policy the president had decided upon in late July. But one of the basic points to emerge, as you search for evidence bearing on this issue, is that the political leadership was probably not nearly as committed to that policy in that period as the standard accounts might lead you to believe. In early July, for example, U.S. leaders were apparently thinking in terms of imposing a full embargo in the event Japan moved into southern Indochina. The British ambassador reported Roosevelt's attitude on July 18, a few days before Japanese forces moved into that area: "President personally definitely contemplates a full embargo on all oil products."[58] A few days earlier, Welles had also made it clear that he favored imposing a "complete economic embargo" on Japan, and Welles, as many scholars point out, was very close to Roosevelt at this time.[59] The idea that the president at this point was determined to avoid extreme action—the sort of action which, by his own account, "would mean war in the Pacific"—is thus very much open to question.

Is that all that can be said, or can you get any evidence that bears directly on the question of whether Acheson was making policy on his own? With that very specific question in mind, you can go back and look specifically at what scholars have to say on this subject. It turns out that Heinrichs, in his account of this episode, gives the impression that Roosevelt was calling the shots. He shows in particular that Acheson was taking orders from Welles.[60] He in fact has a long footnote appended to the passage in which he discussed the question which explicitly takes issue with the Utley argument. (This footnote, buried in the back of the book, might well have escaped your attention, unless you were zeroing in on this subject.) In that footnote, Heinrichs cites a number of documents showing that Acheson had been instructed to grant no licenses for the next week or two—that is, until Roosevelt and Welles had a chance to discuss this issue with Churchill and other British officials at the Atlantic Conference in early August. "Given the close association of Welles and Roosevelt, the fact that Welles was currently Acting Secretary of State, and the vital importance of the issue," Heinrichs concludes, "it seems inconceivable that Welles did not secure the president's approval for this course of action, or inaction."[61]

[58] Halifax to Eden, July 18, 1941, BDFA, Part III, Series E, vol. 4, no. 3361, p. 337 (p. 41 in original print).
[59] Halifax to Eden, July 9, 1941, ibid., p. 330 (p. 34 in original print).
[60] Heinrichs, Threshold of War, pp. 141–42.
[61] Ibid., pp. 246–47.

The reference to the meeting with Churchill, moreover, suggests that British sources might shed some light on the issue. Some key British documents relating to the period have been published, others are readily available on microfilm, and those document collections are so well organized that highly targeted research in these records is very easy to do. When you go through those sources, you learn that the British wanted to take a tough line on the issue and were worried that the U.S. position might be softening.[62] They wanted to make sure that "the economic measures [were] kept up and screwed up."[63] On August 11, at the Atlantic Conference, Churchill brought the issue up with Roosevelt. "It would be essential," Churchill said, "to maintain the full pressure of economic measures which the U.S. Government had already adopted in regard to Japan." Roosevelt's response was clear enough: "The President declared that he had every intention of maintaining economic measures in full force."[64] Welles was even more explicit. His British counterpart pressed him "on the subject of the application of the American freezing orders against Japan." Welles assured him "that the application was very strict." In the case of oil, Welles said, "no licenses were being granted except for crude oil up to an amount corresponding with that exported in 1935. This quantity had already been reached and therefore no more crude oil would be allowed except sufficient to take Japanese ships from American ports home to Japan. No licenses were being given for the export of aviation gasoline, ordinary gasoline or lubricating oil."[65] All this shows rather conclusively that the key decisions were being made by Roosevelt himself.

You've reached the point now where you can put two and two together. Roosevelt knew what a total oil embargo would mean. He knew that an embargo would put America and Japan on a collision course. He nonetheless opted to impose the embargo. That policy was his doing and had not been engineered by midlevel officials like Acheson acting without his knowledge or consent. Roosevelt had therefore deliberately opted for a policy which he knew would in all probability lead to war with Japan.

This is an important conclusion but it does not solve the more basic problem of explaining why the U.S. government pursued the policy it did. Quite the reverse: the effect of the analysis was to rule out two candidate explanations,

[62] See, for example, the extract from the War Cabinet Conclusions for July 31, 1941, in FO 371/27974, *British Foreign Office: Japan Correspondence, 1941–1945*, series for 1941, reel 15, and also the minutes by key officials on Halifax's telegram 3849 of August 18, 1941, in FO 371/27909, series for 1941, reel 7.

[63] David Dilks, ed., *The Diaries of Sir Alexander Cadogan, O.M., 1938–1945* (London: Cassell, 1971), entry for August 11, 1941, p. 399.

[64] Extract from record of a meeting between the Prime Minister and President Roosevelt on August 11th, 1941, FO 371/27909, *British Foreign Office Japan Correspondence, 1941–1945*, series for 1941, reel 7.

[65] Cadogan minute, August 20, 1941, FO 371/27977, ibid.

the idea that Roosevelt did not understand what he was doing and the idea that he had lost control of policy making, but it does not in itself provide any real answer to the fundamental question of how American policy toward Japan in this period is to be interpreted. And the key issue here, it dawns on you as you think about it, has to do with whether U.S. policy toward Japan is to be understood basically in relatively narrow Asia-specific terms or is instead to be viewed essentially in the broader context of America's global policy, and especially in the context of what was going on in Europe. Was America just so fed up with Japan's aggressive behavior that U.S. leaders had essentially decided that the time had come to bring matters to a head with that country and that what was going on in the rest of the world had relatively little to do with that decision? Or was the decision to pursue that policy toward Japan to be understood in much broader global terms, as related in some fundamental way to Roosevelt's desire to take the United States into the war with Germany?

THE JAPANESE WINDOW

How do you go about answering those questions about American policy toward Japan? To deepen your sense for what was going on in U.S.-Japanese relations, you obviously have to try to understand what Japanese policy was. And indeed a study of *Japanese* policy is bound to throw some light on the question of how *American* policy is to be interpreted. For if it turns out that Japan was highly aggressive and determined to expand even if that meant war with the United States, then you could reasonably argue that the particular policy the U.S. government adopted scarcely mattered—that war between Japan and America was virtually inevitable since the United States had to draw the line somewhere. That view of Japanese policy thus goes hand in hand with a relatively moderate view of American policy, the view that Roosevelt's basic goal throughout that period was "to check Japan without going to war" and that America was simply trying to "find ways to hold off Japan."[66] From that point of view, war came because Japan refused to be "held off." If, on the other hand, you conclude that the Japanese very much wanted to avoid war with America in late 1941, and if in fact your study of Japanese policy convinces you that the Japanese were ready to put an end to their policy of expansion in order to head off a war with the United States, then that would lead you to view U.S. policy in a rather different light. All the key elements of the story are bound up with each other: to understand American policy, you really need to understand what the Japanese were willing to agree to at the time.

[66] Dallek, *Roosevelt*, p. 299, and Weinberg, *World at Arms*, p. 245.

How then is Japanese policy in late 1941 to be understood? That's the issue you now have to focus on, and you proceed as usual by looking at how major authors flesh out their arguments— how they support them with specific claims. Those claims, being narrow enough to be studiable, can then be examined. The analysis having been set up in this way, the conclusions you reach on these specific issues are bound to have general implications—implications, that is, that will throw some light on the fundamental question you are concerned with.

What specific claims then support the idea that Japan was determined "to reach its goals even at the risk of war" with America?[67] That claim rests in part on the interpretation of a specific historical event, the July 2 Imperial Conference decision to expand toward the south, even if that meant war with the United States.[68] The assumption is that that decision can be taken at face value, but that assumption can itself be examined in the light of the evidence. Other specific claims are also testable. "In October 1941," Richard Overy writes, "the new Prime Minister, General Tojo, put Japanese demands to the United States for a free hand in Asia. It was agreed in secret that if America should refuse, which was likely, war would be started on 8 December."[69] One can look at the U.S. documents for that month (or actually the part of that month after Tojo took over as prime minister) and see if such a demand for a "free hand in Asia" was actually put to the Americans at that time. Overy also says that "not even the more conciliatory Japanese leaders were prepared at the time to consider forgoing any of the gains they had already made."[70] Other scholars claim that the Japanese government in November 1941 actually "wanted war" with America, and for that reason totally rejected the idea of a return to the status quo ante—that is, to the situation that had prevailed prior to the Japanese move into southern Indochina.[71] Again, these assertions can be examined in the light of the evidence, especially the evidence (if any) those authors cite to support those specific claims.

The general view that Japan was willing to go to war with America rather than abandon its expansionist program, you note, is often supported by a particular view of the role of the military in Japanese policy making. Control of Japanese policy, it is often claimed, was in the hands of the army and navy. Indeed, real power supposedly lay in the hands of "little-known general staff

[67] Langer and Gleason, *Undeclared War*, pp. 661–62. See also Weinberg, *World at Arms*, pp. 186, 247. Butow also frequently argues along these lines. See Butow, *Tojo*, pp. 203, 221, 242–43, 255–56, 283, 334.

[68] See, for example, Langer and Gleason, *Undeclared War*, p. 631.

[69] Richard Overy, *The Origins of the Second World War*, 2d ed. (London: Longman, 1999), p. 93.

[70] Ibid., p. 92

[71] Weinberg, *World at Arms*, p. 257.

THE 1941 CASE 103

officers serving in the army and navy divisions of imperial headquarters."[72] The senior officers—the army and navy chiefs of staff and the war and navy ministers—were allegedly the "robots of their subordinates."[73] Those staff officers, the argument runs, took a very aggressive line, and the policy they pursued made war with America inevitable.

None of this, of course, has to be taken on faith. You can always ask what evidence supports such claims. But perhaps the key thing to note here is that you would only raise that question in the first place if at least some of these claims struck you as problematic for one reason or another. On the question of the role of the staff officers, for example, you might question the claim that the senior commanders were "robots of their subordinates." It might be hard to believe that as people rose in rank, they became less powerful. Indeed, it might be hard to believe that in any organization, anywhere in the world, things would work that way. Or in trying to learn about Japanese foreign policy before the war, you might have read James Crowley's remarkable study of Japanese policy making in 1937.[74] What Crowley shows is that the army general staff wanted to take a moderate line on the China question but was outmaneuvered by the prime minister, Prince Konoye. It was Konoye who played the key role in taking Japan into the war with China; the army was not in effective control of policy at the time. That in itself might suggest that the claim about the military controlling policy in 1941 is not to be accepted uncritically.

You might feel, moreover, that the basic idea that Japan was intent on expansion regardless of consequence is simply hard to accept on very general grounds. If you have spent any time studying international politics, you develop a certain sense for how things work, and in particular for the role of power considerations in shaping policy. When you look at that view of an uncontainable and undeterrable Japan, part of you says, "it just can't be, states just don't behave that way"—a reaction that shows that a certain theory of international politics has come into play. Everyone knew that in terms of mobilizable war potential, the United States was a vastly stronger country than Japan. The figures for steel production, for example, were common knowledge at the time. So why, you say to yourself, would a country like

---

[72] Butow, *Tojo*, p. 240, and also pp. 86, 251, 255–56, 276.

[73] Butow, *Tojo*, pp. 171, 308. See also Yale Maxon, *Control of Japanese Foreign Policy: A Study of Civil-Military Rivalry, 1930–1945* (Berkeley: University of California Press, 1957), pp. 28, 46–47, 104–15, 216, and Masao Maruyama, *Thought and Behaviour in Modern Japanese Politics*, exp. ed. (Oxford: Oxford University Press, 1969), esp. pp. 107–14 (the term "robots" is used on pp. 92 and 107). For a remark in passing that cites both Butow and Maruyama and also shows that this is something like a consensus view, see Ike, *Japan's Decision for War*, p. 17.

[74] James Crowley, *Japan's Quest for Autonomy: National Security and Foreign Policy, 1930–1938* (Princeton: Princeton University Press, 1966).

Japan, already bogged down in a war with China, insist on pursuing a policy of expansion knowing full well that there was a very good chance that it would lead directly to war with America? It's hard to believe that the Japanese government—or any government, for that matter—would behave that way, no matter what a series of distinguished scholars say. Of course, you are not certain on those general grounds that that view of an uncontainable Japan is wrong. There is no guarantee that countries will behave rationally. But your sense for how international politics works makes you reluctant to accept that argument on faith. You're puzzled, and you know you can resolve the puzzle only by looking at the empirical evidence—the evidence that bears directly on the specific claims about Japan that people make, claims that support that general view of an uncontainable and undeterrable Japan. You have, in other words, found a loose thread in the fabric of received interpretation, and it is a certain theoretical perspective that enabled you to find it. Maybe if you pull on it, that whole fabric will begin to unravel, and you might be able to replace it with a rather different understanding of what was going on.

Your approach to this whole set of problems is also affected by the fact (which you soon note as you get into the subject) that not everyone who has written on the topic accepts the view that Japan was uncontainable in 1941. What this means is that you are not just pitting your own general theoretical sense for how things work against the view that everyone with an empirical grasp of the subject has reached. If that were the case, it would be hard to avoid feeling a little intimidated by the historiographical consensus. But when serious commentators are divided, you feel less intimidated by the weight of authority and more able to proceed by weighing arguments against each other.

It turns out that two of the writers who rejected the idea of an uncontainable Japan (and thus of an inevitable war) were the American and British ambassadors to Japan before the war, Joseph Grew and Sir Robert Craigie. Given the positions they held, each was in a position to comment knowledgeably on what had happened, and both men were quite critical of the policies their own governments had pursued toward Japan before Pearl Harbor. And you note that their general arguments turned on claims about specific episodes.

Grew focused on the U.S. government's handling of the Japanese proposal for a meeting between President Roosevelt and Prime Minister Konoye. When the embargo was imposed, Konoye, according to Grew, "for the first time began to see the handwriting on the wall." He understood his country "was heading for disaster." Konoye had been largely responsible for the position Japan now found itself in, Grew wrote, "but he was the only Japanese statesman capable of reversing the engine, and this, prompted by dire necessity, he did his best to accomplish." His plan was to meet with Roosevelt on

American territory. He made it clear to Grew that "he was prepared at that meeting to accept the American terms whatever they might be."[75] Japan, it seemed, was even willing to withdraw from China.[76] Grew was convinced that Konoye meant what he said, that he was prepared to follow through with this policy, and that with the emperor's support would be able to get the agreement with Roosevelt accepted at home.[77] For a prime minister of Japan, Grew wrote, "to offer to come, hat-in-hand so to speak, to meet with the President of the United States on American soil seemed to us in the Embassy a gauge of the determination of the then Japanese Government to undo the vast harm already accomplished in alienating our powerful and progressively angry country," and indeed the proposal for a meeting seemed pointless "unless the Japanese Government were ready to make far-reaching concessions."[78] The problem, according to Grew, was the "uncompromising attitude of our Government." "So far as we in the Embassy could perceive," he wrote, "the policy of the Administration during this critical time was almost completely inflexible."[79] The State Department showed little interest in the Konoye proposal and the plan for a leaders' conference eventually collapsed. Grew's conclusion was that a chance for peace—indeed, for a settlement on American terms—had tragically been allowed to slip away.

Craigie's account focused on a different episode, but his bottom line was much the same.[80] Like Grew, Craigie emphasized the shock effect of the economic sanctions imposed in late July: "The very effectiveness of these economic measures imposed on Japan a time-limit within which she must

[75] Grew to Roosevelt, August 14, 1942 (unsent), pp. 2, 4, and 8, Joseph Grew Papers, Houghton Library, Harvard University, Cambridge, Mass.; available by mail from Houghton Library. See also the account in Joseph Grew, *Turbulent Era: A Diplomatic Record of Forty Years, 1904–1945*, 2 vols. (Boston: Houghton Mifflin, 1952), 2:1301–75, which quotes from key documents (also published in FRUS) and on occasion uses much the same language. On this point, see especially the italicized passage on p. 1359.

[76] Grew to Roosevelt, August 14, 1942 (unsent), p. 5, Grew Papers, Houghton Library; Grew, *Turbulent Era*, 2:1356–57, 1373–74; Robert Fearey, "Tokyo 1941: Diplomacy's Final Round," *Foreign Service Journal*, December 1991, pp. 22–30.

[77] Grew to Roosevelt, August 14, 1942 (unsent), Grew Papers, Houghton Library; Grew, *Turbulent Era*, 2:1316n, 1327–28, 1332–33.

[78] Grew, *Turbulent Era*, 2:1302, 1311.

[79] Ibid., 2:1333-34.

[80] Final Report by Sir R. Craigie on Conclusion of His Mission to Japan, February 4, 1943, FO 371/35957, Public Record Office, Kew, and published in BDFA, Part III, Series E, vol. 6, in the section "Further Correspondence respecting Far Eastern Affairs, Part 22," pp. 127–53 in the original *Confidential Print* pagination, equivalent to pp. 407–33 in the pagination introduced in that published volume. The general line Craigie took in that report has been noted in a number of historical accounts, for example, Thorne, *Allies of a Kind*, pp. 74–75, and Woodward, *British Foreign Policy in the Second World War*, 2:177–78. Craigie also argued along these lines, albeit in somewhat milder form, in his published memoir, *Behind the Japanese Mask* (New York: Hutchinson, 1945).

decide either for or against war with the United States. The issue for Japan was no longer how far southwards in Eastern Asia she could expand without provoking America to war, but by what means—whether by negotiation or by war—she could remove an economic stranglehold which was rapidly becoming intolerable."[81] Japan, he argued, was willing to go quite far to achieve that goal. The key thing here, for Craigie, was the Japanese proposal of November 20, 1941, for a "modus vivendi." In exchange for a resumption of oil deliveries, the Japanese actually offered to *withdraw* from southern Indochina. The basic goal, Craigie thought, was the "virtual restoration of the *status quo ante*": the aim, that is, was to turn back the clock and return to the situation that had existed prior to the Japanese move into southern Indochina in late July.[82] To be sure, the Japanese plan also seemed to call on America to suspend aid to China, but Craigie did not think this was as great a real stumbling block as it appeared to be. "According to my information at the time," he later wrote, it was "doubtful" that the Japanese would have insisted on this condition if the Americans had accepted the rest of the plan.[83] The modus vivendi proposal, in his view, was of fundamental importance.[84] The western powers' failure to respond positively to that proposal, he argued, had led to a war that certainly could have been postponed and quite possibly could have been avoided entirely.[85]

It is also important to note that diplomats like Grew and Craigie are not the only ones to argue along these lines. Some very able scholars took much the same view. Paul Schroeder's *The Axis Alliance and Japanese-American Relations, 1941* endorses Grew's basic point of view and essentially shares Craigie's assessment of the modus vivendi proposal.[86] The Japanese, Schroeder writes, were "realistic about their position throughout; they did not suddenly go insane. The attack [on Pearl Harbor] was an act of desperation, not madness. Japan fought only when she had her back to the wall as a result of America's diplomatic and economic offensive."[87] Prior to the embargo, according to Schroeder, America's goal had been basically defensive, but after July U.S. policy shifted. The Americans were no longer interested in simply "holding the line against Japanese advances and of inducing Japan to draw away from an alliance [with Germany] which the United States considered menacing." "The chief objective of American policy now," he argued, "was to

---

[81] Craigie Report, para. 65 (on p. 153 in the *Confidential Print* version).

[82] Craigie to Eden, February 4, 1953 (covering letter for his report), para. 15 (p. 131 in the *Confidential Print*), and para. 42 in the report (p. 146 in the *Confidential Print*).

[83] Craigie, *Behind the Japanese Mask*, p. 130.

[84] Craigie Report, para. 45 (p. 147 in the *Confidential Print*).

[85] Craigie Report, para. 66 (p. 153 in the *Confidential Print*).

[86] Schroeder, *Axis Alliance*, pp. 76–85, 203–08, 215–16. Schroeder does, however, think that Grew was "over-optimistic about Konoye's capacity to carry through a peaceful policy" (pp. 205–6).

[87] Ibid., pp. 200–201.

push Japan back, to compel her to withdraw from her conquests."[88] The original goals—the containment of Japan and the breaking of Japan's alliance with Germany—were both reasonable and attainable. But with both goals within reach, the Americans shifted course and focused now on a third goal, the liberation of China. The result, he concluded, was "an unnecessary and avoidable war."[89]

The fact that serious writers differ among themselves on this key issue—the question of how containable Japan was and how avoidable war was—simply underscores the point that to get to the bottom of the question, you have to look in a very targeted way at the empirical evidence. These writers differ among themselves not just on basic issues; they also interpret specific episodes differently, and those specific interpretations play a key role in supporting their larger arguments. Those are the issues you therefore want to focus on. It is worth emphasizing yet again that the specific claims you find in the literature, claims that play a key role in supporting larger arguments, determine what to focus on when you go through works that contain empirical evidence on the subject. If the modus vivendi affair is of central importance, you zero in on what various writers have had to say on that issue, noting in particular the evidence they give to support their claims. The same point applies to claims about the "irreversibility" of the July 2 decision, or about the Konoye proposal for a leaders' conference, or about the role of the military in Japan in late 1941.

But where do you find the evidence? All the books you read present some empirical evidence, but to answer the questions you have in mind, you would like to find some books that are loaded with detail, replete with references to, and quotations from, the original sources, something equivalent to Luigi Albertini's extraordinary account of the immediate origins of the First World War.[90] Unfortunately, nothing of the sort exists, but it turns out that there is one English-language book that makes ample use of Japanese sources: Tsunoda Jun's *The Final Confrontation*.[91]

So a number of questions have taken shape in your mind as a result of your reading so far of the historical literature in this area. What emerges when you look at the evidence presented in works like the Tsunoda book with those questions in mind? It quickly becomes clear that the idea that the armed services were a unified bloc, intent on expansion even if it meant war with

---

[88] Ibid., p. 177.

[89] Ibid., p. 203.

[90] Luigi Albertini, *The Origins of the War of 1914*, 3 vols. (London: Oxford University Press, 1952–57). The second and third volumes deal basically with the crisis of July 1914.

[91] The standard reference for this work is: James W. Morley, ed., *The Final Confrontation: Japan's Negotiations with the United States, 1941* (New York: Columbia University Press, 1994). Although he was the author of this volume, Tsunoda's name (as noted above) does not appear on the title page; the book is also unusual in that it contains a long introduction by the translator, David Titus, criticizing Tsunoda's argument.

the United States, does not hold up in the light of the evidence. To be sure, certain officers were quite warlike, but given what you had been led to believe about the Japanese military, evidence that points in the opposite direction is most striking. Many leading admirals, for example, knew that Japan had little chance of winning such a war. Practically everyone who studies the subject knows that Admiral Yamamoto, commander in chief of the Combined Fleet, thought that a war with America would end in the defeat of Japan: "[I]n the end, we shall not be able to stand up to them."[92] This, however, is often treated as an isolated case. But as Yamamoto himself pointed out, four other fleet commanders shared his view, and Admiral Inouye, chief of naval aviation, was also quite pessimistic.[93] On October 5, naval operations division chief Fukudome made what Tsunoda calls a "statement of great importance": at a meeting of army and navy bureau and division chiefs, he announced that he had "no confidence" in the outcome of naval operations.[94] This is of particular interest because Fukudome was identified as one of a handful of key staff officers who were supposedly calling the shots in Japanese military circles before the war.[95] Naval affairs bureau chief Oka, another key staff officer, and navy minister Oikawa, took the same general view.[96] On October 7, Oikawa told War Minister Tojo directly: "I am not confident." But Oikawa was unwilling to take that position officially. It was "not possible," he said, "for the navy to state clearly and openly that we are opposed to this war from a navy standpoint."[97]

The army, however, understood well enough how those top naval officers felt. Could war, it wondered, still be contemplated if the navy was in no position to fight such a war successfully? Wouldn't the whole issue of the southern advance and of war with the United States have to be reconsidered? As one high official explained on October 17, "even the army fully understands that it is impossible for Japan to plunge into a war with the United States without genuine resolve on the part of the navy."[98] General Tojo, the war

---

[92] Ibid., pp. 286–87; see also pp, 107, 225, 273, 288.

[93] Ibid., pp. 114 , 287.

[94] Ibid., pp. 212–13. Fukudome had earlier in the year taken a tougher line, but up to the time of the oil embargo, warlike words might have had a purely instrumental purpose: as the army suspected at the time, and as some historians have later argued, those positions may have been adopted as a way of helping the navy fight its budgetary battles with the army. See Butow, *Tojo*, p. 221, and Michael Barnhart, *Japan Prepares for Total War: The Search for Economic Security, 1919–1941* (Ithaca: Cornell University Press, 1987), pp. 140, 168–69, 174–75, 210, 244.

[95] See Maxon, *Control of Japanese Foreign Policy*, pp. 46–47.

[96] Tsunoda, *Final Confrontation*, pp. 213, 216, 221–22, 225. See also Barnhart, *Japan Prepares*, p. 244.

[97] Tsunoda, *Final Confrontation*, pp. 216, 221–22, 228. See also Arthur Marder, *Old Friends, New Enemies: The Royal Navy and the Imperial Japanese Navy*, vol. 1, *Strategic Illusions, 1936–1941* (New York: Oxford University Press, 1981), pp. 175–78, 252–61.

[98] Ibid., p. 221; see also p. 214.

minister, agreed with that official's view that "so long as the navy is not confident and determined, the utmost caution must be taken before plunging into
a great war that will put the nation's destiny on the line."[99] The army made it
clear in fact that all the navy had to do was to say explicitly that it was in no
position to take on the United States. If it did, the army would go along with
that no-war policy, and the threat of discontent from within the army would
not prevent the army leadership from doing so. The army's view, as expressed
by another key staff officer, Muto, was straightforward: "If the navy is loath to
go to war, then I want them to say that clearly, straight from their own
mouths. If they do that, we will put a stop to the pro-war arguments in the
army."[100] Oka was told bluntly: "If the navy says 'no can do,' we will get the
army under control one way or the other."[101] The army understood how the
navy felt and was frustrated that it could not get a straight answer: "Oikawa
doesn't say he isn't confident," Tojo told army chief of staff Sugiyama on October 14, "but he seems to talk that way. The matter can't be decided because
he won't speak plainly. If the navy can't come out in favor of war, then we
must think of a different way of proceeding based on that."[102] And it seems
quite clear from Tsunoda's evidence that the army leadership really wanted
the navy to come out and take a clear stand against war. Muto told chief cabinet secretary Tomita, a key intermediary in this affair, that he wanted the
navy to say openly that the official policy had to be abandoned and war had
to be avoided:

> It looks like the navy really hasn't made up its mind. If the navy really doesn't want
> war, then the army will have to reconsider. But the navy does not outwardly oppose
> war and tells the army that it's up to the prime minister. I can't get things under
> control in the army merely by saying that it's for the prime minister to decide, but
> if the navy came out and told the army formally that it doesn't want war, then I
> can get the army under control. Can't you get the navy to come out and say this
> for me?[103]

These were hardly the words of a fire-breathing staff officer.

Muto, and General Tojo himself, were willing to take that line in part because they, like everyone else, knew how strong the United States was in
terms of war-making potential.[104] But another part of the reason was that
they were deeply loyal to the emperor, and it was evident the emperor

[99] Ibid., p. 230.
[100] Ibid., p. 222.
[101] Ibid.
[102] Ibid., pp. 227–28.
[103] Ibid., p. 228.
[104] See, for example, Ike, *Japan's Decision*, pp. 187–88; Peter Wetzler, *Hirohito and War: Imperial Tradition and Military Decision Making in Prewar Japan* (Honolulu: University of Hawaii Press, 1998), p. 53; Tsunoda, *Final Confrontation*, p. 164.

wanted to avoid war.[105] After an extraordinary imperial conference at which the emperor made his feelings clear, Muto exclaimed to a member of the Military Affairs Bureau, "War is absolutely out of the question! Listen up now. His Majesty told us to reach a diplomatic settlement on this, no matter what it takes. We've got to go with diplomacy."[106] Tojo was also prepared to follow the emperor's lead on this issue. Colonel Ishii, a member of the army general staff, "received a communication on 16 October from the throne to the army minister saying they should drop the idea of stationing troops in China and that an imperial command (to form a cabinet) was conceivable. Ishii quickly wrote a reply justifying the necessity of stationing troops in China and gave it to Tojo for his audience with the emperor on the afternoon of 17 October. Whereupon Tojo told Ishii: 'If the emperor said it should be so, then that's it for me. One cannot recite arguments to the emperor. You may keep your finely-phrased memorandum.'"[107]

So it's a mistake to argue that the military was intent on war regardless of consequence. The real feeling of army leaders like Tojo was that Japan found itself in a very difficult and painful situation. On the one hand, it was obvious that the United States was a much stronger country than Japan, and that in a long war Japan would simply not be able to stand up to America. On the other hand, the Americans were demanding that Japan give up its position in China and withdraw its troops from that country. After all those years of sacrifice, could Japan really just capitulate to America in that way? Tojo in particular was torn between conflicting emotions: "We have lost 200,000 souls in the China Incident, and I cannot bear to give it all up just like that. But when I think of all the lives that will be further lost if there is a war between Japan and the United States, we must even think about withdrawing troops. That will be hard to decide."[108]

What is extraordinary here was that capitulation on the China issue was not out of the question, even for Tojo. If that was the view of the military leadership, what that implies is that the efforts of the political leadership to avoid war with America are not to be written off with the argument that, whatever their personal preferences, the political leaders would never be allowed by the military to make serious concessions, or even to move away from the "irrevocable" July 2 decision to expand toward the south regardless of consequence. Tsunoda, in fact, shows in some detail how after the oil embargo Prime Minister Konoye and Foreign Minister Toyoda "gutted" that decision in various ways.[109] You get the strong impression from the evidence he presents that they were searching desperately for a way to avoid war with the United States.

[105] Tsunoda, *Final Confrontation*, pp. 174, 176, 240–41.

[106] Ibid., p. 177.

[107] Wetzler, *Hirohito and War*, pp. 51–52. See also Tsunoda, *Final Confrontation*, p. 241.

[108] Tsunoda, *Final Confrontation*, p. 217. See also p. 250.

[109] Ibid., pp. 151–52, 156, 158.

So you've done a certain amount of spadework, and you now have to deal directly with Grew's argument about Konoye's plan for a leaders' conference. When you look at the evidence bearing on this affair, it really does seem that Konoye was willing to go very far indeed. Grew, as I noted, had the distinct impression that Konoye was prepared in the final analysis to accept America's terms, no matter what they were. This, he thought, was the whole point of Konoye's proposal to meet with President Roosevelt on American territory. "Prince Konoye," he wrote in an unsent letter to the president, "was pinning all his faith on his proposed meeting with you in Alaska and he had told me with unquestionable sincerity that he was prepared at that meeting to accept the American terms whatever they might be."[110] Japan was even prepared to withdraw practically its entire army from China. Konoye had given him an "unqualified assurance" that "he would and could bring his country to meet *whatever requirements*" Roosevelt "might lay down at the proposed meeting with him."[111]

The issue is important, so you look for more evidence. One source that turns up when you search for works by people who might have had some direct knowledge of the affair is the transcript of an oral history interview with Eugene Dooman, the American chargé in Tokyo at the time.[112] Dooman gives basically the same account as Grew and adds some additional details. Konoye told him directly, he reports, that "as soon as I reach an agreement with the President I will report immediately to the emperor and it will be the emperor who will command the army to suspend hostilities."[113] That view of what Konoye intended is supported by other accounts given after the war by Admiral Toyoda, the foreign minister in 1941; by Tomita Kenji, chief cabinet secretary at the time; by an account of what Konoye told one of his intimates, Izawa Takio; and by other evidence you come across in your work.[114]

But what about the arguments on the other side? The leaders' meeting was never held, mainly because the U.S. State Department reacted coolly to the idea, but most scholars believe that even if the two leaders had met, things would not have worked out very differently. Herbert Feis, for example, insisted that the written documents that became available after the war did not

---

[110] Grew to Roosevelt, August 14, 1942 (unsent), p. 4, Grew Papers, Houghton Library.

[111] Ibid., p. 8. (emphasis in original).

[112] The search, in this case, was conducted in Eureka, the union catalogue of the Research Libraries Group, available in most American research universities. More information how this source can be used to find unpublished material is included in appendix II, p. 241 below.

[113] "Reminiscences of Eugene Hoffman Dooman,"(1962), p. 95, oral history interview, available through interlibrary loan from the Columbia University Oral History Research Office,New York.

[114] Oka Yoshitake, *Konoe Fumimaro: A Political Biography* (New York: Madison Books, 1992), p. 166–67; and Tsunoda, *Final Confrontation*, pp. 193, 219; and Sagan, "From Deterrence to Coercion to War," p. 74, citing evidence presented in Marder, *Old Friends, New Enemies*, 1:175.

support the view that "a real chance of maintaining peace in the Pacific" had been missed. Those documents, he thinks, showed what Japanese policy really was. They showed that the Japanese were simply not prepared to go far enough to satisfy the Americans, especially on the China issue. Konoye, he writes, was a "prisoner, willing or unwilling, of the terms precisely prescribed in conferences over which he presided." He was bound by the formal policy documents that had been agreed upon, documents in which Japan's minimum demands had been spelled out. He could not go further even if he had wanted to; the military services would see to that.[115]

That claim, however, has to be weighed against Grew's response. Those documents, Grew argues, are not to be taken at face value. They have to be interpreted in the light of the fact that Konoye needed to "get the leaders of the armed forces to play along," that there was no way that he was going to reveal to them how far he was prepared to go, and that his plan was to present them with something like a fait accompli.[116] Dooman, basing his conclusions in part on a long conversation he had in 1953 with Ushiba Tomohiko, a close personal friend of Konoye's and his private secretary, agrees with that interpretation. "I think it is quite clear," he said, "that what Konoye had in mind was actually a double-crossing of the army and navy."[117]

How do you go about getting to the bottom of this issue? You break the question down into its component parts. First of all, there's the issue of whether the documents show that Konoye was bound by conditions others had imposed and would therefore not have been able to go very far in his dealings with Roosevelt. What's to be made of the Feis argument on this point? It's really not very strong. There's no reason to assume that a document has to be taken at face value. The existence of certain written documents does not in itself discredit Grew's argument. Indeed, the whole premise of his argument was that Konoye intended to outmaneuver those who were opposed to what he was trying to do; with a strategy of that sort, written documents need not be taken as sacrosanct. On the issue of whether Konoye intended to go as far as he had to to avoid war, the preponderance of the evidence seems to support Grew's argument. It is hard, for example, as Grew argued, to understand why Konoye was prepared to press so hard for a leaders' conference unless he was prepared "to make far-reaching concessions."[118] Given the obvious fact, moreover, that war with America would be an extraordinarily risky undertaking, it is not hard to believe that Konoye, who felt

---

[115] Herbert Feis, *The Road to Pearl Harbor: The Coming of the War between the United States and Japan* (Princeton: Princeton University Press, 1950), pp. 274–76. See also Barnhart, *Japan Prepares*, pp. 241–42.

[116] Grew, *Turbulent Era*, 2:1374

[117] Dooman oral history, pp. 120–21.

[118] This was Grew's argument at the time. See *Turbulent Era*, 2:1311.

personally responsible for the desperate situation his country was now in, would want to take unprecedented and extreme action.

And then there's the question of whether Konoye could have pulled it off. Suppose he had met with Roosevelt, had made whatever concessions were needed to head off war, and then had tried to present his country with a fait accompli. Would the military authorities have allowed him to accept the American terms, no matter what they were?[119] Suppose the Americans had insisted on a complete withdrawal from China. Would the army have agreed to that, even if Konoye had gotten the emperor to issue the necessary orders? Konoye, it seems, thought there was a good chance he could succeed, and he was obviously in a good position to assess political realities in Japan. Other well-placed Japanese observers also thought he could have carried the country with him.[120] But perhaps the most important body of material bearing on the question is the evidence Tsunoda gives on the attitude of the military establishment. If you reach the conclusion that many top military and naval officers were not eager for war and in fact were looking hard for a way out, then that suggests that Konoye would not have been overthrown by the military if he had reached an agreement with Roosevelt, above all if, as seems very likely, that agreement had been endorsed by the emperor.

But if the goal in looking at the Japanese side of the story is to learn a bit more about American policy, it's not really necessary to answer such questions. The real issue is not whether the Japanese would have agreed to withdraw from China as the Americans demanded, but rather simply whether Japan could have been contained—that is, whether it could be kept from continuing its advance to the south (and kept also from attacking the USSR in the north). And the story of the leaders' conference is of interest not just because of the light it sheds on the question of whether Japan could have been made to withdraw from China, but even more because of what it tells us about whether Japan could have been contained or whether a U.S.-Japanese war was unavoidable. On that question, the implications of this story are quite clear. If key Japanese leaders were surprisingly open to the idea of accommodating the United States even on the China issue, and if even some of

---

[119] See, for example, Schroeder, *Axis Alliance*, pp. 205–06, and Butow, *Tojo*, p. 261.

[120] Thus, for example, former prime minister Hirota, Grew wrote Roosevelt in his unsent August 1942 letter, "who was in close touch with and carried important influence in military and political circles, said (not to me but to others) that Prince Konoye could not possibly afford to allow the proposed meeting to result in failure. Mr. Hirota added that this meant that Prince Konoye would unquestionably have to accept your terms, and that under the existing circumstances he could and would carry the entire Japanese nation, including the military, with him. No statesman in Japan was in a better position than Mr. Hirota to gauge the situation, but the same opinions were held and expressed to me by other influential Japanese at the time." See also Grew, *Turbulent Era*, 2:1359; in that passage, Grew says that Hirota did express those views to him directly.

Japan's top military leaders did not rule out the idea of doing whatever was necessary to avoid war with America, then certainly Japan would have agreed to a much more palatable U.S. demand that it simply forgo further expansion as the price of peace.

That same question (of whether the Pacific War was avoidable) also lies at the heart of your analysis of the second key issue, the question of whether a modus vivendi could have been reached in the weeks before Pearl Harbor. The Konoye government fell after the collapse of the plan for a leader's conference and was replaced in October by a new government headed by General Tojo. The new foreign minister, Togo Shigemori, wanted to see if an agreement could be worked out essentially on the basis of a return to the status quo ante—that is, to the situation that had existed prior to the Japanese move into southern Indochina in July. Japan would withdraw its troops from that area and the flow of oil would resume.[121] A plan outlining an arrangement of this sort was presented to the Americans in November. At the insistence of the army high command, a provision had been included in that plan calling on the United States not to "engage in such actions as may hinder efforts toward peace by Japan and China." The plan was not Japan's final word; Togo, with Tojo's support, was prepared to make further concessions in order "to bring the negotiations to a successful conclusion."[122]

People like Craigie thought that something along those lines could, and indeed should, have been worked out. Those in the west who opposed it said it would have constituted "appeasement." The provision about China was interpreted as a demand that military assistance to that country be ended, and this neither America nor Britain could accept. For that reason, it is often argued, this proposal had no chance of leading to an agreement that would have headed off the war.

The issue is important because it reveals how far each side was willing to go to avoid war and is thus worth examining closely. And when you look at how it's dealt with in the literature, it becomes clear that the two sides were not nearly as far apart on the China issue as they were later made to seem.[123] The Japanese explained what they had in mind by the provision about China soon after the plan had been presented to the Americans. Togo, in a meeting with Grew, alluded to President Roosevelt's idea that the United States might serve as an "introducer" between Japan and China. After being "introduced," the two countries would enter into an armistice and begin peace negotiations. At that point the U.S. government would suspend military aid deliveries to

---

[121] Japanese draft proposal, November 20, 1941, FRUS Japan 2:755–56.

[122] Tsunoda, *Final Confrontation*, pp. 261–65, 370. See also Togo Shigenori, *The Cause of Japan* (New York: Simon and Schuster, 1956), p. 144.

[123] See Langer and Gleason, *Undeclared War*, pp. 879–83, and Schroeder, *Axis Alliance*, pp. 76–89.

Chiang Kai-shek.[124] As some scholars point out, the State Department at this time was also considering a plan of this sort.[125] The two sides, as Heinrichs says, had moved "within negotiating range of each other."[126] But the Americans in the final analysis were not interested in working out this kind of an arrangement. Japan was clearly willing to be contained. Indeed, Japan was willing to withdraw from territory it had occupied as part of the southern advance. But with a settlement on that basis within reach, the Americans decided that it was just not good enough.

EXPLAINING U.S. POLICY: THE INDIRECT APPROACH

In exploring the Japanese side of the question, you are once again struck by the central problem. If Japan was not "uncontainable" or "undeterrable," then maybe war came because the U.S. government was insisting on something more than containment. And in fact it seems quite clear that the Americans were insisting that Japan capitulate on the China issue. But why did they opt for such a policy? Until quite recently, they had been willing to live with what Japan was doing in China. They certainly did not like what the Japanese were doing there, but they were not prepared to go to war to force them out of China. But their policy had shifted dramatically, and that shift had taken place just as the situation with Germany was becoming very serious indeed.

The whole story is quite puzzling. America certainly had a real interest in East Asia. The United States, as Schroeder notes, had a major interest in putting a stop to Japan's southern advance and in weaning Japan away from its alliance with Hitler. But both of those goals, as he argues, were attainable without war. By late 1941, he writes, the United States had reached the point "where the achievement of these two goals was within sight." The puzzle is that at that very moment, with the United States "on the verge of a major diplomatic victory," America "abandoned her original goals and concentrated on a third, the liberation of China"—a new goal that "rendered war inevitable." The United States, Schroeder concludes, thus "forfeited the diplomatic victory which she had already virtually won."[127] And this is in fact the nub of the problem. How is that *American* policy to be explained?

---

[124] Grew to Hull, November 24, 1941, FRUS Japan 2:763; Schroeder, *Axis Alliance*, pp. 82–83.

[125] Langer and Gleason, *Undeclared War*, p. 871 (for the point that the United States would suspend aid to China as soon as China and Japan entered into an armistice and began peace talks), and p. 880 (for the similarity with Japan's own plan): "it is difficult to understand the depth of Mr. Hull's indignation over Japanese-sponsored suggestions which in many respects resembled ideas current in the State Department itself." See also Schroeder, *Axis Alliance*, p. 81 n. 27.

[126] Heinrichs, *Threshold of War*, pp. 208–09.

[127] Schroeder, *Axis Alliance*, p. 203.

Schroeder's own answer was that the American government was a prisoner of its own ideology. The adoption in July of a "new offensive policy" might have led to war, he says, but that course of action was not really the product of "the reasoned decision of policy makers."[128] American policy, he says, was too inflexible, too moralistic. The Americans were just too unwilling to take political realities into account. Secretary of State Hull played a particularly destructive role. "His all-or-nothing attitude," Schroeder says, "constituted one of his major shortcomings as a diplomat."[129] And Roosevelt can be blamed for "allowing Hull and others to talk him out of impulses and ideas which, had he pursued them, might have averted the conflict." But Hull and Roosevelt were not the only ones responsible. Indeed, for Schroeder the blame has to be borne essentially by the country as a whole. "The mistake (assuming that it was a mistake)," he writes, "of a too hard and rigid policy with Japan was, as has been pointed out, a mistake shared by the whole nation, with causes that were deeply organic. Behind it was not sinister design or warlike intent, but a sincere and uncompromising adherence to moral principles and liberal doctrines."[130]

This is an important argument, and it echoes certain major themes in American realist thought. George Kennan, in particular, in his very influential *American Diplomacy*, argued eloquently along these lines.[131] American policy in the Cold War, or in Vietnam, is often interpreted in similar terms.[132] Perhaps you've done some work in those areas and as a result have developed a certain degree of skepticism about that kind of argument.[133] If so, you might be more inclined than you otherwise might be to take Schroeder's general

[128] Ibid., pp. 182.

[129] Ibid., p. 207.

[130] Ibid., pp. 202–03.

[131] George Kennan, *American Diplomacy, 1900–1950* (Chicago: University of Chicago Press, 1951), esp. p. 73. Kennan, however, was not quite prepared to let Roosevelt off the hook in this way. For his rather negative assessment of Roosevelt's policy in late 1941, see his comment on three papers on "Allied Leadership in the Second World War," including one by Dallek on Roosevelt, in *Survey* 21 (Winter–Spring 1975): esp. pp. 29–31. For Dallek's response, see Dallek, *Roosevelt*, p. 531.

[132] See, for example, Michael Howard, *The Causes of Wars and Other Essays* (London: Temple Smith, 1983), pp. 41–42, and Brian VanDeMark, *Into the Quagmire: Lyndon Johnson and the Escalation of the Vietnam War* (New York: Oxford University Press, 1991), pp. xiii–xiv.

[133] On the Cold War, the key body of evidence that convinced me that U.S. leaders were perfectly capable of thinking in realistic spheres of influence terms and of conducting a policy on that basis was United States Department of State, *Foreign Relations of the United States: The Conference of Berlin (The Potsdam Conference) 1945* (Washington, D.C.: GPO, 1960), vol. 2. On Vietnam, the two most important works showing that key U.S. leaders, and above all President Kennedy, were by no means prisoners of the U.S. Cold War ideology, are David Kaiser, *American Tragedy: Kennedy, Johnson, and the Origins of the Vietnam War* (Cambridge Mass.: Harvard University Press, 2000), and Fredrik Logevall, *Choosing War: The Lost Chance for Peace and the Escalation of War in Vietnam* (Berkeley: University of California Press, 1999).

interpretation of U.S. policy as a product of the American ideology with a grain of salt. But even if you were coming to the question without any general views in this area, you still might feel that you needed to come to terms with Schroeder's general argument about the basic taproot of American policy in 1941. The fundamental issue here is obviously of central importance. Was what Schroeder views as a mistaken approach to foreign policy so deeply embedded in American culture that U.S. leaders were simply incapable of thinking along different lines—incapable, that is, of thinking in realist terms?

One obvious way to explore that issue would be to see how these questions were debated, if at all, within the government. How much of a consensus was there? Did everyone take it for granted that policy had to be based on moral principle? In that context, it would make sense to look first at the advice Roosevelt was getting from his chief advisers—from Hull on the political side, and from Army Chief of Staff Marshall and Chief of Naval Operations Stark on the military side.

The case of Hull is of particular interest because the secretary of state is often portrayed as the administration's ideologue in chief. And yet Hull, you notice, when you read the relevant texts and documents with this specific issue in mind, was quite interested in reaching some kind of agreement with Japan and even thought that an acceptance of the Japanese position in Manchuria, a direct violation of American "principle," might be part of such an agreement.[134] In late 1941 Hull also thought it had been a mistake to reject the Konoye proposal for a leaders' conference and said he did not want to make that same kind of mistake a second time.[135] He was therefore quite serious about exploring the possibility of a modus vivendi. He in fact wanted to ignore Chinese and British objections and move ahead with the negotiations. When Roosevelt overruled him, Hull was livid. He really wanted to try to avoid war, and "taking a firm stand on principle" was not his preferred course of action.[136]

The advice Roosevelt was getting from America's top military officers also pointed toward a moderate policy toward Japan. The story of American

[134] See Halifax to Foreign Office (no. 4550), October 3, 1941, with minutes, FO 371/27910, *British Foreign Office: Japan Correspondence, 1941–1945*, series for 1941, reel 7. The point is alluded to in some historical works, but is scarcely given the kind of attention it deserves. See, for example, Heinrichs, *Threshold of War*, p. 193.

[135] Halifax to Foreign Office (no. 5380), November 25, 1941, para. 7, FO 371/27912, *British Foreign Office: Japan Correspondence, 1941–1945*, series for 1941, reel 8.

[136] Sherwood, *Roosevelt and Hopkins*, pp. 428–29; Blum, *Years of Urgency*, p. 387; and especially the evidence in John Costello, *Days of Infamy: MacArthur, Roosevelt, Churchill—The Shocking Truth Revealed: How Their Secret Deals and Strategic Blunders Caused Disasters at Pearl Harbor and the Philippines* (New York: Pocket Books, 1994), pp. 127–29, 388. This latter citation incidentally provides a good example of how even a not-very-scholarly book can be mined for important information on a key point.

strategic thinking in the year or so before Pearl Harbor, beginning with Admiral Stark's "Plan Dog" memorandum of November 12, 1940, and climaxing in the Joint Board's "Victory Program" of September 11, 1941, is of quite exceptional interest, and Mark Stoler gives a superb account in his book on U.S. grand strategy during the Second World War.[137] The information he gives is intriguing enough to make you want to look up the key documents and read them yourself. It is well known, of course, that the basic conclusion the strategists reached was that, in the event of war, the United States would be well advised to adopt a "Europe-first" strategy. But what was really important here for our present purposes is not that particular conclusion but the sort of thinking you find in those documents—the line of argument about what even prewar U.S. policy had to be.

The strategists' basic premise, and this was very much in line with Roosevelt's own thinking, was that the U.S. government could no longer afford to think in purely continental or even hemispheric terms. The United States, it was assumed, would not be secure if Britain collapsed and all of Europe fell under German control. A German superpower, the argument ran, in command of the resources of the entire continent of Europe, and no longer blocked by British naval power, would threaten the security of the Western Hemisphere. "A very strong pillar of the defense structure of the Americas," Stark wrote, "has, for many years, been the balance of power existing in Europe. The collapse of Great Britain or the destruction or surrender of the British Fleet will destroy this balance and will free European military power for possible encroachment in this hemisphere."[138] To be sure, a Germany triumphant in Europe might not want to go to war with America right away. After having conquered all of Europe, according to the authors of the Victory Program, Nazi Germany "might then wish to establish peace with the United States for several years, for the purpose of organizing her gains, restoring her economic situation, and increasing her military establishment." But in doing those things, the Germans would be preparing for "the eventual conquest of South America and the military defeat of the United States."[139] The whole analysis was framed in geopolitical terms. Indeed, this whole way of thinking was based very explicitly on a balance of power approach to the problem. A

[137] Stoler, *Allies and Adversaries*, chap. 2 and 3.

[138] "Plan Dog" memorandum, November 12, 1940, p. 19. This document is available online at the following URL: http://www.fdrlibrary.marist.edu/psf/box4/folo48.html.

[139] The "Victory Program" of September 11, 1941, officially entitled "Joint Board Estimate of United States Over-All Production Requirements," and signed by Army Chief of Staff George Marshall and Chief of Naval Operations Harold Stark, was published in *American War Plans, 1919–1941*, ed. Steven Ross, vol. 5 (New York: Garland, 1992), pp. 160–89 for the main study, and pp. 190–201 for the appended "Estimate of Army Ground Forces." The passage quoted here is on p. 4 of the main study, p. 163 in the Garland volume. Extensive quotations from the Victory Program also appear in Sherwood, *Roosevelt and Hopkins*, pp. 410–18.

major U.S. objective, according to the Victory Program, was the "eventual establishment in Europe and Asia of balances of power"; and Stark wrote that "a balance of power in the Far East is to our interest as much as is a balance of power in Europe."[140]

What all this implied to those military leaders was that the United States had to intervene in the war against Germany. Japan, being a lesser threat, could best be dealt with in a different way, so that American efforts could be focused on the German problem. Some officers involved in these discussions took the argument even further, and said (after Germany attacked the Soviet Union in June 1941) that America had to intervene not just to stop Germany, but to prevent any single power from dominating Eurasia. "Germany and Russia are fighting for world domination," one of them wrote, and "which ever wins will be a long way on the road to domination." That in turn would pose a grave threat to America: "*if any one power dominates Asia, Europe and Africa, our country will ultimately become a second class power even if we gain South America and the whole of North America*."[141] It was on the basis of this kind of thinking, which Roosevelt largely shared, that even officers of an isolationist bent (as Stoler points out) were coming to view U.S. intervention in the war against Germany as essential.[142]

An even more important point was that the United States would not just have to intervene massively—even if (and the logic of the argument would imply especially if) Britain were "completely defeated"[143]—but that America would have to intervene relatively *quickly*. The authors of the Victory Program were very worried that Germany would defeat the USSR, occupy much of that country, destroy the basis of remaining Soviet power through air attack on areas it did not occupy, and then gradually mobilize the resources of the areas under its control (in Russia and in the rest of Europe), thus building up its military power to quite extraordinary levels. But it would take a while before Germany's conquests in the east would lead to a dramatic expansion of German military power. According to the Victory Program, it would probably take "a full year to bring order out of chaos in the conquered areas," and Germany would not be able to profit economically even from a total defeat of Russia until mid-1943.[144] That meant that for the United States, a vital window of opportunity was now open. For America to wait until the Germans had their hands free in the east and had harnessed the resources of conquered Europe to their war machine would make its job much more difficult. It

[140] Victory Program, p. 3 (p. 162 in the Garland volume); "Plan Dog" memorandum, p. 3.

[141] Colonel Paul Robinett, of the army general staff, diary entry for September 12, 1941, quoted in Stoler, *Allies and Adversaries*, p. 50 (emphasis in original).

[142] See Stoler, *Allies and Adversaries*, pp. 49–50.

[143] Victory Program, p. 9 (p. 168 in the Garland volume).

[144] Victory Program appendix, "Estimate of Army Ground Forces," p. 4 (p. 193 in the Garland volume).

therefore made sense to opt for "a rapidly accelerated all-out effort with a view to conducting decisive, offensive operations against the enemy before he can liquidate or recoup from his struggle with Russia"; this was the only alternative to a "long drawn-out war of attrition."[145] "Time is of the essence," the authors of that key strategy document argued, and "the longer we delay effective offensive operations against the Axis, the more difficult will become the attainment of victory." "It is mandatory," they wrote, "that we reach an early appreciation of our stupendous task, and gain the whole-hearted support of the entire country in the production of trained men, ships, munitions, and ample reserves. Otherwise, we will be confronted in the not distant future by a Germany strongly intrenched economically, supported by newly acquired sources of vital supplies and industries, with her military forces operating on interior lines, and in a position of hegemony in Europe which will be comparatively easy to defend and maintain."[146]

U.S. military leaders thus took it for granted that the specter of a German-dominated Europe was the real threat that needed to be faced. The threat posed by Japan was in their view of purely secondary importance. If Germany were defeated, Japan would not pose much of a problem; indeed, following the defeat of Germany, a triumphant America would probably be able to get Japan to come to terms rather easily. (This, incidentally, was an argument Grew and Craigie had also made to support their own relatively moderate policy recommendations.)[147] The implication was that the western powers would be well advised to deal much more gently with Japan than with Germany. It was this kind of thinking that lay at the heart of the basic argument of the Victory Program, a conclusion reflected in the one passage that was underlined in the original document: *"the principal strategic method employed by the United States in the immediate future should be the material support of present military operations against Germany, and their reenforcement by active participation in the war by the United States, while holding Japan in check pending future developments."*[148] Admiral Stark, a year earlier, had also called for a "positive effort to avoid war with Japan."[149] The basic concept of a balance of power in Asia to his mind in fact implied that Japanese power did have an important

---

[145] Ibid., pp. 4–5 (pp. 193–94 in the Garland volume).

[146] Ibid. Stark also thought the country had to move quickly, and in fact told the president right after Germany had invaded Russia that he considered "every day of delay in our getting into the war as dangerous." Stark to Cooke, July 31, 1941, quoted in Feis, *Road to Pearl Harbor*, p. 240.

[147] Victory Program, p. 9 (p. 168 in the Garland volume); Craigie Report, para. 66, p. 153 in the *Confidential Print* volume cited in note. 80 above; Grew quoted in Langer and Gleason, *Undeclared War*, p. 849. "Why on earth should we rush headlong into war?" Grew asked. "When Hitler is defeated, as he eventually will be, the Japanese problem will solve itself."

[148] Victory Program, p. 10 (p. 169 in the Garland volume).

[149] "Plan Dog" memorandum, p. 25.

role to play in the East Asian political equation.[150] Again, Grew saw things much the same way. "While we would undoubtedly win in the end," he wrote Roosevelt in September 1941, "I question whether it is in our own interest to see an impoverished Japan reduced to the position of a third-rate Power."[151]

Given that whole way of thinking, it is scarcely surprising that the military authorities were opposed to the policy toward Japan the administration adopted at the end of July 1941. As Welles pointed out in August, "in the opinion of both the War and Navy Departments of the United States the chief objective in the Pacific for the time being should be the avoidance of war with Japan inasmuch as war between the United States and Japan at this time would not only tie up the major portion of if not the entire American fleet but would likewise create a very serious strain upon our military establishment and upon our productive activities at the very moment when these should be concentrated upon the Atlantic."[152] The undeclared naval war with Germany began the next month, and with the embargo the United States at that time also seemed to be heading toward war with Japan. The military leadership was deeply out of sympathy with that latter policy. "With hostilities in progress and escalating in the Atlantic," Stoler writes, "from a military perspective the president and the State Department seemed to be insanely willing to provoke a second war in the Pacific."[153] In November, during the modus vivendi discussions, the military leaders pleaded for U.S. flexibility. One key army officer told Hull on November 21 that it was a matter of "grave importance to the success of our war effort in Europe that we reach a *modus vivendi* with Japan."[154] The top commanders, Marshall and Stark, wanted to put off a war with Japan for at least a few months. As they told Roosevelt at that point, "the most essential thing now is to gain time."[155]

---

[150] Ibid., p. 3. See also Stoler, *Allies and Adversaries*, p. 30. The army went ever further. Its complaint about the "Plan Dog" memorandum was that Stark went too far in calling for the containment of Japan. Stoler, *Allies and Adversaries*, p. 33.

[151] Grew to Roosevelt, September 22, 1941, FRUS 1941, 4:469.

[152] Quoted in Hearden, *Roosevelt Confronts Hitler*, p. 213.

[153] Stoler, *Allies and Adversaries*, p. 58. Admiral Stark's view, however, was a bit more nuanced than this quotation might suggest. In a September 1941 memorandum—a document which Sherwood says "was highly refreshing to the President"—Stark said that in his opinion "the United States should enter the war against Germany as soon as possible, even if hostilities with Japan must be accepted." The argument was not that the U.S. government should pursue a provocative policy vis-à-vis Japan if that was the only way of getting into the European war quickly. Stark's point was simply that since Germany and Japan were allies, Japan might feel obliged to go to war against America if the United States declared war on Germany—but that the U.S. government should not hold back for that reason. The quotation, however, does suggest that in Stark's view a war with Japan would not be a total disaster if it brought the United States into the war with Germany. For a long extract from the document, see Sherwood, *Roosevelt and Hopkins*, pp. 379–80.

[154] Heinrichs, *Threshold of War*, p. 213.

[155] Stoler, *Allies and Adversaries*, p. 61.

So you can see how you can assess one fundamental and very influential interpretation of American policy, the idea that policy makers were prisoners of America's liberal ideology, that they had to stand up for their moral beliefs, and that they were incapable of conducting a policy based on realist principles. It turns out that the range of choices was much wider than you had been led to believe, that key policy makers were perfectly capable of thinking in balance of power terms, and indeed that strategic realities played such a fundamental role in shaping thinking that even officers of an isolationist bent were drawn toward a strong interventionist policy.

But where does all this get us, in terms of the larger problem? The goal is to understand American policy in late 1941. If Schroeder's explanation does not really stand up, how *is* U.S. policy toward Japan to be interpreted? After all, there has to be *some* explanation for what the U.S. government was doing, *some* reason why the U.S. government was not willing to settle for a policy of containment. You weigh the possible explanations against each other, assessing them not just in terms of the direct evidence but also in terms of their basic plausibility. Was Roosevelt, for example, simply fed up with Japanese aggression? Was it for that reason that he opted for a hard line—that is, for a policy that led directly to war? You assess the basic plausibility of that sort of interpretation. At a time when Roosevelt was moving toward war with Germany, would he have wanted a second war with Japan—a Japan willing to accommodate to American power and forgo further expansion—simply because he was fed up with that country? Someone with real political sense would never behave in that way, and it is quite clear that Roosevelt *had* political sense. That interpretation is just not plausible. So by a process of elimination, you are pushed toward the conclusion that his policy toward Japan has to be understood in the context of his policy toward the far more important problem of the European war.

It's in that way that you go about getting a handle on the key historical problem of explaining U.S. policy in late 1941. You make your own judgment about whether the basic view laid out in documents like the Victory Program made sense. Suppose you think it did, and suppose you think it was so compelling that Roosevelt could not possibly have dismissed it out of hand. The president, after all, agreed that Germany was the main problem, and he clearly wanted to take the United States into the European war. Why then would he have wanted to fight a second war against Japan? Why didn't he limit America's East Asia policy to a simple policy of containment? The military leaders had drawn the conclusion that America should do no more than keep Japan in check. That conclusion followed logically from their basic analysis of the geopolitical problem the United States faced. That argument seems compelling, and Roosevelt shared many of the geopolitical premises on which it was based. And yet he did not draw the same conclusion as the military leaders. He did not, in the final analysis, opt for a policy of simply containing Japan. One has to assume, especially given the cogency of the argument that the military authorities were making, that that policy decision could not have been made frivolously. Given the seriousness of these problems, Roosevelt would have had to think these matters through with great care. So *something* must have come into play that for him tipped the balance in the opposite direction, *something* that the military leaders had not taken into account when drawing their own conclusions about what America's Japan policy should be. What then could that *something* actually be?

Is it out of the question that Roosevelt not only accepted the argument of the Victory Program but took it one step further? Perhaps Roosevelt agreed that America had to be brought into the war against Germany quickly, but given public opinion at home and given Hitler's unwillingness to opt for war in response to what the U.S. Navy was doing in the Atlantic, he calculated that the only way the United States could be brought in quickly enough was by taking advantage of the situation with Japan? The very notion, of course, that Roosevelt's Japan policy was rooted in a desire to take the United States into the European war through the "back door" is generally dismissed out of hand by serious scholars, even by those historians who are quite critical of U.S. behavior in the months before Pearl Harbor.[156] It is tainted by its association with the absurd and baseless charge that Roosevelt had arranged things so that the American forces at Pearl Harbor would be the victims of a Japanese surprise attack—that he did so in order to bring an angry, unified, and vengeful nation into the war. But the baselessness of that particular claim does not mean that the more general argument about Roosevelt possibly using the East Asian situation as a way of bringing America into the European war is not worth taking seriously. Isn't that possibility, you might think, worth considering on its own terms?

But how do you go about figuring out what to make of the back-door argument? Your analysis so far might give you a certain basis for taking that argument seriously, but to form a more solid opinion you need to go into the question in greater depth. You are not going to find direct evidence bearing on the issue. No document will turn up showing Roosevelt saying, in effect, "I am pursuing this policy toward Japan because it is the only policy that will bring America into the war against Germany quickly enough." If any such document existed, you would certainly have heard about it already.[157] And if Roosevelt had *not* opted for his Japan policy for that reason, that negative

[156] Schroeder, *Axis Alliance*, pp. 182, 202–03

[157] It is not inconceivable, however, that direct evidence bearing on the question will eventually become available. Certain still-classified British materials, including a copy of one of the two telegrams Churchill sent Roosevelt on November 26, 1941, might, for example, shed some light on the issue. See Warren Kimball, *Forged in War: Roosevelt, Churchill, and the Second World War* (New York: William Morrow, 1997), p. 357 n. 3. Kimball refers here to the way the withholding of that body of material has fueled speculation about Churchill's role in this affair, and he alludes

point could scarcely be proved by direct evidence. So you have no choice but to look for indirect evidence—for straws in the wind that might have some bearing on the issue. If you get enough evidence of that sort, you might be able to arrive at some kind of conclusion, and how much confidence you have in that conclusion will depend on how strong that mass of evidence is.

How then do you do that kind of work? One way is by identifying specific arguments relating to the back-door theory and then by examining those arguments in the light of the evidence most directly related to the issues at hand. It is sometimes said, for example, that Roosevelt could scarcely have opted for a back-door strategy since he had no way of knowing what Germany would do if Japan attacked the United States. That argument is based on a particular assumption about what Roosevelt knew. So to get at the issue, you'll want to see whether that assumption is well founded. You'll want to look into the question of what Roosevelt thought Germany would do if America and Japan went to war, and you'll want to look in particular at the intelligence side of the story. What assurances, if any, was Germany giving Japan, and what did U.S. intelligence know about what the Germans were saying?

So you look for works that might throw some light on these relatively narrow questions. One source that turns up quickly is the volume Ernest May edited on strategic intelligence before the two world wars.[158] The title of David Kahn's article in that volume, "United States Views of Germany and Japan in 1941," suggests that that essay might give you the information you are looking for. Kahn, as you might already know if you have been working in this field for any length of time, is a leading authority on code-breaking and signals intelligence, and given his eminence you might be tempted to take his judgment as definitive. Kahn says that Hitler's decision to declare war on America "was unpremeditated and partly irrational, precipitated by the Pearl Harbor attack. There was therefore no way in which any intelligence agency could have obtained foreknowledge of it."[159] The first solid intelligence on Hitler's intentions, he says, came only on December 8, the day after the Pearl Harbor attack. If Kahn is right in this regard, that would pose a major problem for the back-door theory. And you are inclined to think that Kahn must know what he is talking about.

But for something this important, you wouldn't want to just leave it at that. It makes sense to cast a wider net. So you explore the literature on strategic intelligence. You identify a number of other accounts likely to have

in particular to the account given in James Rusbridger and Eric Nave, *Betrayal at Pearl Harbor: How Churchill Lured Roosevelt into World War II* (New York: Summit Books, 1991); the passage relating to the Churchill telegram is on p. 141 in that book.

[158] Ernest May, ed., *Knowing One's Enemies: Intelligence Assessment before the Two World Wars* (Princeton: Princeton University Press, 1984).

[159] Ibid., p. 496.

relevant information. F. H. Hinsley's very detailed official study of *British Intelligence in the Second World War* seems to be of fundamental importance, so you get it and look up the section bearing on this issue. You quickly note that Hinsley's account is very different from Kahn's. "Germany's response to Pearl Harbour," Hinsley says, "came as no surprise. In August 1941 the Japanese Ambassador in Berlin had reported to Tokyo a conversation in which Hitler had assured him that 'in the event of a collision between Japan and the United States Germany would at once open hostilities with the United States'"; that decrypt, Churchill was informed, had also been sent on to Washington.[160] Hitler, you note from other accounts, had probably given those assurances in order to stiffen the Japanese in their dealings with America. He knew about the U.S.-Japanese talks that were going on and was worried about the prospect of a settlement between those two countries.[161] This point you file away in the back of your mind. It may be important later on as you try to construct the larger story of what was going on in this period.

You might be able to supplement the Hinsley evidence with other evidence you find in the literature dealing with strategic intelligence in this period. It turns out, for example, that in early November, U.S. authorities received important information from Germany's acting ambassador in Washington, Hans Thomsen, who was working as an American informant. Thomsen told the Americans that if war broke out between America and Japan, Germany would declare war on the United States.[162] The signals intercepts yielded additional evidence. Some scholars refer to a very specific assurance that Germany's foreign minister, Ribbentrop, gave the Japanese ambassador in Berlin in late November.[163] In light of that information, it is reasonable to suppose that Roosevelt calculated (at least at some point before Pearl Harbor) that if Japan attacked the United States, Hitler for his part would also, in all probability, go to war with America.

But what does all this actually prove? A critic of the back-door theory might have little trouble responding to everything that has been said so far. Yes, that critic would say, the Americans *eventually* found out about the assurances, but Roosevelt had opted for a hard line toward Japan well *before* he had any of this information about what Germany would do. And if he had no way of knowing in July 1941 what Germany would do in the event of a U.S.-Japanese war, how then can the policy he adopted at that time be understood

---

[160] F. H. Hinsley, *British Intelligence in the Second World War: Its Influence on Strategy and Operations*, vol. 2 (London: HMSO, 1981), p. 75. Carl Boyd, in his book *Hitler's Japanese Confidant: General Oshima Hiroshi and MAGIC Intelligence, 1941–1945* (Lawrence: University Press of Kansas, 1993), p. 31, also quotes from the decrypt, which he found in the U.S. National Archives.

[161] See, for example, Boyd, *Oshima*, p. 32.

[162] Anthony Cave Brown, *The Last Hero: Wild Bill Donovan* (New York: Vintage, 1982), p. 191.

[163] See, for example, Boyd, *Oshima*, p. 35; Weinberg, *World at Arms*, p. 1001 n. 298; and Sherwood, *Roosevelt and Hopkins*, p. 441.

in terms of his supposed desire to take the United States into the European war through the back door? That point calls for a response. You think about the issue. Does this line of argument really discredit the back-door theory? Roosevelt, you agree, probably did not know when the embargo was imposed in late July what Germany would do if Japan attacked the United States, but at that point he was not irrevocably committing himself to anything. The situation, you assume, would certainly be monitored as the crisis with Japan deepened, and policy toward Japan could be relaxed if it was not producing the "right" results from the "back door" point of view—that is, if it looked like Germany was going to stay out of a U.S.-Japanese war. In other words, this counterargument would run, the initial policy choice in July was not in itself decisive. That policy could have been altered at any point. What was of fundamental importance was that the policy was maintained intact. And the fact that it was maintained intact might have had something to do with what the U.S. government was learning from the intercepts: it chose to stay the course after finding out about what the Germans had promised Japan.

So the back-door theory is able to clear a certain hurdle, but there's a second line of argument you still have to consider. This time the issue is not whether (and when) German promises were made, but rather how seriously those promises were to be taken. Could the Americans really be certain that Hitler would not renege on his promises to Japan, no matter what commitments he had made? If there was a real chance that Hitler would not keep his word—and no one viewed him as a man of honor—wouldn't a back-door strategy have been too risky from Roosevelt's point of view for that reason alone? And the greater the risk that Germany would stay out of a U.S.-Japanese war, the less plausible the back-door theory would be.

You deal with that problem again by focusing on a key assumption—in this case, on the idea that a back-door strategy could work only if *Hitler* decided to intervene in a U.S.-Japanese war. But wasn't it possible that the decision for war might be made by the *Americans*—that if Japan attacked the United States, Roosevelt might have been able to use the occasion to take America into the war against Germany, whether Hitler declared war on the United States or not? You then ask yourself whether you've seen any evidence bearing on this question, and perhaps you do recall certain pieces of evidence. You might remember, for example, that the U.S. government had evidently decided by early 1941 that if war broke out with Japan, the United States would (in the words of one key document) "at once engage in war with Germany and Italy."[164] If that was U.S. policy, doesn't that mean that a

[164] Leutze, *Bargaining for Supremacy*, pp. 225, 242. Note also the extract from a staff paper of January 1941 that served as the basis for the military talks that began that month with the British: "if forced into a war with Japan, the United States should, at the same time, enter the war in the Atlantic." Quoted in George Dyer, *The Amphibians Came to Conquer: The Story of*

German declaration of war was perhaps not nearly as important as you had been led to believe?

But here again you have to consider a counterargument: even if Roosevelt would have liked to pursue such a policy, could he have pulled it off, given political realities in the United States at the time? Could he really have gotten the country to go to war with Germany after a Japanese attack, if Hitler at that point refused to declare war on America? That's clearly an important question, so you look for evidence that might help you answer it. It turns out there's a book called *Hitler Attacks Pearl Harbor: Why the United States Declared War on Germany*, which, as you can tell from the reviews and the discussion in H-Diplo, the email discussion network for diplomatic historians, deals with this very issue. It's not a very good book, but it does present some interesting evidence on American opinion in December 1941. Among other things, the author shows that according to a Gallup poll taken after Pearl Harbor but before the German declaration of war four days later, 90 percent of those polled favored a U.S. declaration of war on Germany.

But the views that came to the surface in the immediate post–Pearl Harbor period did not just emerge out of nowhere. The idea that the Japanese were in league with Hitler had been in place for some time. According to Paul Schroeder, the signing of the Tripartite Pact was of fundamental importance in this context. That agreement, signed by Germany, Japan, and Italy in September 1940, "caused a profound hardening of American opinion toward Japan—a once-for-all identification of the Empire with the Axis, with Hitler and the whole program of world conquest and the menace of aggression which America was sure he represented." The Axis alliance, in fact, came to be seen as much tighter than it actually was. And it was in large part for that reason that Pearl Harbor was widely blamed on the Axis as a whole. Indeed, many people throughout the country—a lot more than you might have thought—were convinced at the time of the Pearl Harbor attack that the Japanese were "Hitler's puppets."[165] And Roosevelt, of course, would not have been unaware of something this basic. It is safe to assume that he would have taken those popular beliefs and attitudes into account when deciding on a particular course of action. He might well have reached the conclusion that Germany would not be able to stay out of a U.S.-Japanese war, no matter

---

Admiral Richard Kelly Turner (Washington, D.C.: U.S. Marine Corps, 1991), pp. 159–60. Roosevelt approved and actually even edited that document. See Simpson, *Stark*, pp. 75–76, and Eric Larrabee, *Commander in Chief: Franklin Delano Roosevelt, His Lieutenants, and Their War* (New York: Harper and Row, 1987), p. 50.

[165] Schroeder, *Axis Alliance*, pp. 22–23. Richard F. Hill, *Hitler Attacks Pearl Harbor: Why the United States Declared War on Germany* (Boulder, colo.: Lynne Rienner, 2003), p. 209 n. 37 (the Gallup poll) and chap. 6 (for the evidence on the common view in December 1941 that the Japanese were "Hitler's puppets"—the phrase itself is from a December 8 *Washington Post* article cited on p. 114).

what decision Hitler made. And what this means is that a back-door strategy, if that is what it was, might well have been workable in that political context.[166]

So you've made certain judgments. You've considered certain arguments against the back-door theory and you've reached certain conclusions. But the core historical problem hasn't really been resolved. You certainly haven't been able to come up with anything that actually proves Roosevelt was pursuing a back-door strategy. So in a sense you're no further along than you had been when you first started to consider those anti-back-door arguments. And yet it's not as though this exercise was entirely worthless. You've obviously learned something, and what you've learned gets factored in as your general understanding of what was going on in 1941 takes shape.

When you're working out an interpretation, you have to do many exercises of this sort. There are all kinds of relatively narrow issues you need to concern yourself with. What, for example, can you find out about Roosevelt's general political style? Was he the type of person who was capable of behaving in a relatively Machiavellian way? That sort of issue has an obvious bearing on the question at hand, but can you find evidence that might shed some light on that issue? You might remember from some of the historical works you've read that Roosevelt was certainly capable at times of maneuvering for advantage. In the talks with Japan, he was willing to "baby" the Japanese, to string them along, to "play for time."[167] Secretary of War Stimson, in a widely quoted October 16 diary entry, referred to a meeting Roosevelt had called at the White House that day to consider the Japan problem: "and so we face the delicate question of the diplomatic fencing to be done so as to be sure that Japan was put into the wrong and made the first bad move—overt move."[168] In another frequently cited diary entry, Stimson quoted Roosevelt as saying on November 25 that "the question was how we should maneuver them [the Japanese] into the position of firing the first shot without allowing too much danger to ourselves."[169] Such comments, of course, do not prove that Roosevelt thought that such maneuvering was needed to bring on an otherwise avoidable war with Japan.[170] He might have thought war was inevitable

---

[166] It should also be noted in this connection that U.S. leaders apparently took it for granted, right after the Pearl Harbor attack, that war with Germany was imminent. They were in fact relieved by this prospect and were not particularly worried about whether Hitler would actually declare war on America. See Sherwood, *Roosevelt and Hopkins*, p. 172.

[167] On the issue of "babying" the Japanese, see FRUS 1941, 4:372–74. On "playing for time," note the Hugh Dalton diary, entry for August 26, 1941, in *The Churchill War Papers*, ed. Martin Gilbert, vol. 3 (London: Heinemann, 2000), p. 1111.

[168] Henry Lewis Stimson Diaries [microfilm edition] (New Haven: Yale University Library, 1973), entry for October 16, 1941.

[169] Ibid., entry for November 25, 1941.

[170] See Richard N. Current, "How Stimson Meant to 'Maneuver' the Japanese," *Mississippi Valley Historical Review* 40, no. 1 (June 1953): 67–74. Note also Langer and Gleason, *Undeclared War*, p. 886; and Dallek, *Roosevelt*, pp. 303–04, 307.

and simply wanted to be sure that it began in what was for America the best way. But there is one key piece of evidence suggesting quite clearly that he did want to maneuver the *Germans* into war. This is the record of what Roosevelt told Churchill at the Atlantic Conference on August 19: as I noted, the president said there that "he would wage war, but not declare it, and that he would become more and more provocative. If the Germans did not like it, they could attack American forces."[171] What this evidence shows is that U.S. leaders were perfectly capable of thinking in tactical terms—of maneuvering, of calculating, of pursuing their objectives in a less-than-absolutely-straightforward way.

Roosevelt's reaction to the Pearl Harbor attack is another important indicator. The president had been worried that the Japanese would limit their attack to British and Dutch possessions and avoid contact with American forces. He knew that in such circumstances it might be hard for him to bring the American people into the war with Japan. "Hence his great relief," as his close adviser Harry Hopkins put it a few weeks later, "at the method Japan used."[172] When the news of the Pearl Harbor attack was received, the president called a meeting of his top advisers. "The conference met in not too tense an atmosphere," Hopkins wrote, "because I think that all of us believed that in the last analysis the enemy was Hitler and that he could never be defeated without force of arms; that sooner or later we were bound to be in the war and that Japan had given us an opportunity."[173] This is not quite the same as saying that Roosevelt had deliberately taken advantage of the Far Eastern situation to bring the country into the European war, but it does suggest that U.S. leaders were pleased by the way things had developed—by the situation which, as they well knew, their own policy had played a key role in producing.[174]

Churchill's attitude at this point is another indicator. The British prime minister was elated by the news of the Pearl Harbor attack. "So we had won after

---

[171] Quoted in Reynolds, *Anglo-American Alliance*, p. 214.

[172] Sherwood, *Roosevelt and Hopkins*, pp. 428–31. For additional evidence on Roosevelt's reaction, see Dallek, *Roosevelt*, p. 311.

[173] Sherwood, *Roosevelt and Hopkins*, p. 431. Note that this also shows that his top advisers, well before Hitler's declaration of war, took it for granted that America would soon be at war with Germany. That might have been a war the United States would have initiated, with Roosevelt taking advantage of popular anger about Pearl Harbor to get the Congress to declare war on Germany. But privy to the intelligence about Hitler's intentions, the government decided to wait for a German declaration of war, which in fact came a few days later. See Hearden, *Roosevelt Confronts Hitler*, p. 221.

[174] Stimson's attitude on the eve of the war is also worth noting in this context. On December 2, knowing that things seemed to be coming to a head, he told Chiang Kai-shek's representative in Washington to tell the Chinese leader "to have just a little more patience, and then I think all things will be well." In context, what this suggests is that the coming of war (through a Japanese attack) was to be welcomed. Quoted in Thorne, *Allies of a Kind*, pp. 83–84; for the original source, see the Stimson Diaries, reel 7, entry for December 2, 1941.

all!" he thought. "Hitler's fate was sealed." "Being saturated and satiated with emotion and sensation," he wrote, "I went to bed and slept the sleep of the saved and thankful."[175] The day after the Pearl Harbor attack, he "was in highest spirits at America and Japan."[176] He later wrote that Craigie's argument that war with Japan could have been avoided was entirely off-base because it was a "blessing that Japan attacked the United States and thus brought America wholeheartedly into the war."[177] Again, this does not prove that Churchill had pressed for a hard-line policy toward Japan with the goal of bringing the United States into the European war, but it does point in that direction.

Churchill's principal objective throughout 1941 had, of course, been to bring the United States into the war against Germany.[178] Ideally he would have loved to bring America in without America and Britain having to fight a war with Japan at the same time. As he put it at the time, that outcome would have been the "first prize." But a war in which America and Britain fought both Japan and Germany was the "second prize," better in his view than if both countries were to remain at peace with Japan, but with America staying out of the European war.[179] And on the principle that a bird in the hand was worth two in the bush, Churchill was prepared to do what he could to land that second prize. At a war cabinet meeting on October 2, Churchill "questioned the statement that it was not in our interests that the United States should be involved in war in the Pacific."[180] Although hesitant at times—there was always the risk that Japan might attack just the British and Dutch possessions and leave the Americans alone—his government in the final analysis therefore pressed for a relatively tough policy toward Japan and played a key role in sabotaging the plan for a modus vivendi.[181] The net effect of British policy was thus to help the British achieve their fundamental goal of bringing the United States into the war. You then wonder whether this was simply a coincidence. Given your understanding of the way governments operate, you might find it hard to believe that an element of calculation was not involved.

The point is important for our purposes because a study of *British* policy can provide a certain window into *American* thinking. If you think the two

[175] Quoted in Dallek, *Roosevelt*, p. 312. See also Foreign Secretary Eden's account in *Churchill War Papers*, 3:1579.

[176] Oliver Harvey diary, entry for December 8, 1941, *Churchill War Papers*, 3:1586.

[177] Quoted in Thorne, *Allies of a Kind*, p. 75.

[178] See Leutze, *Bargaining for Supremacy*, p. 241.

[179] Charles Eade, notes of a luncheon with Churchill, November 19, 1941, *Churchill War Papers*, 3:1474. See also War Cabinet minutes, confidential annex, November 12, 1941, ibid., p. 1445.

[180] Peter Lowe, *Great Britain and the Origins of the Pacific War* (Oxford: Clarendon, 1977), p. 173

[181] See, for example, ibid., pp. 260–61. One of the key documents in this episode, Chiang Kai-shek's letter of protest, was later said by the British ambassador to China "to have been drafted by him." Thorne, *Allies of a Kind*, p. 70n.

countries' core interests were essentially the same, and if you think that Roosevelt and Churchill, taking those common interests as their point of departure, had basically come to share the same general view about how things were to be managed, then the evidence on Churchill's thinking about a war with Japan does feed into an overall estimate of what Roosevelt was trying to do. By looking at what the British were thinking, you can perhaps get some insight into what American policy was. The impression you get from the British sources is thus one of the indicators you can take into account in deciding how to interpret what the Americans were doing.

It's in that way that you gradually form your own opinion. In the absence of strong direct evidence, you proceed as best you can. The indirect evidence is suggestive rather than compelling. You look at a particular straw in the wind, and in itself it may prove nothing. But if you gather enough evidence of this sort, you're able to assess the plausibility of a given argument. Every small brushstroke makes a difference and gradually a larger picture takes shape.

THE LARGER STORY

Suppose you reach the conclusion that Roosevelt used the situation with Japan as a way of bringing the United States into the European war. This conclusion is important for a all sorts of reasons. If true, it tells you something fundamental about the nature of U.S. policy—namely, that geopolitical imperatives can play a truly decisive role in shaping American behavior. It might also have certain broader implications about international politics as a whole. It might suggest that, as a general rule, war is to be understood as the outcome of a political process rather than as the product of aggression pure and simple: if, even in the case of a conflict with countries as aggressive as Germany and Japan in 1941, the decision to go to war with America is not to be viewed as a "gratuitous" act, then war in general is not to be understood as resulting from a simple decision on the part of the aggressor power to start one.

But as important as that conclusion about Roosevelt's East Asian policy is, it's just one element in a much broader interpretative structure. It's not as though you just reach that conclusion and the analysis stops. You've constructed a building block which then has to be lowered into place. The conclusion about Roosevelt has to be fit into a larger argument about what was going on in the world of the great powers not just in late 1941 but in a longer period—the period, say, from September 1939 to December 1941.

In constructing that broader interpretation, one question leads to another. If you think that Roosevelt in 1941 wanted to bring the United States into the war against Germany (and put America on a collision course with Japan as a means of doing so), you then have to think about why he opted for that policy. What did it have to do with his understanding of German policy?

What was his view of Hitler's long-term goals, and how exactly did that view take shape? These questions lead to yet further questions about Hitler, about what *his* goals were, and about what his plans were for achieving them. Did he think that if he won in Europe, a struggle with America for world domination would be inevitable? If he did sometimes talk in that vein, are such remarks to be dismissed as idle speculation, or was he seriously contemplating war with the United States in the not-too-distant future?

Such issues are studiable in the usual way. You look to see what historians say, and you try to assess those arguments in terms both of their internal logic and of the adequacy of the evidence supporting them. Some scholars argue that Hitler did not intend in his lifetime to enter into such a struggle with America, and that in his view the war between the United States and Germany for world domination would take place only in the "dim, indefinite" future.[182] Others take a different view, and once again you wonder who is right. You make an assessment based on the preponderance of the evidence cited, and it turns out that some of the most crucial evidence has to do with Hitler's armaments policy. Even before the war broke out in Europe, Hitler, it seems, had decided to prepare for a major conflict with the United States. A great oceangoing navy and a powerful long-range air force were to be built. "The naval programme," Richard Overy notes, "and the strategic bomber plans, including the 'Amerikabomber' which Messerschmidt began work on in 1939, and the range of advanced technological projects on which German research was working, all indicate clearly the drift of Hitler's strategy"; the "major programmes" were to be "completed by 1943–5."[183] The plans had to be put aside when, contrary to Hitler's wishes, war broke out prematurely in September 1939. But whenever it looked like the war in Europe would soon be over—after the defeat of France in June 1940 and then again in July 1941 when it looked like Russia would soon collapse—Hitler revived preparations for a final confrontation with America.[184] This suggests that Hitler did think that matters would come to a head with America not in the distant future but

---

[182] Meir Michaelis, "World Power Status or World Dominion? A Survey of the Literature on Hitler's 'Plan of World Dominion' (1937–1970)," *Historical Journal* 15, no. 2 (June 1972): 352; see also pp. 353, 359.

[183] Richard Overy, *War and Economy in the Third Reich* (Oxford: Clarendon, 1994), pp. 194–95. It is important to note in this context that the United States had also begun to develop an intercontinental bomber (what would eventually become the B-36) before it went to war with Germany. On the origins of the B-36 program, see Robert Lovett's testimony in 81st Cong., 1st sess., House Armed Services Committee hearings, *Investigation of the B-36 Bomber Program* (Washington, D.C.: GPO, 1949), pp. 24–26.

[184] Overy, *War and Economy*, pp. 194–95; Richard Overy (with Andrew Wheatcroft), *The Road to War* (London: Macmillan, 1989), p. 282; Andreas Hillgruber, "Der Faktor Amerika in Hitlers Strategie 1938–1941," *Aus Politik und Zeitgeschichte* (supplement to *Das Parlament*), May 11, 1966, p. 507; and Weinberg, *World at Arms*, pp. 86, 238–39, 250.

in the course of the next few years—preferably not right away, but after his European enemies had been crushed and he had built up his own military strength to a level that would enable him to take on the world's greatest industrial power, say by 1943–45.

Learning about Hitler's goals then helps bring the questions about America into focus. How did Roosevelt view the problem? What did the president know about Hitler's intentions and in particular about German armaments policy? There are many indications that the president was worried about the threat Germany would pose if it conquered all of Europe and was able to mobilize the vast resources of that continent—indeed, that he was worried about how the United States would fare if war with a triumphant Germany broke out at some future point.[185]

Clearly, the sense that their core interests were imperiled pushed the Americans toward intervention. But wouldn't the growing specter of American involvement inevitably affect *Hitler's* calculations? With that question in mind, you look at the literature on Hitler's policy during the war and, in particular, at the literature on his decision to attack the USSR. That question helps you draw out one key point buried in that literature: you note that his decision in 1940 to attack the Soviet Union the following spring was evidently rooted at least in part in his sense that America was growing stronger and more determined to enter the war and that time was working against him. His own "window of opportunity," that is, was closing rapidly; all continental European problems had to be solved in 1941, he said, "because beginning in 1942, the USA will be in a position to intervene."[186] But if Russia was conquered, Germany, with no power in the east to worry about and with the vast resources of virtually the entire continent of Europe under its control, would be in a position to deal with the United States.[187] Window logic, it seems, was thus a major factor in shaping *both sides'* policies. The prospect of an enormous growth of German power in the near future, as

---

[185] Note in this connection Sherwood, *Roosevelt and Hopkins*, pp. 125–26. See also Joseph C. Harsh, "The 'Unbelievable' Nazi Blueprint," *New York Times Magazine*, May 25, 1941, with key passages marked up by hand, almost certainly by President Roosevelt himself (http://www.fdrlibrary.marist.edu/psf/box31/a296L01.html). In assessing the impact on Roosevelt of the Harsh article, one notes that the president picked up on one of Harsh's arguments—the point that *Japan* would be threatened by a German triumph in Eurasia, and thus had a certain geopolitical interest in joining with America to resist Germany—and used it in a meeting with the Japanese ambassador on July 24, 1941 (FRUS Japan 2:530). This is a typical "straw in the wind" that you use to reach at least tentative conclusions on such issues.

[186] Quoted in Hillgruber, "Faktor Amerika," p. 515, and in R.A.C. Parker, *Struggle for Survival: The History of the Second World War* (Oxford: Oxford University Press, 1989), p. 63. Hitler had also argued along these lines on November 4, 1940. Barry Leach, *German Strategy against Russia, 1939–1941* (Oxford: Clarendon, 1973), p. 77n.

[187] Antony Read and David Fisher, *The Deadly Embrace: Hitler, Stalin and the Nazi-Soviet Pact, 1939–1941* (New York: Norton, 1988), p. 549. See also Weinberg, *World at Arms*, pp. 204–05.

the Germans mobilized the resources first of central and western Europe and then even of the Russian heartland, spurred on the Americans, and the prospect of American intervention played a key role in pushing Germany forward.

"Window logic"? Where did *that* come from? The term refers to the sorts of pressures that result from the opening and closing of "windows of vulnerability" and "windows of opportunity"—from the calculations generated by the sense that the strategic balance is moving in one way or another, from the sense, for example, that it might be a question of "now or never" and that it might be important to act before it is too late. You can see this kind of logic at work when you study in the pre–Pearl Harbor period, but the term itself comes from international relations theory. The concept plays a key role in the writings of contemporary international relations theorists like Stephen Van Evera and Dale Copeland.[188] And you can see from this one case why it pays for the historian to develop a certain familiarity with that body of thought. If you've been exposed to these sorts of arguments and then come across a document like the Victory Program, it's as though a bell is rung. The key historical points are more likely to register in your mind. You're more likely to say, "this is important, this really matters." You're much better able to understand the larger significance of the sort of thinking laid out in such documents than if you had come to the issue cold, without any exposure to this literature at all.

With a prepared mind, you're thus much better able to see the sort of logic that was at play. But you can't just stop at that point. You're aware of the relative thinness of the evidence on which this sort of interpretation is based, and you want, if you can, to build on a much more solid foundation. So you need to flesh out that basic interpretation and develop it in much greater depth. You need to look at the specific areas in which that sort of logic might have come into play—for example, German armaments (and especially air and naval) policy, or German policy toward northwest Africa and the islands in the eastern and mid-Atlantic (Madeira, the Azores, and the Canary and Cape Verde islands). In each case, you would like to see what the Germans were doing in those areas and the extent to which their efforts were directed against the United States. In particular, you would like to know the degree to which they were preparing for what they saw, and indeed could rationally see, as a growing American threat to their position in Europe. So you look at the literature, for example, on German policy toward northwest Africa and the Atlantic islands—especially Norman Goda's *Tomorrow the World*—and you are struck by the fact that German policy in this area was shaped by a mix of

---

[188] See Stephen Van Evera, *Causes of War: Power and the Roots of Conflict* (Ithaca: Cornell University Press, 1999), esp. chap. 4, and Dale Copeland, *The Origins of Major War* (Ithaca: Cornell University Press, 2000).

offensive and defensive considerations vis-à-vis America.[189] And again if you've been exposed to international relations theory—in this case, to a well-known line of argument developed by Robert Jervis—you're in a better position to deal with some of these issues: you understand something about what happens in a situation in which offensive and defensive strategies cannot be distinguished from each other.[190]

Of course, you can't just limit yourself to an examination of the German side of the story. The key issue that lies at the heart of this kind of interpretation is the degree to which the two sides influenced each other. So you have to ask the same kinds of questions about American policy as you ask about German policy. To what extent was Roosevelt, in moving ahead with an active policy in these areas, essentially trying to beat the Germans to the punch?[191] This is the sort of issue you can try to get at by studying American sources. What did Roosevelt know about what the Germans were doing with regard to northwest Africa and the Atlantic islands? What did he think their intentions in this area were? How did he interpret whatever evidence he had? Did he fit it into some sort of larger interpretative framework? Did he, for example, link Germany's interest in that area (and especially in Dakar) to German designs on Latin America (given how close Brazil was to the west African bulge)? To what extent was he thinking of the need to preempt a possible German move into northwest Africa and the islands? To what extent, that is, did he think it was important to move before it was too late? All these questions are open to study, and in fact those questions frame the research effort. And because they are the product of this sort of thought process, the way they are answered will give you insight into some really fundamental historical and indeed theoretical issues.

Once sensitized to the importance of window logic, moreover, you naturally pay particular attention when you see historians arguing along those

[189] Norman Goda, *Tomorrow the World: Hitler, Northwest Africa, and the Path toward America* (College Station: Texas A&M University Press, 1998), esp. pp. 67, 69, 177, 195–96. How, incidentally, can you identify a work of this sort? Just use your library's search engine, and search for titles including the words "Hitler" (or "Nazi" or even "Germany") and "Africa." Note also that once you have identified this single work, you can then do more extensive study by looking up various works cited in Goda's superb bibliography.

[190] See especially Robert Jervis, "Cooperation under the Security Dilemma," *World Politics* 30, no. 2 (January 1978): esp. pp. 199–206. The indistinguishability problem was particularly acute in the area of air strategy, since defense against air attack could be achieved most effectively by the "destruction of enemy aviation at its bases," as a March 1939 U.S. Army Air Corps memorandum put it. The effect was that each side in a conflict would be led to reach for aircraft of greater and greater range, meaning that it would be increasingly difficult to infer strategic intent from the type or location of the force each side deployed. For the March 1939 memorandum and for a discussion of the increasing range of planned U.S. bombers before the war, see Craven and Cate, *Army Air Forces*, 1:119–20.

[191] Note his formal justification of the need to occupy French North Africa, cited in Goda, *Tomorrow the World*, pp. xiii–xiv.

lines. In Overy's view, for example, window logic probably played a major role even in 1939. The British and French governments, he argues, felt at that point that their current "high levels of arms spending could be sustained for only a short time." That fact, he says, "pushed both western governments towards the conclusion that it would be better to take decisive action, even war, sooner rather than later," and that in turn was a key factor leading to war in 1939, a war which Hitler would have preferred to put off for a few years.[192] If Hitler had had his way, and if Germany had "enjoyed a further four or five years of peace," history, in Overy's view, might have taken a totally different course. Germany, he says, would have developed into "one of the military superpowers of the 1940s."[193]

The basic point suggested by this and other accounts is that the coming of war in 1939 had set off a dynamic which Hitler was unable to control and which eventually overwhelmed him. The idea here, as Andreas Hillgruber argues, is that by December 1941 the Nazi leader had essentially resigned himself to the fact that the United States was going to go to war against him and, in declaring war on America, was simply trying to make the best of a bad business.[194] If war with America was inevitable in any event, he might as well take advantage of the opportunity he now had, after Pearl Harbor, to firm up his alliance with Japan. To wait for Roosevelt to move first, moreover, would be taken as a sign of weakness. A declaration of war might therefore be his best option. But the conclusion to be drawn from these accounts is that for him war with America at that point was not a happy solution.

So you come to see how one thing leads to another. War breaks out in 1939 as the western powers see their window of opportunity closing; Germany's early victories lead to a deepening U.S. involvement; and Hitler's fear of an eventual U.S. intervention is a major factor pushing him forward. His moves, in turn, generate more pressure on America to enter the war, and U.S. policy toward Japan has to be understood in that context. The conflict with Japan comes to a head with the attack on Pearl Harbor, and within days the United States and Germany are officially at war. There is a logic tying all these things together, a logic in which power considerations play a key role, and to understand the story—to make these events intelligible, in Hanson's sense—is to work out what that logic is.

So gradually, as you put these things together, a certain sense for the larger story, or at least for one major strand in that larger story, takes shape in your

---

[192] Overy, *Origins of the Second World War*, pp. 62, 69–73, and Richard Overy, "Germany, 'Domestic Crisis' and War in 1939," *Past and Present*, no. 116 (August 1987): 167–68, reprinted in Overy, *War and Economy*, pp. 231–32.

[193] Overy, *War and Economy*, p. 195.

[194] Hillgruber, "Faktor Amerika," pp. 522–23. See also Gerhard Weinberg, "Germany's Declaration of War on the United States: A New Look," in his *World in the Balance: Behind the Scenes of World War II* (Hanover, N. H.: University Press of New England, 1981).

mind. That sense may be very rough and imperfect, but you know how you can deepen your understanding of what was going on. You know that the particular elements of the story can be studied more closely. In this case, all the things I just talked about can be fleshed out by looking at the specific claims on which basic arguments rest, and those specific claims can then be studied by looking at the empirical evidence, especially the evidence cited in the works in which those claims are made.

How far do you take this process? The answer depends on what your goals are. But even if you want to go into these questions in considerable depth, it still makes sense to try to work out early on, in a relatively rough way, what the basic structure of the historical problem is. What you are able to come up with might be little more than a sketch. But as you proceed with your work, it's vitally important that you have *something* to go on, some sense, however rudimentary, for what the overall story was. Little of that interpretation may remain intact by the time you are done, but it is the process that is important. As you do this sort of work, you come to understand at a much deeper level how things fit together. You get a better sense for the texture of the historical process you are studying—a better feel for what was actually shaping the course of events.

And note the role that a certain familiarity with international relations theory plays in this process. I've touched on this issue a number of times before. My basic point in those passages is that by grappling with the fundamental conceptual issues—and in particular by coming to terms with the arguments developed in the theoretical literature—the historian is able to appreciate the importance of various elements of the story that might otherwise go unnoticed. A few paragraphs back I gave the example of "window logic." But the general point is so important for our present purposes that I'd like to give a couple of other examples here.

One of the most basic ideas in contemporary American international relations theory has to do with what is called the "security dilemma"—that is, with the idea that states might be led to adopt aggressive policies for purely defensive purposes. Their aim might be simply to provide for their own security, but they might, as Robert Jervis puts it, be "trapped by the logic of the situation." And that problem, the argument runs, is particularly serious in situations where the offense is believed to have the upper hand, where a premium is placed on offensive as opposed to defensive military operations.[195]

So suppose you're familiar with that body of thought when you study American policy in 1941. You note that President Roosevelt and other top

---

[195] See Jervis, "Cooperation under the Security Dilemma," esp. pp. 186–99, and Van Evera, *Causes of War*. For a recent survey of this body of work, see James D. Morrow, "International Conflict: Assessing the Democratic Peace and Offense-Defense Theory," in *Political Science: The State of the Discipline*, ed. Ira Katznelson and Helen Milner (New York: Norton, 2002).

officials defined defense in very expansive terms. They thought it would be foolish for the Americans to sit on their hands until their homeland was attacked. They assumed by 1941 that it was important to move against Germany before it was too late. They took it for granted that Germany was so great a threat that "*any* action" that the United States took against that country was "necessarily one of self defense and could never be considered as aggression."[196] You note that that general view was linked to their understanding of the basic nature of modern warfare—that, for Roosevelt especially, U.S. policy had to be rooted in an understanding of the "lightning speed of modern warfare."[197] And you're struck by the fact that they felt the nation was threatened by Germany's offensive military capabilities and that it therefore had to develop offensive forces of its own.[198] You're struck in particular by what you see going on in the very important area of air warfare—by the fact that each side understood that the best way to defend against air attack was to destroy the enemy air force on the ground, that each side was therefore under pressure to develop aircraft "whose range outdistanced the striking ability of potential enemies," and that each side was therefore led to build bombers of greater and greater range and thus to adopt a more threatening offense-oriented posture. Indeed, you're struck by the fact that both Germany and America had begun to develop intercontinental bombers even before they went to war with each other. And you note that Roosevelt's understanding of the importance of these developments helps explain why his policy took the shape it did.[199]

If you're familiar with the theoretical arguments, you take special notice when you see these things—when you see people saying in effect that their country needs to act aggressively for defensive purposes, and when you see how that attitude is linked to their understanding of modern warfare. You take special notice because you sense that what you see is not just an isolated historical artifact, a way of framing the issue specific to this particular case. You sense that something more general is at work—that the sort of dynamic the theorists have discussed at a more abstract level is at work in this particular

[196] Turner in meeting with Japanese ambassador Nomura, July 20, 1941, reported in Turner to Stark, July 21, 1941, FRUS Japan 2:519, quoted and discussed in Deborah Miner, "United States Policy toward Japan 1941: The Assumption That Southeast Asia Was Vital to the British War Effort" (Ph.D. diss., Columbia University, 1976), pp. 243–44. (emphasis added).

[197] Radio address announcing the proclamation of an Unlimited National Emergency, May 27, 1941, Roosevelt, *Public Papers*, 10:188–89.

[198] Craven and Cate, *Army Air Forces*, 1:117–18; Roosevelt, *Public Papers*, 9:198, and the other documents in this collection cited in note 13 above.

[199] In addition to the sources cited in notes 183 and 190 above, see Robert Frank Futrell, *Ideas, Concepts, Doctrine: Basic Thinking in the United States Air Force, 1907–1960* (Maxwell Air Force Base, Montgomery, Ala.: Air University Press, 1989), 1: 109–11; and Thomas Greer, *The Development of Air Doctrine in the Army Air Arm, 1917–1941* (Washington D. C.: Office of Air Force History, 1985), pp. 93 (for the quotation), 94, 100–101, 118–19.

case. To understand means to see the general in the specific, and that's what the theory has helped you do.

But here I'm looking at the issue from the historian's point of view. For the political scientists, the connection is the same, but it works the other way. When you see what was going on in 1941—when you see the sort of thinking that lay at the heart of American policy—key theoretical points come to life. They take on a certain reality quality. You come to see that in doing theoretical work you're not just playing a sort of intellectual game. You're not just dealing with abstract intellectual constructs. You're dealing with ideas that help you understand how international politics actually works.

So history is important for the theorist, and theory is important for the historian. To sort out a particular problem, the historian has to do a lot of thinking, and the theoretical literature can provide a certain degree of support. And it's little short of amazing how much the theorist can learn by studying the historical issues the way they need to be studied—by going into them in some depth and by analyzing historical claims in terms both of their internal logic and of the adequacy of the evidence that supports them.

Chapter Five

WORKING WITH DOCUMENTS

FOR MOST PURPOSES, the method outlined in the previous two chapters will take you as far as you need to go. But suppose you wanted to go further still. Suppose your goal was to get to the bottom of some historical issue—or at least to go into that issue as deeply as you could. In that case, you'd have to spend a lot of time working with primary sources. You'd certainly want to look at published collections of documents. You might also want to use material available on microfilm or microfiche or in some electronic format. You might even want to examine archival sources, both in your own country and abroad.

How do you do that kind of work? The amount of material available to you might be massive. Where do you start and how do you proceed? How are particular documents to be assessed? And how do you go about drawing meaning from the sources you examine?

PRIMARY SOURCE RESEARCH: GENERAL PRINCIPLES

If you want to study a problem in the light of the sources generated at the time, you would not want to approach those sources in a totally mindless way, just plunging in at some randomly chosen point and reading document after document until the story takes shape in your mind. You would want, as always, to approach the sources with a set of questions in mind, questions that will help you see what's important in the documents you read. And knowing what the questions are will give you a better sense for which collections you'll want to focus on and for the order in which you'll want to examine them.

You can come up with a set of questions in basically two ways. You could study what scholars have had to say about the subject you're interested in. You could use the technique I talked about in the two preceding chapters. By analyzing the historical literature, you develop a sense for the structure of a historical problem. You come to understand how general arguments rest on certain relatively narrow claims, which in turn are supported by certain specific bodies of evidence. You then ask: what's to be made of those general arguments? Are those specific claims valid? What does the evidence cited actually show? When scholars disagree among themselves on key issues, you can ask: who's right? And to decide those issues, you can go beyond simply weighing arguments against each other, looking only at the evidence presented in those texts. You can examine the evidence yourself. And in fact you might remember that in the previous chapter we went into the primary sources (albeit in a highly targeted way) to help decide some major issues. You could use that basic technique, but more extensively and more systematically.

Or you could try to think through the core historical problems on your own. You do that by focusing on fundamentals. The key point to bear in mind here is that international politics is about conflict. It's about what happens when different countries want different things and when those desires clash with each other. So in studying international politics in a particular period, you can start with the basics: What does each country *want*? What sort of *policy* is it pursuing? What kind of *thinking* is that policy rooted in? What does each side actually *do*, and how does each react to what the others are doing? What, in other words, is the basic *story* here? And by "story" I mean not just a mindless chronicle of all the different things that happened. I mean a story with some sort of causal structure—a story that gives some sense for why things took the course they did, for how we got from point A to point B.

If those are the basic questions, how do you go about answering them? You can begin in various ways, and it's generally not a bad idea to move ahead on at least two different fronts more or less at the same time. On the one hand, you want to begin to piece things together—to see what the major developments were and what one thing had to do with another. And to do that you could read the diplomatic documents dealing with a certain question in chronological order, or even read (say) the foreign ministry files dealing with a particular issue during a specific period from beginning to end. You could also examine the most accessible open sources—newspapers and magazines, speeches and press conferences, and other sources of that sort. You'd be surprised by how much you can learn just by reading the relevant listings in the *New York Times Index*—not the *Times* itself, just the *Index*.

But at the same time, you should probably try to get at what the basic thinking was. You should try, that is, to look at the world through the eyes of those who controlled policy and who played key roles in deciding what a particular state actually did. One of the first things you would want to look at are the documents recording the thinking of key policy makers and, above all, the thinking of the political leadership within each country. Those documents might be formal, like the records of meetings of the U.S. National Security Council (NSC), the British cabinet, or the Politburo in Communist countries. They might be informal, like documents recording one-on-one meetings involving top officials in particular governments. They might be purely internal documents, or documents recording high-level intergovernmental meetings—and in fact those latter documents are often of quite extraordinary interest. And records of meetings are not the only documents that will give you insight into these issues. The diplomatic correspondence, for example—the correspondence between key foreign ministry officials and a country's representatives abroad—is often of great importance in this context.

So one of the basic principles governing your research strategy is that you should start at the top and proceed from there. What that implies in practice is that it makes sense fairly early on to examine the great collections of diplomatic documents which many of the more important countries publish—the U.S. State Department's *Foreign Relations of the United States* (FRUS) series, the *Documents diplomatiques français* (DDF), the various series published by Britain and Germany and a variety of other countries.[1] The documents published in these collections were not originally written for public consumption; as a very rough rule, they were made public about thirty years after they were written. One of the reasons these collections are so useful is that the editors, often professionally trained historians, tend to select relatively important documents for publication. And although published by foreign offices, they often include non–foreign ministry material. The notes of NSC meetings, for example, are often published in FRUS.

There are other published sources—diaries, collections of the personal papers of key policy makers, and so on—that you might want to consult relatively early on in a project to get some insight into the thinking of certain individuals who play a major role in your story. Those sources, of course, do not have to be read cover to cover, and you can often zero in on key issues by using the index. But there is a limit to how far you can go just using published sources. You may need to examine documents that are available on microfilm, microfiche, or in some electronic format. For example, the NSC records, available on microfilm, include the notes of many meetings that were never published in FRUS or published there only in part. You might be amazed by how much material of this sort is readily available. In the last section of this chapter and in appendix II, I'll talk more about how you go about finding and working with such sources.

For the most serious projects, you'll want to go deeper still. To develop the sort of understanding you hope to achieve in such cases, you'll almost certainly need to do real archival research. This is not nearly as scary as many people think. Archives are as a rule very pleasant places to work. But in doing archival work, where do you start? In the United States, some of the richest sources—the sources relating to the highest level of policy making—are at the presidential libraries, so you might well want to visit one or two of those repositories fairly early on. In Britain, you would probably want to start by working with certain classes of material in the British National Archives (formerly called the Public Record Office)—cabinet records, records of the prime minister's office, and so on. In other countries, it's generally not hard to

---

[1] These collections will be discussed at greater length in the final section of this chapter and in appendix II, pp. 217–218 below.

figure out what the most important collections of material are. Key manuscript collections can also be consulted; you get some sense for who the key figures are as you do your historical work, and often those individuals have left collections of papers you can study. Again, I'll talk more about this toward the end of the chapter and in appendix II.

You may wonder how you can tell who the key people actually are. You cannot, of course, just go by titles. In the American system, for example, the president may or may not play a major role in shaping policy. A secretary of state might be a key figure, or might be a tool in the hands of his or her subordinates. But as you study your subject closely, these questions about who really mattered tend to answer themselves. You can see who defers to whom, who plays the leading role, who feels excluded or chooses not to participate in policy making in a major way, and whom foreign governments deal with.

So it's generally not hard to see who played the leading roles and thus which sources are most valuable for your purposes. But that does not mean that you'll want to limit yourself to those sources. You can begin to spread out soon after you start a project. You might notice how military considerations get factored in to some policy decision, so you might feel that you need to understand the military side of the story better. That means you need to go into the military sources, and once again the basic rule is to start at the top and work your way down. You begin, that is, with the records kept by the civilian and military heads of the defense establishment. In the case of the United States, that means starting with the records of the Joint Chiefs of Staff and the Office of the Secretary of Defense. As you work in those sources, you might decide that you need to study some particular issue more deeply; you might therefore need to look at the records of the army staff, or study the papers of some key military commander, like the NATO commander in the late 1950s, General Norstad. You go into such materials with specific questions in mind. Those questions determine the particular volumes or boxes of documents you zero in on. (You can generally tell roughly what each box or volume contains from the finding aids.) The same basic method applies to foreign office or intelligence agency material. And such materials are often available on microfilm or in some electronic format.

The key thing to note here is that a research project tends to take on a life of its own. You may think you are running the show, but you soon discover that that is not quite true. Questions take shape as you do your work, and those questions have to be answered. You're on the trail of a problem, and you can't quite tell in advance what sorts of questions will turn up as you try to figure out what was going on. You basically just have to allow the project to take its own course.

Let me give a few examples to show how this works in practice. The first relates to the Cuban missile crisis. In studying that crisis, you may notice (perhaps on your own, or perhaps because other scholars have pointed it out) that on October 22, 1962, when President Kennedy gave his speech an-nouncing that the Soviets had sent missiles to Cuba, the United States seemed to be thinking in terms of a "prolonged struggle"—that is, of a crisis that would last for months—but that within a few days, that view changed dramatically.[2] By October 25 there was a much greater sense of urgency. The crisis, U.S. leaders now felt, needed to be settled quickly. How is that shift to be explained? The issue is important because it bears on the key question of why the crisis came to a head as it did. And putting this question at the cen-ter of your research effort allows you to work in a more focused way. It allows you to draw meaning from the sources you examine more efficiently.

Or to take another example from that same episode: you see from the doc-uments you study that Kennedy's plan was to get work on the missile sites to stop and then to enter into a negotiation with the Soviets. But there was no negotiation. Instead, the Soviets accepted the terms the Americans pre-sented to them on the evening of October 27. It's hard to understand why they would end up acceding to a virtual ultimatum if a more moderate U.S. offer had been on the table. Does this mean that they were not aware of Kennedy's plan? But in that case, how could they have remained ignorant of Kennedy's intentions? Again, this is a relatively narrow, studiable issue, and in answering it you get a better sense for why the crisis took the course it did.

Or suppose you were studying the coming of the First World War during the July crisis in 1914. You note that Russia's initial policy in that crisis was to advise the Serbs not to resist an Austrian invasion but to entrust their fate "to the judgment of the Great Powers."[3] If that position had remained intact, a great European war might well have been avoided. But you also note that within days after taking that position on July 24, the Russian line had shifted. Now an Austrian invasion would mean a European war. How, you wonder, is that very specific shift in policy to be explained?

Or to take another case involving Russian policy in that crisis: the Russian government ordered general mobilization on July 30 because it felt war was imminent; the Russian mobilization led to a German mobilization, and for Germany mobilization meant war. But the Germans had decided that they would not be the first to mobilize. They wanted to be able to point to Russia as the country that had taken the crucial step that had made war inevitable. Would the Russian government, you might wonder, have ordered general mobilization if it had understood that it was Germany's policy not to mobilize

---

[2] See Theodore Sorensen, *Kennedy* (New York: Harper and Row, 1965), p. 712, and Alexander George, "The Cuban Missile Crisis, 1962," in *The Limits of Coercive Diplomacy,* ed. Alexander George et al. (Boston: Little Brown, 1971), pp. 104–5.

[3] Special Journal of the Russian Council of Ministers, July 24, 1914, in Geiss, *July 1914,* p. 187. See also Sazonov to Strandtmann, July 24, 1914, and Memorandum of the Day of the Russian Ministry of Foreign Affairs, July 24, 1914, ibid., pp. 187–88, 189–91.

first? If the Russians had understood what German policy was, then (you might calculate) they might have been under less pressure to act. So the question of what the Russians knew about that German policy has a certain importance. This narrow issue is in principle studiable. You even have some ideas about the sort of source you would like to consult—for example, the reports of the Russian military attaché in Berlin—in order to get to the bottom of the issue.

In studying questions of this kind, you are not simply accumulating detailed information for its own sake. These issues are important because they have a certain bearing on broader issues of interpretation. Note once again the basic technique here: your goal is to see how big issues of interpretation turn on relatively narrow, relatively concrete, and therefore more readily studiable problems. To take another example from the July crisis: on July 29 the Russians ordered a partial mobilization against Austria, and the German chancellor reacted by sending his famous "world on fire" telegram to Vienna. "We must decline," he wrote, "to let ourselves be dragged by Vienna, wantonly and without regard to our advice, into a world conflagration."[4] It seemed that the German government, now aware that war was a very real possibility, was trying to pull back from the brink. But just fourteen hours after that telegram was sent, the Russians ordered general mobilization, and after that war became virtually inevitable. You can thus get at the huge issue of the origins of the First World War by focusing on the very narrow question of what happened, or failed to happen, during that fourteen-hour period, and why. You think about what the German chancellor would have had to do if he had really wanted to follow through on the policy of the "world on fire" telegram; you note that he took no serious action to head off the war during that period and you look for evidentiary clues that might explain his inaction in this specific case.

So you're not just dotting the i's and crossing the t's. You're not just gathering data as a kind of end in itself. You're actively looking for answers. You're actively trying to get a sense for what the story was. It's not as though you just read the documents and the important conclusions fall like ripe fruit into your lap without any real intellectual effort on your part. You have to do some real thinking. You have to think about what was puzzling about the particular episode you're examining. You have to put yourself in the shoes of the people you are studying and then perhaps ask what you would have done. That kind of exercise helps sensitize you to the problems they faced and helps generate the questions that provide focal points for your own research.

In the process of sorting things out, you almost automatically develop a deeper understanding of your subject. Without quite realizing what is going

---

[4] Luigi Albertini, *The Origins of the War of 1914*, 3 vols. (London: Oxford University Press, 1952–57), 2: 504, 522–25.

on, your basic sense for what was happening tends to be transformed. You move away from the simple clichés that had perhaps framed your initial understanding of the subject: in the case of the Cuban crisis, for example, that this was a simple confrontation in which the two sides stood eyeball-to-eyeball until one side blinked, or in the case of the July crisis that war came because the crisis just "spun out of control." You come to see that what was going on cannot be understood in such simple terms. You develop a sense for the texture, for the complexity, of a particular episode.

The process of developing an interpretation in this way is thus fairly straightforward. You begin by raising questions. You then try to answer them by examining the evidence. As you do that, new questions take shape, and those new questions themselves need to be answered. You just go where the process takes you. There's really no mystery to it at all.

Assessing the Evidence: Some Techniques

Historians take it for granted that an interpretation is built essentially on a close study of the documentary evidence. But if the documents are so important, don't you need some sort of method for judging the reliability of specific pieces of evidence?

Historians as a general rule are not particularly concerned with this problem. The question of source reliability—that is, of whether a document accurately records something that really happened—does arise from time to time. But historians generally concern themselves with this sort of issue only when they sense that there's something odd about a specific piece of evidence— that is, when it doesn't fit in well with the larger picture as those scholars understand it. When doubts arise, the historian can then ask fairly targeted questions about that document. If it purports to record a meeting, does one find other evidence showing that that meeting was actually held (in the logs or appointment books of those who attended the meeting)? If this was an intergovernmental meeting, are there other records of the meeting in the files of the other governments represented? Does the sort of language supposedly used ring true in terms of what you know about those who were recorded as talking a particular way? You apply various commonsense tests of that sort and reach a conclusion about the reliability of a particular document.[5]

---

[5] For a recent case in point, see "Did Truman Meet with NATO Foreign Ministers on 3 April 1949? A Cold War Mystery," ed. William Burr, including the text of an email from Stephen Schuker to Melvyn Leffler discussing the issue, and with a link to the document in question (http://www.gwu.edu/~nsarchiv/nsa/DOCUMENT/200008/). See also my own comment on this issue posted on H-Diplo on August 25, 2000 (http://www.polisci.ucla.edu/faculty/trachtenberg/cv/hdiplo.html). The document was originally included in a microfiche supplement to the State

But such problems rarely come up, and historians assume that the documents they find in the archives (and elsewhere) can normally be taken as genuine—in the sense, for example, that if someone is reported as saying something in some official document, then that person probably did actually say something of the sort. Documents, after all, are generated for a government's own internal purposes, and what would be the point of keeping records if those records were not even meant to be accurate? It's just hard to believe that a major goal, when a document is being drafted, would be to deceive historians thirty years later—that is, at a time when no one would really care much about the issue at hand. The point here is very general, and I of course don't mean to imply that records of this sort are going to be perfect—that a record of a meeting, for example, is going to give you a complete and absolutely accurate account of everything that was said. This is obviously not to be expected, and in fact documents might be distorted in various ways. An account of a meeting, for example, might not include material that would have shown some powerful figure in an unfavorable light and certain things might be omitted for political reasons. And certain types of sources—diary entries, for example—have to be taken with a grain of salt. But if an official document records someone as actually saying something, you can be reasonably sure that it's not a pure fabrication.

That judgment about the basic reliability of official documents that were secret at the time and were made available to the public decades later is supported by the impressions you get spending years working with historical sources. You often come across more than one record of the same meeting, and it is easy to compare those records with each other. An account, for example, of President Kennedy's January 22, 1963, remarks to the National Security Council was published in volume 8 of the *Foreign Relations of the United States* series for 1961–63, and three other accounts are available in the

---

Department's *Foreign Relations of the United States* series, "Memoranda of Conversations of the Secretary of State, 1947–52" (Washington, D.C.: GPO, 1988). It was republished in Cees Wiebes and Bert Zeeman, "Eine Lehrstunde in Machtpolitik: Die Vereinigten Staaten und ihre Partner am Vorabend der NATO-Gründung," *Vierteljahrshefte für Zeitgeschichte* 40, no. 3 (July 1992): 413–23.

For another example of how questionable evidence can be dealt with, see the discussion of the German diplomat Eckardstein's dispatches in William Langer, *The Diplomacy of Imperialism, 1890–1902*, 2 vols. (New York: Knopf, 1935), 2:501–2, 727–31. Note also Albertini's references to the "suppressions, alterations, and falsifications" found in the French *Yellow Book*, the collection of documents relating to the outbreak of the First World War that the French government published in 1914. For the analysis supporting that characterization, see Albertini, *The Origins of the war of 1914*, 2:322 (for the quotation), 575, 593, and 616; 3:163–64; and the many references under "France, *French Yellow Book*" in the indexes to both volumes (2:701 and 3:744). Note finally Albertini's reference to the omission of an important sentence from the version of a document published in the *Blue Book*, the collection of documents the British published in 1914, in 3:163n, which he characterizes there as "symptomatic."

microfiche supplement to that volume; a fifth account can be consulted at the Kennedy Library.[6] There is both a French and an American record of Secretary of State Dulles's meeting with the French foreign minister on November 19, 1957.[7] There are both British and American minutes of the Nassau conference of December 1962.[8] Many other examples can be given, and in fact one of the less frequently emphasized reasons for doing multi-archival work is that it often enables you to get more than one record of the same meeting. As you do the comparisons, you not only arrive at conclusions about the reliability of the specific accounts you examined but also reach general conclusions about the reliability of particular kinds of sources.

Let me give some examples of how this process works. The first has to do with the Potsdam Conference of July–August 1945. The Potsdam Conference is a particularly interesting case because the American, British, and Soviet notes of the same top-level meetings have all been published. Indeed, we have two sets of American notes, the minutes taken by Llewellyn Thompson, then first secretary in the American embassy in London, and by Benjamin Cohen, special assistant to Secretary of State Byrnes. What do you find when you compare these records with each other? Take, for example, the notes of the twelfth plenary meeting, which took place on August 1, 1945. At that meeting, Stalin, Byrnes, Truman, and British foreign secretary Ernest Bevin dealt with the issue of how various German assets were to be divided up among the victor powers. Here is how the four accounts report one key part of that discussion.

Thompson Minutes

> MR. STALIN suggested that they might reach agreement along the following lines. The Russians would not claim the gold which their Allies had found in Germany. With regard to shares and foreign investments, perhaps the demarcation line between the Soviet and western zones of occupation should be taken as the dividing line and everything west of that line would go to the Allies and everything east of that line to the Russians.
>
> THE PRESIDENT inquired if he meant a line running from the Baltic to the Adriatic.
>
> STALIN replied in the affirmative and said that with respect to foreign investments,

[6] "Remarks of President Kennedy to the National Security Council Meeting of January 22, 1963," U.S. Department of State, *Foreign Relations of the United States* (FRUS), 1961–63, vol. 8 (Washington, D.C.: GPO,1996), doc. 125 and p. 457n; microfiche supplement to FRUS 1961–63, vols. 7–9 (Washington, D.C.: Department of State, 1997), docs. 284–86.

[7] Dulles-Pineau meeting, November 19, 1957, 740.5/11-1957, State Department Central Files, Record Group 59, U.S. National Archives, and *Documents diplomatiques français, 1957* (DDF) (Paris: Imprimerie Nationale, 1991), 2:712.

[8] The U.S. records are in FRUS 1961–63, vol. 13 (Washington, D.C.: G-PO, 1994), pp. 1091–112; the British records are in Prem 11/4229 at the British National Archives (formerly called the Public Record Office), Kew.

all investments in Europe west of this line would go to the Allies and all investments in Eastern Europe to the Russians. He said that for example German investments in Rumania and Hungary would fall to the Russians.

MR. BEVIN asked if German investments in other countries would be theirs.

MR. STALIN replied that they would and mentioned France, Belgium, and America as examples.

MR BEVIN said he agreed and asked if Greece would belong to Britain.[9]

Cohen Notes

STALIN: We don't claim gold. As to shares in foreign investments everything west of the military demarcation line is relinquished by us. Everything east of the line should go to us.

TRUMAN: That implies [applies?] only to German investments east of the line.

STALIN: For example, German investments in Rumania and Bulgaria.

ATTLEE: I agree.

BEVIN: Greece belongs to the British.[10]

British Notes

The Soviet Government [Stalin said] were ready to renounce all claim to shares in undertakings in the western zones, gold found by the Allies in the western zones, and a corresponding share of German external assets. This might be expressed by saying that all assets in countries west of the demarcation line between the Russian zone and the western zone of occupation should be at the disposal of Great Britain and the United States, while all assets to the east of that line should be at the disposal of the Soviet Union. Thus, assets in e.g. France, Belgium and Holland and the Western Hemisphere would be at the disposal of Great Britain and the United States; those in Finland, Bulgaria and Roumania, for example, would be at the disposal of the Soviet Union.

MR. BEVIN asked whether Premier Stalin's suggestion might be expressed by saying that all German external assets located in the areas occupied by the Russian Armies would be at the disposal of the Soviet Union, while all such assets located elsewhere would be at the disposal of Great Britain and the United States; PREMIER STALIN agreed.[11]

---

[9] Thompson Minutes of August 1, 1945, plenary meeting, United States Department of State, *Foreign Relations of the United States: The Conference of Berlin (The Potsdam Conference) 1945*, 2 vols. (Washington, D.C.: GPO, 1960), 2:566–67.

[10] Cohen notes of August 1, 1945, plenary meeting, ibid., 2:579. Attlee was the British prime minister at the time.

[11] *Documents on British Policy Overseas*, ed. Rohan Butler and M. E. Pelly, Series I, vol. 1, *The Conference at Postdam, July–Augut 1945* (London: HMSO, 1984): 1128.

Soviet Notes

> STALIN: Can we not agree on the following: the Soviet delegation waives its claim
> to gold; as for shares of German enterprises in the Western zone, we also waive
> our claim to them, and will regard the whole of Western Germany as falling
> within your sphere, and Eastern Germany, within ours.
>
> TRUMAN: We shall have to discuss this proposal.
>
> STALIN: As to the German investments, I should put the question this way: as to
> the German investments in Eastern Europe, they remain with us, and the rest,
> with you.
>
> TRUMAN: Does this apply only to German investments in Europe or in other coun-
> tries as well?
>
> STALIN: Let me put it more specifically: the German investments in Rumania,
> Bulgaria, Hungary and Finland, go to us, and all the rest, to you.
>
> BEVIN: The German investments in other countries go to us?
>
> STALIN: In all the other countries, in South America, in Canada, etc., all this is
> yours.
>
> BEVIN: Consequently, all German assets in other countries lying west of the zones
> of occupation in Germany will belong to the United States, Great Britain and
> the other countries? Does this also apply to Greece?
>
> STALIN: Yes.
>
> BYRNES: How does this apply to the question of shares of German enterprises?
>
> STALIN: In our zone they will be ours, and in your zone, yours.[12]

When you compare these accounts, you get a fairly clear sense for what the
gist of the discussion was. German assets were being divided between east and
west, and an agreement on those economic issues had certain political over-
tones. The accounts differ, of course, in certain ways, but even when they do,
that does not mean that you cannot form an opinion as to what was actually
said. The two American accounts, for example, report Bevin as asking for
Greece; the Soviet notes also show him raising the issue of Greece. In the
British notes, however, Greece is not mentioned by name. It is reasonable to
conclude that Bevin did actually mention that country explicitly, since the
absence of an explicit reference to Greece in the British minutes is quite un-
derstandable. Western governments, even in their internal documents, prefer
to show their leaders dealing with these issues in a more discreet way. This is
not to say, of course, that Bevin actually said, "Greece belongs to the British."
He might well have been less direct in his phrasing. But for a notetaker trying
to get at the gist of what he was saying, it is not hard to see how his raising of
the issue would have legitimately come across that way.

---

[12] *Tehran Yalta Potsdam: The Soviet Protocols*, ed. Robert Beitzell (Hattiesburg, Miss.: Academic
International, 1970), p. 288.

A second example has to do with the December 1959 Rambouillet meeting of western heads of government. All four of the heads of government who took part included descriptions of this meeting in their memoirs, a very unusual and thus quite interesting case, and we also have the British and French minutes of those meetings.[13] One can thus compare the memoir accounts both with each other and with the minutes as found in the archives and in the published diplomatic documents, and one can also compare the British and French minutes with each other. What conclusions emerge when you do this exercise? The memoir accounts are wildly different from each other, and, for the most part, from the British and French minutes as well. Those minutes, on the other hand, give remarkably similar accounts of what was said. In such circumstances, it is not hard to reach a judgment as to which sources are suspect and which can be considered reliable. Eisenhower, for example, in the memoirs he published a few years after leaving office, has himself rejecting French president Charles de Gaulle's proposal that the French, American, and British governments establish "themselves as a kind of triumvirate to promote their common interests throughout the world."[14] The British record, however, has Eisenhower, with very little prodding from de Gaulle, suggesting "the establishment of a tripartite machinery to operate on a clandestine basis with the object of discussing questions of common interest to the three Governments," and the French record also has Eisenhower at this point calling for the establishment of a tripartite "mécanisme 'clandestin.'"[15]

So what's to be trusted, what the memoirs say or what the documents show? Memoirs are going to be read by a lot of people, and an author has to take that basic fact into account in deciding what to say. But those who prepare the official record do not have to worry so much about how people will react. They can better afford to be honest. A document is written on the basis of notes

---

[13] For the sections on the Rambouillet conference in the memoirs of the four leaders who attended, see Charles de Gaulle, *Memoirs of Hope: Renewal, 1958–62* (London: Weidenfeld and Nicolson, 1971), pp. 222–24; Harold Macmillan, *Pointing the Way, 1959–1961* (London: Macmillan, 1972), pp. 100–114; Dwight Eisenhower, *Waging Peace, 1956–1961* (Garden City, N.Y.: Doubleday, 1965), pp. 508–9; Konrad Adenauer, *Erinnerungen 1959–1963: Fragmente* (Stuttgart: Deutsche Verlags-Anstalt, 1968), pp. 23–28. For the French records, see *Documents diplomatiques français 1959* (DDF) (Paris: Imprimerie Nationale, 1995), 2:749–75 (doc. 295). The British documents are in Prem 11/2996 in the British National Archives (BNA) in Kew outside of London and are also available in a number of American university libraries on CD-ROM: *Macmillan Cabinet Papers, 1957–1963* (London: Adam Matthew Publications, 1999).

[14] Eisenhower, *Waging Peace*, p. 508.

[15] Eisenhower–Macmillan–de Gaulle meeting, December 20, 1959, p. 1, Prem 11/2996, BNA. These British notes were given to the U.S. State Department—the U.S. government had kept no official record of its own—and the portion of the document in which this comment was made was published in FRUS 1958–60, 7, part 2 (Washington, D.C.: GPO, 1993), p. 319. The passage in the French record is in DDF 1959, doc. 295, beginning of part IV.

taken at the time. A memoir is written years later, and people's memories, of course, fade with time. So even in a one-on-one confrontation between a document and a memoir, the document should win. But when you have two independently prepared documents, released years after the event by two separate governments, and each of those documents shows much the same thing going on, there is no contest at all. The documents win hands down.

Let me give a third example. This case is perhaps the most interesting of the three because here you can compare the official records of meetings with what was actually said. During the Cuban missile crisis, President Kennedy met with his top advisers to talk about what needed to be done. Those discussions were recorded (without the knowledge of most of the participants), and transcripts of those recordings were eventually published. Official minutes were also prepared at the time by an NSC official, Bromley Smith, who knew nothing about the recordings. Those minutes were made available at the Kennedy Library beginning in 1978 and were also eventually published. You can compare the minutes with the corresponding transcripts. You can even listen to the tapes themselves. You can thus judge for yourself how reliable minutes of that sort are as a historical source.[16]

As you do that comparison, it becomes clear that Smith's goal was not to recount every comment that was made, in the precise order in which those remarks were made, as though they were all of equal importance. His aim instead was to give as clear a sense as he could of the gist of the discussion. The discussion is thus made to sound more focused than it actually was. But that is what makes a record of this kind different from a transcript. It does not mean that this sort of record was in any fundamental way inaccurate. If you

[16] For the Bromley Smith minutes for the period of the crisis, see FRUS 1961–63, vol. 11 (Washington, D.C.: G-PO, 1996), docs. 73, 79, 90, 94, 97. Copies of the tapes are available on audiocassette from the Kennedy Library in Boston, and some of the tapes have been put online. See, for example, the "History and Politics Out Loud" website (http://www.hpol.org/), and also the WhiteHouseTapes.org website (http://whitehousetapes.org/). Certain transcripts were released by the Kennedy Library beginning in the early 1980s. In the mid-1990s, new transcripts were made and were published in *The Kennedy Tapes: Inside the White House during the Cuban Missile Crisis*, ed. Ernest May and Philip Zelikow (Cambridge, Mass.: Belknap Press of Harvard University Press, 1997). But it was charged that those transcripts were full of errors, some quite serious. See especially two articles by Sheldon Stern: "What JFK Really Said," *Atlantic Monthly* 285, no. 5 (May 2000), and "Source Material: The 1997 Published Transcripts of the JFK Cuban Missile Crisis Tapes: Too Good to Be True?" *Presidential Studies Quarterly* 30, no. 3 (September 2000): 586–93. A revised set of transcripts was published in 2001: Philip Zelikow, Ernest May, and Timothy Naftali, eds., *The Presidential Recordings: John F. Kennedy, vols. 1–3, The Great Crises* (New York: W. W. Norton, 2001). But those transcripts, Stern charged, still contained many errors. See the appendix to his book *Averting "The Final Failure," John F. Kennedy and the Secret Cuban Missile Crisis Meetings* (Stanford: Stanford University Press, 2003), and his review article "The JFK Tapes: Round Two," *Reviews in American History* 30, no. 4 (December 2002): 680–88. The editors naturally defended themselves, and other scholars weighed in with comments. See the list of articles in http://whitehousetapes.org/pages/news_articles.htm

go through the minutes sentence by sentence, in practically every case you can find at least one, and often more than one, passage in the transcript that shows that Smith had given an essentially accurate account of what was said. What this implies is that for most purposes, the Bromley Smith minutes can be taken as a fairly reliable source.

As you do these sorts of exercises—and in historical work you generally end up doing lots of them—you are not just taking your measure of particular sources. You are not just judging the reliability of Thompson's notes of the Potsdam Conference, or Eisenhower's memoirs, or the Bromley Smith minutes. You are learning something about the reliability of the sorts of records you find in the archives and in published collections of documents. You are learning something about the reliability of memoir sources in general. You are learning something about what constitutes good evidence, and about the sort of evidence that is not quite as good.

For most historians, the documentary record—the body of material generated at the time and kept under wraps for many years—is far and away the best source there is. Yes, you sometimes need to read the open sources—that is, the sort of material that entered the public record at the time—but you can't be too quick to take what someone said in public as representative of his or her real thinking. Everyone knows that people tend to express themselves more freely in private, and everyone knows why. When speaking in public, people tend to concern themselves more with how other people will react. They know what constitutes acceptable public discourse and what is expected of them. Being familiar with the conventions of their own political culture, they know they cannot be too frank.

When dealing with questions of foreign policy, political leaders face a particular problem. The people at the top of any political system live in two separate worlds. On the one hand, they live in the world of international politics. They're more exposed to the realities of international politics than most of their compatriots are, so they're under a certain pressure to adjust their thinking to the realities of that world. But they also live in the world of domestic politics and thus need to defend their policies to people at home, people who are more shielded from the realities of the international system than they are and who thus tend to approach foreign policy in a more parochial way—that is, people whose approach to foreign policy is more rooted in the values of their own national culture. Political leaders thus have a strong incentive to package their policies in a way that takes that fact into account—an incentive, that is, to frame their policies in a way that reflects the set of values that that culture officially embraces. The rhetoric they adopt, in other words, corresponds to what the public expects to hear and does not necessarily reflect the real thinking of the policy maker. So public discourse, not just in a democracy but in any political system, is inherently suspect. The real thinking is more likely to be revealed by what people say in private, as recorded in documents they believe will not become publicly available for many years.

This does not mean, of course, that open sources are devoid of value. When you're studying recent events, you in fact may have little choice but to rely heavily on such sources, and it is possible to do very good work using sources of that sort. Arnold Wolfers' *Britain and France between Two Wars* and E. E. Schattschneider's *Politics, Pressure and the Tariff* are two excellent cases in point, and both are worth reading just to see how work of this sort can be done, although few scholars today would want to study the issues Wolfers and Schattschneider were concerned with just using the sources they used.[17] For a more recent example, you might want to look at Richard Kohn's "The Erosion of Civilian Control of the Military in the United States Today."[18] This article is of exceptional interest in substantive terms, but it is also worth reading because it shows how far you can go in certain cases by using open sources—how far you can go, in fact, by bringing the method and sensibility of a historian to bear on the analysis of a contemporary issue. But, as a general rule, open sources have to be used with some care.

Open sources are of particular interest when they record a line of argument at odds with what you think people at the time probably wanted to hear—when, for example, a policy maker pushes the envelope a bit and runs a certain political risk by taking a certain line in public. Some of Roosevelt's most interesting public statements in 1940 and 1941 fall into this category.

The same basic set of considerations also applies to another kind of source: interviews with former (or even present) policy makers. You can, of course, learn a lot, especially about contemporary issues, by conducting interviews, above all if you learn everything you can about a particular subject before you meet with the people you are interviewing. James Goldgeier's *Not Whether but When: The U.S. Decision to Enlarge NATO* (1999), a first-rate scholarly work based largely on interviews, is a good case in point. But you obviously have to be wary of what people say when you are interviewing them. Memories are fallible, and the level of honesty varies from person to person. The interviewees, moreover, often have a real interest in getting you to see things in a certain light. So as a general rule you cannot quite take what people tell you at face value, and what you learn in this way is not quite as solid as what you learn from the documents.

Not everyone takes that view. Richard Neustadt, for example, once said that if "forced to choose between the documents on the one hand, and late,

---

[17] Arnold Wolfers, *Britain and France between Two Wars: Conflicting Strategies of Peace since Versailles* (New York: Harcourt, Brace, 1940); E. E. Schattschneider, *Politics, Pressures and the Tariff: A Study of Free Private Enterprise in Pressure Politics, as Shown in the 1929–1930 Revision of the Tariff* (New York: Prentice-Hall, 1935).

[18] Richard H. Kohn, "The Erosion of Civilian Control of the Military in the United States Today," *Naval War College Review* 55, no. 3 (Summer 2002).

limited, partial interviews with some of the principal participants on the other," he would be "forced to discard the documents."[19] But this is the sort of comment that makes most historians' jaws drop. They, and quite a few political scientists as well, are not comfortable with "a research method that permits participants to put excessive spin on the past"—a research method, in fact, that unduly discounts the value of the written evidence.[20]

But even if written documents are the best sources we have, are they really good enough for our purposes? A document may be a reliable record, in the sense that people really did say essentially what they are recorded as saying. You might be reasonably certain that a document is not a pure fabrication and that the record has not actually been falsified. But even if you know what people said, do you really know what was in their minds at the time? They may have actually said certain things in particular meetings, but how can you tell if what they said is in fact correct?

You reach a judgment in this area the same way you make any historical judgment: namely, by looking at as much evidence as you can. Suppose, for example, you read the record of a December 16, 1962, meeting of high U.S. officials dealing with the Skybolt affair. According to that record, Secretary of Defense Robert McNamara opened that meeting by reviewing the talks he had just had in London with his British counterpart, Defence Minister Peter Thorneycroft. He noted "the insistent desire of the British to obtain a categorical assurance that the United States was in favor of the independent British nuclear deterrent, and his own refusal to give such an assurance."[21] Is that comment to be taken at face value? You look at other sources related to this episode. The Neustadt Report on the Skybolt affair, perhaps the most important of those sources, refers to notes of the McNamara-Thorneycroft meeting taken down by John Rubel, a U.S. Defense Department official. According to those notes, Thorneycroft asked whether McNamara was "prepared to state publicly that the United States is willing to do everything possible to assist Britain to keep its independent nuclear deterrent," and McNamara replied, "Yes, I would"—which directly contradicts the account McNamara give at the December 16 meeting in Washington.[22] Well, which

[19] Quoted in Graham Allison, *Essence of Decision: Explaining the Cuban Missile Crisis* (Boston: Little, Brown, 1971), p. 181. See also Richard Neustadt, *Alliance Politics* (New York: Columbia University Press, 1970), p. 7.

[20] J. Garry Clifford, "Bureaucratic Politics," *Journal of American History* 77, no. 1 (June 1990): 164.

[21] Meeting of high U.S. officials, December 16, 1962, *FRUS 1961–63*, 13:1088.

[22] Rubel, notes of McNamara-Thorneycroft meeting, December 11, 1962, p. 4, Neustadt Papers, box 19, John F. Kennedy Library, Boston; also available online in Declassified Documents Reference System, document number CK3100078274. McNamara, however, did go on to say: "Of course, we would have to consider Germany, France and, for that matter, you and your commitments to the Common Market."

version are you to believe? The Rubel notes have the flavor of a real conversation; Rubel doesn't seem to have any reason to distort what was said; but McNamara, on December 16, was giving an account to a group that included Under Secretary of State George Ball, who you know (since you have done a lot of work on the subject) would have been quite upset to hear that McNamara said he would publicly support the idea of an independent British nuclear deterrent. So you can be reasonably sure that the Rubel notes are reliable, and that McNamara's account of what he had said was not accurate.

But even if you did not have the Rubel notes, you could still make a judgment. You could look for British notes of that meeting, perhaps in the official files at the Public Record Office or maybe in Thorneycroft's personal papers. You might find the record of a meeting between Thorneycroft and Prime Minister Macmillan (or with some other official) at which Thorneycroft gave an account of what McNamara had said. You could search for records made by other participants in that meeting, both British and American. You could also draw whatever conclusions you could from less direct indicators—those giving you some sense for McNamara's general policy views, and those giving you some idea about what he was like as a person, and in particular about whether he was the sort of person who always tried to tell the truth. The basic principle here is very simple: you make an assessment by looking at the whole picture—that is, by looking at something in as large a context as possible.

This case is of particular interest because it shows in a very clear way how you go about dealing with this kind of problem. But the case itself is somewhat extreme. Normally you are not trying to see whether someone is lying. Normally your goal is much broader. You are trying to figure out what to make of something someone says in a meeting, or in a memorandum, or in instructions to an ambassador—that is, you are trying to figure out how to interpret a document. You are trying, above all, to figure out the connection between what was said and what actually happened. But the basic point I made about the McNamara material applies to this more general case as well. You proceed by casting as wide a net as you can. If you are interested in seeing what a key policy maker was actually thinking, you do not want to focus too narrowly on just one particular document. You want to see whether that policy maker said much the same thing in a wide variety of contexts, over a considerable period of time, and whether particular points were made with real feeling. And you want to see whether the words corresponded to what was actually done.

Suppose, for example, you see President Eisenhower talking about the need for America to pull out of Europe and for Europe to become an independent force in world affairs. How can you tell if such comments are to be taken seriously? For one thing, you see him talking in that vein over and over again, in all kinds of situations and to all kinds of people, before he became president, throughout his presidency, and after he left office. You see him at times making that point quite passionately. You work out what the implications of that sort of thinking would have had to be if the president were serious about it, and you look to see what was actually done. You do this sort of work and draw whatever conclusions you think are appropriate.

How to interpret the evidence you have is not the only problem you need to deal with when you are working with documents. Another basic set of problems has to do with the fact that the documentary record is always incomplete. Many conversations and thoughts are never recorded in the first place. Records of meetings might not include important comments that were made at those meetings, perhaps because the person who prepared the record was told not to include them. Even when documents are produced, scholars might not be allowed to see them, even decades after they were written. Or the material is released but in a highly selective way.[23] The most damaging material might not appear in the published diplomatic documents, no matter how important it is in historical terms. Key documents might be withdrawn before particular files are made available to the public. Or documents might be released in what is called "sanitized" (i.e., redacted) form. But that very term shows that the goal is to get rid of the "dirt" before historians get a chance to see it. The heart of the problem here is that since we are interested above all in government behavior, we have to rely mainly on the sort of material that helps us understand why governments did what they did, namely, documents produced by, and thus controlled by, the governments themselves. If what is contained in that material is considered politically sensitive—and the most important evidence often is, sometimes even many years later—governments will decide what to make available with those political concerns in mind. And sometimes important material has actually been destroyed, perhaps in the course of the very war whose origins those documents might have helped illuminate, perhaps for political or bureaucratic reasons. The minutes of the meetings of the U.S. Joint Chiefs of Staff, for example, for practically the whole of the Cold War period from 1947 on, were destroyed by military officials.[24] How then can a historian build an accurate interpretation on an evidentiary base of that sort?

---

[23] One very famous case involves the documents the German government published during the Weimar period on the origins of the First World War. On this episode, see Holger Herwig, "Clio Deceived: Patriotic Self-Censorship in Germany after the Great War," *International Security* 12, no. 2 (Autumn 1987): esp. 13–17; note also the sources cited in n. 21 of that article.

[24] The official rationale for the destruction of those records was that the JCS secretary had determined that "the transcripts generated did not constitute official minutes of the meetings but were merely working papers reflecting the reporter's version of events." McBride to Hastings, January 25, 1993, linked to http://www.gwu.edu/~nsarchiv/nsa/DOCUMENT/940228.htm.

Other cases become known from time to time. See, for example, "C.I.A. Destroyed Files on 1953 Iran Coup," *New York Times*, May 29, 1997. Note also the files on "Destruction of Documents" and "18 1/2 minute Gap," in the "Records of the Executive Assistant Pertaining to

These problems, though serious, are by no means entirely unmanageable. You can hope to get some real insight into major historical issues even when there are major gaps in the record. An archaeologist can get some sense for what a prehistoric community was like just by examining the relatively small number of artifacts that survive, and an astrophysicist can get some insight into the origins of the universe by studying the vestiges of cosmic events that took place "billions and billions" of years ago. In much the same way, the historian can hope to reach conclusions about certain historical problems, even when only limited evidence is available. Every piece of evidence is a window into the same historical reality, and you don't need to look through every window to get some sense for what that historical reality is.

How do you deal with the problem of limited source material? You just make the most of whatever evidence you do have. You look for whatever sources shed light—even indirect light—on the problem you are concerned with.[25] Suppose, for example, you can't answer key questions about Roosevelt's policy in 1941 just by examining the material in the U.S. archives. But you might be able to answer those questions about *American* policy by looking at *British* sources.[26] Or suppose you want to see what Soviet policy on the German question was right after World War II, and you don't have access to the Soviet archives. You can still form an opinion by looking at non-Soviet sources. You ask various questions. Were the Soviets interested, in the immediate postwar period, in setting up a unified German state, and indeed one not necessarily ruled by the Communists? Well, what would you have done if you were the Soviet ruler at that time and you wanted to work out an arrangement of that sort? At the very least you would have approached the western powers and made it clear to them that you were interested in working out that kind of arrangement. You have access to the archives of the western powers. You note the absence of such overtures. By studying the western sources, you note various other things the Soviets either did or failed

Presidential Tape Recordings," box 3, U.S. National Archives, College Park, Maryland; see http://www.archives.gov/research_room/independent_counsel_records/watergate/presidential_ta pe_recordings.html. Another case that turned up recently involves the United Nations. In March 2005 it was revealed that UN Secretary-General Kofi Annan's chef de cabinet had authorized the destruction of important files shortly after an "independent, high-level" committee had been appointed to look into the charges that had been leveled against the UN's Oil-for-Food program for Iraq. Independent Inquiry Committee into the United Nations Oil-for-Food Programme, *Second Interim Report*, March 29, 2005 (http://www.iic-offp.org/documents/Interim-ReportMar2005.pdf), pp. 81–82.

[25] On this point of method, see Jon Tetsuro Sumida, "A Matter of Timing: The Royal Navy and the Tactics of Decisive Battle," *Journal of Military History* 67, no. 1 (January 2003): esp. 129–30.

[26] For an important example, see James Leutze, *Bargaining for Supremacy: Anglo-American Naval Collaboration, 1937–1941* (Chapel Hill: University of North Carolina Press, 1977), pp. 202–5.

to do, and you draw whatever inferences you reasonably can from what you have noted. You are thus able to reach certain conclusions about what Soviet policy on the German question in 1945–46 actually was—perhaps not as rock-solid as you would like your conclusions to be, but a whole lot better than nothing.[27]

That's basically how you deal with the problems you face when whole bodies of source material are simply unavailable. But what do you do when you have evidence, but evidence that has been released in a way that reflects the political agenda of those who have made it available? If certain kinds of information are systematically excluded for political reasons from the corpus of available evidence, doesn't that mean that our understanding of the subject that evidence covers will necessarily be distorted—and distorted in a way that conforms to the objectives of the censors?

Again, there's a method for dealing with problems of this sort. It's based on the idea that if you can figure out what the bias of the declassifiers is, you can control for it when you are working out an interpretation. How then do you go about identifying the nature of the bias introduced into the body of available evidence by the fact that declassification is frequently a highly politicized process? The answer has to do with the fact that the historian is not dealing with a single highly efficient censor, who always does things exactly the same way. In the United States, for example, a particular document is often found in more than one file and in more than one repository. Those different copies are sometimes declassified differently by different people working at different times. We thus often get variant versions of the same document. You might think that newer versions are invariably more complete than older versions, but in fact earlier releases are sometimes less sanitized than later ones. This happens more frequently than you might think. Take, for example, the Bowie Report, an important document from 1960. The version declassified on July 20, 1989, although containing deletions, was actually more complete than the version published in FRUS in 1993; and a complete version of the document, with no deletions at all, was released in 1980.[28] This is just one example of the irrationality of the process, but it's important

---

[27] See Marc Trachtenberg, A Constructed Peace: The Making of the European Settlement, 1945–1963 (Princeton: Princeton University Press, 1999), pp. 30–31.

[28] Bowie Report, "The North Atlantic Nations: Tasks for the 1960's," August 1960, FRUS 1958–60, 7, part 1: 622–27. The version declassified in 1989 is available through the Declassified Documents Reference System (see esp. doc. nos. CK3100280059, CK3100280079, CK3100280087) and can be consulted online through subscribing libraries. The full unsanitized version was released through the Nuclear History Program in 1991; according to the declassification stamp on the title page of the NHP version, this document had been declassified in full by the State Department in July 1980. To see some of the passages that were sanitized out in the FRUS version, log on to the following URL: http://www.polisci.ucla.edu/faculty/trachtenberg/documents/ bowie.html.

to realize that you can use the method I'm going to talk about only because the process is not entirely rational.

In principle, that method is very simple. You just compare different versions of the same document, all of which may have been "sanitized" in various ways. Doing those comparisons gives you some sense for the bias of the declassifiers. Once you identify the bias, you can control for it when you're developing an interpretation.[29]

The fact that you can use this method only when you come across various versions of the same document is reason in itself for doing very extensive archival work—in this case, in various American archives. But it also makes sense when you're dealing with this sort of problem to do research in the archives of more than one country. People interested in U.S. foreign policy often think that all they need to do is use the American sources. But non-U.S. materials can be of enormous value, even if you are just interested in American policy. The use of non-U.S. sources allows you to make the sorts of comparisons I'm talking about here—comparisons which are possible in part because different governments have different declassification policies. The British, for example, do not go in for sanitizing documents, U.S.-style. When they release a document, they almost invariably release it in full.

Let me give a couple of examples that show how this method works. The first example has to do with the record of a meeting between Secretary of State John Foster Dulles and his German counterpart, Foreign Minister Heinrich von Brentano, that took place on November 21, 1957. Dulles made some very interesting comments on the nuclear question that were sanitized out of the version of the document published in FRUS in 1986.[30] In fact, only two brief passages were left in:

NUCLEAR WEAPONS

As to nuclear weapons, the Secretary said it seemed to us that it would be a very wasteful use of our combined assets if at this stage one country after another were to undertake the long and expensive process of trying to make such weapons. . . .

Making these weapons is, of course, a very costly process. United States production was increasing both the quality and quantity. We were getting them clean and making them smaller. We were doing this at enormous cost and it would be folly for all the countries of NATO to attempt to do this.

These extracts make it seem that Dulles wanted to keep the Europeans from acquiring nuclear capabilities, and indeed that was how that passage in the sanitized document was interpreted by some distinguished European

---

[29] For a more general discussion of this method, which I call "declassification analysis," see http://www.polisci.ucla.edu/faculty/trachtenberg/documents/doclist.html

[30] Dulles-Brentano meeting, November 21, 1957, *Foreign Relations of the United States, 1955–1957*, vol. 4 (Washington, D.C.: GPO, 1986), p. 202.

scholars.[31] But when you look at the full document as found in the archives, a very different picture emerges.[32] Dulles seems to be saying, in fact, that the U.S.-produced nuclear weapons in Europe could not remain under exclusive American control. The Europeans, he says (in one of the deleted passages), "needed to be assured of use to a greater extent than heretofore." The issue needed to be treated "on a basis of impartiality": "as far as we were concerned, we did not think it possible to contemplate a situation in which there were first and second class powers in NATO." He then went on to point out that when the London and Paris agreements had been worked out in 1954—very important agreements which among other things severely limited what the Germans could do in the nuclear area—"atomic weapons were regarded as something apart, both from a political and moral viewpoint." But "he did not think this would always be the situation." Nuclear weapons, in his view, were becoming normal weapons: "in the course of time, the distinction between nuclear and other weapons would gradually break down." The implication was that the 1954 constraints were not to be viewed as permanent, that movement into a fully nuclearized world was unavoidable, and that the U.S. government actually wanted to help the Europeans get more control of nuclear weapons. Indeed, after making the comment included in the FRUS version about the "folly" of the Europeans trying to replicate what the United States was doing in the nuclear area, Dulles went on to note that "the converse of this was that there must be confidence that the weapons would be available for our NATO Allies in time of war." All this is rather different from what the sanitized version of the document might have led you to think.

The obvious point to draw from this exercise is that if you can do so, you should by all means try to examine the full version of the document, and that point is certainly valid. This case shows quite clearly why, for really serious scholarly work, you should not rely exclusively on published sources and why you might need to do archival work. But there is another and perhaps more subtle point to be made. By doing this comparison, you are also learning something about the sort of thing the censors might want to keep you from finding out about—namely, the fact that the Eisenhower administration's attitude on European nuclear weapons was a good deal more liberal than you had been led to believe. In other words, you have learned something about the bias of the

---

[31] See, for example, Maurice Vaïsse, "Aux origines du mémorandum de septembre 1958," *Relations internationales*, no. 58 (Summer 1989): 261–62, and Peter Fischer, "Die Reaktion der Bundesregierung auf die Nuklearisierung der westlichen Verteidigung (1952–1958)," *Militärgeschichtliche Mitteilungen* 52, no. 1 (1993): 127–28.

[32] For the relevant excerpts from the full version of the document, with the passages sanitized out of the published version highlighted in red, see http://www.polisci.ucla.edu/faculty/trachtenberg/documents/brentano.html; the full document itself can be found in the State Department Central Files, Record Group 59, 740.5/11-2157.

declassifiers and thus about the way the body of available evidence has been distorted. You can now discount for that bias. You can interpret the evidence in the light of what you now know about the declassification process.

The second example has to do with the British and American records of a meeting between President Kennedy and Prime Minister Macmillan at Nassau on December 19, 1962. If you compare the British notes as found in the British National Archives with the U.S. minutes as published in FRUS, you can readily identify the passages in the British account that correspond to the passages sanitized out of the U.S. document. It turns out that most of those passages had to do with Germany. The U.S. censors did not want people to see how sensitive the American and British governments were to the whole question of Germany acquiring nuclear weapons.[33] Once again, you can identify the way the evidence was distorted, and once you identify the bias, you can control for it when you develop your own interpretation.

So while problems with evidence are real, there are certain methods you can use to deal with them. The key point—and this is the common thread that runs through all the examples I have given in this section—is that you want to cast as wide a net as possible. In assessing the evidence, context is everything. You want to develop a sense for the larger picture, but you also want to pay special attention to documents that are closely related to the specific documents you are interested in, including different versions of the same document that you find in different places.

This is one reason why, when you're doing really serious historical work, you want to go into the issues you are dealing with as deeply as you can. You go into a subject in that way not because your aim is to absorb a great mass of detailed information as a kind of end in itself. You do that kind of work because you want to develop as deep a sense as you can for the larger picture.

THE NUTS AND BOLTS OF HISTORICAL RESEARCH

In working with the primary sources, some of the most important skills you need to develop are quite mundane in character. You have to learn how to identify important sources relating to your topic. You have learn how particular sources can be used. You have to learn what to do when you set foot in an archive. You have to learn a lot of things of that sort. In this section, I want to talk a bit about these relatively prosaic matters. The discussion here, however, will just deal with some of the basics. More detailed information will be provided in appendix II.

---

[33] For a copy of the British notes with the passages that correspond to the deletions in the U.S. document highlighted, see http://www.polisci.ucla.edu/faculty/trachtenberg/documents/nassau.html. The sanitized U.S. record of this meeting is in FRUS 1961–63, 13:1091–101.

I'll be talking here about three kinds of sources: published (meaning in this context printed) sources, then microform and electronic sources, and finally archival sources. That order is not totally arbitrary. When you do research, it makes sense, as a general rule, to begin by examining the material that is most readily accessible and easiest to use, and that means that when you start to study the sources, you'll want to begin by looking at what has been published.

The most important of those sources are the great collections of diplomatic documents that a number of governments put out. These collections are of absolutely fundamental importance for our purposes, so let me spend a little time talking about them. The main American collection, which I have referred to a number of times before, is the State Department's *Foreign Relations of the United States* series, or FRUS. This currently covers the period from 1861 to 1976. It used to be that one or more volumes were published for any given calendar year. But beginning with the 1952–54 series, a given set of volumes would cover a three- or four-year period. Each volume in a particular series deals with a specific subject (like national security affairs or economic matters) or with a particular region of the world. The series includes not just State Department documents but also documents produced by other agencies of government, including presidential documents. There are certain special volumes, or collections of volumes, that were also published in the *Foreign Relations* series: for example, the series on the Paris Peace Conference of 1919, the volume on Yalta, the two volumes on Potsdam, and so on. Some special collections were published on microfiche—for example, the secretary of state's memoranda of conversation for the Truman and early Eisenhower periods—and in recent years some of the printed volumes have been published along with microfiche supplements. A full list is available online.[34] A number of volumes are also available online, as is a list of volumes currently available for purchase from the Government Printing Office.[35] By consulting the FRUS website, you can also see which volumes are scheduled to come out in the near future and when.[36]

The British have also published a number of important collections of documents: *British Documents on the Origins of the War, 1898–1914* (11 volumes); *Documents on British Foreign Policy, 1919–1939* (65 volumes); and *Documents on British Policy Overseas* (15 volumes so far, dealing with certain aspects of the post–World War II period down to 1975). Volumes in that latter series sometimes come with microfiche supplements. There is also an important privately published collection of British documents called *British Documents on Foreign Affairs*. This extraordinary collection covers the period from the

[34] http://www.state.gov/r/pa/ho/frus/c4035.htm.

[35] http://www.state.gov/www/about_state/history/frusonline.html; http://www.state.gov/r/pa/ho/frus/gpo/.

[36] http://www.state.gov/r/pa/ho/frus/c10996.htm.

mid-nineteenth century to 1950. It includes the documents considered important enough to be included in what was called the "confidential print"—documents that were printed and circulated to key British officials at the time—and is very extensive. The original printed documents are reproduced in facsimile. More than 500 volumes have been published so far. A list of what has been published is available online.[37]

The collections of French diplomatic documents, like the British ones, are broken down into a number of parts, but unlike their British counterparts, they all have the same title. The *Documents diplomatiques français* (DDF) for 1871–1914, published many years ago, contained 41 volumes. A number of DDF volumes dealing with the 1914–39 period have been published. Most of the volumes in this series (32 of them) deal with the 1932–39 period, but volumes covering the 1914–19, 1920–32, and 1939–44 periods are also being published. There are two DDF series devoted to the post–World War II period. In the 1944–54 series, 10 volumes have already come out. In the series that covers the period from 1954 on, 28 volumes, dealing with the period up to 1965, have been published so far. For a list, and ordering information, see the website that was set up for this collection.[38]

There are also collections dealing with German foreign policy. The collection covering the Weimar and Nazi periods, the *Akten zur deutschen auswärtigen Politik, 1918–1945*, is divided into five series and includes 62 volumes. Two of those series were also published in English translation: the *Documents on German Foreign Policy, 1918–1945* contained 18 volumes, covering the period from 1933 to 1941. The *Akten zur auswärtigen Politik der Bundesrepublik Deutschland* covers the period from 1949 on. At least one volume is published for each year, and so far over 30 volumes have been published, dealing with the 1949–53 and 1963–74 periods. There are also collections dealing with German policy before 1914, most notably the famous *Die grosse Politik der europäischen Kabinette, 1871–1914* (40 volumes in 54), and translated extensively into French as *La Politique extérieure de l'Allemagne, 1870–1914* (32 volumes). There is also a volume of German documents from the crisis that led to the Franco-Prussian War that was published in English translation in 1957: *Bismarck and the Hohenzollern Candidature for the Spanish Throne*, edited by Georges Bonnin.

The major collections of diplomatic documents are absolutely basic, but there are many other important published sources, too many in fact to even begin to list here. Many diaries and collections of papers have appeared in print. For example, 68 volumes of the *Papers of Woodrow Wilson* have been published, and 21 volumes of the *Papers of Dwight David Eisenhower* have appeared so far. To locate sources of this sort, one little trick is to do an

---

[37] http://www.lexisnexis.com/academic/2upa/Isiaas/BritishDocumentsForeignAffairs.asp.

[38] http://www.france.diplomatie.fr/archives/service/publications/doc-diplos/doc-diplos.html.

advanced search on your library's search engine and put the name of the individual you are interested in in two or three search fields simultaneously, say the author, title, and subject fields. You may be surprised by what turns up. Or you could search in the author field for a particular last name, and at the same time search in the title field for words like "papers," "correspondence," "letters," "writings," "diaries," and "works" (linking them together, if possible, with the Boolean connector "OR"). Extracts from diaries and personal papers can also often be found in biographies: Alistair Horne's biography of Macmillan is a good case in point.[39]

For certain purposes, you might want to go beyond the published material and dig a little deeper. And that means that you will probably want to use microfilm and microfiche sources, or sources available on CD-ROM or on the internet. Many such sources are available, and these sources are not hard to use. Most microfilm and microfiche collections come with printed guides, and by using those guides you can generally tell very quickly which reels or fiche, and often even which frames, to go to. And at most libraries you can use readers that allow you to make photocopies of the documents that interest you simply by pressing a button.

How do you find the collections relating to the topic you are interested in? You might want to start by browsing through some general guide listing which sources of this sort are generally available. Just about the best guide I have found is the guide the University of Chicago library has prepared covering its own collections; those materials will probably also be available either at your own institution or through interlibrary loan.[40] As a next step, you might want to browse through the online catalogues of the main private publishers of microform and CD-ROM material of interest to people in our field—University Publications of America, Scholarly Resources, Thomson Gale, and Adam Matthew, and you would probably also want to look at one of the catalogues of microfilm publications put out by the U.S. National Archives. These catalogues, as well as some of the more important collections themselves, are discussed in more detail in appendix II.

But as valuable as these nonarchival sources are—and it is sometimes amazing how much you can learn from sources of this sort—you might need to go into a subject at a deeper level, and that means that you might actually need to do some archival research. Many people find that prospect daunting. They stand in awe of work that is based essentially on archival research, as though archival work is the sort of thing only a highly trained scholar can do.

[39] Alistair Horne, *Macmillan*, 2 vols. (London: Macmillan, 1988–89).

[40] Frank Conaway, comp., "Guide to Microform and CD-Rom Sources for History and Political Science in the University of Chicago Library" (http://www.lib.uchicago.edu/e/su/hist/mfguide.html). See also "Major Microform Collections in the Combined Arms Research Library" (http://www-cgsc.army.mil/carl/resources/microform.asp).

But doing archival work is in principle no harder than doing any other kind of historical work. There is nothing mysterious about working in archives. No arcane set of skills is needed. And it is not hard to explain how this sort of work is actually done. First you identify the collections you would like to see. Then you get the finding aids for those collections—that is, the guides that tell you what they contain, box by box or volume by volume, and sometimes even folder by folder. When you decide which boxes or volumes or folders you want to see, you fill out and submit an order form for those materials. This can often be done electronically nowadays, and sometimes you are allowed to phone in your order a day or so in advance of your visit. The material is then pulled from the stacks. You pick up what you have ordered and go through the material in those volumes or boxes or file folders, xeroxing, scanning, or taking notes on the documents that strike you as important for your purposes (and making sure, in the case of the documents you've copied, that you note their exact archival locations, in case you need to cite them later on).

To use certain collections, you may have to get permission in advance, or you may have to come in with certain letters vouching for your bona fides as a researcher or with certain forms of identification, but it is generally not hard to find out what is required. The basic rules about what you need to do are normally laid out on an archive's website, and sometimes you can actually fill out whatever application is required on that website and submit it electronically.

How do you figure out which collections might be worth looking at? The official sources are located as a rule in fairly obvious places: a country's national archives, or perhaps the archives of its foreign ministry, or in special repositories like the presidential libraries in the United States or the various places where military records are kept. Those institutions generally have printed or online guides describing their collections. More detailed information about major official repositories is given in appendix II.

In many cases, you will also want to look at collections of private papers. Sometimes, in fact, these are the most important collections available. One of my favorite books, George Monger's *The End of Isolation*, was based mainly on sources of this sort. Sometimes a private archive is built around the papers of one key individual—the Institut Mendès France, for example—but more normally a given repository will include many such manuscript collections. In the United States, the Library of Congress houses a large number of important collections, as do various libraries and institutions connected with major research universities. In Germany, key collections are often housed in institutions connected with the main political parties. A particular individual's papers might also be found in one of the official repositories, like the Archives nationales in France or the British National Archives. Sometimes there are several collections of papers associated with one individual. There are, for example, collections of Acheson Papers at the Sterling Library at Yale, at the Truman Library in Missouri, and with the State Department materials at the National Archives in College Park, Maryland.

A particular individual's papers can be located in various ways. For papers in American repositories, you can consult the National Union Catalogue of Manuscript Collections (NUCMC). You can also search the material in the Research Library Group's Union Catalog by using the RLG's Eureka search engine (also sometimes called RLIN). Information on private British collections is available on the British National Archives website. Information on German collections is available online through the German Historical Institute in Washington. There are various gateway websites with links to important repositories, both official and unofficial, in Europe and indeed all over the world. I'll talk more about all of this in appendix II.

You can get leads about major sources in other ways as well. The specific archival locations for particular documents are usually given in the published diplomatic documents (or in other sources, like the Declassified Document Reference System, which I'll also talk about in appendix II). You can often tell from those annotations what the richest files are, and you can then go and look at those files yourself. Relevant archival collections are sometimes listed in the introduction to a published volume of documents or in editorial notes included in a particular volume. Historical works, including especially official histories (both published and unpublished) generally give their sources in footnotes and bibliographies; those leads can also point you in the right direction. You can also talk with people—both archivists and other scholars—to get ideas about sources. And there are various articles that discuss the archive situation in particular parts of the world (especially the former Soviet bloc) that you might find helpful in this regard.[41]

Once you figure out which collections you want to see, you then have to consult the corresponding finding aids to see which boxes or volumes to order. If you actually go to an archive, the archivists will show you where the finding aids are and show you how to fill out and submit an order form. But to save time or to be able to plan a research trip more effectively, you might want to check out the finding aids in advance. An increasing number of them have been put online, and I'll give references to the more important ones in appendix II. Many can be consulted by using the *National Inventory of Documentary Sources* (NIDS). NIDS was originally a collection of finding aids on microfiche with a hard-copy guide describing what was available, but it is now available online through subscribing libraries. There are also versions of NIDS for the British isles and for Canada. It is generally relatively easy to

---

[41] See, for example, Patricia Grimsted, "Archives of Russia Seven Years After," Cold War International History Project Working Paper No. 20 (2 parts) (Washington, D.C.: CWIHP, 1998) (http://wwics.si.edu/topics/pubs/ACF518.pdf and http://wwics.si.edu/topics/pubs/ACF51B.pdf).

locate and use finding aids, especially once you are at an archive. The situation at the U.S. National Archives in College Park, however, is a bit more complicated; I'll talk more about how the system there works in appendix II.[42]

Those are the basics. You'll learn more as you actually do archival work. You should make a point of talking with the archivists. They'll sometimes tell you about collections you did not know existed (since not everything that exists is listed in the guides). They can sometimes provide you with finding aids that are not on the open shelves. And you'll learn a few things just by looking at the documents. The State Department, for example, used to use a decimal system for organizing the records in its Central Files and that system could be a little arbitrary at times. It is sometimes hard to tell from the general filing scheme exactly where the documents dealing with a particular subject are to be found. The material on the First World War, for example, is filed under the decimal heading for political relations between Austria and Serbia, which is not exactly where you might expect it to be. So it's important to know that cross-references to particular files are often penciled in in the margins of documents; those notations tell you where other documents dealing with the subject covered in a particular passage are to be found.[43]

These are the kinds of things you learn as you do archival research. You just learn the ropes as you go along. There is nothing particularly difficult about any of this, and no one should be the least bit afraid to set foot in an archive. Archival work is in principle very simple and, to my mind at least, is also by far the most enjoyable thing a historian gets to do.

[42] See pp. 243–248 below.

[43] See, for example, the two cross-references penciled in in the margin of the extract from the record of the November 21, 1957, Dulles-Brentano meeting, reproduced in http://www.polisci. ucla.edu/faculty/trachtenberg/documents/brentano.html.

Chapter Six

STARTING A PROJECT

Suppose you're a political scientist and your goal is to get a handle on a certain theoretical issue by studying it in some specific historical context. How in practice do you proceed? How do you get such a project off the ground? What do you actually do when you begin a project of this sort?

In this chapter, I want to talk a bit about how the kind of project can be done, and I'm going to do that by taking you through a couple of exercises. I'll be talking in some detail about two specific projects and about the kinds of things you actually do in the early phases of those projects. Both of those projects have to do with the relative gains issue—that is, with the arguments relating to the idea that countries find it hard to cooperate with each other because they're afraid others will benefit more from those cooperative arrangements than they will. There's nothing particularly special about this issue; in fact, it's typical of the sort of issue you can study using the techniques I'll be using here.

So let's say that you've come across the relative gains argument in one context or another and feel it's worth analyzing in a serious way. How would you proceed? You'd probably want to approach it on two levels—first on the conceptual and then on the empirical level. You'd begin, therefore, by examining the theoretical literature on this subject. You'd want to look at the arguments that are made and see how they stack up against each other. You'd try to analyze them in terms of their internal logic: your goal would be to see whether they made sense in their own terms. In general, you'd want to see what was to be made of that whole body of thought.

But to do that, you first have to see what the literature in this area is, especially see what the important works are. But that you can do relatively quickly. You use some of the techniques I talk about in chapter 3 and in appendix I. The most obvious way to start is to do a title search for "relative gains" first in JSTOR and then in the Social Science Citation Index.[1] In JSTOR, ten titles turn up when you do a basic search for that term in the political science journals included in the JSTOR database.[2] By doing an advanced

---

[1] For a discussion of how these search engines are used, see appendix I, pp. 208–211 below.

[2] The figures given in this chapter are from searches done in late 2004. The searches discussed here were done using the MELVYL search engine (http://melvyl.cdlib.org/), the union catalogue for the University of California library system.

search, you can cast a somewhat broader net, and search for titles that contain both "relative" and "gains," but not necessarily right next to each other. This yields an eleventh title, Peter Liberman's "Trading with the Enemy: Security and Relative Economic Gains," which came out in *International Security* in the summer of 1996. A title search in the SSCI yields fifteen hits, the larger number here having to do with the fact that many of the JSTOR journals have a "moving wall": the issues for the last three years, or five years, are not available through JSTOR. And if you do a simple topic search in the SSCI for "relative gains"—that is, if you don't check the "title only" box— you'd get eighty-nine hits, many less directly related to the issue at hand than the listings that turned up in the title search, but still worth noting.

You can also do a Google search for "relative gains."[3] If you do, be sure to go into the advanced search window and limit the search results to files from the "edu" domain and perhaps also to files in pdf or doc format. That search turns up a number of recent academic papers and course syllabi with sections (and selected readings) dealing with the issue. Or alternatively (or in addition) you could search for "relative gains" in Google Scholar.[4] That search also yields a number of listings in this area ordered by relevance, many of which are linked to the text of the articles cited. In either case, you then look at the more recent articles and academic papers, focusing on the first few pages in each. In those introductory sections, authors commonly try to summarize the existing academic literature on the subject with a view to showing how their own works fit in. So reading those introductory passages, you quickly get a sense for the shape of the field—a sense, in particular, for which articles are of fundamental importance.[5] And that sense is reinforced by what you find in the syllabi that have turned up in the search.

What then are the most important works in this area? A handful of articles (by Grieco, Powell, and Snidal) are cited over and over again in those introductory passages and in the syllabi you've seen, and a passage on page 105 of Waltz's *Theory of International Politics* is also frequently quoted. You can then do a "cited reference search" for each of those articles in the SSCI to see whether there are more recent works dealing with the subject that you might find of interest—works that happen not to have the term "relative gains" in their titles.[6] Just reviewing the titles of the articles that come up in these "cited reference searches" gives you a certain sense for the sort of resonance

[3] http://www.Google.com.

[4] http://www.scholar.google.com/.

[5] For a particularly good example of an introductory passage of this sort, see one of the papers listed toward the top of the Google search: Robert Franzese and Michael Hiscox, "Bargains, Games, and Relative Gains: Positional Concerns and International Cooperation" (1998; http://www-personal.umich.edu/~franzese/rg15.pdf), pp. 1–3.

[6] There's no point searching for references to the Waltz book, since a very large number is bound to come up, most of them having little to do with the issue at hand.

the relative gains concept has had and for the general flavor of the literature on this question. From those lists of article titles, you can learn something about the way the concept has been applied to particular areas. You might be particularly interested, for example, in the way the relative gains argument has been referred to in articles dealing with Sino-American or Japanese-American or European-American relations.[7] It's not hard to look up the articles in question, find the footnote where the relative gains works are cited, and read the corresponding text. You may also note that some review articles turn up in the search; these are, of course, of particular value for your purposes at this point.

You can also do a full-text search for "relative gains" in JSTOR. You'll get many hits—265 for political science journals, 558 if you expand the search to include economics and finance journals. That's quite a few listings to go through, but it's important to note that the articles cited are listed according to "score"—that is, by how often and how close to the start of the article the search term appears. And this list allows you to see fairly easily how leading scholars—and that means above all scholars whose names you recognize—have reacted to the relative gains argument. Each listing actually includes a link for "page of first match," so you can go to the relevant passage very quickly. That again will give you a certain sense for how the field as a whole views this concept.

As you use these search engines, you're able to put together a file of the most interesting references very easily. You can often save full-text versions of the most interesting articles without much trouble. Pretty soon you'll have a fairly sizable collection of material, which you might want to save in a special file. This is something you'll want to come back to later when it's time to analyze the literature in a more systematic way.

Sometimes, as you do this bibliographical work with the goal of just developing a certain sense for what this particular area of scholarship is like, you come across real gems—passages you know will be very useful toward the end of the project when you're writing up your findings. One of the articles that turned up in the SSCI search was Robert Jervis's "Realism, Neoliberalism, and Cooperation: Understanding the Debate," which appeared in the summer 1999 issue of *International Security*. The "greatest deficiency in the relative/ absolute gains literature," Jervis wrote in that article, "is that it has remained largely at the level of theory and prescription, with much less attention to when decision makers *do* in fact exhibit relative-gains concerns."[8] If you're

---

[7] For example; H. Fukui, "The U.S.-Japan Alliance: Past, Present, and Future," *Journal of Japanese Studies* 26, no. 2 (Summer 2000): 520–26; P. A. Papayoanou and S. L. Kastner, "Sleeping with the (Potential) Enemy: Assessing the U.S. Policy of Engagement with China," *Security Studies* 9, no. 1–2 (Fall 1999): 157–87; Mark Sheetz, "Exit Strategies: American Grand Designs for Postwar European Security," *Security Studies* 8, no. 4 (Summer 1999): 1–43.

[8] Robert Jervis, "Realism, Neoliberalism, and Cooperation: Understanding the Debate," *International Security* 24, no. 1 (Summer 1999): 47 n. 14 (emphasis in original).

writing a paper or an article that does in fact try to deal with this issue in a specific empirical context, it's very nice to be able to introduce your substantive discussion with a quotation of that sort, especially one that comes from one of the most distinguished people in the field.

That's the sort of thing you just file away somewhere, knowing that you'll want to use it later on. For now, you're focusing mainly on a certain body of theory. You're trying to figure out what to make of it, but you're also trying to figure out how you can get a handle on the questions that lie at the heart of these theoretical discussions. And that basically means that you'll want to figure out some way of tying the analysis of these issues to the examination of some body of empirical evidence.

Questions of this sort are of fundamental importance, particularly at the start of a project. How exactly should the conceptual and empirical sides of the project be related to each other? Why exactly is a particular empirical subject worth focusing on? Does it give you a good handle on the basic conceptual problem? Given the key theoretical claims you've identified, what exactly would you expect to find in a particular historical context? Can you find any explicit claims laid out in the theoretical literature that you can examine in the light of the empirical evidence? You'll want to spend some time thinking about these kinds of questions fairly early on.

What else would you like to get out of the empirical work you'll be doing on the subject? Maybe you began with a vague sense that there was something wrong with a particular line of argument. Doing the empirical work might help you bring your thoughts into focus. Or it might help you see things of a general nature you hadn't seen before—things, perhaps, that no one who had written on the issue had been able to see.

THE TECHNOLOGY TRANSFER ISSUE: THE U.S. CASE

So you're going to have to choose some empirical issue to investigate, but what should it be? If the relative gains theorists are basically right, you'd expect countries to hoard their economic assets; if they have a technological edge over countries, you'd expect them to try to hold on to it. You'd in particular expect them to try to maintain their lead in technologies that have major military applications. To get at the issue, you might want to look at U.S. policy in this area. How does the U.S. government feel about the export of American technology, especially defense technology? How does it feel about technology-sharing arrangements that might benefit America, but which might benefit other countries even more?

How do you go about studying that issue? One way to start is with a Google search, say for "export military technology." This turns up a number of interesting hits. For one thing, the Center for Strategic and International

Studies (CSIS), a well-known research institute in Washington, D.C., had a project in 2000-2001 on "Technology and Security in the 21st Century: Study on Military Export Control Reform."[9] The website for that project has many interesting leads. In particular, it lists the names of people involved with the project—people you might eventually want to talk to, if you really get into the subject. The Google search also turns up a link to the Center for Technology and National Security Policy at the National Defense University, also in Washington.[10] You can see what various members of its staff have published. One of them, Daniel Burghart, wrote a book on a related question: *Red Microchip: Technology Transfer, Export Control and Economic Restructuring in the Soviet Union* (1992).

That book can serve as a kind of entrée to the literature. You look it up in the library catalogue and note the subject entries it's listed under. One of them is "Technology transfer—Soviet Union." So now you know what subject heading to look for. You lop off the "Soviet Union" and browse the subject headings that begin with the term "technology transfer." Those that contain the word "bibliography" are especially interesting at this point.[11] Some headings, like "Technology transfer—United States," have more entries than you want to go through, so you try to figure out some way to limit what gets listed. Maybe you could search for books in this category that also have the word "defense" or "security" in their titles? This yields a reasonable number of hits. Most of them are at best of only limited interest, but there are a couple that seem directly related to the topic you're interested in.[12] What distinguishes these books is that they're listed not just under the "technology transfer" subject headings but also under the subject headings for "national security." So you search for those two subject terms simultaneously. The list that comes up contains a whole series of relevant works, including a large number of congressional hearings and reports. And that list can be readily expanded by going into the subject links for some of the more interesting works that turn up in this search.

[9] http://www.csis.org/export/projdescript.htm.

[10] http://www.ndu.edu/ctnsp/about.html.

[11] Here are some titles listed under such subject headings: Stephen Stillwell, *Technology Transfer and National Security: A Bibliography of Journal Articles*, CSIA working paper no. 89-5 (Cambridge, Mass.: Center for Science and International Affairs, John F. Kennedy School of Government, Harvard University, 1989); Betty Taylor, *Transfer of Technology: A Bibliography of Materials in the English Language: International Law Bibliography* (New York: Oceana Publications, 1985); and John Chumack, ed., *Global Technology Transfer: Issues and Bibliography* (New York: Nova Science Publishers, 2002).

[12] For example, Gary K. Bertsch and John R. McIntyre, eds., *National Security and Technology Transfer: The Strategic Dimensions of East-West Trade*, Westview Special Studies in National Security and Defense Policy (Boulder, Colo.: Westview Press, 1983), and Herman Kahn, *National Security Policy Issues in U.S.-Soviet Technology Transfer* (Croton-on-Hudson, N.Y.: Hudson Institute, 1974).

So in an hour or two of work, you're able to identify a fairly substantial list of sources. The congressional material alone will provide a lot of grist for your mill. And some of the books that turn up are of interest for particular purposes. Michael Mastanduno's *Economic Containment*, for example, is worth looking at for a variety of reasons.[13] First of all, it was published in the Cornell series in Political Economy, and that tells you right away that it's of high quality. And Mastanduno, you may remember, was the author of one of the main articles that turned up when you did your search for "relative gains" in the periodical literature, so you figure there's a good chance he'll be sensitive in that book to the kinds of issues you're concerned with. The book, moreover, will give you some ideas about how a political scientist goes about developing an argument in this area, and some ideas also about the sorts of sources that can be used in the type of study you want to do. Other works are of interest for other reasons. Martin Tolchin's *Selling Our Security: The Erosion of America's Assets* has a certain polemic flavor—or at least that's what the title seems to suggest—and so that book (along with the reviews it got when it came out) might tell you something about the broader resonance of relative gains concerns in the country as a whole.[14] And some works—for example, the Office of Technology Assessment (OTA) report *Arming Our Allies: Cooperation and Competition in Defense Technology*—are of particular interest because they relate to the whole question of collaboration with allies.[15] This is worth focusing on because there is nothing particularly surprising about the control of militarily important exports to adversaries. But if you see a country worrying about allies getting too strong, that perhaps *would* be surprising—and therefore of particular importance in this context.

But this collection of sources, as important as it is, is just a beginning. There is still a certain hit-or-miss quality to it, and you'd like if you can to get something more comprehensive. So you go to the library stacks, and especially to those sections in the stacks where the call numbers in the list of books you've generated tend to cluster—in this case, the HF 1414.5 section most notably, but also the HC 110 area—and you look not just for the books on your list but other books related to the subject you're interested in, especially recent books put out by reputable publishers. And when you find them, you look especially at introductions, footnotes, and bibliographies.

You gradually develop, even as you do purely bibliographical work, a certain sense for who the important people in this field are—not just the authors

[13] Michael Mastanduno, *Economic Containment: CoCom and the Politics of East-West Trade,* Cornell Studies in Political Economy (Ithaca: Cornell University Press, 1992).

[14] Martin Tolchin, *Selling our Security: The Erosion of America's Assets* (New York: Knopf, 1992).

[15] U.S. Congress, Office of Technology Assessment, *Arming our Allies: Cooperation and Competition in Defense Technology* (Washington, D.C.: GPO, 1990).

of books but people who play a major role in particular projects, such as the CSIS project noted above or the OTA study that produced the *Arming Our Allies* report. You can see if those people wrote other things, in newspapers and magazines, or if they testified before or wrote studies for Congress, using, for this purpose, the various search engines discussed in the "open sources" section toward the end of appendix II. You can also do Google searches on these people. To give but one example: William W. Keller is listed as staff director for the OTA project that produced the *Arming Our Allies* study. When you do a Google search on him, the first link that turns up takes you into a website in which his publications are listed. One of them happens to be right on target for your purposes, an article Keller coauthored with Janne Nolan called "Mortgaging Security for Economic Gain? U.S. Arms Policy in an Insecure World," which came out in *International Studies Perspectives* in May 2001. And you also develop a certain sense for the keywords you can use to identify various additional sources— "FSX," for example, since the FSX affair was the subject of a number of books that turned up in the search.

The basic principle here is quite simple: as you do this kind of work, one source leads to another. To again take the example of the *Arming Our Allies* study: you note that it was done by the Office of Technology Assessment's International Security and Commerce Program. The very title of that program suggests that it might have produced other reports that you might want to see. You could do an author search for that program, but when you saw the original catalogue listing for *Arming Our Allies*, you might have noticed that it was available online. If you click into the link given in the catalogue listing, not only does the original text of the report come up, but you can also see from the URL how you might be able to get other OTA reports related to your project. The full URL for the report is http://govinfo.library.unt. edu/ota/Ota_2/DATA/1990/9005.PDF, but you can do what Bill Arkin, in his guide to national security sources on the internet, refers to as "URL surgery." You snip off the document-specific part of the internet address and try out the stripped-down URL http://govinfo.library.unt.edu/ota/. The link works. You're taken to a search engine for all the OTA reports maintained by the University of North Texas Libraries' "Cybercemetery," a partnership between the UNT Libraries and the Government Printing Office to provide permanent access to websites and publications of government agencies that no longer exist. (The OTA was closed down in 1995.) So you go into the "Cybercemetery" OTA webpage and then search for "International Security and Commerce Program." A manageable seventy listings turn up, all readable (and downloadable) in pdf. It turns out that many of those documents are directly related to the subject you're interested in.

You may have noticed, however, that this whole search process began in a rather peculiar way, with the Google search that turned up the Burghart book. But one of the points to bear in mind here is that what you're ultimately able to come up with does not depend on the particular point of entry you use. You could start the search in all sorts of ways, but sooner or later you'll end up seeing the same subject lists. You could, for example, have done various title, subject, and keyword searches, using words like "technology," "military," "security," "export," "policy," and "control," and combining them in different ways using multiple search fields. Or you have searched for a standard subject like "United States—foreign economic relations," and simultaneously searched for subjects (or even titles) that contained words like "technology" or "security." You might have to go into the subject links for some of the books that turn up when you do searches of this sort—indeed, you might have to repeat that process once or twice—but eventually some of the listings you identify will be linked to the technology transfer subject lists. So no matter how you start, you'll end up seeing the same titles I mentioned before.

Another point is that as you accumulate references, you notice that many of the books fall naturally into subcategories. Quite a few books and congressional materials relate to U.S. policy toward China; a number relate to U.S. policy toward Japan; a few have to do with Europe. This in itself suggests that you might want to organize your project in a particular way; indeed, it helps you see how the paper or article you'll produce might be structured. You could have a general section, followed by a section on China, a section on Japan, and a section on Europe. Maybe that would work? And seeing how the references cluster around regions might suggest something else. It occurs to you that you might be able to get additional sources by looking at bibliographies organized by geographical area. For example, to learn about the historical literature on U.S.-Japanese economic relations, you could look at the chapter on "The United States, Japan, Korea, and the Pacific since 1961" in Robert Beisner's *American Foreign Relations since 1600: A Guide to the Literature*, and then read the section on Japan, "Trade and Other Economic Issues," on pages 1572–73.

As those ideas take shape in your mind, you continue the search for sources. So far you have concentrated on books, but now it's time to begin generating a list of articles dealing with the technology transfer issue. The SSCI is your basic tool here, and you could begin your search with some of the articles that have turned up so far—articles cited in the footnotes and bibliographies of the books you've seen—or with the names of people who have written books on the subject or who have been prominently mentioned in other ways. Or you could do ordinary keyword searches. You're bound to generate quite a few listings this way. And then on to the dissertations and book reviews using the methods outlined in appendix I.

You also might want to see what's available on microfilm, using the technique described in appendix II. It turns out that there's a UPA series that might be useful: "International Trade: Special Series, 1971–1988," a collection of think tank studies. It's clear from the description that the issue of technology transfer looms large in this collection.[16]

So far you've been focusing on secondary sources. You may want to start thinking, even at this point, about whether there is any primary source material you can use. You've identified certain primary sources already, mainly congressional materials. But are there any executive branch sources you might consult? Certain volumes in the *Foreign Relations of the United States* series deal with foreign economic policy. Perhaps those are worth looking at for documents or for references. Perhaps you can find something in the *Declassified Documents Reference System*. Maybe you could do some archival research.

The goal, as you gather all this material and begin to examine it, is not just to get a sense for what was actually done in the technology transfer area— that is, for what controls were actually applied. You're even more interested in the sort of thinking that was going on, not only in the government but in semiofficial circles and in the country as a whole. And as you try to sort these issues out, you want to make sure that you have clear questions in mind and that you've worked out in your mind why exactly you want to focus on those particular questions.

BRITISH TRADE POLICY IN THE NINETEENTH CENTURY

Perhaps you're interested in the relative gains question, but you don't want to choose a topic having to do with contemporary U.S. policy. You might think that people have, in a sense, paid too much attention to the American case— that it's not right that our understanding of international politics should rest to so great an extent on the analysis of just one case, no matter how important it is in its own terms. You might therefore be looking for something to study from some other period in history. If so, the case of Britain in the early nineteenth century might come to mind. Britain, as everyone knows, was "the first industrial nation." And yet the British (you might have been taught at some point) did not adopt a policy designed to keep other countries from catching up: the old mercantilist controls were dismantled at that time; the British opted for a very liberal policy, and it didn't seem to matter much to them how exactly the benefits of free trade were divided up.

That story is at odds with what the relative gains theory would lead you to expect, and perhaps you're tempted to choose this case for that very reason. You might dislike the relative gains argument and you might think the British case could serve as a kind of battering ram, but that's not a good way to approach the problem. You never get much out of a project if you think you know the answers in advance. It's much better to frame the questions in

---

[16] http://www.lexisnexis.com/academic/2upa/Abe/SpecialStudiesInternationalTrade.asp.

such a way that the answers are not known in advance but turn instead on what the evidence shows. In this case, for example, you might want to see what role, if any, security considerations played in the making of British foreign economic policy, or how they entered into the policy discussion at the time.

How then do you proceed? You can begin by doing a search in the library catalogue for something obvious, something like "history British trade policy." A title search does not turn up much, but a keyword search yields eighty-three hits. Some listings seem especially relevant, but others—even if they deal with different periods—help you see which subject headings to search under. Here are some of the basic subject headings that turn up:

> Free trade—Government policy—Great Britain—History
> Great Britain—Commercial policy—History
> Great Britain—Commercial policy
> Great Britain—Coreign economic relations
> Great Britain—Foreign economic relations—History

As you go through those subject lists, either the full lists or versions that you pare down in some way, a number of titles catch your eye. They might be of particular interest because they deal directly with the question of how economic and political issues relate to each other. Or maybe you want to check out a particular study because it covers a fairly broad period and you hope it will give you a good overview of the topic. Or perhaps you're interested in some books because they seem to have a certain political science flavor (which is important, given the way you've set up the project). In some cases, you might want to look at certain books simply because you think their bibliographies are worth checking out. Here are a number of titles that fall into these various categories:

> D. C. M. Platt, *Finance, Trade, and Politics in British Foreign Policy, 1815–1914* (Oxford: Clarendon Press, 1968)
> Judith B. Williams, *British Commercial Policy and Trade Expansion, 1750–1850; with a Bibliographical Chapter by David M. Williams* (Oxford: Clarendon Press, 1972)
> Cheryl Marie Schonhardt, *A Model of Trade Policy Liberalization: Looking Inside the British "Hegemon" of the Nineteenth Century* (Ph.d. diss., UCLA, 1991)
> Steven E. Lobell, *The Challenge of Hegemony: Grand Strategy, Trade, and Domestic Politics* (Ann Arbor: University of Michigan Press, 2003)
> Alexander Brady, *William Huskisson and Liberal Reform: An Essay on the Changes in Economic Policy in the Twenties of the Nineteenth Century* (London: Oxford University Press, 1928)

You note where the books you found cluster in the stacks—in this case, the HF 1533 and HF 2044–HF 2045 areas seem particularly promising—and you can check out what's in those locations, focusing especially on the bibliographies in the books you find there. But suppose you want to cast a broader net. You can use some of the other techniques I've already mentioned. You can try, for example, to do a Google search. Maybe if you search for something as straightforward as "history of British trade policy," something will turn up? As it happens, you do get a couple of hits when you search for that phrase. It turns up, in fact, in the footnote to a paper on the World Trade Organization that's been posted online: "For a comprehensive political history of British trade policy in the nineteenth century, see A. C. Howe, *Free Trade and Liberal England, 1846–1946* (Oxford: Clarendon, 1998)." This book seems to be quite a find, but you probably would have found it anyway, even without the Google search, if only because it has an HF 2045 call number.

You can get leads in all kinds of ways. You might, for example, want to look at the bibliographies at the end of various general histories of Britain in that period. And you can identify a number of book-length bibliographies simply by adding the term "bibliography" to the various subject headings that turn up as you do this bibliographical work, or by doing a subject search for one or another of those headings in one search field and using "bibliography" as a search term in a second search field. Using this method, a number of bibliographies turn up:

David Nicholls, *Nineteenth-Century Britain, 1815–1914*, Critical Bibliographies in Modern History series (Hamden: Archon Books, 1978).

Lucy M. Brown and Ian R. Christie, eds., *Bibliography of British History, 1789–1851* (Oxford: Clarendon Press, 1977)

Ian R. Christie, *British History since 1760: A Select Bibliography* (London: Historical Association, 1970)

Robert Goehlert, *Resources for the Study of British Politics* (Monticello: Vance Bibliographies, 1979)

And other bibliographies—for example, R. C. Richardson and W. H. Chaloner, *British Economic and Social History: A Bibliographical Guide* (1996)—are referred to in one or another of the books you look at in this phase of the project.

You'll get many other leads when you go to the parts of the stacks where the books you're interested in are found and read their introductions and bibliographies. For example, E. L. Woodward's *The Age of Reform, 1815–1870*, a general history of Britain, whose importance is reflected in the fact that it went through a number of editions, is in the DA 530 section of the stacks. But John Clarke's general survey of British foreign policy in the 1782–1865 period also has a DA 530 call number, and you come across it as you're browsing in the area where Woodward's *Age of Reform* is located. You then look up "free trade" in the index to the Clarke book and you find a ten-page passage dealing with that question. Clarke talks about a number of works there, and he also lists a whole series of important works dealing with trade issues in the paragraph in his bibliography devoted to that subject.[17] One of the books he talks about is Bernard Semmel's *The Rise of Free Trade Imperialism*.[18] Semmel, at the very beginning of that book, discusses a number of works on the subject, the first of which is an older book by R. L. Schuyler, which, Semmel says, was about "the dismantling of the system of mercantilist colonialism."[19] Near the Semmel book in the stacks is the Howe book I referred to before, and Howe, also in the first couple of pages of his book, talks about the older literature and cites (among other works) the Schuyler book. Howe, moreover, lists a whole series of works in his bibliography, including more detailed studies, such as A.J.B. Hilton's *Corn, Cash, and Commerce: The Economic Policies of the Tory Governments, 1815–1830*.[20] And near the Semmel and Howe books in the stacks is *Protection and Politics: Conservative Economic Discourse, 1815–1852*, by Anna Gambles, a book with other references to the literature on this question—for example, to C. Schonhardt-Bailey's *The Rise of Free Trade*.[21] And doing a Google search for that latter author and title, you find a link to a recent review article on the subject, an article that might enable you to get up to speed on the literature very quickly.[22] As you go from book to book and from reference to reference, you gradually identify a whole series of works that didn't turn up when you did the regular bibliographical work with the library catalogue. Some of them—for example, Albert Imlah's *Economic Elements in the Pax Britannica*—seem to be of fundamental importance.[23]

And on it goes: there's no limit to number of ways you can attack the problem. You could, for example, pick up some general economic history or some history of technological change—David Landes's wonderful book, *The Wealth and Poverty of Nations* (1998), is one very well-known work of this sort—and see what the author has to say about the spread of technical knowledge and

[17] John Clarke, *British Diplomacy and Foreign Policy, 1782–1865* (London: Unwin Hyman, 1989), pp. 300–309, 344–45.

[18] Bernard Semmel, *The Rise of Free Trade Imperialism* (Cambridge: Cambridge University Press, 1970).

[19] R. L. Schuyler, *The Fall of the Old Colonial System: A Study in British Free Trade, 1770–1870* (New York: Oxford University Press, 1945), p. 1.

[20] A.J.B. Hilton, *Corn, Cash, and Commerce: The Economic Policies of the Tory Governments, 1815–1830* (Oxford: Oxford University Press, 1977).

[21] Anna Gambles, *Protection and Politics: Conservative Economic Discourse, 1815–1852* (Rochester: Boydell Press, for the Royal Historical Society, 1999); C. Schonhardt-Bailey, ed., *The Rise of Free Trade*, 4 vols. (London: Routledge, 1997). Volume 4 is titled: *Free Trade Reappraised: The New Secondary Literature*.

[22] Kevin H. O'Rourke, "British Trade Policy in the Nineteenth Century: A Review Article," *European Journal of Political Economy* 16, no. 4 (November 2000): 829–42.

[23] Albert Imlah, *Economic Elements in the Pax Britannica: Studies in British Foreign Trade in the Nineteenth Century* (Cambridge, Mass.: Harvard University Press, 1958).

about efforts to control it. Landes, for example, has a chapter ("The Wealth of Knowledge") dealing with the question, and in that chapter he relies heavily on the work of another scholar, John Harris. Eleven works by Harris, most of them dealing with this issue, are in fact cited in Landes's bibliography.

You can now switch gears and search for articles. Your basic tool here, again, is the Social Science Citation Index. You can in fact use some of the articles cited in the books you've seen (e.g., the Harris articles) as jumping-off points for SSCI searches. The whole process is not terribly systematic, but as you do this sort of work, you gradually find yourself seeing the same works mentioned over and over again. When that happens, you sense that you've probably identified most of the important writings dealing with the subject.

In the course of doing this work, moreover, you come across a number of primary sources. You see a reference to a four-volume collection edited by Lars Magnusson called *Free Trade: 1793–1886*,[24] a work that might be worth checking out. Why? In part simply because it's been published fairly recently. For that reason alone, the introduction might be worth reading and the references might be particularly good. And maybe the documents themselves might have something of real value for your purposes.

Of the various primary sources you come across as you do this bibliographical work, a couple stand out above all the others. First of all, there's the *Goldsmiths'-Kress Library of Economic Literature*, a massive collection of microfilmed materials covering the period through 1831 and containing 24,246 items (with a multivolume hard-copy guide). And then there's another source that turns up when you search simultaneously for the two subject terms "Great Britain—Politics and government" and "sources":

Papers of the Prime Ministers of Great Britain, 459 reels of microfilm, with guide (Brighton: Harvester Microform, 1981–)
  Series 1. Papers of William Pitt the Younger
  Series 2. Papers of Sir Robert Peel
  Series 3. Papers of Lord Liverpool
  Series 4. Papers of the Duke of Newcastle
  Series 5. Papers of Lord North
  Series 6. Papers of George Grenville
  Series 7. Papers of Spencer Perceval
  Series 8. Papers of William Ewart Gladstone

But these are sources you'd only want to approach after you've learned the basics about the period—how the political system worked, who the important people were, and so on.

So that's what you can come up with in the course of about five hours of bibliographical work. Other sources are, of course, available—the *Parliamentary*

---

[24] Lars Magnusson, ed., *Free Trade: 1793–1886* (New York: Routledge, 1997).

Debates, for example, and periodicals like the *Times* of London, the index for which goes back to the eighteenth century. And it's a safe bet that many other sources will turn up as you do your work—that is, as you see which sources other people have used. But even now you can be confident that there's enough material available in or through your home library to sustain a serious research effort in this area.

Chapter Seven

WRITING IT UP

You BEGIN a major historical research project—one based, that is, on extensive research in original sources—by trying to get a sense for the scholarly "lay of the land." Your first goal when you start a project is to see what scholars have had to say about the subject you're interested in—to see where they differ and what specific claims lie at the heart of those disagreements. You want to see what the key questions are and how those questions relate to each other. The aim, in other words, is to develop a certain sense for the "architecture" of the problem. And as you do that work, as you analyze the historical literature in that way, you're automatically preparing yourself for phase two of the project, the research phase.

That phase is obviously of fundamental importance. It's by doing research that questions get answered, that problems get solved, that you come to understand what was going on. That phase, in fact, looms so large in your project that when you're done with your research, you may feel that your work is nearly over. You know you'll probably have to write something up. In fact, you'll probably *want* to bring the project to completion by pulling your thoughts together and presenting your conclusions in a relatively formal and well-organized way. You may think that's fairly easy and that it shouldn't take too long to put your conclusions down on paper.

But as any experienced scholar can tell you, it's not easy to write something up. It's not easy because to write is to think. When you write, you're virtually forced to think seriously about what of any importance has emerged from all the work you have done. You ask yourself, as you prepare to write up your findings: what do I have to say that's worth saying? Why should anyone care about the conclusions I've reached? And when you decide *what* you want to say, you still have to figure out *how* exactly you want to say it. A given thought can be put into words in all kinds of different ways; the various points you want to make can also be put together in any number of ways. How you do these things matters enormously. How you express a thought and how you structure a text are not mere "matters of style" that do not deserve much attention. These "matters of style" are far more important than you might think.

"Style," the well-known historian Peter Gay once wrote, "is not the dress of thought but part of its essence."[1] The famous jurist Benjamin Cardozo

---

[1] Peter Gay, *Style in History* (New York: Basic Books, 1974), p. 189.

made the same basic point. Form, he said, was no mere adornment: "The strength that is born of form and the feebleness that is born of lack of form are in truth qualities of substance. They are the tokens of the thing's identity. They make it what it is."[2] This insight applies with particular force to historical work. Suppose a historical text just rambles along. When there's no real point to the discussion, the message is that there is no rhyme or reason to the story—or, if there is, that the author has not been able to see it. But a clear and well-constructed text gives a very different message. The reader gets a sense for what was driving things, a sense for what really mattered. So if your goal is to bring out what is important, you need to write as clearly as you can.

You thus have to concern yourself with matters of style both at the microlevel and at the macrolevel. In practice that means you're probably going to have to spend a lot of time working on your text. This is something that just has to be done, whether you like doing it or not. As Jacques Barzun and Henry Graff point out in their well-known guide to historical research and writing: "care lavished on expression is not some optional embellishment bestowed upon your work; it is the means through which your work begins to exist."[3]

You may find this point somewhat depressing. You may think that an ability to write is a gift or a talent—that it's something you're either born with or not—and you may feel that if you're not one of the lucky ones, you'll probably never be able to write well. But an ability to write is a skill that can be developed. It in fact can be developed in three ways: through practice, through example, and through precept. Of these, practice is by far the most important. You see what works for you. If something works, you add it to your bag of tricks. If something doesn't work, you avoid it.

You can also learn about style from the books and articles you read. Whenever you read a historical text, pay attention to what the author is doing *as a writer*: to how the argument is structured, to how the text is written, to the various rhetorical devices that are being used. If you dislike the way a particular work of history is written, try to put your finger on why you dislike it. That again will give you some sense for what to avoid in your own work. On the other hand, if you like the way a historian does something, make a mental note of that too. You might want to use that technique in your own work.

---

[2] Benjamin N. Cardozo, "Law and Literature," in *Selected Writings of Benjamin Nathan Cardozo*, ed. M. Hall (New York: Matthew Bender, 1975), pp. 339–40; the essay was originally published in 1925. In the passage from which this quotation is taken, Cardozo quotes Henry James: "Form alone takes, and holds and preserves substance, saves it from the welter of helpless verbiage that we swim in as in a sea of tasteless tepid pudding."

[3] Jacques Barzun and Henry Graff, *The Modern Researcher*, 5th ed. (New York: Harcourt Brace, 1992), p. 34.

This applies even to little things, like beginning the text with a good quotation or ending a section with a one-sentence paragraph.

You can also develop a certain skill as a writer by approaching the issue on a more abstract level. You can try to understand in a general way what makes for good historical writing. What should a historical text look like? What should you aim for when you are ready to write something up? You can try to learn a bit about the nuts and bolts of historical writing—about how in general to go about designing a historical text and how in practice to go about writing it.

What to Aim For

When you write a work of history, what exactly are you trying to do? Suppose you've come to understand certain things, and say you want to produce a text that allows you to pass those insights on to the reader. What would such a text look like?

To answer that question, you first need to think about what it means to understand something. Do you remember how that issue was dealt with in the first two chapters of this book? The point there was that understanding essentially meant seeing how things fit together. The past has a certain structure, and in developing an interpretation the aim is to show what that structure is—to "provide patterns within which data appear intelligible."[4] You can't give any sense for what that *structure* is, for what those *patterns* are, if you present everything you found in the sources. Your presentation has to be selective. You have to bring out what is truly important, and that means that relatively trivial matters cannot receive much attention. Your goal, after all, is not to present a picture that is as complex as reality itself: "the more like a reflection a map becomes," as Hanson said, "the less useful it is as a map."[5]

If your goal is to explain something, you need to show how the main elements in the story are related to each other causally—how one thing led to another, how one thing followed from another "as a matter of course." In other words, you want to show, drawing on your understanding of how the world works, why, at least to a certain extent, they *had* to happen the way they did—why what you observe is in a certain sense natural. You don't want to push the point too far, but to the extent you can, you want to give a sense for a certain element of *necessity* in the story, and that means that you want to get at the basic *logic* underlying the course of events.

[4] N. R. Hanson, *Patterns of Discovery: An Inquiry into the Conceptual Foundations of Science* (Cambridge: Cambridge University Press, 1958), p. 90.

[5] Ibid., p. 28. See also N. R. Hanson, *Observation and Explanation: A Guide to the Philosophy of Science* (New York: Harper, 1971), pp. 79–83.

Those two last italicized words I'm juxtaposing on purpose. Remember the Hanson argument I talked about in chapter 1? "The necessity sometimes associated with event-pairs construed as cause and effect," he said, "is really that obtaining between premises and conclusions in theories which guarantee inferences from the one event to the other."[6] It was the "logical guarantee that theories place upon causal inferences that explains the difference between truly causal sequences and mere coincidences."[7] History, of course, is very different from physics; the logic of historical change is fairly loose, and the element of necessity is relatively weak. But when we do historical analysis—when we're developing a historical interpretation—we still talk to a certain extent about the way things *have to be*; and in doing so we draw on our understanding of the way the world works.

Suppose, for example, I wanted to write about great power politics in the late 1960s and early 1970s. I could talk about the deterioration of Sino-Soviet relations in the 1960s in one section and then go on to talk about détente in Europe and improving U.S.-Soviet relations in other sections. The reader might learn a lot about various issues but would not see how these developments were linked. Or I could talk about how relations between Russia and China deteriorated and how this was one of the main factors that led to détente in Europe, using language that suggests that events just happened to take that course and could easily have developed differently. Or I could pull these sections together by arguing that the deterioration of Sino-Soviet relations was bound to have an effect on relations between the USSR and the west. That third approach would have a stronger interpretive bite, precisely because it evokes a certain element of necessity.

When I say that there *had to be* a certain connection between the coming of détente in Europe at the end of the 1960s and the deterioration of Sino-Soviet relations in the course of that decade, what exactly do I mean? As I pointed out earlier in the book, that sort of language is not to be taken literally. It's just a shorthand way of saying that strong pressures could be presumed to come into play in such a case, not that such pressures were in any fundamental sense irresistible. But even when I talk loosely about the way things "had to be," that sort of talk still reflects the fact that I'm making a kind of deduction: in making that claim, I'm essentially drawing on my general sense for how international politics works. I'd be drawing, that is, on a kind of "theory."

So Hanson's basic point applies to historical work, and that point is very important for our present purposes. Historical explanation is historical argument: to explain is to reach for some kind of deductive structure. If the goal is

---

[6] Hanson, *Patterns of Discovery*, p. 90.

[7] N. R. Hanson, *Perception and Discovery: An Introduction to Scientific Inquiry* (San Francisco: Freeman, Cooper, 1969), pp. 285ff., 295, 309–10 (the quotation is on p. 309).

to show how things are linked *causally*, the points the historian makes about them have to be linked *logically*. So for example: if I want to explain why hundreds of U.S. nuclear weapons ended up under the control of America's European allies by the end of the Eisenhower period, I would begin by talking about how Eisenhower did not want the defense of Europe to rest forever on America's shoulders. I would go on to point out that *this implied* that the Europeans ultimately had to stand on their own—that Europe, to use Eisenhower's phrase, had to become a "third great power mass" in world affairs. It was *inconceivable*, this argument would run, that the Soviets could be allowed to take over all of Europe because of the effect that would have on the global balance of power and thus on America's position in the world; there *therefore* had to be a counterweight to Soviet power on the continent, and if America was not going to provide it, the Europeans would have to balance Soviet power by themselves. But *if* the Europeans were to stand up to a great nuclear power like the USSR without direct American support, *then* they would have to have a nuclear capability of their own. Eisenhower *therefore* wanted to help them develop that capability, and to that end he wanted the Europeans to get effective control of many of the American weapons deployed on their territory.

Notice the words I've just italicized. They're the sort of words you use when you're developing an argument—that is, when you want your text to have a kind of deductive structure. You can also see from that passage that I'm drawing on a kind of theory, on my basic understanding of how international politics works. This is typical of the kind of argument that lies at the heart of many historical works. And that's no accident: if the goal is to explain something, this is the sort of structure—the sort of feel—a text should have. This is true even in the case of narrative history. A historian may, of course, want to explain something by telling a story, but that story has to have a certain *logic* to it. The goal in that case is to bring out the different elements of that story and show how they're related to each other, how key developments follow naturally, *logically*, from other things that have already been shown. And the goal ideally is to explain things that the reader might find perplexing (like the Europeans being allowed to get effective control of American nuclear weapons) by showing how they follow naturally from other things that are much easier to understand (America not wanting to have to carry the burden of European defense forever). "An event," as Hanson says, "is explained when it is traced to other events which require less explanation."[8]

This fundamental idea—that if you want to explain something, some kind of deductive structure should lie at the heart of your analysis—has a number

---

[8] Hanson, *Patterns of Discovery*, p. 94. See also his *Observation and Explanation*, pp. 39–40, and his comment on p. 43 of that book: "[L]inking the unfamiliar with the familiar has always been a glory of theoretical science."

of implications about how a text should be written. The text, first of all, should have the flavor of an argument. Transitional passages, the connective tissue that ties the different elements of the text together, are of particular importance in this regard. They have to reflect your real understanding of how those elements are in fact related. But to make sure that you are bringing out those logical connections, you may want to make a point of using words like "so," "thus," and "therefore," the "if . . . then" construction, and phrases like "this implied that," "it followed that," and "what this meant was that" in passages of this sort. If they're missing, and especially if you introduce those passages with words like "another" and "also," words that often signal weak structure, that's a sign that you have not pulled things together as well as you might have. In that case, you might want to go back and think more deeply about how your points are connected to each other.

The basic point that the text needs a conceptual core, that some sort of argument should lie at the heart of the text, has a major bearing on how you deal with empirical evidence. A text is not a Thanksgiving turkey, to be stuffed with as much detail as possible. Empirical evidence should never be presented for its own sake or because you think it "speaks for itself." Every empirical fact needs a conceptual peg to hang on. You use empirical evidence to make a point, and as a general rule you do not want to present a piece of evidence if it does not relate to your argument in a fairly direct way. Indeed, even if a piece of evidence *does* relate directly to some point you are making, you still might not want to include it in the text. Too much evidence might weigh down your argument. You don't want your text to be a "long, hard slog," to use a phrase Donald Rumsfeld made famous in another context. So when you're making a point, it's often best to give only strong evidence in the text. (Weaker evidence can still be cited in footnotes.) The same point applies to quotations. A good quotation is like gold in your hands. But quotations, and especially block quotations, need to be used sparingly. They lose their value if you use too many of them.

This does not mean, of course, that the empirical side of an argument is to be slighted. Every serious historian knows that hard evidence is of absolutely fundamental importance and that historical analysis has to have real empirical depth. What you are saying obviously has to be grounded in reality; your points have to be supported effectively by evidence found in the sources. And while you may try to reach for a kind of deductive structure, you know that you cannot push that effort too far. You cannot impute a tighter logic to historical reality than is warranted by your sense for what was actually going on. History is not like mathematics or even physics. The logic of historical change is fairly loose; elements of chance and of choice always come into play; and to explain why events took the course they did, you have to talk a lot about the specific choices that were made, about the kind of thinking that happened to exist at the time, about the way chance events affected what happened. So you of course have to present a lot of factual material, and you have to talk about many things that cannot be explained in purely deductive terms.

It's all a question of balance, and the art of doing historical work consists in large part of knowing how to strike the right balance between the conceptual and the empirical sides of the analysis—between logic and argument on the one hand and evidence on the other. You don't want to lean too heavily in either direction. You certainly don't want to slight the importance of the empirical evidence. But to the extent that you reasonably can, you want to throw into relief what was really important. The conceptual core of the text should not be hard to see.

And if the goal is to highlight what really mattered, the text obviously needs a relatively clear and simple structure. You do not want to develop such a complex picture that the reader drowns in an ocean of detail and can no longer understand what was going on. If you develop your interpretation to the point where it is as complex as the evidence appeared when you first encountered it, you end up "destroying the very thing" an interpretation is "meant to achieve—namely, the provision of an 'awareness of structure' absent from the original confrontation with a complex of phenomena."[9] Patterns cannot emerge if the text is too complex: to provide an "awareness of structure," a certain premium has to be placed on clarity and on simplicity. The text has to be lean, focused, and relatively easy to follow and to absorb.

Four key points follow from these basic principles. The first is that you need to emphasize fundamentals. International politics is about conflict. Say you are studying a specific episode, and a particular conflict lies at the heart of the story there. So you ask: what is that conflict *about*? What does each side *want*? What sort of *policy* does it adopt? What kind of *thinking* is that policy rooted in? Those questions will direct your attention to what really matters and thus to what needs to be highlighted in the text.

The second point is that you need to apply a very strict rule of relevance to everything you put in the text. How does a given passage relate to the argument as a whole? If it's only minimally relevant, maybe it should be dropped, no matter how interesting you think it is in its own right. How does it relate to what comes immediately before or after it? If it does not fit in well at a particular point, you have to find some other place to put it. If it does not fit in well anywhere, you might have to put it in a footnote or in an appendix or even drop it entirely. It is vitally important not to break the flow of the argument. The last thing you want is to have the text come across as disjointed or hard to follow.

The third point has to do with what I call the "principle of concentration"—that is, with the idea that the evidence and arguments you have bearing on

---

[9] Hanson, *Observation and Explanation*, p. 81. In the original passage, Hanson was talking about models in general; I am applying his point here to historical interpretation in particular.

one specific point should be concentrated in a one tightly constructed passage in the text. The "principle of concentration" was originally one of the old "principles of war." The idea was that forces were not to be scattered all over the battlefield but were to be concentrated in places where they would be most effective. In historical writing it also makes sense to concentrate your firepower at key points in the text. If you pull related points together, you will have a simpler, leaner structure, and your core argument will be stronger because the pillars on which it rests will be stronger.

The fourth point is that a big part of your job as a historian is to draw from the great mass of evidence you've examined a small number of things you think are important. The reader should never get the sense that a massive amount of raw data is being dished out. The text needs to have a more finished, a more "digested" feel.[10] Since the facts never just speak for themselves, part of your job is to make them "speak" by drawing out their meaning and providing appropriate commentary—that is, by bringing out the handful of major points you want the reader to note. But just a handful: you want your text to have a relatively simple structure because that's the only way to convey a sense for the structure of historical reality—a sense, that is, for what was really important in the story.

How to Do It

Suppose then that you have a general sense for the kind of text you'd like to produce. But how in practice do you go about producing it? What do you actually do when you're ready to write something up? In this section, I'm going to describe the method that works for me. It may not work for everyone. But if you're not sure how to write up your findings, it helps to have at least something to go on.

My basic premise here is that a work of history needs to be *designed*—that before you begin writing, you need some sort of *plan*. This point might strike you as obvious, but not everyone agrees that this is the case. The argument is sometimes made that after having worked on a topic for some time, you can sit down with pen and paper and plunge into the writing. The ideas, it is said, just flow. A draft gets written, and only then do you switch gears and rework it into something you're happy with. That method might work for some people, but it strikes me as a terribly inefficient way to proceed. Sooner or later you'll have to think seriously about what you want to say and how you want to say it, and it seems to me that the sooner you do it, the better.

---

[10] For a wonderful example of a short passage that sums up a vast amount of material, see the very first paragraph in the second volume of Bernadotte Schmitt's *The Coming of the War, 1914* (New York: Scribner's, 1930).

How then do you come up with a plan? You do it in two stages. First, you try to figure out what you want to say—that is, the *points* you want to make. Second, you try to figure out how those points can be related to each other. You try to figure out, in other words, how a text based on those points can be structured.

So the first goal is to develop at least a rough sense for the points you want to make, but how do you go about doing that? It's important to remember that you are not just starting from scratch. Certain ideas have already taken shape in your mind. When you did your research, you were not just gathering data "like pebbles on the beach," mindlessly absorbing factual information. You had approached the subject with certain questions in mind. Presumably you were able to come up with some answers. You were engaged in a thought process, and that process had led somewhere. What were those answers? Where exactly did that thought process lead? You can certainly jot a few things down.

And then you can ask yourself a number of other key questions. What's interesting or important or surprising about what you came up with, and how does the view you now hold differ from the conventional wisdom in this area? Does your work pass the "so what?" test, the "who cares?" test, the "why does this matter?" test? How would you explain to someone new to the subject why exactly your findings do matter? How has your own understanding of the subject changed in the course of your work? What impact has your work had on your understanding of international politics on a more general level? What do you want the reader to "take away" from your account, and why? What of any importance did you personally "take away" from the work you did? The answers to all these questions will help determine the points you want to make, and when a point occurs to you, again, you just jot it down on a piece of paper.

Finally—and I'll come back to this later on—you might also be able to sharpen your sense for what you want to say by reading through your notes and the materials you gathered during the research phase.

But getting some idea for the points you'd like to make is just a first step. Your next goal is to pull at least some of those points together—you don't need to use all of them—into a single overarching argument. You're looking for some sort of structure, for some sort of framework for your text, and using the points you've come up with as raw material, you now begin to construct it. You start by trying to see connections between the various points you've jotted down. In looking for connections, again, you are not starting from scratch. Various connections have taken shape in your mind already. In the course of your work, you developed a certain sense for the "architecture" of the historical problem you're concerned with—that is, for how different issues relate to each other. That means that you will almost automatically be able to see how the points you can make about those issues relate to each other. You came, for example, to see how general arguments rest on specific claims, and you've examined some of those specific claims in the light of the evidence. You thus have points to make about those specific claims, and because of the way your thought process developed, you already understand how those points relate to the more general issues you're dealing with.

So a structure takes shape, and to a certain extent that structure emerges without any great effort on your part. The real thinking, or at least most of it, took place during the earlier part of the project. So at this point, it's generally not hard to see what your major arguments are going to be and how various relatively narrow points you would like to make relate to those more general arguments. Take the case of the research project about America's road to war in 1941 that I talked about in chapter 4. Three major arguments had emerged as the issues related to that question were sorted out. First, there was an argument about American policy: that the U.S. government had deliberately put the United States on a collision course with Japan. Then there was an argument about Japanese policy: that the Japanese were much more interested in avoiding war with America than was commonly assumed. And finally there was an argument about the relationship between U.S. policy toward Japan and U.S. policy toward Germany: that U.S. policy toward Japan has to be understood in the context of Roosevelt's policy of bringing the United States into the European war. And in the course of the project a whole series of narrower points had emerged: about the modus vivendi, for example, or about the bureaucratic politics interpretation of the oil embargo. At this point, now that the bulk of the research has been done, it's easy to see how those specific points relate to those more general claims. It's not hard to see, for example, how the point that President Roosevelt was still in charge of policy—that policy had not been hijacked by midlevel officials like Acheson—related to the more general argument about U.S. policy toward Japan in late 1941. So to a certain extent, as you try to design a text, a structure emerges in a fairly straightforward way.

To a certain extent, but by no means entirely, and as a general rule, there are many decisions about how a text should be put together that have to be made. Your points have to be developed in a certain order, and it is often not obvious what that order is. In the 1941 case, for example, is it best to begin by talking about U.S. policy toward Germany or by talking about U.S. policy toward Japan? In principle, you could do it either way, but doesn't one way work better than the other? You have to make a judgment, and to make it, you have to think about how well each of those two structures would work. And you also have to worry about where various specific points ought to be put. Should you discuss the modus vivendi in your section on Japanese policy or in the section on U.S. policy toward Japan? It might fit well in both sections, but you generally don't want to have to discuss it twice. So where's the best place for it?

There are many such issues you need to think about, and the easiest way to provide yourself with a framework for thinking about them is by writing an outline. An outline does not lock you into anything. It's simply a sketch, and writing one up is a low-cost method for assessing a particular way of structuring the text. You read a particular outline and try to imagine how well a text with that kind of structure would work. Will the argument flow as well as you would like? Does it feel disjointed? If there are problems with that particular approach, can they be solved by moving things around? If a particular approach does not work well at all, you can try out another approach by writing another outline. To do that, you may have to go back and rebuild from the ground up: what do you really want to say? What exactly are you trying to do?

You play around with different ways of structuring the argument, and you eventually come up with the best outline you can. And that outline can help in all kinds of ways when you actually start to write. An outline, for example, gives you a certain sense for the larger picture, for what the text as a whole will look like, as you work on a particular passage. It thus helps you figure out how to frame the argument in that passage—how to make it fit into the text as a whole.

But an outline is just a tool. It should never be taken as a straitjacket. A text has a life of its own. As you write, you develop a sharper sense for what you want to say, so as you move along, new outlines often have to be drawn up. In the end, there might be an enormous gap between the text you produce and the outline you started out with. But this does not mean that the whole process of outlining has not served an important purpose. As Eisenhower said (in a very different context to be sure, but the point applies here as well), "plans are worthless, but planning is everything."

What this means is that when you start to write, all you need is a relatively simple outline. Since your outline is very much subject to change, and also since one of its main functions is to help you hold on to some sense of the larger picture, a picture you want to keep relatively simple, there is generally little point to making it too elaborate. You may have specific points you want to include in particular sections. You can simply note those points in the corresponding part of the outline. At this stage, you are just sketching out your basic argument, and you do not really have to work out what you are going to say in any detail.

So you begin to write, and it's only when you have to write a particular passage that you need to come up with some sort of specific plan for that passage. And again you do that by working up an outline for that passage, building on what you have already done earlier in the project. Your building blocks here are the notes you've taken and the other materials you've assembled during the research phase. So how you proceed at this point depends on how you've done your research. What sort of notes have you taken? Have you xeroxed a lot of documents? How have you dealt with the material that you've assembled?

How then is research in this very mundane sense to be done? The answer used to be very straightforward. You were supposed to take careful notes when you did research. You were allowed to use either index cards or notebooks, but you were supposed to take extensive notes on what you read. And this in fact is the way research traditionally had to be done. But when it became possible to photocopy materials inexpensively, a researcher could proceed in a very different way. Instead of taking extensive notes, he or she could simply xerox whatever material was considered important. But this method is sometimes frowned upon. Barzun and Graff, for example, explicitly advise researchers against it.[11]

My own view is very different. I think that if you want to do serious work in this area, it makes sense to xerox quite extensively. It's not just that it takes so much time to transcribe key passages by hand, or that all kinds of errors tend to creep in when you copy text that way. The more basic point is that it is hard to know the first time you read a document which passages are worth transcribing or what sort of note to make about the meaning of the document as a whole. The meaning of a document might only become clear later on when you have done a lot more work on the subject, and in practice you often need to come back and reread a document in its entirety, preferably in conjunction with a whole series of related documents. So I think it's much better to work with xeroxed material than with index cards or notebooks. But let me explain how I use that material and you can decide for yourself whether that method makes sense for you.

First, this is how I deal with published sources. I take notes on the books and articles I read—nothing too extensive (since I don't want to be swamped by detail), just the bare minimum I need to note what I think is important. I take notes on the volumes of documents I go through in much the same way. If I own those books, I'll mark up key passages in pencil, often writing brief comments in the margins. If I don't own them, I'll xerox key passages and mark up those xeroxed pages in much the same way. The notes and xeroxes (if any) for that particular source will then be stapled together. The top page in that packet will include whatever information I'd need if I ever had to cite that work in something I was writing. That material I then arrange alphabetically by author's last name or, in a separate file, by title if it is something like a published collection of documents.

I handle unpublished material—archival material and material available on microfilm, microfiche, or in some electronic format—a little differently. I photocopy or print out whatever documents I find of interest, taking care to write the full archival or other reference at the bottom of the first page.

---

[11] Barzun and Graff, *The Modern Researcher*, p. 25n.

When I read a photocopied document, I mark it up and then attach a "Post-it" self-stick note sheet to its first page. On that sheet, I note as succinctly as I can what is important about the document, indicating the pages on which key passages can be found. (These are generally the passages I've marked up.) On the top right-hand corner of the first page I write the date of the document—this serves mainly as a document identifier—and then I file the documents in chronological order. If I have more than one document with a given date, I'll put letters after the date—9/12/50a, 9/12/50b, and so on—so that different documents can be distinguished from each other.

When it's time to write, I read through all this material—the documents (arranged in chronological order) and the notes and photocopied pages from books and articles. This serves two purposes. First, it gives me a stronger sense for what the story is and for the points I'd like to make, and thus helps me with the design of the text as a whole. Second, it helps me organize everything I've gathered so I'll be able to see which documents and other material relate to which specific issues, and thus to which specific passages in the text I intend to produce. A particular document or passage from a book or article will generally relate to one or two particular topics—something like "Yalta Agreement" or "German nuclear question." So going through those piles of material enables me to see what those topics are. I then devote a separate piece of paper to each of them, and on each of those topic sheets, I list those documents (identified by date alone) and other sources (generally identified by author, maybe with short title), indicating very briefly how this source bears on the issue in question. For example, if a document is of interest mainly because it shows what French president Charles de Gaulle's views were on the question of a West German nuclear capability, on the "German nuclear question" sheet I'll give the date of the document and write "deG on Ger nuc."

I'll have those topic sheets in hand when I'm ready to write a particular passage. At that point, I get out the relevant topic sheet, pluck out all the material listed there from the files I've compiled, and reread that material. I read the documents in chronological order, to get what sense I can for how things developed over time. I then think about what's important in what I've just read, and this helps me decide which specific points I'll need to make in that passage. I then try to work out an outline for that passage, and as I draft that passage with all these materials at hand, I can easily quote from key texts. The footnotes will also be easy to write up, since I'll have the exact references at hand.

That method can be used to write passage after passage, and eventually a draft is complete. But this first draft is just a beginning. Even after a first draft has been written, you'll almost certainly still have a long way to go. The revision process is of fundamental importance, and there is no getting around the fact that it's also generally quite time-consuming. You have to revise at both the macro- and the microlevel. Your text might pass through a whole series of drafts before you are satisfied even with its basic structure. The revision process, especially in its early stages, can be quite radical. A second or even a third or fourth draft might have to be written essentially from scratch. And even after you are satisfied with the basic structure of your text, you probably still have a lot of work to do. Passages that block the free flow of the argument might need to be moved around or deleted; the logic tying the different elements in the text together might need to be brought out more clearly. Particular sentences might seem a bit "off" and will have to be reworked or even dropped.

Deletions, in fact, are of central importance at this point. When people sit down to write, they often like to include everything that occurs to them, and first drafts frequently have a kind of "kitchen sink" quality. But during the revision phase, a very different set of considerations has to come into play. The overall character of the text—its coherence, its smoothness, it clarity—needs to become the fundamental concern. At this point, it often becomes clear that including even a perfectly valid point might do more harm than good, and deleting certain points might actually strengthen the text. And so from one draft to another, a good deal of material ends up getting dropped.

You do the revising, in other words, basically by turning yourself into an editor and a critic. You can take the method outlined in chapter 3 and apply it to your own work. What's your basic argument in the text? Does it come through clearly enough? What sort of structure does the text have? What stands out in your mind right after you read it? How would a reader summarize what you've written, and how hard a time would a reader have doing that? As you think about these things, you might hit upon an entirely different structure—a better structure—for your argument, and so you write a new draft, perhaps using (people sometimes say "cannibalizing") some of the passages found in the previous draft. When the basic structure is as good as you can make it, you then work on the text at the microlevel. Again, you read it with a critical eye. Are the transitions good enough? Is it too repetitive? Can the argument be tightened up? Can you prune the text in any useful way? You work on sentence structure, on word choice, and so on. You pay special attention to "guideposts"—the title, the subtitle, chapter or section titles, the introduction, the conclusion (if any), first and last paragraphs in chapters and sections and in the work as a whole, first and last sentences, and so on. Are they doing the job you want them to do? You work on the text until everything you read sounds right and everything is as it should be—that the references, for example, are written up the right way. There are standard rules governing these things, and if you're not sure about how something is done, you should look up the rule in the University of Chicago Press's *A Manual of Style*.

What all this means is that you have to develop a certain skill as a writer, and fortunately there are some very good books that can help you do this.

The Elements of Style by William Strunk and E. B. White is a little gem—
brief, to the point, and easy to absorb. I also like *Style: Toward Clarity and
Grace* by Joseph Williams, a more demanding book, but very much worth
reading. If you need to work on your writing but are pressed for time, you
should at least read pages 17–79 and 135–50 in that book.[12] The best time to
read those sections is when you're about to begin revising your first draft.
And there are various specialized books you might want to consult at some
point for one purpose or another—for advice on usage, for example, or if you
have to write a grant proposal, or if you want to turn your dissertation into a
publishable manuscript.[13]

This, of course, is just one of the skills you need to do historical work. In
previous chapters I've discussed some of the others. I tried to show what they
are and how you can go about developing them. The basic point there, and
indeed the basic point of this book as a whole, is that there's no great mystery
to any of this. History is a craft, and a craft is something you can learn.

---

[12] Joseph M. Williams, *Style: Toward Clarity and Grace* (Chicago: University of Chicago Press, 1990). See also Williams's *Ten Lessons in Clarity and Grace*, 6th ed. (New York: Longman, 2000).

[13] On usage, the two most famous works are H. W. Fowler, *A Dictionary of Modern English Usage* (many editions) and Wilson Follett, *Modern American Usage* (New York: Hill and Wang, 1966). See also Theodore Bernstein, *The Careful Writer: A Modern Guide to English Usage* (New York: Atheneum, 1965). On writing grant proposals, see Lynn Miner and Jeremy Miner, *Proposal Planning and Writing* (Westport, Conn.: Greenwood, 2003). UC Berkeley's Institute of International Studies has a website devoted to the subject (http://globetrotter.berkeley.edu/DissPropWorkshop/). On turning a dissertation into a book, see Beth Luey, ed., *Revising Your Dissertation: Advice from Leading Editors* (Berkeley: University of California Press, 2004), esp. chap. 1, 4, and 7; note the other works cited in this book's bibliography.

Appendix I

IDENTIFYING THE SCHOLARLY LITERATURE

IN THIS APPENDIX, I'm going to discuss some specific sources of bibliographical information and how they can be used. Because many of the sources covered here are only available online, I've posted an online version of this appendix with direct links to those sources[1] as well as a short bookmarkable webpage listing the links included in this appendix.[2] Both webpages will be updated periodically.

I. BIBLIOGRAPHIES, GUIDES, AND RELATED WORKS

There is no bibliography—not that I could find, at any rate—that covers the history of international relations as a whole. One general work, however, is still worth looking at, even though it's by now a little out-of-date:

> Byron Dexter, ed., *The Foreign Affairs 50-Year Bibliography: New Evaluations of Significant Books on International Relations 1920–1970* (New York: R. R. Bowker for the Council on Foreign Relations, 1972). This has relatively lengthy reviews of what at the time of publication were the most important works in this area.

For a more comprehensive listing of works, mainly in English, French, and German, dealing with international politics in the twentieth century, check out the very important bibliography put out as a supplement to the most important German journal in this area, the *Vierteljahrshefte für Zeitgeschichte*:

> Institut für Zeitgeschichte, *Bibliographie zur Zeitgeschichte*. This running bibliography was originally published over a two-year cycle but now comes out annually. A cumulative version, including the material that had been listed between 1953 and 1980, was published under the same title (Munich: K. G. Saur, 1982–83).

---

[1] http://www.polisci.ucla.edu/faculty/trachtenberg/methbk/AppendixI.html.
[2] http://www.polisci.ucla.edu/faculty/trachtenberg/methbk/AppendixI(links).html.

If you're interested in finding out about relatively minor conflicts, at least in the post-1945 period, you might want to look at:

James Ciment, ed., *Encyclopedia of Conflicts since World War II* (Armonk, N. Y.: Sharpe Reference, 1999). This has relatively brief articles on many conflicts; each article has a short list of other works bearing on those conflicts.

Most bibliographical or historiographical works deal with either the foreign policy of a single country or with specific topics. By far the largest number of such works relate to American foreign policy:

Robert Beisner, ed., *American Foreign Relations since 1600: A Guide to the Literature,* 2 vols. (Santa Barbara, Calif.: ABC-CLIO, 2003)

Richard Dean Burns, ed., *Guide to American Foreign Relations since 1700* (Santa Barbara, calif.: ABC-CLIO, 1983)

Michael Hogan, ed., *America in the World: The Historiography of American Foreign Relations since 1941* (Cambridge: Cambridge University Press, 1995) (surveys originally published in the journal *Diplomatic History*)

Michael Hogan, ed., *Paths to Power: The Historiography of American Foreign Relations to 1941*(Cambridge: Cambridge University Press, 2000) (historiographical articles originally published in *Diplomatic History*)

Gerald Haines and J. Samuel Walker, eds., *American Foreign Relations: A Historiographical Review* (Westport, Conn.: Greenwood, 1981)

Gordon Martel, ed., *American Foreign Relations Reconsidered, 1890–1993* (New York: Routledge, 1994)

Robert Schulzinger, ed., *A Companion to American Foreign Relations* (Malden, Mass.: Blackwell, 2003)

Warren I. Cohen, ed., *Pacific Passage: The Study of American–East Asian Relations on the Eve of the Twenty-first Century* (New York: Columbia University Press, 1996)

Some very useful lists of books are available online. See, for example:

Richard Immerman's *Bibliography on U.S. Diplomatic History, 1918–1975*[3]

"Contemporary China: A Book List" (Lynn White and Valerie Cropper). Seventy-seven pages, with sections on Sino-American relations, China's policies toward Russia and Japan, collections of documents, and so on.[4]

Books page from Nick Sarantakes' *U.S. Diplomatic History Resources Index.*[5]

The Sarantakes website is a very valuable resource for people in our field. In one part of the website, in fact, Sarantakes lists a whole series of bibliographies available online dealing with specific topics relating to international

---

[3] http://astro.temple.edu/~rimmerma/461bib.html.

[4] http://www.wws.princeton.edu/~lynn/Chinabib.pdf.

[5] http://faculty.tamu-commerce.edu/sarantakes/stuff-books.html.

affairs and U.S. foreign policy.[6] This I think is one of the handful of lists you will certainly want to look at as you begin a new project in this area.

There are also a couple of encyclopedias you might find useful:

> Bruce W. Jentleson and Thomas G. Paterson, eds., *Encyclopedia of U.S. Foreign Relations*, 4 vols. (New York: Oxford University Press, 1997)
>
> Alexander DeConde, Richard Dean Burns, and Fredrik Logevall, editors in chief, and Louise B. Ketz, executive editor, *Encyclopedia of American Foreign Policy*, 2d ed., 3 vols. (New York: Scribner, 2002)

The first of these, prepared under the auspices of the Council on Foreign Relations, has relatively brief articles on a wide range of topics. The second has longer articles on a number of subjects related to international politics, not just U.S. policy. In each case, the articles include a handful of bibliographical references.

Don't forget that if your library uses the Library of Congress cataloguing system (as most research libraries nowadays do), you can find books dealing with U.S. relations with a particular country by going directly to the E183.8 section of the stacks. The part of the call number that follows the "E183.8" will begin with the same letter that that country's name begins with. Books, for example, dealing with U.S. relations with China will begin with "E183.8 C6," and those dealing with U.S.-Canadian relations will start with "E183.8 C2" and so on.

To find bibliographies dealing with the foreign relations of countries other than the United States, you could take one of the bibliographies I just listed—the Beisner book, for example—and then look it up in your library catalogue. You could see which subject headings it is listed under and then do a subject search, substituting for "United States" in the subject heading the name of that particular country. The following are typical of the sorts of listings that can be found with this method:

> Sadao Asada, ed., *Japan and the World, 1853–1952: A Bibliographic Guide to Japanese Scholarship in Foreign Relations* (New York: Columbia University Press, 1989)
>
> Thomas Hammond, *Soviet Foreign Relations and World Communism: A Selected Annotated Bibliography of 7,000 Books in 30 Languages* (Princeton: Princeton University Press, 1965)
>
> William E. Echard, *Foreign Policy of the French Second Empire: A Bibliography* (New York: Greenwood Press, 1988)
>
> Andrew R. Carlson, *German Foreign Policy, 1890–1914, and Colonial Policy to 1914: A Handbook and Annotated Bibliography* (Metuchen, N.J.: Scarecrow Press, 1970)
>
> Abraham J. Edelheit and Hershel Edelheit, *The Rise and Fall of the Soviet Union: A Selected Bibliography of Sources in English* (Westport, Conn.: Greenwood Press, 1992)
>
> Donna Evleth, *France under the German Occupation, 1940–1944: An Annotated Bibliography* (New York: Greenwood Press, 1991)

[6] http://faculty.tamu-commerce.edu/sarantakes/stuff-bib.html.

There is also an important series of guides—the "Guides to European Diplomatic History Research and Research Materials"—covering the period from 1918 to 1945. These works discuss both primary and secondary sources, and although some of them are getting a little out-of-date, practically all of them are still worth looking at:

Robert H. Johnston, *Soviet Foreign Policy, 1918–1945: A Guide to Research and Research Materials* (Wilmington, Del.: Scholarly Resources, 1991)

Sidney Aster, *British Foreign Policy, 1918–1945: A Guide to Research and Research Materials* (Wilmington, Del.: Scholarly Resources, 1984)

George W. Baer, *International Organizations, 1918–1945: A Guide to Research and Research Materials* (Wilmington, Del.: Scholarly Resources, 1981)

Alan Cassels, *Italian Foreign Policy, 1918–1945: A Guide to Research and Research Materials* (Wilmington, Del.: Scholarly Resources,1981)

Christoph M. Kimmich, *German Foreign Policy, 1918–1945: A Guide to Research and Research Materials* (Wilmington, Del.: Scholarly Resources, 1981)

Robert J. Young, *French Foreign Policy, 1918–1945: A Guide to Research and Research Materials* (Wilmington, Del.: Scholarly Resources, 1981)

There are also useful guides dealing with particular subjects. These can often be found by doing a title search for a particular phrase (like "Cold War") and, simultaneously, for a word like "guide," "bibliography," "handbook," or "survey." Or they can be found by tacking on the word "bibliography" to a specific subject heading and then doing a subject search, or perhaps by adding that word in a second search field as a separate search term. Here are some examples of bibliographies that turn up in this way:

Michael Kort, *The Columbia Guide to the Cold War* (New York: Columbia University Press, ca. 1998), which contains a 104-page annotated bibliography (pp. 207–310)

J. L. Black, *Origins, Evolution, and Nature of the Cold War: An Annotated Bibliographic Guide* (Santa Barbara, Calif.: ABC-CLIO, 1986)

Sino-Soviet Conflict: A Historical Bibliography (Santa Barbara, Calif.: ABC-CLIO, ca. 1985)

Ronald M. DeVore, *The Arab-Israeli Conflict: A Historical, Political, Social & Military Bibliography* (Santa Barbara, Calif.: Clio, 1976)

Sanford Silverburg, *Middle East Bibliography* (Metuchen, N.J.: Scarecrow, 1992)

The United States in East Asia: A Historical Bibliography (Santa Barbara, Calif.: ABC-CLIO, 1985)

James S. Olson, ed., *The Vietnam War: Handbook of the Literature and Research* (Westport, Conn.: Greenwood, 1993)

David L. Anderson, *The Columbia Guide to the Vietnam War* (New York: Columbia University Press, 2002)

Lester H. Brune and Richard Dean Burns, *America and the Indochina Wars, 1945–1990: A Bibliographical Guide* (Claremont, Calif.: Regina, 1991)

If you're interested in the Vietnam War, there's a very good bibliography available online:

Edwin E. Moïse's "Vietnam War Bibliography"[7]

And if you're interested in the Cold War, you might want to look at the list available on the Parallel History Project on NATO and the Warsaw Pact's website:

Parallel History Project, "Selective Bibliography on the Cold War Alliances"[8]

There's also a series of guides that you might find useful for some purposes: the *International Relations Information Guide* series put out by Gale in the late 1970s and early 1980s. These guides dealt with particular areas of the world and with some specific questions. Here are some of the titles:

John J. Finan and John Child, *Latin America, International Relations: A Guide to Information Sources* (Detroit: Gale, 1981)

Richard J. Kozicki, *International Relations of South Asia, 1947–80: A Guide to Information Sources* (Detroit: Gale, 1981)

J. Bryan Collester, *The European Communities: A Guide to Information Sources* (Detroit: Gale, 1979)

Mark R. Amstutz, *Economics and Foreign Policy: A Guide to Information Sources* (Detroit: Gale, 1977)

Alexine L. Atherton, *International Organizations: A Guide to Information Sources* (Detroit: Gale, 1976)

Even though these books are a bit out-of-date by now, you might be able to use them to find more recent works of this sort in these areas. Just look them up in your library's catalogue, then click into the links for the subject headings they're listed under. For example, in the MELVYL catalogue, the union catalogue for the University of California system, the Finan and Child book is listed under the subject heading "Latin America—Foreign relations—Bibliography," and one of the other books listed under that heading is more recent:

G. Pope Atkins, *Handbook of Research on the International Relations of Latin America and the Caribbean* (Boulder, Colo.: Westview Press, 2001)

Two general areas have their own literature—military affairs and intelligence—and various guides can help you find your way around. For works on U.S. military history, you can check out the following works:

Daniel K. Blewett, *American Military History: A Guide to Reference and Information Sources* (Englewood, Colo.: Libraries Unlimited, 1995)

[7] http://www.clemson.edu/caah/history/FacultyPages/EdMoise/bibliography.html.
[8] http://www.isn.ethz.ch/php/services/selective_bibliography.htm.

Susan Kinnell, *Military History of the United States: An Annotated Bibliography* (Santa Barbara, Calif.: ABC-CLIO, 1986)

Jack C. Lane, *America's Military Past: A Guide to Information Sources* (Detroit: Gale, 1980)

There's also a very good list of important works in this area available online:

Eliot Cohen's "Strategic Studies Core Readings"[9]

You might also want to take a look at the list of military history bibliographies on the Institut de Stratégie Comparée website.[10]

Note also the more than twenty bibliographies that have come out as part of Garland Publishing's Wars of the United States series, a collection covering the historical literature dealing with many of America's wars. Examples include:

Benjamin Beede, *Intervention and Counterinsurgency: An Annotated Bibliography of the Small Wars of the United States, 1898–1984* (New York: Garland, 1985)

Dwight L. Smith, *The War of 1812: An Annotated Bibliography* (New York: Garland, 1985)

Anne Cipriano Venzon, *The Spanish-American War: An Annotated Bibliography* (New York: Garland, 1990)

David R. Woodward and Robert F. Maddox, *America and World War I: A Selected Annotated Bibliography of English-Language Sources* (New York: Garland, 1985)

John J. Sbrega, *The War against Japan, 1941-1945: An Annotated Bibliography* (New York: Garland, 1989)

Keith D. McFarland, *The Korean War: An Annotated Bibliography* (New York: Garland, 1986)

Louis A. Peake, *The United States in the Vietnam War, 1954–1975: A Selected Annotated Bibliography* (New York: Garland, 1986)

On intelligence matters, you might want to take a look at some of the following references:

The U.S. Intelligence Community: Information Resources (Columbia University Library), which lists important works plus bibliographies dealing with the subject[11]

Mark M. Lowenthal, *The U.S. Intelligence Community: An Annotated Bibliography* (New York: Garland, 1994)

Neal H. Petersen, *American Intelligence, 1775–1990: A Bibliographical Guide* (Claremont, Calif.: Regina Books, 1992)

Literature of Intelligence: A Bibliography of Materials, with Essays, Reviews, and Comments (J. Ransom Clark)[12]

[9] http://www.sais-jhu.edu/programs/ir/strategic/cohen/docs/corereadings.pdf.
[10] http://www.stratisc.org/pub/biblio_Bibliographie3_5.html.
[11] http://www.columbia.edu/cu/lweb/indiv/lehman/guides/intell.html.
[12] http://intellit.muskingum.edu/.

Scholars' Guide to Intelligence Literature: A Bibliography of the Russell J. Bowen Collection in the Joseph Mark Lauinger Library, Georgetown University, ed. Marjorie W. Cline et al. (Frederick, Md.: University Publications of America for the National Intelligence Study Center, 1983)

Diplomacy, International Affairs, & Intelligence (Georgetown University collections), in which the section on intelligence is toward the bottom of the page[13]

International Intelligence History Association[14]

Loyola Homepage on Strategic Intelligence[15]

Bibliography of the John E. Taylor collection (books about espionage and intelligence)[16]

Federation of American Scientists Intelligence Resource Program website[17]

If you're interested in this subject, be sure to check out the material on the CIA's Center for the Study of Intelligence website.[18] If you click into the link for "publications" you'll get some very good material, including some original documents. Much of this material is available in pdf and can be easily downloaded and printed out. You can also ask to be put on the mailing list for the CSI's *Bulletin*, which has a lot of interesting information. Just call the CSI at (703) 613-1751.

Finally, if you would like to learn about the political science literature in the whole international relations area, there are a number of guides you should know about. One important source is:

Ira Katznelson and Helen Milner, eds., *Political Science: The State of the Discipline* (New York: Norton for the American Political Science Association, 2002)

This volume has five articles dealing with the international relations literature, some of which refer the reader to other review articles. The APSA has actually published a series of volumes on *The State of the Discipline*, all of which contain review articles. Note also:

Walter Carlsnaes, Thomas Risse, and Beth Simmons, eds., *Handbook of International Relations* (London: Sage, 2002)

Ted Robert Gurr, ed., *Handbook of Political Conflict: Theory and Research* (New York: Free Press, 1980)

Manus Midlarsky, ed., *Handbook of War Studies* (Boston: Unwin Hyman, 1989)

Philip Tetlock, Jo Husbands, Robert Jervis, Paul Stern, and Charles Tilly, eds., *Behavior, Society, and Nuclear War* and *Behavior, Society, and International Conflict,*

[13] http://gulib.lausun.georgetown.edu/dept/speccoll/diplo.htm.
[14] http://www.intelligence-history.org/.
[15] http://www.loyola.edu/dept/politics/intel.html.
[16] http://www.archives.gov/research_room/alic/bibliographies/taylor_collection.html.
[17] http://www.fas.org/main/content.jsp?formAction=325&projectId=6.
[18] http://www.odci.gov/csi/index.html.

3 vols. (New York: Oxford University Press for the National Research Council of the National Academy of Sciences, 1989–93)

The *Annual Review of Political Science* (available online through many libraries), which contains many survey articles covering the international relations literature—for example, James Fearon's "Domestic Politics, Foreign Policy, and Theories of International Relations," which appeared in the *Annual Review* in 1998

There are in addition many volumes in which leading practitioners present their views about various subfields—about what's been accomplished lately, about problems they see with the work that's currently being done, and about where the field is going. The articles in those volumes often cite what are considered the more important works in that particular area. For some recent examples of this genre, see Michael Brecher and Frank Harvey, eds., *Millenial Reflections on International Studies* (2002); A.J.R. Groom and Margot Light, eds., *Contemporary International Relations: A Guide to Theory* (1994); Edward Mansfield and Richard Sisson, eds., *The Evolution of Political Knowledge* (2004); and Ken Booth and Steve Smith, eds., *International Relations Theory Today* (1995). Susan Strange's article in that latter volume on "Political Economy and International Relations" is a particularly good case in point. This is exactly the sort of article you would want to read if you were new to the field and wanted to develop a certain sense for what work in International Political Economy (IPE) is like. There are also books in which a single author surveys the whole field of international relations; chapters in such books often deal with particular subfields. For a very good recent book of this sort, see Chris Brown, *Understanding International Relations*, second edition (2001). At the end of each chapter are suggestions for further reading. Scholarly journals sometimes have special issues devoted to this sort of stocktaking: see, for example, "International Organization at Fifty: Exploration and Contestation in the Study of World Politics," *International Organization* 52, no. 4 (Autumn 1998).

Collections of readings (published mainly for undergraduates) can also provide useful entrées into particular fields of scholarship. Note, for example, John Baylis and James Wirtz, eds., *Strategy in the Contemporary World: An Introduction to Strategic Studies* (2002). The articles here (on topics like terrorism) will help you get started if you know nothing about the subject; they all have short lists of works on the subject they cover. A few collections of readings dealing with IPE are listed at the start of the Higgott article on "International Political Economy" in the Groom and Light book I just cited; in that passage, a few major texts dealing with the subject are also listed. Chris Brown, in the book of his I mentioned in the previous paragraph, also lists a number of collections of this sort in his end-of-chapter suggestions for further reading. For a somewhat older compilation of the many edited volumes dealing with international relations (in which the readings each volume contains are also listed), see Dorothy LaBarr and J. David Singer, *The Study of International Politics: A Guide to the Sources for the Student, Teacher, and Researcher* (1976), pp. 28–78.

II. THE PERIODICAL LITERATURE

Let me begin here by listing some important journals you might want to examine when you're starting a research project in this field. This list, which includes both history and political science journals, is very short. Most of the important journals are available electronically, and in the online version of this appendix I give links for those listed here, along with dates of coverage. More extensive lists of journals in this area accessible in this way (generally through subscribing libraries) are available online. The University of Pennsylvania Library has a list of journals in international relations available online;[19] the University of Chicago Library has lists of journals available electronically in both history[20] and political science.[21] The website for the Zurich-based International Relations and Security Network (ISN) also has lists of links to journals in the international relations area in its "Links Library." Journals are listed there by subject and also by regional focus.[22]

> *Comparative Strategy*
> *Diplomacy and Statecraft*
> *Diplomatic History* (regularly carries survey-of-the-literature review articles)
> *Foreign Affairs* (basically a policy journal but with a regular section on "recent books on international relations"; the "browse book reviews" window on the website's books page is browsable by region or topic).[23]
> *Historical Journal* (very broad coverage but with review articles that relate to international politics)
> *Intelligence and National Security*
> *International Affairs* (London)
> *International Journal of Intelligence and Counterintelligence*
> *International Organization*
> *International Security*
> *International Studies Quarterly*
> *Journal of American–East Asian Relations*
> *Journal of Cold War Studies*
> *Journal of Contemporary History*

[19] http://www.library.upenn.edu/cgi-bin/res/sr.cgi?community=38&resourcetype=17.
[20] http://www.lib.uchicago.edu/e/su/hist/hisejl.html.
[21] http://www.lib.uchicago.edu/e/su/polsci/polejl.html.
[22] http://www.isn.ethz.ch/.
[23] http://www.foreignaffairs.org/book/.

Journal of Military History (formerly *Military Affairs*) (has a section on "recent journal articles")
Journal of Strategic Studies
Relations internationales
Security Studies
Vierteljahrshefte für Zeitgeschichte
World Politics

There are, of course, many other journals that carry articles of interest to people working on international affairs. Not only are there general journals (like the *American Political Science Review*) that publish articles on international politics, but there is a large periodical literature devoted to all kinds of specialized questions even in this area. One guide to intelligence periodicals, for example, describes about 150 intelligence and intelligence-related journals:

Hayden B. Peake, *The Reader's Guide to Intelligence Periodicals* (Washington, D.C.: NIBC Press, 1992)

But when you're trying to find your way around a field, you can't read everything, and it's best to start with the handful of periodicals most likely to give you what you need.

You can, however, approach this basic problem in a somewhat different way. You can use various search engines to find out about journal articles that have been published on a particular subject—and, indeed, about which articles are particularly important. I'll talk here about three in particular: the *Social Science Citation Index* (part of the *Web of Science*), the *Expanded Academic ASAP*, and JSTOR. These are subscription services, but you can generally get access to those search engines through your university library's website. You can also use publicly available search engines like Google to do work of this sort (as noted in chapter 6.)

Web of Science (including the Social Sciences Citation Index [SSCI])[24]

This search engine is a lot of fun to use once you get the hang of it. It allows you, first, to identify articles relating to topics you're interested in, and then, using those articles as a kind of base, it allows you to "spread out" and identify related works. Once you identify a particular article, you can see quickly which works that article cites in its footnotes. But you can also go the other way and see which articles in the SSCI database cite the particular article you've started out with. You can then do the same thing with the new articles you've identified, again spreading out in both directions. In that way you can generate a "web of citations," and in the course of doing so, you develop a

[24] http://isi3.isiknowledge.com/portal.cgi/wos.

certain feel for that particular area of scholarship. You see which articles and authors are cited a lot, which journals are important, and so on.

How do you use the SSCI? When you first click into the *Web of Science*, the first thing you should do is choose which database (or databases) you want to search in by checking one or more of them on the bottom of the homepage. Since no one can quite decide whether history is a social science or one of the humanities, if you're searching for a topic that has a certain historical dimension, you should probably check the boxes for "Social Sciences Citation Index" and "Arts and Humanities Citation Index," but leave "Science Citation Index Expanded" unchecked. Then, unless you're searching for a particular article that you've already identified, it's probably best to click the box for "general search."

A search page then appears. You can search, for example, for works by a particular author (in which case you normally give the last name, followed by first initial and an asterisk). Or you can search for a particular topic—"Cuban missile crisis," for example. You can limit those searches in various ways—for example, to articles that have appeared in a certain journal. When you do the search, a number of listings appear. You can either click into the particular listings you're interested in, or you could mark the listings that seem worth checking out. To create a list, you then just click the "submit" button on the right. A "Marked List" icon will soon appear on the top right. Clicking into that will enable you to see the list of saved references whenever you like. Note, incidentally, that the listings are often linked directly to your university's holdings, and quite frequently just by clicking a button or two the full text of the article you're interested in will show up on your computer, to be read, saved, or printed out.

But however you proceed—whether you go into the listings directly or prefer to work from a marked list—you're now ready to click into the listings for particular articles. When you do that, you'll see a link for "cited references" and another link for "times cited." By clicking into those links, you'll see (respectively) which sources the author of the article used, and *some of the places* where that article has been cited. If, at this point, you want a more inclusive list of places where that article is cited, you should now do a "cited reference search" by clicking into the icon at the top of the page and then searching for that particular article. Often a lot more references now turn up. Click the boxes for what you're interested in (or click "select all"), then click the "finish search" box. Now a longer list of articles appears, and again you can either go directly into the links for any or those articles or you can mark and save whatever you're interested in.

So that's how you proceed when you want to work your way up—that is, when you want to see where a particular article you're interested in has been cited. But for any of these articles you can also work your way down, by clicking into the "cited references" link for any particular listing. When you do that, a list of all the sources the author has used turns up, and you'll note that those sources are of two different kinds. The ones in blue are themselves linked, and when you click "view record" for any of them, you'll be taken to the regular listing for that article. You can't do that with the ones in black, but by leaving them checked, you can still see where they've been cited—and you can do this quickly, without having to do a "cited reference search" for every one of them you're interested in. You do this just by checking the "find related records" box. And again a list of linked titles comes up, and you can mark and save what you're interested in.

When you do a topic search, there are various things you can do to increase the number of hits. To see what they are, click into the "more examples" link just above the topic field on the general search page. One of the most useful ones is the "SAME" search operator. This enables you to search for topics containing words not necessarily right next to each other but which are found in the same listing. For example, if you searched for "relative SAME gains" you'd be able to locate Peter Liberman's article "Trading with the Enemy: Security and Relative Economic Gains," which wouldn't turn up if you just searched for "relative gains"—even if you didn't check "title only."

By using these search operators, along with parentheses and "wildcards" like the asterisk (to catch word variants—i.e., "China" as well as "Chinese"), you can cast a fairly wide net when you do topic searches. For example, suppose you're interested in the Sino-Soviet conflict. You could search directly for "Sino-Soviet conflict." (When I did this search, I got twenty-four hits.) But you know that the words might be separated from each other, or that variant terms (like "dispute") might be used, or that some titles might refer to "China" and others to "Chinese," and so on. So knowing all these things, and not wanting to do a whole series of searches with heavily overlapping results, you could construct a single term: (sino-soviet OR ((Soviet OR Russia* OR USSR) SAME Chin*)) SAME (relations OR dispute OR conflict OR schism). (When I searched for this term, I got 237 hits; I got 193 hits when I checked "title only.") Many hits might be irrelevant for your purposes, but you can generally tell from the titles which articles you'd want to check out.

You can also identify articles dealing with a particular topic by using Google Scholar.[25] Just enter a term in the search field (e.g., "relative gains") and run the search. Various articles are listed, along with links to other articles and unpublished papers in which those articles were cited. Many of these works are available here in full-text versions. This is by no means a substitute for the SSCI, but you might want to use it as a supplement.

[25] http://www.scholar.google.com/.

Expanded Academic ASAP (Infotrac)[26]

This is a good source for searching both the scholarly and the general interest periodical literature on relatively recent issues. You can search in various ways using the drop-down menus on the advanced search page. This search engine often, although by no means always, provides you with the text of the articles that turn up in the search. You can limit the search by date, and also mark and save articles of interest. The search engine also allows you to use "proximity operators" to catch listings that contain search terms that occur within a certain number of words of each other. Suppose, for example, you wanted to see what Kissinger's position was on the Iraq war. If you did a "full text" search for "Kissinger n10 Iraq," you'd get articles where the words "Kissinger" and "Iraq" were within 10 words of each other. If you do a subject search (e.g., for "Kissinger") and an inordinately large number of listings turn up, you may want to do a "Subject Guide Search" for the same term. The listings you're led to will be divided up into more easily usable subdivisions ("Ethical Aspects," "Records and Correspondence," and so on).

JSTOR

JSTOR is probably the most important electronic archive for scholarly journals. People use it mainly to read specific articles they've already identified, articles that were published in one of the JSTOR journals. But you can also use it to identify articles dealing with particular topics. It has a very simple search engine.[27] You can search in particular journals or in, say, just history or just political science journals (or both). You can search by author or by title (meaning by words or phrase in a title), and you can also do a full-text search. If you click into the "expert search" window, you can do all kinds of things. Suppose, for example, you wanted to see what leading political scientists had to say about the relative gains issue. You could begin by trying to see what Robert Jervis had to say about the issue. So you enter a query for "au:jervis AND "relative gains"" and a number of listings turn up. There is even a link for the "page of first match"—that is, the first place Jervis in a particular article talks about relative gains. To learn more about the construction of queries, consult the "search help" page.

It's important to develop a certain familiarity with those three general search engines. By knowing how to use them, you will be able to identify articles in any area of scholarship you happen to be interested in. But there are

---

[26] http://web4.infotrac.galegroup.com/itw/infomark.
[27] http://www.jstor.org/search.

two more narrowly framed search engines you should know about. First there is CIAO (Columbia International Affairs Online).[28] This subscription service, available through many research libraries, allows you to search for scholarly works dealing with a specific topic. The editors control what gets included in the CIAO database, so not everything is included here. But the CIAO database includes things (like working papers) you can't get elsewhere, and much of what turns up in a CIAO search is available in full-text format. The Lancaster Index to Defence and International Security Literature—"an on-line bibliographic database, indexed and cross-referenced, of journal articles and monographs dealing with military and security affairs"— is another search engine you might want to check out, especially if you are interested in military affairs.[29] If you're interested in such questions, you might also want to check out the list of "National Security Portals and Links" on SAIS's Center for Strategic Education (CSE) website.[30]

Other websites are available at if you're interested in certain specific issues. Charles Lipson lists a number of them on his website:[31] YaleGlobal Online (globalization);[32] University of Minnesota Human Rights Library;[33] Federation of American Scientists websites on such issues as Terrorism and Weapons of Mass Destruction (WMD);[34] and various websites related to issues like nuclear nonproliferation and international political economy. Lipson also has a page of his own, loaded with links, devoted to questions relating to the Middle East (including terrorism issues).[35] Bill Arkin has a page of links to information sources related to September 11 and related issues on the CSE website.[36]

III. Dissertations

Dissertations as a rule have excellent bibliographies and lists of sources, so getting hold of a good one allows you to save a lot of time when you're doing bibliographical work. And dissertations, as it turns out, are easy to identify and easy to get hold of. They're made available by a private company, University Microfilms Incorporated, or UMI, now part of ProQuest.

To identify them, you need to use the search engine on the UMI website.[37] (Your library has to be a subscriber.) When you enter the website, you can

---

[28] http://www.ciaonet.org.

[29] http://www.mpr.co.uk/scripts/sweb.dll/li_home.

[30] http://sais-jhu.edu/centers/cse/online_supplement/section4.html.

[31] http://www.charleslipson.com/.

[32] http://yaleglobal.yale.edu/index.jsp.

[33] http://www1.umn.edu/humanrts/index.html.

[34] http://www.fas.org/terrorism/wmd/index.html.

[35] http://www.charleslipson.com/News-Mideast.htm.

[36] http://sais-jhu.edu/centers/cse/links/september11links.html.

[37] http://wwwlib.umi.com/dissertations/gateway.

choose between the basic and the advanced search. The advanced search is actually easier to use. You begin building a query by entering keywords in the boxes in the lower part of the screen. Be sure you select "keyword" from the drop-down menu. When you do the search, the search engine will look for keywords in the title and in the abstract for the dissertations in the database. Every time you enter one or more keywords, click the "add" button and the keyword will appear (preceded by the word "KEY") in the search box in the top half of the screen. You can combine keywords (using connectors like "and" and "or"), and you can also combine search terms with parentheses. You can use "wildcards"—this search engine uses a question mark for this purpose—and you can edit the search box directly. Here's what one such search term (for dissertations relating to the Sino-Soviet dispute) might look like:

KEY((sino-soviet) OR (soviet and chin?)) AND KEY(dispute OR conflict)

Then click the blue search button. A number of listings appear. For each listing, you can read an abstract and selections from the text and also see whether that title is available in pdf—a valuable feature, since, if it is available that way, you can get hold of it very quickly. You can also mark it for saving, put it in your shopping basket, or purchase it right then and there.

You could also begin by clicking "browse" on the top left. Then click "social sciences" and under "social sciences" click the link to the right of whatever field you want to search in—for example, "International Law and Relations (0616)." That will take you into the basic search window; when you get there, that subject heading will be already marked. And by entering terms in the other fields, you can search within that subject. You can limit the search in various ways. You have the option, for example, of limiting the search to dissertations that were finished during a particular time period.

IV. Syllabi

You can often get a good sense for what a particular area of scholarship is like by looking at syllabi that have been prepared for courses in that area. A syllabus will list what the instructor considers to be the most important works in the field, or at least the relatively small number of works that students new to the field should read. If you read a series of syllabi, you'll also notice that the same works tend to get listed over and over again, and this, of course, gives you a certain sense for what is considered important in the field.

Syllabi are not hard to get hold of nowadays. Quite a few of them are available online. You can often find them by going into a history or political science department or university registrar website and looking at course listings. The syllabus for a particular course will often be linked to the course listing. Or you can go into a department website and look at the listing for a faculty member in the field you're interested in; the faculty member might have a website with links to the courses he or she has taught or is teaching. To save you a bit of trouble, I've collected, or provided links to, a number of good political science syllabi.[38] For diplomatic history course syllabi, you can check out the linked list on the Sarantakes website;[39] there's another collection of such syllabi on the SHAFR website.[40] The Center for Strategic Education at SAIS also has a good list of syllabi on its website.[41] Finally, you might be interested in the sort of syllabi that were used thirty-odd years ago. It turns out that a collection of such syllabi was published in 1970:

> Charles F. Hermann and Kenneth N. Waltz, ed. and comp., *Basic Courses in Foreign Policy: An Anthology of Syllabi* (Beverly Hills, Calif.: Sage Publications, 1970)

V. Book Reviews

It's always interesting to see what people think of the books you've read, are reading, or even are just thinking of reading. And it's not hard to locate book reviews and get access to them electronically.

To get reviews of scholarly and semischolarly books, you can use some common computerized search engines, including three I've talked about before. Here's how to use them for this purpose.

To find book reviews published in a JSTOR journal: first, go into the JSTOR advanced search window,[42] put a phrase from the title in the "exact phrase" field, check the box for "title" and the box for "review," and click "search." You can also limit your search to journals in a particular discipline, or even to a single journal.

Next, to find reviews published in one of the journals covered by Project MUSE, another important electronic scholarly journal archive, go into the MUSE website, click "search," and then in the "search for" box, type in the name of the author or the title of the book you're interested in.[43] In the drop-down menu in the next box, click "author reviewed" (or "title reviewed," if you typed in the title) and then click the search button.

The third search engine you can use is the *Expanded Academic ASAP.* Using either the basic search or the advanced search window, do a keyword search, typing the following into the entry box: the author's last name, a word or a short phrase from the book's title, and then the phrase "and book reviews" (without the quotation marks). For example, type in "Waltz and

---

[38] http://www.polisci.ucla.edu/faculty/trachtenberg/guide/SelSyl.html.

[39] http://www.tamu-commerce.edu/coas/history/sarantakes/stuff-coursematerial.html.

[40] http://www.shafr.org/syllabusinitiative.htm.

[41] http://www.sais-jhu.edu/centers/cse/syllabi/index.html.

[42] http://www.jstor.org/search/AdvancedSearch.

[43] http://muse.jhu.edu/index.html.

spread of nuclear and book reviews," to get reviews of the book Kenneth Waltz co-authored with Scott Sagan on *The Spread of Nuclear Weapons*.[44]

You can also use the *Web of Science* (i.e., the SSCI) to find book reviews.[44] Click "general search." Then, in the topic field, type in the title and check the box "title only." At the bottom of the page, where it says "restrict by languages and document types," select "book review." Then click "search."

For less scholarly reviews, various online sources are listed in AcqWeb's *Directory of Book Reviews on the Web*.[45] This has links to such sources as the *Atlantic*, *New York Review of Books*, *New York Times Book Review*, *Washington Post Book World*, *Los Angeles Times Book Review*, *London Review of Books*, *Washington Monthly*, *Boston Review*, *Le Monde–Livres*, and so on.

You can also search for reviews posted on one of the h-net historians' email discussion groups.[46] A particular book, in fact, might be discussed in one of the h-net groups in a more informal way. To see if it's been discussed, you can search for that title on the general h-net advanced search page.[47] You should probably choose to search by phrase (rather than by keyword). You can limit the search by particular discussion list—you could select h-diplo, for example—and also by date. You can search either in the whole text or in the subject line. Alternatively, you could log onto the h-diplo homepage[48] and click into the links (on the left) for "H-Diplo Reviews"[49] (listed there alphabetically by author's last name) and "H-Diplo Roundtables"[50] (discussions on what were considered the most important books). What turns up is often quite interesting.

H-Diplo, I should also note in this context, regularly publishes discussions of articles published in the main journals in the field. Some of them, like the discussion of Eduard Mark's article on "The War Scare of 1946 and Its Consequences" (*Diplomatic History* 21, no. 3 [Summer 1997]), are of quite extraordinary interest. To view a particular thread of this sort, go into the general h-net advanced search page,[51] type in (in quotation marks) a key phrase from the title (e.g., "War Scare of 1946"), select "phrase" and then "h-diplo" as the list to be searched in, select "subject line" as the search field, and then click "search."

There's one last thing you might want to do when you're trying to get a feel for what a given area of scholarship is like. You can actually watch or listen to people giving talks on some subject you're interested in. In some cases, those people are prominent scholars—people whose books and articles you

---

[44] http://isi3.isiknowledge.com/portal.cgi/wos.

[45] http://acqweb.library.vanderbilt.edu/bookrev.html.

[46] http://www.h-net.org/reviews/search.html.

[47] http://www.h-net.org/logsearch/.

[48] http://www.h-net.msu.edu/~diplo/.

[49] http://www.h-net.msu.edu/reviews/showlist.cgi?lists=H-Diplo.

[50] http://www.h-net.msu.edu/reviews/showlist.cgi?lists=H-Diplo.

[51] http://www.h-net.msu.edu/reviews/showlist.cgi?lists=H-Diplo.

might already be familiar with—and seeing them in action will give you a much stronger sense for what's distinctive about their approach to the subject. Listening (or, better yet, watching) these talks, it's as though a whole new dimension of meaning opens up: people express themselves quite freely when they're talking informally (whereas in written work, they tend to be more guarded), and both tone of voice and body language can also be quite revealing. This sort of source is particularly useful if you are dealing with some contemporary topic. Here are links to some of the more interesting sources of this sort:

MIT World: In the "video finder" on the top right, choose a category like "international affairs" or "national security affairs" or choose a host like the Center for International Studies. There are good videos here on such topics as the North Korea nuclear problem (Gallucci) and the future of U.S.-China relations (Christensen, Van Evera).[52]

Berkeley Webcast course on "Issues in Foreign Policy after 9/11":[53] Click into link for "resources," then the link under "Webcast lectures," for terrific video lectures by people like Kenneth Waltz, John Mearsheimer, Robert Gallucci, and Josef Joffe.

Institute of Politics, JFK School of Government, Harvard University, JFK Jr. Forum Video Archive. Videos of panel discussions and lectures of topical issues go back to 1998.[54]

Johns Hopkins School of Advanced International Studies: Links to recent talks, in audio (with some also in video versions) are given on the SAIS homepage; for archived events, click into the link at the bottom of the page.[55]

[52] http://mitworld.mit.edu/index.php.
[53] http://webcast.berkeley.edu/courses/archive.html?prog=115&group=59.
[54] http://www.iop.harvard.edu/events_forum_archive.html.
[55] http://www.sais-jhu.edu/.

Appendix II

WORKING WITH PRIMARY SOURCES

I$_N$ THIS APPENDIX, I want to talk about some of the most important collections of source material, especially material that I didn't discuss in chapter 5, and I want to show you how to go about identifying other sources related to your topic.

The discussion here is broken down into a number of parts. First, I'll talk about the published documents, and then I'll discuss collections that are available in some semipublished form: on microfilm or microfiche, on CD-ROM, or through the internet. After that, I'll give some information about archival sources, and then I'll talk about various open sources—sources that were never secret and are available today in a variety of formats. Finally I'll tell you what you need to know about using the Freedom of Information Act, putting in Mandatory Declassification Review requests, and in general about what you have to do if you'd like to see still-classified material.

Many of the sources and finding aids I discuss here are available online, and—as was the case with appendix I—an online version of this appendix (with direct links to those materials) has been made available.[1] That online version will be updated periodically. I've also posted a short webpage listing many of the links cited in this appendix.[2]

I. PUBLISHED COLLECTIONS OF DOCUMENTS

The collections of diplomatic documents published by major governments are of fundamental importance and for that reason were discussed at some length in the final section of chapter 5. Rather than rehash that discussion, let me just give some of the key references here:

Foreign Relations of the United States (FRUS)
List of volumes published[3]
Volumes available online[4]

---

[1] http://www.polisci.ucla.edu/faculty/trachtenberg/methbk/AppendixII.html.
[2] http://www.polisci.ucla.edu/faculty/trachtenberg/methbk/AppendixII(links).html.
[3] http://www.state.gov/r/pa/ho/frus/c4035.htm.
[4] http://www.state.gov/www/about_state/history/frusonline.html.

Volumes available for purchase[5] (you're probably better off phoning in your order to the GPO at (866) 512-1800 than using the online form)

Status reports (publication schedule)[6]

British Documents on the Origins of the War, 1898–1914 (11 volumes)

Documents on British Foreign Policy, 1919–1939 (65 volumes)

Documents on British Policy Overseas (for post-1945 period; 15 volumes so far)

British Documents on Foreign Affairs (confidential print, privately published, covering roughly the period from 1850–1950, more than 500 volumes published so far, a list of which is available online)[7]

Documents diplomatiques français (various series, covering from 1871 through the 1960s, listed by series and ordering information)[8]

Die grosse Politik der europäischen Kabinette, 1871–1914 (40 volumes in 54). French translation: *La Politique extérieure de l'Allemagne, 1870–1914* (32 volumes)

Akten zur deutschen auswärtigen Politik, 1918–1945 (62 volumes in 5 series). Two of those series also published in English translation: *Documents on German Foreign Policy, 1918–1945* (18 volumes, covering the period from 1933 to 1941)

Akten zur auswärtigen Politik der Bundesrepublik Deutschland (covers the period from 1949 on, with at least a single volume for each year; over 30 volumes published so far, dealing with the 1949–53 and 1963–74 periods)

Die internationalen Beziehungen im Zeitalter des Imperialismus: Dokumente aus den Archiven der zarischen und der provisorischen Regierung (prerevolutionary Russian documents published during the Soviet period)

Krasnyĭ arkhiv (106 volumes)

You should remember, of course, that other governments—Australia, Italy, and Belgium to name just a few of the western ones—also publish collections of documents. And there are many published collections of documents that are not put out by governments at all. Some deal with particular topics. Some are collections, often multivolume collections, of a particular individual's papers. These can generally be found using the techniques outlined in chapter 5, especially the technique of using the word "sources" as one of your subject words when you do a subject search in a library catalogue, and the technique of putting words like "papers" and "correspondence" in the title field at the same time as you search for a particular subject. Important collections are also cited in the bibliographies of the books and dissertations you look at, and are sometimes also cited in the major collections of diplomatic documents that I just listed. They can in addition be found in bibliographies like the *Bibliographie für Zeitgeschichte*, interspersed with listings of books and articles dealing with the same general subject.

[5] http://www.state.gov/r/pa/ho/frus/gpo/.
[6] http://www.state.gov/r/pa/ho/frus/c10996.htm.
[7] http://www.lexisnexis.com/academic/2upa/Isiaas/BritishDocumentsForeignAffairs.asp.
[8] http://www.france.diplomatie.fr/archives/service/publications/doc-diplos/doc-diplos.html.

II. Microfilm, Microfiche, and CD-ROM Material

It's amazing how much material you can examine without having to spend a single night away from home. A vast amount of material is available on microfilm, microfiche, and CD-ROM, and in recent years a very large and growing body of material has been put online.

Let me begin by talking about those first three types of sources. You can usually get access to them even if your home library doesn't own them. To order them through interlibrary loan, first request the finding aids. (They're generally published as supplements to the original microform or CD-ROM publications.) From the finding aids you'll be able to see which reels or fiche or CDs to request. You can locate those guides and collections and make your interlibrary loan request by using Eureka, the union catalogue for the Research Libraries Group (also sometimes called RLIN).

How do you identify material of this sort you might be interested in? The basic library search engines are not very good for this purpose. Some, although by no means all, of them allow you to limit your search, for example, to microform material. But you just can't count on such a search to turn up the material of this sort included in that particular database. Harvard's HOLLIS catalogue, for instance, allows you to select "microforms" in the drop-down menu for "Format" on the lower left of the "expanded search" page, but if you did a search for "Joint Chiefs of Staff" and selected "microforms" in that way, you'd get five listings, three of them not microforms at all—but not including the *Records of the Joint Chiefs of Staff* microfilm collection, which the Harvard library not only owns but which it lists elsewhere in HOLLIS. Other "microform" searches yield better results, but the point here is that this type of search is simply not reliable—and HOLLIS is actually better than most university library search engines.

You might have more luck with the Library of Congress catalogue.[9] When you log in, you choose the "Command Keyword" option from the "search type" menu and then use the search term "microform" in conjunction with other search terms (e.g., "Japan AND foreign AND microform"). If your keyword is a phrase, make sure you enclose it in quotation marks or the search won't work. Once you do find something, you can go into the "full record" and click into the links for the subject headings under which the sources you're interested in are listed.

So you can find things with this method, but there is no getting around the fact that it's still a little hit-or-miss. How well you do really depends on your ability to guess the right keywords. So is there another way of proceeding? Well, you could begin by going through the two online guides I referred to in chapter 5: Frank Conaway's "Guide to Microform and CD-Rom Sources for

[9] http://catalog.loc.gov/cgi-bin/Pwebrecon.cgi?DB=local&PAGE=First.

History and Political Science in the University of Chicago Library"[10] and the list of "Major Microform Collections in the Combined Arms Research Library."[11] Those two guides will give you a general sense for what is available in this area.

You might also want to take a look at the *Guide to the Microform Collections in the Humanities and Social Sciences Division* of the Library of Congress.[12] The online version of that guide builds on a number of earlier published versions, most recently one edited by Patrick Frazier:

> *Guide to the Microform Collections in the Humanities and Social Sciences Division of the Library of Congress*, ed. Patrick Frazier (Washington, D.C.: Library of Congress, 1996)

To use the online guide, first click into one of the halves of the index—either the A–J or the K–Z half—and either scroll through to see what is available, look up the name of a particular country or subject you are interested in, or do a Ctrl F search for a country's name or other keyword. Particular collections are listed under various subject headings in that alphabetical index. Once you have identified a particular collection, click into the letter that the title of that collection begins with. (The links for each letter are at the top of the index pages.) For example, if you scroll down to "Japan" toward the bottom of the A–J part of the index, you will see two headings, "Japan—Foreign relations" and "Japan—History." Say you are interested in the first collection listed under "Japan—Foreign relations," namely "Archives in the Japanese Ministry of Foreign Affairs." So you click into the "A" list. The collections are listed there in alphabetical order by title.

Of course, you'll also come across references to particular collections of this sort as you do your regular bibliographical work. But you may want to do a more systematic search for what is available, so let me talk a bit about how that can be done.

You can search systematically because microfilm, microfiche, and CD-ROM collections are published by just a handful of major private firms and governments—and by "governments" I mean mainly the U.S. government, which, in fact, has made available not just its own records but massive amounts of material produced by certain other countries. So you just go through the catalogues describing these products one by one.

University Publications of America (now part of LexisNexis) is the first firm you should know about.[13] Under "international studies" in the very middle of its homepage, you'll see a list of about twelve categories. Click into

---

[10] http://www.lib.uchicago.edu/e/su/hist/mfguide.html.

[11] http://www-cgsc.army.mil/carl/resources/microform.asp.

[12] http://www.loc.gov/rr/microform/guide/indexa-j.html.

[13] http://www.lexisnexis.com/academic/2upa/upaMnu.asp.

every one of them that is of interest to you. You'll then see the particular collections in that area that they've published. When you find one that you think you might want to see, just bookmark (or save) that link, maybe keeping those bookmarks (or saved files) together in a single folder.

Some of the collections that turn up are of really fundamental importance. I personally find the collections of JCS and NSC material to be particularly useful. The first two parts of the *Records of the Joint Chiefs of Staff* cover the period from 1942 to 1953; this includes about 120 reels of microfilm. UPA has also begun to put out a third part, covering the period from 1954 to 1960; the section that has just come out deals with the Far East.

If you work with the JCS material, you might want to use it in conjunction with the various histories that the JCS Historical Office has produced. The series that office published on *The Joint Chiefs of Staff and National Policy* is particularly important. Seven volumes in that series, covering the period from 1945 to 1960, have come out so far. But there are other JCS histories worth knowing about. Some have been published—to see what they are, just do a title search in a good library catalogue for "History of the Joint Chiefs of Staff"—and others have been declassified and are available in the archives. The unpublished JCS "History of the Indochina Incident," for example, I found to be of particular value: it summarized documents that were considered too sensitive to declassify and include in the regular boxes of JCS papers that were made available to the public. Such histories are particularly useful if you're doing archival work, because their footnotes tell you what the richest files are. Various other JCS histories exist but have not been declassified, and there are classified versions of some of the JCS histories that have been published.[14] If you find out about something of interest, you can ask to see it under the Freedom of Information Act, which I'll be talking about at the end of this appendix.

The NSC material is composed of two collections: *Documents of the National Security Council* and *Minutes of Meetings of the National Security Council*. Each of these includes the original publication plus a number of supplements. These two collections should be used in conjunction with each other.

How do you use the NSC material? The microfilm collections come with guides. You can either use those guides or, better yet, you could use a very good 721-page cumulative index to both collections: *Index to Documents of the National Security Council*. This covers the material through the first supplement of the *Minutes of Meetings* and the fourth supplement of the *Documents*. This is quite a chunk: some of this material was produced during the Reagan period.

If you're working with the NSC material, there are a few other lists you should know about. There is a list of the numbered NSC documents through

[14] For a partial list, see http://www.polisci.ucla.edu/faculty/trachtenberg/guide/jcshist.html.

the end of the Eisenhower period in Gerald Haines, *A Reference Guide to United States Department of State Special Files*, pp. 38–62. I'm also posting a somewhat shorter list of numbered NSC documents, arranged by subject, also limited to documents from the Eisenhower period.[15] For pdf lists of the various categories of NSC documents (including NSAMs, NSDMs, and PDs), go to the University of Michigan Document Center's list of Federal Government Resources: President of the United States and click into "directives."[16] For the NSC meetings, I found a list of the NSC summaries of discussion for the Eisenhower period, which I've also made available online.[17]

Here are some other interesting UPA collections:

John F. Kennedy National Security Files, 1961–1963
Lyndon B. Johnson National Security Files, 1963–1969
Memos of the Special Assistant for National Security Affairs McGeorge Bundy to President Johnson, 1963–1966
Vietnam: National Security Council Histories
Papers of the Nixon White House

Scholarly Resources, Inc., is a second firm that puts out this kind of material.[18] When you log on to its website, click the link for "catalog" at the top, and then click into the link under "browse" on the left for "microfilm/ other media." A number of subject headings appear, and you can go into the links for "diplomatic history," "international relations," and "military history," among others. Many titles appear. Or instead of going into "browse," you could click the link for "search" and search for a particular keyword. Many of the SR collections are based on the holdings of the U.S. State Department and the British Foreign Office, although quite a few other interesting collections are included here—the Dean Acheson Papers, the George Ball Papers, and so on.

Thomson Gale is the next major company whose online catalogue you might want to look at.[19] When you log on to its website, just click into the "browse our catalog" link on the top left, then click the "media type" icon, then click "microform." It currently has 1,205 collections of all sorts listed under that category, not broken down by subject, but still you might want to go through the list to see what it has. It has some interesting collections of mainly British material. It has a couple of collections of Churchill Papers ("The Sir Winston Churchill Papers"; "Churchill at War"), a collection of

[15] http://www.polisci.ucla.edu/faculty/trachtenberg/guide/nsc%28jfkl-list%29. html.
[16] http://www.lib.umich.edu/govdocs/frames/fedprsfr.html.
[17] http://www.polisci.ucla.edu/faculty/trachtenberg/guide/nsc.html.
[18] http://www.scholarly.com/.
[19] http://www.gale.com/.

Chamberlain Papers, a collection of "Papers of the Prime Ministers of Great Britain," and various other items of interest. It has also come out with two major collections of Russian and Soviet archival material. The collection called "Russian Archives" actually includes 17 separate collections of Russian archival material going back to the period of the Napoleonic Wars. The Soviet collection, "The Departmental Records of the Central Committee of the Communist Party of the Soviet Union, 1953–1966," is also quite important.

Incidentally, there is another important collection of Soviet archival material available on microfilm: the *Archives of the Soviet Communist Party and Soviet State,* an enormous collection that can be consulted at the Hoover Institution at Stanford University and at the Lamont Library at Harvard.[20]

Next let me talk a bit about Adam Matthew Publications.[21] This is a British firm and mainly puts out collections of British material. When you go to its website, click into "Publication A–Z List," and then "U.S. Dollar version." A long list of publications, not divided up by category, then appears on the screen. Here's a list of some items that might be of interest to people in our field:

Cabinet Papers (actually both Cabinet and Prime Minister's Office papers)
Curzon, India and Empire
The First World War: A Documentary Record
Foreign Office Files (broken down into collections dealing with China, Cuba, Japan, Post-War Europe, the USSR, and the United States)
Macmillan Cabinet Papers (available online, but was originally sold on CD-ROM, and that CD-ROM version is still available in certain libraries)
Nuclear Policy and the Cold War
Treasury Papers (of John Maynard Keynes)

Those are the most important private publishers of this kind of material, but before I go on to tell you about what the U.S. government puts out, let me just note the existence of a couple of other important sources of the sort. First, there's a very important source called the *Declassified Documents Reference System.* As its name suggests, the people who run it put out a selection of important declassified documents. For years, those documents were made available on microfiche, with hard-copy guides published periodically, and that material is still available in many libraries. But the microfiche version was replaced by an online version, and so I'll discuss this source in the section of the appendix dealing with online materials.

The same basic point applies to a second source of this sort. The National Security Archive, a private organization based in Washington, D.C., puts out a series of collections of documents on microfiche dealing with various topics related to national security and foreign policy. The documents assembled come from a variety of different sources, gathered by very skilled "archive hounds" and vigorous "FOIA requesters." Those microfiche collections are still quite useful, but today you can also consult these collections online. That online series, available through subscribing libraries, is called the "Digital National Security Archive," and I'll talk about the DNSA in the section on online materials.

Let me conclude this section by talking briefly about microform materials put out under official auspices. This means mainly the microfilm collections published by the U.S. National Archives, now officially called the National Archives and Records Administration, or NARA. There are other microform sources that could be mentioned in this context. The major collections of diplomatic documents, for example, sometimes have microfiche supplements. The FRUS microfiche supplements, for example, are listed in the volumes section in the FRUS website, cited above. (To locate them, do a Ctrl F search for "microfiche" on that webpage.) Microfiche supplements have also been published in conjunction with the *Documents on British Policy Overseas*. But NARA is by far the most important official producer of this sort of material.

NARA periodically publishes a catalogue of their microfilm publications:

National Archives Microfilm Publications for Research: A Comprehensive Catalog (Washington, D.C.: NARA, 2000)

There is also an online version of the NARA microfilm catalogue.[22] If you use the online version, you can search by keyword or by record group. (NARA's holdings are divided into more than 500 record groups.) As it turns out, only a small number of record groups are of interest for our purposes—I'll tell you what they are in the section about archives—and there are microfilm publications listed for only a handful of them. And of those, only two are of really fundamental importance:

RG 59: General Records of the Department of State (1,100 publications)
RG 242: National Archives Collection of Foreign Records Seized (93 publications)

There are, however, a number of interesting microfilm publications based on material found in various other record groups:

RG 225: Records of Joint Army and Navy Boards and Committees
RG 226: Records of the Office of Strategic Services
RG 243: Records of the U.S. Strategic Bombing Survey
RG 260: Records of U.S. Occupation Headquarters, World War II
RG 331: Records of Allied Operational and Occupation Headquarters, World War II
   (records relating to the International Military Tribunal for the Far East)

---

[22] http://www.nara.gov/cgi-bin/starfinder/0?path=micfilm.txt&id=mfilm&pass=&OK=OK.

Using the online catalogue, you can quickly see which microfilm publications have been drawn from material in those last five record groups. As for the State Department material in RG 59, if you don't want to review the entire list of microfilm publications—and there are about 1,100 of them—you could use the online catalogue but conduct a more targeted search. You could, for example, put the name of the country you're interested in the keyword field, put "RG059" in the record group field, and then click "Display Search Results." Or you could use NARA's special catalogue of microfilm publications in the diplomatic area.[23] The online version of that catalogue is a little hard to use, so you may want to use the print version, even though it was published a number of years ago:

United States, National Archives and Records Administration, *Diplomatic Records: A Select Catalog of National Archives Microfilm Publications* (Washington, D.C.: NARA, 1986)

Let me end this section with a word about RG 242. This is the record group for foreign material that fell into the hands of the American government. Some of the sources here are very rich. There are 93 microfilm publications listed for this record group, and some of the most important ones have to do with Germany. Probably the most valuable of those is microfilm publication T120, *Records of the German Foreign Office Received by the Department of State*, which contains over 5,800 reels. There are two guides that can be used in conjunction with this collection:

American Historical Association, Committee for the Study of War Documents, *A Catalogue of Files and Microfilms of the German Foreign Ministry Archives, 1867–1920* (Washington, D.C., 1959) (also available as microfilm publication T322)

A Catalog of Files and Microfilms of the German Foreign Ministry Archives, 1920–1945, comp. and ed. George O. Kent, 4 vols. (Stanford, Calif.: Hoover Institution, Stanford University, 1962–72)

The first of those catalogues, according to its preface, "is both a record of the files of the Political Department of the German Foreign Ministry for the period 1867–1920 and a guide to all microfilming programs which have been carried out in these and other related files by the German War Document Program of the American, British, and French Governments, by other governments, and by certain institutions and individuals."

Many other collections of German material from RG 242 have been put out on microfilm. There is, for example, a whole series of publications of the papers of well-known German military figures—Roon, Schlieffen, Gneisenau, Seeckt, Groener, Moltke, and others. Microfilm Publication T291

[23] http://www.archives.gov/publications/microfilm_catalogs/diplomatic/diplomatic.html.

contains the papers of certain German diplomats. For more information about some of these materials, see J. S. Conway, *German Historical Source Material in United States Universities* (Pittsburgh: University of Pittsburgh Council for European Studies, 1973); Anne Hope and Jörg Nagler, *Guide to German Sources in American Archives and Libraries* (Washington, D.C.: German Historical Institute, 1991—available free of charge from the GHI); and Manfred F. Boemeke and Roger Chickering, "Guide to Archives and Historical Collections in the Washington Metropolitan Area. Part II: Research Resources in Modern German and Austrian History" (Washington, D.C.: GHI, 1995).[24]

There are also some Italian collections listed, including collections of Mussolini and Ciano papers. There's a collection of Soviet documents from the Smolensk archive—that material was the basis for Merle Fainsod's famous book, *Smolensk under Soviet Rule* (Cambridge, Mass.: Harvard University Press, 1958)—and even a collection of Grenada material. For more information about these collections, check out the section on RG 242 in NARA's online guide.[25]

Many important British materials are also available on microfilm. You can find a lot of them by doing an advanced search on a standard library search engine like the MELVYL catalogue.[26] If you use that catalogue, be sure to click the link at the top for "advanced" search. In one of the search windows, select "subject" from the drop-down menu and type in something like "Great Britain Foreign relations Sources." Make sure the "no" box is checked under "words as phrase." If you clicked "search" at this point, the search engine would list everything in the database listed under a set of subject headings which taken together contain all those words. But that would yield a lot of nonmicrofilm material. To then limit that search to microfilm sources, in a second search window select "keyword" from the drop-down menu and type in the word "microfilm." Now run the search. You'll turn up quite a few listings, many of which may have also turned up in your search of the various publishers' websites I listed above. You can target the search more narrowly by adding other keywords, like the name of another particular country— "Japan," for example.

But the technique of using "microfilm" (or even "microform") as a keyword does not always work. It would not, for example, turn up many of the very important microfilm collections of British cabinet documents that you can find just by doing an author search for "Great Britain. Cabinet Office" and

[24] http://www.ghi-dc.org/guide7/frame2.html.

[25] http://www.archives.gov/research_room/federal_records_guide/na_collection_of_seized_foreign_rg242.html.

[26] http://melvyl.cdlib.org.

following some of the links that turn up. Here's a list of the most important of those holdings that I found in MELVYL. They're listed in order by class number, classes being the basic units into which departmental collections are divided in the British National Archives. The class numbers themselves (sometimes followed after a slash by what are called "piece numbers," identifying a particular volume or box or bundle of papers) are noted in parentheses. The listings marked with an asterisk are covered by finding aids published by the List and Index Society, which I'll talk about in more detail later in the section on archival research.

Committee of Imperial Defence and Standing Defence Sub-committee minutes, 1902–39 (CAB 2)

*Cabinet Minutes and Memoranda, 1916–1939 (CAB 23 and 24). Also available on microfilm, a *Subject Index of War Cabinet Minutes* is divided into the following parts: (1) 1916 Dec.–1918 Mar.; (2) 1918 Apr.–1919 Dec.; (3) 1939 Sept.–1941; (4) Dec. 1942 Jan.–1945 July. (CAB 23 is indexed in List and Index Society vols. 40, 51, 61, 62, 92, 100; CAB 24 is indexed in List and Index Society vols. 29, 41, 52, 156.)

Imperial War Cabinet, 1917; minutes of meetings 1–14, Mar. 20–May 2, 1917 (with subject index) (CAB 23/40)

Papers and Minutes of the British Secretariat to the Supreme War Council, 1917–1919 (CAB 25)

Proceedings and Conclusions of Anglo-French and Allied Conferences, 1915–1920 (CAB 28)

Cabinet Papers, 1880–1916 (CAB 37/1–162)

Records of the Committee of Imperial Defence, 1888–1914 (CAB 38)

Cabinet Letters in Royal Archives, 1868–1916 (CAB 41/1–37)

Chiefs of Staff Committee, Minutes of Meetings and Papers, 1934–1939 (CAB 53/1–55)

*Cabinet Minutes, 1939–1945 (CAB 65/1–55) (indexed in List and Index Society vols. 71 and 74)

*War Cabinet Minutes and Papers, 1939–1941 (CAB 67) (indexed in List and Index Society vol. 148)

*War Cabinet Minutes and Papers, 1939–1942. Memoranda (WP(G) Series) (CAB 68) (indexed in List and Index Society vol. 148)

Chiefs of Staff Committee, Minutes, 1939–1946 (CAB 79)

Chiefs of Staff Committee, Memoranda and Minutes (CAB 80/1–22, 104–5)

Committees and Sub-committees of the Chiefs of Staff Committee, Minutes and Papers, 1939–1947 (CAB 81) (Note: CAB 81/40 deals with post-hostilities planning, 1939–47)

Joint Planning Committee of the Committee of Imperial Defence and the War Cabinet, Minutes of Meetings (CAB 84)

Chiefs of Staff Committee, Anglo-French Committees: Minutes of Meetings, 1939–1940 (CAB 85/1–64)

Chiefs of Staff Committee Papers, 1942–1947 (CAB 88/1–39)
Commonwealth and International Conferences, Minutes and Papers, 1939–1945 (CAB 99)
Cabinet Minutes (CM and CC Series), 1945–1974 (CAB 128)
Cabinet Memoranda (CP and C Series), 1945–1972 (CAB 129)

III. Online Sources

In the past, a vast amount of very valuable material was published on micro-film or microfiche, but the tendency nowadays is to make this kind of mater-ial available in some electronic format—or, more precisely, to make it avail-able online. In this section, I'd like to talk about some of the main online sources, first those put out by various private organizations and then those put out under the auspices of various government agencies. For a very knowl-edgeable guide to sources of this sort, see William Arkin's *National Security Research on the Internet* (Washington, D.C.: SAIS Center for Strategic Educa-tion, 2000).[27]

The *Declassified Documents Reference System* (DDRS) is the first such source you should know about, especially if you're working on the Cold War period.[28] The people who run it publish a selection of newly released declassi-fied documents. As I noted above, these documents used to be published on microfiche. They're now available online, but only through libraries that sub-scribe to this service.

With the DDRS search engine, you can do either a basic search or an ad-vanced search. You might as well always use the advanced search option; if the only field you fill in is the top one, this is equivalent to doing a basic search anyway. You begin by entering the terms you want to search for in the search fields at the top of the screen. You can search for words found in the title or abstract of a particular document, or in the text of the document it-self. You can also do a "keyword/subject" search: this turns up documents containing the words or phrases you specify in their titles, descriptions, or in their first fifty words. You then use the remaining fields to limit the search in various ways—by date of issue, agency of origin, classification level, and so on. For example, for "Document classification" you can choose "top secret" to get only the documents originally given the highest regular classification; these are presumably the most sensitive, and therefore the most interesting,

---

[27] http://www.sais-jhu.edu/centers/cse/internet_guide/index.html.

[28] You can generally find the link to this source on your library's basic search engine. If your computer is on a system that has access, you might also be able to get access by clicking into the website for the Gale Group (http://infotrac.galegroup.com/menu#) and then clicking into the link for the DDRS at the bottom of the page.

documents available. By holding down the control key, you can select documents in more than one category—for example, both secret and top secret documents.

In theory, this is a very powerful finding aid and can be an effective (and efficient) way to generate source material bearing on particular topics. You can zero in on documents that were produced within a particular time frame, or by a particular agency, or which dealt with a particular subject, or indeed that meet all three criteria. But be careful, because this search engine is by no means perfect. Not all documents dealing with the Cuban missile crisis, for example, are labeled as such, so a subject search for that term would not yield everything in the DDRS database dealing with that episode. Searching by date and perhaps by agency of origin might be a more effective way to generate listings related to that topic.

The *Digital National Security Archive* (DNSA), another subscription service, is the second online source you should know about.[29] The DNSA developed out of the microfiche collections that the National Security Archive published in the 1990s (and continues to publish). The DNSA currently includes about twenty-two collections, each focused on a particular topic:

Afghanistan: The Making of U.S. Policy, 1973–1990
The Berlin Crisis, 1958–1962
China and the United States: From Hostility to Engagement, 1960–1998
The Cuban Missile Crisis, 1962
El Salvador: The Making of U.S. Policy, 1977–1984
El Salvador: War, Peace, and Human Rights, 1980–1994
Iran: The Making of U.S. Policy, 1977–1980
The Iran-Contra Affair: The Making of a Scandal
Iraqgate: Saddam Hussein, U.S. Policy and the Prelude to the Persian Gulf War, 1980–1994
Japan and the United States: Diplomatic, Security, and Economic Relations, 1960–1976
Nicaragua: The Making of U.S. Policy, 1978–1990
The Philippines: U.S. Policy during the Marcos Years, 1965–1986
Presidential Directives on National Security from Harry Truman to William Clinton (Part I)
South Africa: The Making of U.S. Policy, 1962–1989
The Soviet Estimate: U.S. Analysis of the Soviet Union, 1947–1991
Terrorism and U.S. Policy, 1968–2002
U.S. Espionage and Intelligence, 1947–1996
U.S. Intelligence Community, 1947–1989
U.S. Military Uses of Space, 1945–1991
U.S. Nuclear History: Nuclear Arms and Politics in the Missile Age, 1955–1968

[29] http://nsarchive.chadwyck.com/nsaindexhome.htm.

U.S. Nuclear Non-Proliferation Policy, 1945–1991

Terrorism and U.S. Policy, 1968–2002

Presidential Directives on National Security from Harry Truman to George W. Bush (Part II)

These collections are described in detail on the DNSA webpage.[30] Just click into the link on the left for "collections," and then click into the links for whichever collections interest you. Note that some of these collections are linked to certain projects conducted under the auspices of the National Security Archive itself. The collection on U.S.-Japanese relations, for example, was connected to the National Security Archive U.S.-Japan project. That project, incidentally, has its own website, which contains the text of various working papers and oral history transcripts.[31]

The DNSA search page is very easy to use.[32] You can search by collection or you can search in all collections at the same time. You can limit the search by date, by level or classification, and in various other ways. Keywords corresponding to a particular document are noted in the listing for that document, and those keywords themselves are linked, so you can quickly call up other documents related to the subject you're interested in. You have the option of viewing (and saving) particular documents in pdf; this, incidentally, is the case for the DDRS as well.

The DNSA is, as I say, a subscription service, but there are many documents (including documents not in the DNSA) available on the National Security Archive's open website.[33] This material is organized into various "electronic briefing books" dealing with various topics, and containing documents and commentary. Those briefing books are in turn listed by area on the NSA "documents" webpage ("Nuclear History," "China and the United States," "U.S. Intelligence," "Humanitarian Interventions," and so on).[34]

The Cold War International History Project (CWIHP) website is also worth looking at, at least if you are interested in the Cold War period.[35] The CWIHP's "Virtual Archive" is composed of a series of collections of documents, often translated from Russian, east European, or Asian Communist original texts. Those collections ("New Evidence on Sino-Soviet Relations," "Poland in the Cold War," "Stalin's Conversations with Chinese Leaders," and so on) are listed on the Virtual Archive's webpage.[36] Many of those documents were originally published in the CWIHP's *Bulletin* or in one of the

---

[30] http://nsarchive.chadwyck.com/nsaindexhome.htm.

[31] http://www.gwu.edu/~nsarchiv/japan/usjhmpg..htm.

[32] http://nsarchive.chadwyck.com/cgi-bin/starfinder/0/nsaindex.

[33] http://www.gwu.edu/~nsarchiv/.

[34] http://www.gwu.edu/~nsarchiv/NSAEBB/.

[35] http://wwics.si.edu/index.cfm?topic_id=1409&fuseaction=topics.home.

[36] http://wwics.si.edu/index.cfm?topic_id=1409&fuseaction=library.Collection.

CWIHP's working papers. Both the *Bulletin* and the working papers are available online.[37]

Those are perhaps the most important sources of online material made available by private institutions, but this is by no means a comprehensive listing of what can be found on the internet. If you read Russian, for example, you'll certainly be interested in the "online document archive" of Russian-language documents on the Harvard Project on Cold War Studies website.[38] And you'll probably want to take a look at Vladimir Bukovsky's Soviet Archives website[39] and at the material available on the Parallel History Project website[40] ("thousands of pages of unpublished archival documents in facsimile, articles, and research reports with a particular emphasis on the military-political dimensions of the Cold War"). The PHP website also has a good deal of material relating to the NATO side of the conflict.

Now let me turn to the official sources. Many documents have been posted on various (mostly U.S.) government websites. The presidential libraries—and I list their websites below in the section on archives—have put many interesting documents online. For example, at the Kennedy Library website you can see practically all the NSAMs—the National Security Action Memoranda—for the Kennedy period.[41] At the Johnson Library website, you can access a number of oral histories, including the Rusk oral history.[42] The Ford Library also has some important material online. This includes a collection of National Security Study Memoranda and Decision Memoranda,[43] and also a series of memoranda of conversations dealing with foreign policy and national security issues.[44]

The State Department has an Electronic Reading Room which contains more than 50,000 documents released by that agency in accordance with the Freedom of Information Act (FOIA) or in other ways.[45] This is not the easiest search engine to use. You have to search for pages containing particular words and phrases, and that means that you're forced to guess which words or phrases the documents you're interested in are likely to contain. And you can't even limit the search by date of issue, level of classification, or anything like that. This website was created under congressional mandate, and one has

---

[37] http://wwics.si.edu/index.cfm?topic_id=1409&fuseaction=topics.publications&group_id=11900; http://wwics.si.edu/index.cfm?topic_id=1409&fuseaction=topics.publications&group_id=11901.

[38] http://www.fas.harvard.edu/~hpcws/documents.htm.

[39] http://psi.ece.jhu.edu/~kaplan/IRUSS/BUK/GBARC/buk.html.

[40] http://www.isn.ethz.ch/php.

[41] http://www.jfklibrary.org/nsam.htm.

[42] http://www.lbjlib.utexas.edu/johnson/archives.hom/oralhistory.hom/rusk/rusk.asp.

[43] http://www.ford.utexas.edu/library/document/nsdmnssm/nsdmnssm.htm.

[44] http://www.ford.utexas.edu/library/document/memcons/memcons.htm.

[45] http://foia.state.gov/SearchColls/CollsSearch.asp.

the sense that in putting it together, the State Department didn't really have its heart in it.

But if you're interested in certain specific topics—Chile, Argentina, El Salvador, and a number of other subjects—this might be a very useful source. To see what those topics are, click "Collection Descriptions" on the search page. The three collections on Chile are particularly rich. You can check the box corresponding to whichever collection you're interested in, and if you want to see a list of everything they have, click "List All." The documents are then listed in reverse chronological order, and you can then call up the text (in pdf) of whatever documents you're interested in. Toward the bottom of the search page are links to collections of material released by other government agencies (and posted on the Web) as part of the Chile Declassification Project.

Various other collections of government material can be found online. There is even a collection of important NATO strategy documents (assembled by Gregory Pedlow, the SHAPE historian) posted on the NATO website.[46] There's a very useful set of documents relating to the Gulf War on the GulfLink website.[47] The Bundesarchiv has put some of the German Cabinet protocols from the late 1950s on its website.[48] But probably the most useful collections of online material have been put out by the U.S. intelligence agencies. The National Security Agency has posted various collections of material on its website: collections on the Cuban missile crisis, Venona, the USS *Liberty* affair, and so on.[49]

The online CIA collections are even more valuable. I'm *not* referring here to the general search you can do with the CIA's "Electronic Reading Room,"[50] which is a typical keyword-based search engine and is hard to use for the same reason such search engines are in general hard to use: you never really know which keywords will yield all of the documents, and only those documents, that you're interested in. When I say the online CIA collections are valuable, what I'm really referring to are the "special collections." You can get a list of them by clicking into the link with that name on the left of the general search page.

The "Special Collections" page currently lists two collections you can examine online: The National Intelligence Council (NIC) Collection ("analytic reports produced by the National Intelligence Council on a variety of geographical and functional issues since 1946") and the Princeton Collection ("analytic reports produced by the Directorate of Intelligence on the Former

---

[46] http://www.nato.int/archives/strategy.htm.

[47] http://www.gulflink.osd.mil/search/declass.html. To see how this source was used by one scholar, see Avigdor Haselkorn, *The Continuing Storm: Iraq, Poisonous Weapons and Deterrence* (New Haven: Yale University Press, 1999).

[48] http://www.bundesarchiv.de/kabinettsprotokolle/web/index.jsp.

[49] http://www.nsa.gov/public/publi00003.cfm.

[50] http://www.foia.cia.gov/search_options.asp.

Soviet Union, declassified and released for a March 2001 Conference at Princeton University"). Well-organized, browsable online indexes, with direct links to the text of the documents themselves, are available for both collections. And in the lower part of the "special collections" page are links to lists of documents "available at the National Archives":

> *Declassified National Intelligence Estimates on the Soviet Union and International Communism*
> *Declassified Intelligence Estimates on Selected Free World Countries*
> *Declassified Intelligence Analyses on the Former Soviet Union Produced by CIA's Directorate of Intelligence*

Those lists are important. The reference to the National Archives is somewhat misleading, because many of the documents cited in those lists are in fact available online. You just have to look them up in the CIA's normally hard-to-use Electronic Reading Room—only this time the information you've been given on those lists enables you to use that search engine effectively. You're not going blind: your search can be highly targeted. And even if that material is not in the ERR, you still may be able to find it using the DDRS or the DNSA. I should, incidentally, note that if you are interested in the early 1960s, a list of National Intelligence Estimates (NIEs) (and the generally more important Special National Intelligence Estimates, or SNIEs) produced from January 1960 through May 1962 that the NSC staff considered "still generally useful" is available online.[51] That list might also help you search for particular documents.

A great mass of declassified CIA material (8.7 million pages as of November 2003) is also available "online" through what is called the CREST ("CIA Records Search Tool") system—but (for the time being at least) the computer terminals you need to use this source are available only at the National Archives building in College Park (room 3000).[52] The system is very well indexed and is set up so that you can easily print out what you need.

Finally, let me talk about a collection of material that is not quite an online source, but should probably be noted in this part of the appendix anyway: the documents released by the Defense Department under the Freedom of Information Act. I got a list of those documents by filing a FOIA request for it, and I posted that DoD FOIA list online.[53] A somewhat different, but probably more up-to-date list of DoD FOIA documents is available on the DoD website.[54] There are now nearly a thousand documents in the list, but if

[51] http://www.polisci.ucla.edu/faculty/trachtenberg/methbk/nies.pdf.
[52] See http://www.odci.gov/cia/public_affairs/press_release/2003/pr11202003. htm (CIA press release), and http://www.archives.gov/research_room/alic/research_tools/online_databases. html#m4 (NARA information).
[53] http://www.polisci.ucla.edu/faculty/trachtenberg/guide/dodfoia(2002).doc.
[54] http://www.defenselink.mil/pubs/foi/master_reading_list.html.

you're interested in a particular subject you can do a keyword search (if you're using a Windows-based system) with Ctrl F. For example, if you're interested in chemical weapons and chemical warfare, hit Ctrl F and search for "chemical." There are many documents listed there relating to Vietnam and to various nuclear issues. If you find a document you're interested in, you should be able to arrange for the DoD FOIA office to send you a copy. You might want to use the request form found on DOD FOIA website.[55] If you need to discuss matters over the phone, you can contact that office at (703) 696-4689.

IV. ARCHIVAL SOURCES

The basic procedure for working with archival sources is very simple. First you identify the collections you'd like to examine, and then you get the finding aids or inventories for those collections. Using those finding aids, you decide which boxes or volumes of documents you'd like to see. You then submit your request, and the materials are either delivered to you or you pick them up at some central desk a little later. It's all quite straightforward.

How then do you identify the collections that are important for your purposes? You begin by looking at the guides put out by the most important official repositories. The published guides are updated periodically, and most of these repositories by now have also posted versions of their guides on their websites. Those websites, moreover, provide you with all kinds of practical information—about when the archive is open, about what you have to do to get access to its collections, about research grants, and so on.

In the United States, the most important repositories for our purposes are the presidential libraries and the National Archives in College Park, Maryland, although some of the military services have major repositories of their own.

The National Archives (NARA) has a very useful website[56]:

> *Guide to Federal Records in the National Archives of the United States.*[57] A hard copy version, edited by Robert Matchette et al., was published by NARA in 1995. The most important thing to get from the guide is a sense for which record groups you might want to work with. The website has a page listing record groups by clusters that is particularly useful in this context.[58] You might also want to take a look at James E. David, *Conducting Post–World War II National Security Research in Executive Branch Records: A Comprehensive Guide* (Westport, Conn.: Greenwood, 2001). It is important to remember that not every collection

---

[55] http://www.defenselink.mil/pubs/foi/.

[56] http://www.archives.gov/.

[57] http://www.archives.gov/research_room/federal_records_guide/.

[58] http://www.archives.gov/research_room/alic/research_tools/record_ group_clusters.html.

of interest to people in our field and available in the National Archives is listed in the online guide. The Robert S. McNamara papers, for example, is currently not listed, since it is no longer in a numbered record group. But you can often find out about such sources by talking to the archivists (in this case, in Modern Military Records, which in fact has a list of privately donated material of this sort) or to other scholars.

The presidential libraries include:

Roosevelt Library, Hyde Park, New York[59]
    Guide[60]
    Online finding aids[61]
Truman Library, Independence, Missouri[62]
    Guide (includes links to subject guides)[63]
    Truman Papers (many finding aids linked)[64]
    Other collections of papers (many finding aids linked)[65]
Eisenhower Library, Abilene Kansas[66]
    Guide (with many links to finding aids)[67]
Kennedy Library, Boston, Massachusetts[68]
    Guide[69]
    Finding Aids[70]
    White House Tapes: some recordings are available on the "History and Politics Out Loud" website;[71] see also the WhiteHouseTapes.org website.[72] For transcripts, see Philip Zelikow, Ernest May, and Timothy Naftali, eds., *The Presidential Recordings: John F. Kennedy, vols. 1–3, The Great Crises* (New York: Norton, 2001)
Johnson Library, Austin, Texas.[73]
    Guide (with finding aids)[74]
    LBJ phone conversations[75] (some available on the C-SPAN website)

[59] http://www.fdrlibrary.marist.edu/.
[60] http://www.fdrlibrary.marist.edu/collec20.html.
[61] http://www.fdrlibrary.marist.edu/view1.html.
[62] http://www.trumanlibrary.org/.
[63] http://www.trumanlibrary.org/collect.htm.
[64] http://www.trumanlibrary.org/hst-pape.htm.
[65] http://www.trumanlibrary.org/personal.htm.
[66] http://www.eisenhower.utexas.edu/.
[67] http://www.eisenhower.utexas.edu/loh2.htm.
[68] http://www.jfklibrary.org/.
[69] http://www.jfklibrary.org/guide.htm.
[70] http://www.jfklibrary.org/f_aids1.htm.
[71] http://www.hpol.org/.
[72] http://whitehousetapes.org/.
[73] http://www.lbjlib.utexas.edu/.
[74] http://www.lbjlib.utexas.edu/johnson/archives.hom/holdings/content.asp.
[75] http://www.lbjlib.utexas.edu/johnson/archives.hom/Dictabelt.hom/content.asp.

Nixon Presidential Papers (at National Archives, College Park, Maryland)[76]
    Finding aids index[77]
    Kissinger telephone transcripts finding aid[78]
    White House tapes[79] (some phone conversations available on the C-SPAN website)
Ford Library, Ann Arbor, Michigan[80]
    Guide (with links to finding aids)[81]
Carter Library, Atlanta, Georgia[82]
    Guide[83]
Reagan Library, Simi Valley, California[84]
    List of collections[85]
George H. W. Bush Library, College Station, TX[86]
    Guide (with links to finding aids)[87]

The military archives include:

U.S. Army Military History Institute[88]
Air Force Historical Research Agency[89]
    Personal Papers[90]
Naval Historical Center[91]
    Personal Papers[92]

In Britain, the most important repository is now also called the National Archives.[93] It is located in the village of Kew, between Heathrow Airport and central London. Its most important part used to be called the Public Record Office (PRO), and you'll still often see it referred to by that name. You can work with this repository's online catalogue[94] in two ways: by browsing

---

[76] http://www.archives.gov/nixon/about_nixon/about_nixon.html.
[77] http://www.archives.gov/nixon/textual/textual_materials.html.
[78] http://www.archives.gov/nixon/kissinger/index.html.
[79] http://www.archives.gov/nixon/tapes/tapes.html.
[80] http://www.ford.utexas.edu/.
[81] http://www.ford.utexas.edu/library/guides/guide.htm.
[82] http://www.jimmycarterlibrary.org/.
[83] http://www.jimmycarterlibrary.gov/library/pres_materials.phtml.
[84] http://www.reagan.utexas.edu/.
[85] http://www.reagan.utexas.edu/resource/complete.htm.
[86] http://bushlibrary.tamu.edu/.
[87] http://bushlibrary.tamu.edu/research.html.
[88] http://carlisle-www.army.mil/usamhi/.
[89] http://www.au.af.mil/au/afhra/.
[90] http://www.au.af.mil/au/afhra/wwwroot/personal_papers/personal_papers.html.
[91] http://www.history.navy.mil/index.html.
[92] http://www.history.navy.mil/ar/mss.htm.
[93] http://www.nationalarchives.gov.uk/.
[94] http://www.catalogue.nationalarchives.gov.uk/default.asp.

through the listings there or by conducting a search. To browse, you first look up the code for the department of government you're interested in ("FO" for Foreign Office, "CAB" for Cabinet Office, "PREM" for Prime Minister's Office, "DEFE" for the Ministry of Defence, to give the most important ones for our purposes—a much fuller list of department codes is available on its website).[95] You then enter that code in the "go to reference" box and click "go." The holdings that turn up for a particular department are broken down into consecutively numbered classes (like "FO 371," the political correspondence of the Foreign Office), and those classes are in turn broken down into "pieces"—that is, boxes, bound volumes, or even file folders—also numbered consecutively, beginning with 1. The piece-by-piece lists for a particular class give you a certain sense for how extensive the holdings in a particular area are. And this information of course helps you decide which particular pieces are worth looking at.

The PRO published a number of handbooks you may find helpful:

Great Britain, Public Record Office, *The Records of the Foreign Office, 1782–1968,* 2d ed. (Richmond: Public Record Office, 2002)

Great Britain, Public Record Office, *The Records of the Cabinet Office to 1922* (London: HMSO, 1966)

Great Britain, Public Record Office, *Classes of Departmental Papers for 1906–1939* (London: HMSO, 1966)

You might also want to take a look at the list of online research guides available on the (British) National Archives website.[96]

A number of the finding aids that you can consult in the main building at Kew were published in facsimile form by the List and Index Society and can be consulted in American research libraries. If you are going to do research in this repository, these volumes might help you prepare for your stay there. They're in fact a little easier to use than the online guide. Even if none of them relate directly to what you are interested in, you might want to take a look at one or two of them just to get a feel for the sorts of finding aids that will be available to you at Kew. Remember also that some of the collections covered here have been reproduced in microfilm collections discussed in an earlier section of this appendix.

The List and Index Society lists include:

Vols. 29, 41, and 52: *Cabinet Office Subject Index of C.P. Papers (Cabinet Memoranda), 1919–1922* (for part of CAB 24)

Vols. 40, 51: *Cabinet Office Subject Index of War Cabinet Minutes, 1916 Dec.–1919 Dec.* (for part of CAB 23)

---

[95] http://www.catalogue.nationalarchives.gov.uk/popularcodes.asp.

[96] http://www.catalogue.nationalarchives.gov.uk/researchguidesindex.asp.

Vols. 61 and 62: *Subject Indexes of Cabinet Office Conclusions, 1919 Nov.–1921 Dec.* (for CAB 23/18–28)

Vols. 73 and 74: *Subject Indexes of War Cabinet Minutes, 1939 Sept.–1941 Dec. and 1942 Jan.–1945 July* (CAB 65)

Vols. 92 and 100: *Subject Index of Cabinet Conclusions, 1922–Jan.–Oct.* (for part of CAB 23)

Vol. 126: *Prime Minister's Office Class List (PREM 1–6)*

Vols. 131, 140, and 162: *Cabinet Office Class Lists: Parts I* (CAB 1–36; 39, 40), *II* (CAB 43–47, 50–55, 57, 58, 60–100), and *III* (CAB 101–3, 105–11, 115, 117–19)

Vol. 136: *List of War Cabinet Memoranda, 1939 Sept.–1945 July* (CAB 66)

Vol. 148: *Cabinet Office List of War Cabinet Memoranda (WPG & WPR series), 1939 Sept.–1942 Dec.* (CAB 67 and 68)

Vol. 156: *Cabinet Office War Cabinet Memoranda: General Index of GT Papers 1–8412 1916 Dec.–1919 Oct.* (CAB 24/6–90)

Vol. 199: *Ramsay Macdonald Correspondence, 1890–1937* (PRO 30/69)

Vol. 230: *Foreign Office General Correspondence: Political, 1952* (FO 371/96642–102560)

Vol. 239: *Foreign Office General Correspondence: Political, 1954* (FO 371/ 108095–113216)

In France, there are several main repositories you should know about: the Centre historique des Archives nationales[97] (or CHAN, for pre-1958 material and the archives of heads of state), the Centre des archives contemporaires[98] (or CAC, for post-1958 material)—these two repositories are both parts of the Archives nationales—the Foreign Ministry Archives,[99] which is a separate unit, and the Service historique de l'Armée de Terre (SHAT), also not part of the Archives nationales. The CHAN has put some of its inventories online: to get at the list, click the link for "archives" on the CHAN homepage. Two *fonds* are of particular interest: AG. Papiers des chefs de l'État (through Pompidou)[100] and AP. Archives personnelles et familiales[101] (with online inventories and guides by topic).

For the Archives nationales as a whole, you might want to consult some published guides:

Les Archives nationales: Etat général des fonds, ed. J. Favier et al., 5 vols. (Paris: Archives nationales, 1978–88)

Les Archives nationales: Etat des inventaires, ed. J. Favier et al., 4 vols. (Paris: Archives nationales, 1985–2000)

[97] http://www.archivesnationales.culture.gouv.fr/chan/.
[98] http://www.archivesnationales.culture.gouv.fr/cac/fr/index.html.
[99] http://www.diplomatie.gouv.fr/archives/.
[100] http://www.archivesnationales.culture.gouv.fr/chan/chan/fonds/edi/sm/ EDIAG.htm.
[101] http://www.archivesnationales.culture.gouv.fr/chan/chan/fonds/edi/ap/apintro.htm.

Guide des papiers des ministres et secrétaires d'Etat de 1871 à 1974, ed. C. de Tourtier-
Bonazzi and F. Pourcelet (Paris: Archives nationales, 1984)
La seconde guerre mondiale: Guide des sources conservées en France, 1939–1945, ed. B.
Blanc, H. Rousso, and C. de Tourtier-Bonazzi (Paris: Archives nationales, 1994)

For the Foreign Ministry, there are also a number of published guides:

Ministère des Affaires étrangères, *Les Archives du ministère des Relations extérieures
depuis l'origine: Histoire et guide*, 2 vols. (Paris: Imprimerie nationale, 1984–85)
Ministère des Affaires étrangères, *Etat général des inventaires des Archives diplomatiques* (Paris: Imprimerie nationale, 1987)
Paul M. Pitman, *Petit guide du lecteur des Archives du Quai d'Orsay* (Paris: Association des Amis des Archives diplomatiques, 1993) (also available in English)

Various other published guides are listed on Foreign Ministry archives
website.
As for the French military archives, a brief guide to the SHAT[102] is available online, and a more detailed guide to the holdings of that archive has
been published:

France, Armée de Terre, Service historique [Jean-Claude Devos and Marie-Anne
Corvisier-de Villèle], *Guide des archives et sources complémentaires* (Vincennes:
Service historique de l'armée de terre, 1996)

A number of SHAT's inventories have been published. For a listing, do an
author search in a library catalogue (like MELVYL) for "France. Armée de
Terre. Service historique" and, at the same time, search for the word "inven-
taire" in the title field. If you are working on the Cold War period, you might
also want to take a look at Piers Ludlow's article, "No Longer a Closed Shop:
Post-1945 Research in the French Archives," which originally appeared in
the October 2001 issue of *Cold War Studies*.
In Germany, the Foreign Office also has its own archive. A brochure in pdf
describing the holdings there is available on that archive's website.[103] The
website itself contains other very useful information.[104] But quite a few important sources are also available in the Bundesarchiv, Germany's national
archives.[105] Many published finding aids for the Bundesarchiv collections are
listed in the online *Guide to Inventories and Finding Aids at the German Historical
Institute Washington, D.C.* (under "K" for "Koblenz," where the Bundesarchiv is

[102] http://jomave.chez.tiscali.fr/adgenweb/shat.html.
[103] http://www.auswaertiges-amt.de/www/de/infoservice/download/pdf/publikationen/archiv.pdf.
[104] http://www.auswaertiges-amt.de/www/de/infoservice/politik.
[105] http://www.bundesarchiv.de/.

located).[106] Note also Frank Schumacher, *Archives in Germany: An Introductory Guide to Institutions and Sources* (Washington, D.C.: GHI, 2001),[107] and also two guides dealing with the East German archives: Cyril Buffet's *Guide des archives de l'Allemagne de l'Est*, put out by the Centre Franco-Allemand de Recherches en Sciences Sociales in Berlin in 1994, and Bernd Schäfer, Henning Hoff, and Ulrich Mählert, *The GDR in German Archives: A New Resource Guide* (Washington, D.C.: GHI, 2002).[108] The GHI will send hard-copy versions of any of its guides to you for free upon request. Incidentally, any American scholar planning to do historical research in Germany should become familiar with the GHI website, which is packed with useful information, including information about funding.[109]

But many interesting sources are not to be found in those main national repositories. Collections of personal papers are often very valuable. Although some of them, especially in France, can be found in the main national repositories, as a general rule they are housed in all sorts of places. How do you go about identifying collections of papers that might be important for your purposes? You can begin by looking at some of the obvious repositories. In the United States, for example, many important collections can be found in the Library of Congress. You could either browse through the LOC's whole list of manuscript collections[110] or you could look at some of their subject lists[111]—"National security," for example, or "United States—Foreign relations—Great Britain." Many of those listings have finding aids attached. There are other important repositories you might want to check out. The Mudd Library at Princeton,[112] for example, and the Hoover Institution at Stanford[113] each house important archival collections of interest to people in our field.

For a much fuller listing of archival collections in U.S. repositories, your best bet is to use ArchivesUSA,[114] an online publication from ProQuest. (Your library has to be a subscriber for you to use this search engine.) ArchivesUSA brings together the information from two separate sources: the information published in the National Union Catalogue of Manuscript Collections (NUCMC), the standard catalogue of material in this area, which was published in hard-copy from 1959 to 1993; and the information included in ProQuest's own publication, the National Inventory of Document Sources (about which more later). You can search by name or by keyword; links in

---

[106] http://www.ghi-dc.org/guide5/frame1.html.

[107] http://www.ghi-dc.org/guide13/index.html.

[108] http://www.ghi-dc.org/guide14/index.html.

[109] http://www.ghi-dc.org/.

[110] http://lcweb2.loc.gov/faid/repositoryfr.html#MSS.

[111] http://lcweb2.loc.gov/faid/faidctopindex1.html.

[112] http://www.princeton.edu/mudd/.

[113] http://www-hoover.stanford.edu/hila/.

[114] http://archives.chadwyck.com/.

many of the listings will actually give you the "index terms" a particular item is listed under. This allows you to do a keyword search for particular terms that are of interest to you.

This is an important research tool, but it's not quite as good as you might think. I did a spot check, and a couple of collections I've used—the Bernard Brodie Papers at UCLA and the Lauris Norstad Papers at the Eisenhower library—did not even come up when I did keyword searches for Brodie's and Norstad's last names. I also did a search for the Kissinger Papers at the Library of Congress. No listing turned up, even though one did when I searched for "Kissinger" on the Library of Congress's NUCMC catalogue. Still, you can identify many sources using ArchivesUSA.

You can also use Eureka, the Union Catalogue of the Research Libraries Group, to identify archival material. When you get into Eureka, click into the "advanced search" window, select "keyword" from the search menu, and type in the last name of a particular individual in the search window. Then scroll down and check the box for "Archival and Mixed Collections." Then click "search." The list that comes up might well contain some interesting archival material.

This technique, moreover, is particularly useful for identifying archival material dealing with a particular subject. Say you did a search for the keyword "Kissinger" limited to "Archival and Mixed Collections." One of the seventy-four listings that come up is the Kissinger Papers at the Library of Congress. When you click into that listing, you see a whole series of linked subject headings. One of them is "United States—Foreign Relations—China." Click into that subject link and then call up the whole list of works included under that heading. Then click "limit" at the bottom of the window, select "material type," check the box for "Archival and Mixed Collections," and click "Apply Limit." More than a hundred collections are then listed on your screen.

For Britain, you can search for collections of papers using the National Register of Archives,[115] now part of the British National Archives. Click the link for "personal name." You can then search for a particular individual, or even browse through the entire listing of holdings of personal papers. One nice thing about this search engine is that it turns up not just the collection of papers of the individual you are searching for but all collections in the database that contain something written by that individual. Some research guides are also available online, with descriptions of and direct links to the main repositories in a given area. See, for example, the guide to sources for the history of the armed forces. One of the archives mentioned there, the Liddell Hart Centre for Military Archives at Kings College London, has particularly good holdings and a very good website.[116] If you're interested in

[115] http://www.nra.nationalarchives.gov.uk/nra/.
[116] http://www.kcl.ac.uk/lhcma/home.htm.

working with collections of papers in Britain, you might want to check out a couple of published guides:

Royal Commission on Historical Manuscripts, *Surveys of Historical Manuscripts in the United Kingdom: A Select Bibliography*, 2d ed. (London: HMSO, 1994)

Royal Commission on Historical Manuscripts, *Record Repositories in Great Britain: A Geographical Directory* (London: HMSO, 1991)

In Germany, the institutions set up by the main political parties—the Konrad-Adenauer-Stiftung[117] for the CDU and the Friedrich-Ebert-Stiftung[118] for the SPD—are home to the papers of many individuals connected with those parties. If you'd like to cast a somewhat broader net, take a look at Erwin Welsch, *Archives and Libraries in a New Germany* (New York: Council for European Studies, 1994). There's a similar guide for France, by now a little out of date: Erwin Welsch, *Libraries and Archives in France: A Handbook* (New York: Council for European Studies, 1979). A French website called "BORA"[119] ("Base d'Orientation et de Recherche dans les Archives") is worth looking at, if you're interested in collections of private papers in France. It now has references to material of this sort included in official repositories and will eventually include collections of papers found in other kinds of repositories as well.

The Council for European Studies has a webpage with links to various European archives;[120] click into the link for "archives in Europe." There are various other gateway websites of this sort that you might find useful. The University of Idaho Library, for example, has a very good site giving links to "Repositories of Primary Sources";[121] just click into the sections for European repositories. Note also UNESCO's Archives Portal website, which has many links to European repositories.

If you're interested in Russian material, be sure to check out the "Archives in Russia" website.[122] This site is connected to the guide *Archives of Russia: A Directory and Bibliographic Guide to Holdings in Moscow and St. Petersburg*, ed. Patricia Kennedy Grimsted, 2 vols. (Armonk, N.Y.: M. E. Sharpe, 2000). See also Grimsted's two-part CWIHP working paper, "The Russian Archives Seven Years After" (September 1998): part I and part II.[123] Note also the website for the University of Toronto's Stalin-Era Research and Archives Project (SERAP).[124]

---

[117] http://www.kas.de/archiv/acdp/bestand/nachlaesse_deposita/526_webseite.html.

[118] http://www.fes.de/archive/index_gr.html.

[119] http://daf.archivesdefrance.culture.gouv.fr/sdx/ap/.

[120] http://www.columbia.edu/cu/ces/frames/overall.html.

[121] http://www.uidaho.edu/special-collections/Other.Repositories.html.

[122] http://www.iisg.nl/%7Eabb/.

[123] http://wwics.si.edu/topics/pubs/ACF518.pdf; http://wwics.si.edu/topics/pubs/ACF51B.pdf.

[124] http://www.utoronto.ca/serap/.

There is also some very useful information (about both archival and published Soviet sources) in Jonathan Haslam's article, "Collecting and Assembling Pieces of the Jigsaw: Coping with Cold War Archives," *Cold War History* 4, no. 3 (April 2004). This article also contains important information about a number of neglected archival sources (Italian, Brazilian, etc.). It's one of a series of archival review articles published in that journal (which, by the way, is available online in a number of university libraries). That series includes the Piers Ludlow article on French archival sources already cited, an article by Leopoldo Nuti on Italian archival sources (2, no. 3, April 2002), and a number of others.

So those are the basics. That's how you go about identifying the archival sources you might like to examine. But once you've identified particular collections, you'd still like to get some sense for what they contain. Of course, you could wait until you arrived at the archive to see what's in those various collections. The archivists will show you where the finding aids are, and might even provide you with certain finding aids that are not on the open shelves. You could do it that way, but the odds are that you'd like to be able to do this kind of work before you leave home—if only to be able to get some rough sense for how much time you'd need to spend in a particular repository. So is there a way of consulting those finding aids before you actually go to the archives?

Well, sometimes yes and sometimes no. Many of the guides and search engines I've mentioned have links to finding aids. When you find ones that are of interest, you might want to download or at least bookmark them. And you can also try to see what's included in an important publication, available in a number of university libraries and through interlibrary loan: the *National Inventory of Documentary Sources* (NIDS). NIDS is basically a collection of many finding aids from various U.S. sources reproduced on microfiche. You can see what they are by using the hard-copy guide. Or you can use *ArchivesUSA* to see if a finding aid for a collection you're interested in has been included in NIDS. If it has, the "NIDS fiche number" will appear on the listing. If you want to see which finding aids in a particular repository are included in NIDS, just enter the name of the repository in the repository field in the main *ArchivesUSA* search engine and under "search options," select "NIDS Records Only."

But it's basically just a convenience to be able to get finding aids in advance. And whether you can get them in advance or not, the whole process of doing archival research—identifying collections, going through the finding aids, ordering the materials you'd like to see—is on the whole very straightforward. There is, however, one exception to that general rule, and that has to do with the U.S. National Archives in College Park, Maryland.

The National Archives can be a very confusing place until you get the hang of it, so let me explain a little bit about how it works for people in our field. When you arrive at the archives, the first thing you do is get an archives card. There is a small room on your right as you go in the door; the people there set you up at a computer, you show them a picture identification, and soon you'll have your card. You can't take things into the reading room with you without getting them specially stamped, so try to bring in as little as possible. You can drop off your extra stuff in a free locker—you need a quarter to operate it—in the basement. Then you go back to the first floor and through the control gate. After you're checked through, you take the elevator to the second floor and go into the reading room. After you check in there, unless you have material already waiting for you, you'll have to go to another desk down toward your left, to get a pass and an escort to go down to the rooms where the archivists and findings aids are. This is also where you will fill out and hand in your order forms (also called "pull slips" or "service slips"). You will, incidentally, need to fill out a separate form for each box, except if a number of consecutively numbered boxes are ordered, in which case a single form can be used.

There are two such rooms: room 2400 for modern military records (including CIA materials and such sources as the McNamara papers) and room 2600 for civilian records, including the State Department records in RG 59. Say you go to the civilian records division first. You'll check in at the desk and meet with an archivist who will explain the basics to you and set you up with some finding aids. Note when the records are pulled: 9:30, 10:30, 11:30, 1:30, and 3:30. Be sure to hand in your forms by those deadlines; if you miss a deadline, you will have to wait an extra hour or two. This may not be a problem, of course, if you have other work in the finding aids to do, including work in room 2400 (which has the same schedule for pulling boxes), but it's a good idea to order your boxes early, because they sometimes make mistakes pulling boxes. You can get something like eighteen boxes on a truck, which will then be delivered for you to pick up in the main reading room. You can order one truck from the civilian records division, and one from the modern military division, so you can assure yourself of a continuous flow of documents. (As soon as you finish with, say, your State Department records and return that truck, put in your forms for a new State Department batch; you will be able to work on your military records while your new State Department materials are being pulled.)

The State Department records are broken down into two parts: the Central File, and the Lot Files (The Lot Files are generally the records of specific offices in the State Department.) The Central File is itself broken down into two parts, based on method of classification. Until January 1963, a decimal system was used, so these are often called the "decimal files." From 1963 to 1973, the record keepers used a "subject-numeric" system and in 1973 the system was changed again.[125] Various finding aids for parts of the central

---

[125] On these systems, see Gerald Haines and J. Samuel Walker, "Some Sources and Problems for Diplomatic Historians in the Next Two Decades," in Gerald Haines and J. Samuel Walker, *American Foreign Relations: A Historiographical Review* (Westport, Conn.: Greenwood Press, 1981), esp. pp. 336–341.

files are available at the archives—for example, the "Purport Lists for the Department of State Decimal File, 1910–1944," a very detailed, document-by-document list (also available as National Archives microfilm publication M973; 654 rolls). The "Records Codification Manual" for the 1950–63 records is also available on a single roll of microfilm (publication M1275). See also the information given for file 59.2.5 in the section on RG 59 in the National Archives online guide.[126]

The forms for boxes in the State Department Central Files are relatively easy to fill out. For the decimal series, you need to write in, in the big space at the bottom of the form where it says "record identification," the decimal number and the date, something like "740.5611 for 1957–59." For the line above, you also need to fill in the first two boxes, the RG number (59) and the stack area (250)—which is the same for all these records. A typical service slip for the decimal files is available online.[127]

But how do you get the decimal number in the first place? One filing system was used from 1910 to 1949, and a somewhat different classification system was used in the period from 1950 to 1963. There are guides in room 2600 (the archivists will show them to you) describing these systems, but those guides don't always give you what you need. For example, you can't just look up "Euratom" in the index and learn that 840.1901 is where documents on U.S. policy toward Euratom are located. You can ask the archivists to help you, but often they don't know how to find things either. Basically, for that latter period, there are three main series of interest, the 600, 700, and 800 series. 6xx.yy deals with political relations between country xx and yy; 7xx.subj deals with political and military affairs for country (or region) xx; 8xx.subj deals with internal economic and social affairs. Some of the main country codes are: 11 for the United States, 41 for Britain, 51 for France, 62 for Germany, 62a for West Germany, 61 for Russia. The same system is also used for regions: 00 for general, 40 for Europe, 50 for continental western Europe. Some of the main subject codes for our purposes are: 5 for defense, 56 for equipment, 5611 for nuclear, 5612 for missiles, and (for the 800 series) 1901 for atomic energy. But lot of material on U.S.-German relations is not in 611.62, as you might think, but rather in 762.00 ("Germany—General"), and there is some good material also in 740.5. Or who would guess that 740.56 seems to be the main file on nuclear sharing and the FIG agreements (a plan for joint nuclear production between France, Italy, and Germany)?

So it's important to remember that it takes a while to find your way around this source. You get leads in various ways. Often cross-references are written in by hand in the margins of particular documents. Archival references are also given for documents published in the *Foreign Relations* series. Those references will often point the way to the richest files, indeed to boxes of documents you might not otherwise think of ordering. (Most of the volumes in the *Foreign Relations* series are on the open shelves in the middle of the main reading room, so you don't have to lug your own copies from home.)

Now let me talk about the subject-numeric part of the State Department central files, for documents from about February 1963 on. How do you find your way around the subject-numeric files? There is a short guide giving a rough explanation of this system, and again there are the references in FRUS, but your basic entrée here is the box list in the "State Department group" of finding aids in room 2600. The box list, however, gives only a fairly minimal idea of what each box contains, so you may have to grope around a bit. You order by box number. A typical order slip for the subject-numeric files can be viewed online.[128]

The lot files are more difficult to use. There is a book by Gerald Haines describing the lot files:

Gerald Haines, *A Reference Guide to United States Department of State Special Files* (Westport, Conn.: Greenwood, 1985)

You can also often find lists of relevant lot files at the beginning of various FRUS volumes. Your main entrée into the lot files, however, will probably be the finding aids in the "State Department group" in room 2600 (on the left toward the back as you walk in). There are black loose-leaf binders and white loose-leaf binders; they overlap somewhat, and the white binders are much better. When you go through the finding aids in those binders, note the lot number and brief title, the numbers of the boxes you're interested in, and, above all, the location number for that lot file. The location number is generally, but not always, written by hand into the finding aid and looks something like this: 250/D/15/06, or 250/62/23/5. When it's not written in, you can find it by using the new Lot File Database; a terminal is in the finding aids room, and the archivists can show you how to use it. You put the location number, and not the number for the lot file itself, on your order form, in the second through fifth boxes right above the big "record identification" box. (See the example I put online.)[129] But the lot number is often used when the document is actually cited. You of course will also give the box number (or numbers) you're ordering when filling out the order form.

The Lot File Database will also tell you where the finding aid for a particular lot file is located. The mere fact that a finding aid is not available does not in itself mean that the lot file cannot be consulted. Some of these lot files

---

[128] http://www.polisci.ucla.edu/faculty/trachtenberg/guide/usna-slip%283%29.html.

[129] http://www.polisci.ucla.edu/faculty/trachtenberg/guide/usna-slip%282%29.html.

have box lists which the archivists can bring you but which are not available on the open shelves.

Another important binder is labeled "Conference Files." This collection contains the records of meetings held by U.S. officials on trips, mostly abroad. For example, if you order "Conference Files for 1964–66, CF 268–269, boxes 465–466," at 150/68/28/1–7, you'll get the records of the U.S. Balance of Payments Mission to Europe of January 1968. In the back of the Conference Files binder, you'll also see a list of materials under the heading "Executive Secretariat, Briefing Books, 1958–76." This contains some interesting material you might be surprised to find here. Boxes 3–9 in this collection, for example, contain a set of documents on U.S. relations with France, June 1958 through February 1963 (Lot 69D 150, 150/68/1/2–7).

I should note more generally that there are often hidden treasures in RG 59, and it's often hard to know how to go about discovering them. You often just stumble across them in the course of doing something else. For example, there's a part of RG 59 devoted to the State Department's Division of Historical Policy Research and Its Predecessors, and part of this has sixteen boxes of "Special Studies and Reports, 1944–50." It's located in 150/46/08-09/06-07. Box 4 (report no. 84) has about four hundred pages of top secret teletype conferences between the State Department and the London embassy relating to the Berlin blockade affair of 1948. Box 5 has three bound volumes on the Moscow Foreign Ministers' Conference of 1947. Boxes 7–16 have an enormous amount of material on the Middle East, 1946–48. But you only find out about these things by poking around.

Those State Department materials in RG 59 are very important. Certain other record groups might be worth exploring, but there's a good chance you'll be disappointed by what you find in those collections. The NSC documents in RG 273, for example, are not particularly rich. If you're interested in NSC material, you'd be much better off going to the presidential libraries. The National Archives does, however, have a few things that might be worth looking at for certain purposes. There is a card catalogue in Room 2600 listing the formal NSC papers, and, as I said before, there is also a list in the Haines book. Using those lists, you can request files corresponding to particular NSC documents (NSC 68 and so on). You can also request the file for a particular NSC meeting, using (if you're interested in the Eisenhower period) the guide to the meetings I gave you above.[130] But as I say, my experience was that these sources were not particularly rich—not nearly as good as the kind of thing you can see at the presidential libraries.

The military sources, however, are very rich. The most important military source is RG 218, the JCS records. For materials dealing with the period

[130] http://www.polisci.ucla.edu/faculty/trachtenberg/guide/nsc.html.

through 1958, you give your request by citing a CCS number, which derives from the filing system developed for the U.S.-British Combined Chiefs of Staff during World War II. You request, for example, "CCS 092 Germany (5-4-49) for 1958." For the period from 1959 on, a different system was used. There are guides that explain these systems, but it is a very good idea to ask for help from the archivists. I've posted a typical cover sheet from the JCS papers for 1961.[131] Note the list of "cross index numbers" toward the top. This sort of thing can be quite useful for "spreading out" and figuring out which boxes to order next. Another way of getting at this source, as I noted above, is by using the JCS histories, both published and unpublished.

The military affairs division at the National Archives has other record groups that are of some interest, especially for the period prior to about 1954—for example, RG 330, the records of the Office of the Secretary of Defense (OSD). There is an official *History of the Office of the Secretary of Defense*, four volumes of which, covering the 1947–60 period, have been published so far:

> *History of the Office of the Secretary of Defense*, gen. ed. Alfred Goldberg (Washington, D.C.: OSD Historical Office, 1984–)

The footnotes in that series might help you find your way around this source. And you can use whatever help you can get, because this is not a particularly easy record group to find your way around. The same CCS system used in RG 218 is also used here, but apparently in a completely different way.

So how then do you use RG 330? In the finding aid room off of Room 2400, there are two binders (one black, one white), each broken down into two halves (NM-12 and A-1), listing all the available components in RG 330 by entry number. Sometimes an entry number is for an index to a collection listed under another entry number. It turns out, for example, that the most important source in this collection for 1950–51 is Entry 199, OSD materials for July 1950–December 1951. But there is a very large number of boxes in Entry 199. So to identify what you want, you need to go into Entry 198, boxes 7–14, the Index for July 1950–December 1951. This gives you the file (or CD) numbers for files in Entry 199. You then go to the Entry 199 folder in the RG 330 box in the finding aids room, figure out which boxes in Entry 199 correspond to the files (listed by CD number) you've identified from the index in Entry 198, and put in your request for those boxes—getting the stack location numbers from the loose-leaf binders. Is it any wonder that not too many people use this source, especially when you realize that the declassifiers were notoriously conservative in releasing material in this collection? And yet you do come across gems in this collection from time to time, real nuggets of gold unavailable elsewhere.

[131] http://www.polisci.ucla.edu/faculty/trachtenberg/guide/jcscoversheet.html.

V. Open Sources

Some topics—especially those of continuing political importance—cannot be studied effectively on the basis of the sorts of material I've been talking about so far. If you're interested in some episode that has taken place in the very recent past, or in some story that is still unfolding, you'll have to rely on open sources: on newspaper and magazine accounts, on statements made by government officials, on testimony in congressional hearings, and the like. That material is sometimes also worth examining even if you are interested in subjects for which a large amount of previously classified material has been made available. It is always interesting to know how a particular issue was treated in the public discussion at the time, and occasionally even important historical records are published under congressional auspices. So let me talk briefly about material of this sort—first, newspapers and magazines; then the congressional sources; and finally, material released by the executive branch, both in the United States and in other countries.

Newspapers and magazines, or at least those issues that came out from about 1980 on, are now searchable electronically through LexisNexis. This allows you to do full-text searches for articles in major U.S. and non-U.S. newspapers and magazines—more than 350 newspapers (*New York Times, Washington Post, Wall Street Journal, Financial Times, Die Zeit, Le Monde, Le Figaro*, and so on) and more than 300 magazines (*Newsweek, New Yorker, New Republic, National Review, L'Express, Der Spiegel, Economist*, etc.). Three important newspapers—the *New York Times*, the *Los Angeles Times*, and the *Wall Street Journal*—can also be searched via ProQuest Newspapers. In the case of those three newspapers, there are two separate collections, a historical collection and a current collection, but together they provide full coverage from the nineteenth century through the present. Both LexisNexis and ProQuest are subscription services, so you'll need to get access to these sources through your library.

The ProQuest and LexisNexis search engines allow you to do keyword searches, but this, as you know, has its problems. It's hard to know which keywords will give you everything you want but will not generate a mass of irrelevant material at the same time, so when you do keyword searches you pretty much have to grope in the dark. That's why it's important to note that the old-fashioned hard-copy newspaper indexes continue to be published, and those indexes in my view are just terrific. As I said in the text, you can learn a lot just by reading the listings in the *New York Times Index*, and indexes are available for a number of other major newspapers: *Washington Post, Los Angeles Times, Le Monde*, and the *Times* of London. General interest magazines are also quite important, and played a major role in the political culture before television arrived on the scene. The basic guide to that source is the *Reader's Guide to Periodical Literature*; the *Reader's Guide* can now also be searched electronically through the WilsonWeb, another subscription service.

You may want to read certain newspapers and magazines on a regular basis, especially if you are working on some contemporary issue. In that case, you should know about the many periodicals that are available through their own websites. For the European press, there is a good list, with links, on the Council for European Studies website.[132] The State Department's surveys of the foreign media are available online.[133] Charles Lipson has many links to international news sources on his website.[134] For the periodical literature in the military area, check out the page on "National Security Media Sources" in the Center for Strategic Education (SAIS) website.[135] English translations of key articles in some important non-English-language periodicals are available online, at least for a certain period of time following publication of the original; *Der Spiegel*, for example, has an English-language edition available online.[136]

Let me now talk a bit about published congressional sources. If you're studying some contemporary issue, these might well be of fundamental importance. How do you approach this material? The LexisNexis congressional webpage is a good place to start. You can search there in various databases: the CIS (Congressional Information Service) Index, "historical indexes," a "testimony" database, and so on. The CIS index covers the period from 1970 on, and you can search that index by subject (there's a browsable list), by committee, by witness, and in various other ways. The search can of course be limited by date. The listings that turn up sometimes have full-text links, but when they don't, you can use the title of the hearings to do a title search in a regular library catalogue. The historical indexes cover the pre-1980 period. The testimony database, which covers the post-1988 period, is particularly good if you're studying a particular person. A search for Henry Kissinger, for example, turns up sixty references. You also have the option of searching for a particular individual by doing a witness search in the CIS index, which covers a somewhat broader period.

This particular search engine, however, has its problems, and you might also want to use a browsable index, at least as a supplement. This is fairly easy to do, at least for relatively recent material. Just go to the Congress page on the GPOAccess website.[137] You'll find browsable lists of hearings listed by committee both for the current Congress and for previous Congresses going back to 1997. The listings are linked to full-text transcripts of those hearings, and the format is much more readable than what you get with LexisNexis.

For older material, congressional sources are much harder to use. Finding aids exist—note especially the "historical indexes" on LexisNexis—but it's

[132] http://www.columbia.edu/cu/ces/frames/overall.html.

[133] http://usinfo.state.gov/products/medreac.htm.

[134] http://www.charleslipson.com/News-audio.htm.

[135] http://sais-jhu.edu/centers/cse/online_supplement/section5.html.

[136] http://www.spiegel.de/spiegel/english.

[137] http://www.gpoaccess.gov/congress/index.html.

hard to tell what's really important amid all the dross. If you're interested in the early Cold War period, however, there is one guide that you might find useful, at least if you're interested in military affairs:

> *Congressional Hearings on American Defense Policy, 1947–1971: An Annotated Bibliography*, comp. Richard Burt (Lawrence: University Press of Kansas, 1974)

If you'd like to use unpublished congressional material, you should take a look at Andrew L. Johns, "Needles in the Haystacks: Using Congressional Collections in Foreign Relations Research," *SHAFR Newletter* 34, no. 1 (March 2003): 1–7; that article lists a number of indexes, guides, and websites that you might want to consult.

Now, finally, let me outline some of the material that's put out by the executive branch. In the United States, two published collections are often quite useful:

> *Public Papers of the Presidents of the United States* (the online edition starts with the volume for 1992)[138]
> *Department of State Bulletin*

If you're working on a recent topic, you'll probably want to rely heavily on online sources:

> White House website[139]
>> Current news, with links to the news archive[140] (contains the text of official statements, and you can search by issue using the drop-down menu)
> State Department website (post–January 2001 material)[141]
>> Secretary of State's remarks (current administration)[142]
>> Other senior officials (with links to their remarks)[143]
>> Countries and regions[144] (the "releases" links on the regional bureau websites linked here give the text of remarks relating to each region; in the "releases" section, there's also a link to a pre-2001 archive of material related to each area)
>> Foreign media surveys[145]
> State Department Electronic Archive (pre–January 2001)[146]
>> Briefings and Statements (1993–present)[147]

---

[138] http://www.gpoaccess.gov/pubpapers/search.html.
[139] http://www.whitehouse.gov/.
[140] http://www.whitehouse.gov/news/.
[141] http://www.state.gov/.
[142] http://www.state.gov/secretary/rm/.
[143] http://www.state.gov/misc/19232.htm.
[144] http://www.state.gov/countries/.
[145] http://usinfo.state.gov/products/medreac.htm.
[146] http://dosfan.lib.uic.edu/ERC/index.html.
[147] http://dosfan.lib.uic.edu/ERC/briefing.html.

Department of Defense DefenseLink[148]

Transcripts of remarks (current[149]) (archive[150]) (search engine[151])

Many other countries have websites of this sort, with texts often available in English. The French Foreign Ministry website, for example, has a page in English containing the foreign minister's remarks over the past couple of years.[152] The same can be said of the German Foreign Office website.[153] Even the website for the president's office in France has an English-language version containing the text (in English) of President Chirac's speeches.[154] Various embassies in Washington also provide the text of speeches, interviews, and so on on their websites. See, for example, the websites for the French embassy[155] and the German embassy[156] in Washington. It really is quite extraordinary how much material of this sort is available online nowadays.

VI. Getting to See Classified Material

There are various things you can do if you would like to see material that's still classified. You can, above all, try to get that material declassified. And you can go about doing that in a number of ways. You could file a request under the Freedom of Information Act (FOIA), for example, or you could file a Mandatory Declassification Review (MR) request for one or more specific documents.

The particular procedure you use depends on the sort of material you want. If you're interested in material produced by a regular agency of government (like the State Department or the CIA), you're supposed to use the FOIA procedure. The MR procedure is supposed to be used when you're trying to see documents produced by the president's office and its offshoots (and that includes the NSC). What this means in practice is that you'll normally file MRs for documents in the presidential libraries. But if you want to see classified congressional materials—the records, for example, of the Joint Committee on Atomic Energy—you can't use either the FOIA or Mandatory Review procedure. You instead have to get in touch with the Center for Legislative Archives at (202) 501-5350 (or 5353), and they'll tell you how to proceed.

---

[148] http://www.defenselink.mil/.

[149] http://www.defenselink.mil/transcripts/.

[150] http://www.defenselink.mil/transcripts/archive.html.

[151] http://www.defenselink.mil/search/.

[152] http://www.france.diplomatie.fr/actu/actu.gb.asp?DOS=27766&PAG=30.

[153] http://www.auswaertiges-amt.de/www/en/infoservice/aktuelles/.

[154] http://www.elysee.fr/elysee/anglais/speeches_of_president_chirac/2005/2005_speeches_and_documents.27733.html.

[155] http://www.ambafrance-us.org/news/.

[156] http://www.germany-info.org/relaunch/politics/speeches/speeches.html.

How does mandatory review work? The process is quite simple. When a collection is processed, documents that haven't been declassified are withdrawn from the files, and a "withdrawal sheet" is placed at the top of each file folder. The withdrawal sheet lists and describes documents that have been taken out. You look at the withdrawal sheets in the files that are of interest to you, and on the basis of what you see there, you fill out the form the presidential libraries have devised for this purpose. I'm putting a couple of these withdrawal sheets online—one that's "clean"[157] and another that's been through the mill[158]—so you can see what they're like. I'm also putting a blank MR request form online for the same reason.[159] You can list a number of separate documents on a single form, provided they're all from the same file folder. There are limits to the number of MRs you can file—that is, to the number of documents you can ask to have reviewed for declassification—within a particular period of time. You're also not allowed to file an MR request for a particular document if it's already been reviewed fairly recently—information about prior reviews appears on the withdrawal sheet. There are various other rules that might apply and the precise rules change from time to time. The archivists will tell you everything you need to do when you're at the library.

MR requests can take years to get processed, so this is one thing you should do early on in a multiyear project. Just file your forms (making a copy for yourself before you send it in), wait to make sure the library sends you your MR request number so you can keep track of your request (if it doesn't, be sure to call and ask for it), and then forget about this whole business. When the documents come, you'll be pleasantly surprised by whatever they send you. The same point, of course, applies to FOIA requests.

How do you use the FOIA? Again, it's really not that hard to use. You don't send in a list this time. You write a letter. The National Security Archive has a FOIA guide[160] on its website, and so does the Freedom of Information Clearinghouse[161] (Ralph Nader). You can also get "Using the FOIA: A Step by Step Guide" from the Center for National Security Studies in Washington. All of these guides have basic information, sample letters, and lists of addresses for you to send your letters to. (Some of this material is a little out of date, so it might be best to check addresses by phone before you send anything in.) Requests for relatively recent State Department material (as a general rule, material produced since 1975) should now be sent to: Margaret Grafeld, Director, Office of IRM Programs and Services, A/RPS/IPS, Dept. of State SA-2, 515 22nd St. NW, Washington, DC 20522-6001. Older

[157] http://www.polisci.ucla.edu/faculty/trachtenberg/guide/mr%281%29.html.

[158] http://www.polisci.ucla.edu/faculty/trachtenberg/guide/mr%282%29.html.

[159] http://www.polisci.ucla.edu/faculty/trachtenberg/guide/mrform.html.

[160] http://www.gwu.edu/%7Ensarchiv/nsa/foia.html.

[161] http://www.citizen.org/litigation/free_info/articles.cfm?ID=5208.

(i.e., currently pre-1975) material should be requested from the National Archives, with requests sent to the following address: Civilian Records, Archives II, Room 2600, National Archives at College Park, 8601 Adelphi Road, College Park, MD 20740-6001. Department of Defense FOIA requests can now be filed electronically, using a form for this purpose that has been posted on the web.[162] The State Department now has a FOIA website that you might want to check out.[163]

As a general rule, you should try to be as specific as possible in a FOIA request. This may include giving specific archival references, including references to the retired files in the Washington National Records Center in Suitland, Maryland, where materials which are no longer in agency offices but which have not been turned over to the National Archives are generally kept. (You might actually have to go there to get the references; this is what the best FOIA requesters often do.) Also, it doesn't hurt to explain where you found out about the particular source you'd like released (if the lead came, for example, from the footnotes in a declassified historical study) and where that source is likely to be found. You can, of course, request a number of documents in a single letter, providing they're all from the same agency. After you send in your letter, you'll generally get a preliminary response. If that doesn't include the FOIA request number you've been assigned, be sure to get in touch with the office that sent you that letter and ask what it is. If you don't do that, you'll never be able to keep track of your request. And then be prepared to wait. It can, and generally does, take years before you get anything in the mail.

If your goal is just to see classified material—and not necessarily to get it released—you can sometimes proceed in a very different way. For certain classes of documents, you can get a kind of security clearance that allows you to see material of historical interest. For example, the Air Force History Support Office has (or at least at one point had) a program, called "Limited Security Access," which enables scholars to see historical materials under Air Force control classified up to the level of secret.[164] Call (202) 767-5764 or (202) 404-2261 for further information. I used that clearance to see not just certain Air Force materials (especially classified histories) but also to help me get access to the Rand papers, an unusually rich source. (Rand, for the period I was interested in, worked under contract for the Air Force.) You have to re-quest declassification of either specific documents, parts of documents, or of the notes you took on those documents, in order to cite these sources. That takes a little while, but it is a lot faster and more efficient than the FOIA process.

---

[162] http://www.defenselink.mil/pubs/foi/foiarequest.html.

[163] http://www.foia.state.gov/AboutFOIA.asp.

[164] http://www.airforcehistory.hq.af.mil/.

You come across other programs of this sort from time to time. At one point, for example, you had to apply for a security clearance to see the wonderful collection of Dulles State Papers at the Mudd Library in Princeton. This is no longer necessary, since that collection has now been declassified in its entirety. But the point is that programs of this sort exist, and you might want to find out if there is a program of this sort in the area you're interested in that you might be able to take advantage of. Of course, you can always talk with the archivists about what is possible—about whether there is any way to apply for special permission to see still-classified material. This applies not just to American sources but to archival material in other countries as well.

Finally, I should note that when you do archival research, you have to deal with various practical matters, like finding a place to stay while you are away from home and getting funding to pay for your research trips. I included some information on these matters in Part III of my old Cold War history website.[165] To get that information, click into that link and do a Ctrl F search for "housing" or "funding."

[165] http://www.polisci.ucla.edu/faculty/trachtenberg/guide/PART THREE.HTML.

BIBLIOGRAPHY

Albertini, Luigi. *The Origins of the War of 1914.* 3 vols. London: Oxford University Press, 1952–57.

Allison, Graham, and Morton Halperin. "Bureaucratic Politics: A Paradigm and Some Policy Implications." In "Theory and Policy in International Relations," edited by Raymond Tanter and Richand Ullman. *World Politics* 24, Supplement (Spring 1972).

Anderson, Irvine. "The 1941 *De Facto* Embargo on Oil to Japan: A Bureaucratic Reflex." *Pacific Historical Review* 44 (1975).

Appleby, Joyce,; Lynn Hunt, and Margaret Jacob. *Telling the Truth about History.* New York: Norton, 1994.

Atkinson, R. F. *Knowledge and Explanation in History.* Ithaca: Cornell University Press, 1978.

Australia. Department of Foreign Affairs. *Documents on Australian Foreign Policy, 1937–49.* Canberra: Australian Government Publishing Service, 1975–.

Barnhart, Michael. *Japan Prepares for Total War: The Search for Economic Security, 1919–1941.* Ithaca: Cornell University Press, 1987.

Beisner, Robert. *American Foreign Relations since 1600: A Guide to the Literature.* Santa Barbara: ABC-CLIO, 2003.

Blum, John Morton. *From the Morgenthau Diaries: Years of Urgency, 1938–1941.* Boston: Houghton Mifflin, 1965.

Boyd, Carl. *Hitler's Japanese Confidant: General Oshima Hiroshi and MAGIC Intelligence, 1941–1945.* Lawrence: University Press of Kansas, 1993.

British Documents on Foreign Affairs: Reports and Papers from the Foreign Office Confidential Print. Part III (1940–45), Series E (Asia). Bethesda, Md.: University Publications of America, 1997.

Brodie, Bernard. *War and Politics.* New York: Macmillan, 1973.

Butow, Robert. *Tojo and the Coming of the War.* Princeton: Princeton University Press, 1961.

Collingwood, R. G. *The Idea of History.* New York: Oxford University Press, 1956.

Copeland, Dale. *The Origins of Major War.* Ithaca: Cornell University Press, 2000.

Craven, Wesley, and James Cate, eds. *The Army Air Forces in World War II.* Vol. 1: *Plans and Early Operations, January 1939 to August 1942.* Chicago: University of Chicago Press, 1948.

Crowley, James. *Japan's Quest for Autonomy: National Security and Foreign Policy, 1930–1938.* Princeton: Princeton University Press, 1966.

Dallek, Robert. *Franklin D. Roosevelt and American Foreign Policy, 1932–1945.* Oxford: Oxford University Press, 1979. Paperback edition, 1981.

Dilks, David, ed. *The Diaries of Sir Alexander Cadogan, O.M., 1938–1945.* London: Cassell, 1971.

Documents on British Policy Overseas. Edited by Rohan Butler and M. E. Pelly. Series I, vol. 1: *The Conference at Potsdam, July–August 1945.* London: HMSO, 1984.

Donagan, Alan. "Can Philosophers Learn from Historians?" In *Mind, Science, and History*, edited by Howard Kiefer and Milton Munitz. Albany: State University of New York Press, 1970.

———. "The Popper-Hempel Theory Reconsidered." *History and Theory* 1 (1964). Reprinted with minor changes in *Philosophical Analysis and History*, edited by William Dray. New York: Harper and Row, 1966.

Dooman, Eugene. "Reminiscences of Eugene Hoffman Dooman." Columbia University Oral History Collection, 1962. New York.

Dray, William. *Laws and Explanation in History*. Oxford: Oxford University Press, 1957.

———. *On History and Philosophers of History*. Leiden: Brill, 1989.

———. *Philosophy of History*. Englewood Cliffs, N.J.: Prentice-Hall, 1964.

Fearey, Robert. "Tokyo 1941: Diplomacy's Final Round." *Foreign Service Journal*, December 1991.

Feis, Herbert. *The Road to Pearl Harbor: The Coming of the War between the United States and Japan*. Princeton: Princeton University Press, 1950.

Fischer, Fritz. *Germany's Aims in the First World War*. New York: Norton, 1967.

———. *War of Illusions: German Policies from 1911 to 1914*. New York: Norton, 1975.

Geiss, Imanuel, ed. *July 1914: The First World War, Selected Documents*. New York: Scribner's, 1967.

Geyl, Pieter. *Use and Abuse of History*. New Haven: Yale University Press, 1955. Reprint, Archon Books, 1970.

Goda, Norman. *Tomorrow the World: Hitler, Northwest Africa, and the Path toward America*. College Station: Texas A&M University Press, 1998.

Great Britain. Foreign Office. *British Foreign Office: Japan Correspondence, 1941–1945*. Microfilm. Wilmington, Del.: Scholarly Resources, 1978.

Grew, Joseph. *Turbulent Era: A Diplomatic Record of Forty Years, 1904–1945*. 2 vols. Boston: Houghton Mifflin, 1952.

Halévy, Elie. "The World Crisis of 1914–1918." In Elie Halévy, *The Era of Tyrannies: Essays on Socialism and War*. London: Allen Lane, 1967.

Hanson, N. R. *The Concept of the Positron: A Philosophical Analysis*. Cambridge: Cambridge University Press, 1963.

———. *Observation and Explanation: A Guide to Philosophy of Science*. New York: Harper, 1971.

———. *Patterns of Discovery: An Inquiry into the Conceptual Foundations of Science*. Cambridge: Cambridge University Press, 1958.

———. *Perception and Discovery: An Introduction to Scientific Inquiry*. San Francisco: Freeman, Cooper, 1969.

Haskell, Thomas L. *Objectivity Is Not Neutrality: Explanatory Schemes in History*. Baltimore: Johns Hopkins University Press, 1998.

Hattori, Takushiro. *The Complete History of the Greater East Asia War*. Translated by the U.S. Army, 500th Military Intelligence Service Group, 1953. Microfilm. Washington, D.C.: Library of Congress, Photoduplication Service, 1977.

Hearden, Patrick. *Roosevelt Confronts Hitler: America's Entry into World War* II. DeKalb: Northern Illinois University Press, 1987.

Heinrichs, Waldo. *Threshold of War: Franklin D. Roosevelt and American Entry into World War* II. New York: Oxford University Press, 1988.

Hempel, Carl. "The Function of General Laws in History." *Journal of Philosophy* 39 (1942). Reprinted in *Theories of History*, edited by Patrick Gardiner (New York: Free Press, 1959).

———. "Reasons and Covering Laws in Historical Explanation." In *Philosophy and History*, edited by Sidney Hook. New York: New York University Press, 1963.

Hexter, J. H. "The One That Got Away." *New York Review of Books*, February 9, 1967.

Hillgruber, Andreas. "Der Faktor Amerika in Hitlers Strategie 1938–1941." *Aus Politik und Zeitgeschichte* (supplement to *Das Parlament*), May 11, 1966.

Hinsley, F. H. *British Intelligence in the Second World War: Its Influence on Strategy and Operations.* 5 vols. in 6. London: HMSD, 1979–90.

Hook, Sidney, ed. *Philosophy and History: A Symposium.* New York: New York University Press, 1963.

Ickes, Harold L. *The Secret Diary of Harold L. Ickes.* 3 vols. New York: Simon and Schuster, 1954–55.

Ike, Nobutaka, ed. *Japan's Decision for War: Records of the 1941 Policy Conferences.* Stanford: Stanford University Press, 1967.

Jervis, Robert. "Cooperation under the Security Dilemma." *World Politics* 30, no. 2 (January 1978).

Kahn, David. "United States Views of Germany and Japan in 1941." In *Knowing One's Enemies: Intelligence Assessment before the Two World Wars*, edited by Ernest May. Princeton: Princeton University Press, 1984.

Kellner, Hans. *Language and Historical Representation: Getting the Story Crooked.* Madison: University of Wisconsin Press, 1989.

Koyré, Alexandre. *Newtonian Studies.* Cambridge, Mass.: Harvard University Press, 1965.

Kuhn, Thomas. *The Essential Tension: Selected Studies in Scientific Tradition and Change.* Chicago: University of Chicago Press, 1977.

———. *The Structure of Scientific Revolutions.* 2d ed. Chicago: University of Chicago Press, 1970.

———. *The Trouble with the Historical Philosophy of Science.* Cambridge, Mass.: Harvard History of Science Department, 1991.

Lakatos, Imre. "Falsification and the Methodology of Scientific Research Programmes." In *Criticism and the Growth of Knowledge*, edited by Imre Lakatos and Alan Musgrave. Cambridge: Cambridge University Press, 1970.

———. "History of Science and Its Rational Reconstructions." In *Method and Appraisal in the Physical Sciences: The Critical Background to Modern Science, 1800–1905*, edited by Colin Howson. Cambridge: Cambridge University Press, 1976.

———. "Lectures on Scientific Method." In Imre Lakatos and Paul Feyerabend, *For and Against Method: Including Lakatos's Lectures on Scientific Method and the Lakatos-Feyerabend Correspondence*, edited by Matteo Motterlini. Chicago: University of Chicago Press, 1999.

Langer, William, and S. Everett Gleason. *The Undeclared War, 1940–1941.* New York: Harper, 1953.

Leach, Barry. *German Strategy against Russia, 1939–1941.* Oxford: Clarendon, 1973.

Leutze, James. *Bargaining for Supremacy: Anglo-American Naval Collaboration, 1937–1941.* Chapel Hill: University of North Carolina Press, 1977.

Logevall, Fredrik. *Choosing War: The Lost Chance for Peace and the Escalation of War in Vietnam*. Berkeley: University of California Press, 1999.

Malachowski, Alan, ed. *Reading Rorty: Critical Response to Philosophy and the Mirror of Nature (and Beyond)*. Oxford: Blackwell, 1990.

Maruyama, Masao. *Thought and Behaviour in Modern Japanese Politics*. Expanded edition. Oxford: Oxford University Press, 1969. Originally published 1953.

Matloff, Maurice, and Edwin Snell. *Strategic Planning for Coalition Warfare, 1941–1942*. Washington, D.C.: Center of Military History, 1999.

Maxon, Yale. *Control of Japanese Foreign Policy: A Study of Civil-Military Rivalry, 1930–1945*. Berkeley: University of California Press, 1957.

Michaelis, Meir. "World Power Status or World Dominion? A Survey of the Literature on Hitler's 'Plan of World Dominion' (1937–1970)." *Historical Journal* 15, no. 2 (June 1972).

Morrow, James D. "International Conflict: Assessing the Democratic Peace and Offense-Defense Theory." In *Political Science: The State of the Discipline*, edited by Ira Katznelson and Helen Milner. New York: Norton, 2002.

Neustadt, Richard. *Report to JFK: The Skybolt Crisis in Perspective*. Ithaca: Cornell University Press, 1999.

Newell, R. W. *Objectivity, Empiricism and Truth*. London: Routledge, 1986.

Novick, Peter. *That Noble Dream: The "Objectivity Question" and the American Historical Profession*. Cambridge: Cambridge University Press, 1988.

Oakeshott, Michael. *Experience and Its Modes*. Cambridge: Cambridge University Press, 1933.

Oka Yoshitake. *Konoe Fumimaro: A Political Biography*. New York: Madison Books, 1992.

Overy, Richard. "Germany, 'Domestic Crisis' and War in 1939." *Past and Present*, no. 116 (August 1987). Reprinted in Overy, *War and Economy in the Third Reich*.

———. *War and Economy in the Third Reich*. Oxford: Clarendon, 1994.

Overy, Richard (with Andrew Wheatcroft). *The Road to War*. London: Macmillan, 1989.

Parker, R.A.C. *Struggle for Survival: The History of the Second World War*. Oxford: Oxford University Press, 1989.

Public Papers and Addresses of Franklin D. Roosevelt. Compiled by Samuel Rosenman. Vol. 9, New York: Macmillan, 1941. Vol. 10, New York: Harper, 1942.

Reynolds, David. *The Creation of the Anglo-American Alliance, 1937–41: A Study in Competitive Co-operation*. Chapel Hill: University of North Carolina Press, 1982.

Rohwer, Jürgen. "Die USA und die Schlacht im Atlantik 1941." In *Kriegswende Dezember 1941*, edited by Jürgen Rohwer and Eberhard Jäckel. Koblenz: Bernard and Graefe, 1984.

Roosevelt Letters. Edited by Elliott Roosevelt with Joseph Lash. Vol. 3. London: Harrap, 1952.

Rorty, Richard. *Objectivism, Relativism, and Truth*. Cambridge: Cambridge University Press, 1991.

———. *Philosophy and the Mirror of Nature* Princeton: Princeton University Press, 1979.

Ross, Steven, ed. *American War Plans, 1919–1941*. Vol. 5. New York: Garland, 1992.

Schelling, Thomas. *Arms and Influence*. New Haven: Yale University Press, 1966.

———. *The Strategy of Conflict*. Cambridge, Mass.: Harvard University Press, 1960.

Schroeder, Paul. *The Axis Alliance and Japanese-American Relations, 1941*. Ithaca: Cornell University Press, 1958.

Searle, John. *The Construction of Social Reality*. New York: Free Press, 1995.

Sherwood, Robert E. *Roosevelt and Hopkins: An Intimate History*. New York: Harper, 1948.

Simpson, B. Mitchell. *Admiral Harold R. Stark: Architect of Victory, 1939–1945*. Columbia: University of South Carolina Press, 1989.

Stoler, Mark. *Allies and Adversaries: The Joint Chiefs of Staff, the Grand Alliance, and U.S. Strategy in World War II*. Chapel Hill: University of North Carolina Press, 2000.

Taylor, A.J.P. *The Origins of the Second World War*. New York: Atheneum, 1962.

Tehran Yalta Potsdam: The Soviet Protocols. Edited by Robert Beitzell. Hattiesburg, Miss.: Academic International, 1970.

Thorne, Christopher. *Allies of a Kind: The United States, Britain and the War against Japan, 1941–1945*. New York: Oxford University Press, 1978.

Toulmin, Stephen. *Foresight and Understanding: An Enquiry into the Aims of Science*. New York: Harper, 1961.

———. "From Form to Function: Philosophy and History of Science in the 1950s and Now." *Daedalus* 106, no. 3 (Summer 1977).

———. *Human Understanding*. Vol. 1. Princeton: Princeton University Press, 1972.

Trachtenberg, Marc. *A Constructed Peace: The Making of the European Settlement, 1945–1963*. Princeton: Princeton University Press, 1999.

———. *History and Strategy*. Princeton: Princeton University Press, 1991.

Tsunoda Jun. *The Final Confrontation: Japan's Negotiations with the United States: Japan's Road to the Pacific War*. Vol. 5 of *Japan's Road to the Pacific War*, edited by James Morley. New York: Columbia University Press, 1994.

Tuchman, Barbara. *The Guns of August*. New York: Macmillan, 1962.

United States. Department of State. *Foreign Relations of the United States: The Conference of Berlin (The Potsdam Conference) 1945*. 2 vols. Washington, D.C.: GPO, 1960.

United States. Department of State. *Foreign Relations of the United States: Japan, 1931–1941*. 2 vols. Washington, D.C.: GPO, 1943.

Utley, Jonathan. *Going to War with Japan, 1937–1941*. Knoxville: University of Tennessee Press, 1985.

———. "Upstairs, Downstairs at Foggy Bottom: Oil Exports and Japan, 1940–41." *Prologue* 8 (1976).

Van Evera, Stephen. *Causes of War: Power and the Roots of Conflict*. Ithaca: Cornell University Press, 1999.

Walsh, W. H. *An Introduction to the Philosophy of History*. London: Hutchinson's, 1951.

Waltz, Kenneth. "Evaluating Theories." *American Political Science Review* 91, no. 4 (December 1997).

———. *Theory of International Politics*. New York: McGraw-Hill, 1979.

Weinberg, Gerhard. "Germany's Declaration of War on the United States: A New Look." In Gerhard Weinberg, *World in the Balance: Behind the Scenes of World War II*. Hanover, N.H.: University Press of New England, 1981.

———. *A World at Arms: A Global History of World War II*. Cambridge: Cambridge University Press, 1994.

White, Hayden. *The Content of the Form: Narrative Discourse and Historical Representation*. Baltimore: Johns Hopkins University Press, 1987.

———. *Metahistory: The Historical Imagination in Nineteenth-Century Europe*. Baltimore: Johns Hopkins University Press, 1973.

———. *Tropics of Discourse: Essays in Cultural Criticism*. Baltimore: Johns Hopkins University Press, 1978.

Woodward, Llewellyn. *British Foreign Policy in the Second World War*. 5 vols. London: HMSO, 1970–.

INDEX

Acheson, Dean, 97–100, 192; papers of, 167, 222
Adam Matthew (publisher), 223
"architecture" of a problem or argument, 32, 59, 63, 64, 95, 183, 191
archival sources, 165–68, 234–48; British, 236–38; French, 238–39; German, 239–40; Russian, 167, 231, 242–43; U.S., 234–36, 240–41, 243–48. *See also* manuscript sources
Arkin, William, 212, 228
Atlantic Conference (1941), 81–82, 99–100

"back door" theory, 123–28
Bacon, Francis, 15–16, 27
Barzun, Jacques, 184, 194
Baudrillard, Jean, 12
Baumont, Maurice, 55
Beisner, Robert, 57, 176
bibliographies and research guides, 57–58, 199–207
Bibliographie zur Zeitgeschichte, 58, 199
book reviews, 53, 214–15
Bowie, Robert: report on NATO, 159
Brodie, Bernard, 37, 46–49, 93
bureaucratic politics theory, 74–77, 96n.46

Cardozo, Benjamin, 183–84
Center for Strategic Education, 212, 214, 250
Churchill, Winston, 81–82, 99–100, 129–31, 222–23
CIAO (Columbia International Affairs Online), 212
classified material, access to, 252–55
Cohen, Eliot, 204
Cohen, Warren, 56
Cold War International History Project, 230–31
Collingwood, R.G., 4–6, 15–16
Copeland, Dale, 134
Craigie, Robert, 104, 120; and proposed modus vivendi, 105–6, 114, 130
Crowley, James, 103
Cuban missile crisis, 143–44, 146, 152–53

Dallek, Robert, 81–82, 90
Darwin, Charles, 43

Declassified Documents Reference System, 223, 228–29
Digital National Security Archive, 229–30
dissertations, 56, 212–13
documents: available online, 228–34; destruction of, 157–58, 157n.24; diplomatic, collections of, 163–65, 217–18; gauging reliability of, 146–53, 155–57; on microfilm and microfiche, 165, 219–28; other published, 164–65; working with, 140–68, 217–55. *See also* archival sources; manuscript sources; open sources
Dooman, Eugene, 111, 112
"dramatic" findings, 36, 37–38, 42; "gold in your hands," 36
Duhem, Pierre, 17n.63, 41n.20
Dulles, John Foster, 160–61

Einstein, Albert, 17, 42, 43, 44n.31
Eisenhower, Dwight, 28, 151, 156; on plans, 193
EUREKA (Research Libraries Group union catalogue), 53, 167, 219, 241
Expanded Academic ASAP, 53, 211, 214–15
explanation: and deduction, 1, 4, 24, 28–29, 186–87; and the element of necessity, 24, 32, 34, 185–87; role of theory in, 25. *See also* historical interpretation; theory

Feis, Herbert, 111–12
Fischer, Fritz, 67–73
Foreign Relations of the United States, 163, 217–18
Foucault, Michel, 10, 12
France: archival sources, 238–39; diplomatic documents, 164, 218; manuscript collections, 242
Freedom of Information Act (FOIA), using, 252–54
Fukudome Shigeru, 108

Galileo, 20n.81, 41, 44n.31
Gay, Peter, 183